The Cities on the Hill

STUDIES IN POSTWAR AMERICAN POLITICAL DEVELOPMENT

Steven Teles, *Series Editor*

Series Board Members
Jennifer Hochschild
Desmond King
Sanford Levinson
Taeku Lee
Shep Melnick
Paul Pierson
John Skrentny
Adam Sheingate
Reva Siegel
Thomas Sugrue

The First Civil Right: Race and the Rise of the Carceral State
Naomi Murakawa

How Policy Shapes Politics: Rights, Courts, Litigation, and the Struggle Over Injury Compensation
Jeb Barnes and Thomas F. Burke

Ideas with Consequences: The Federalist Society and the Conservative Counterrevolution
Amanda Hollis-Brusky

No Day in Court: Access to Justice and the Politics of Judicial Retrenchment
Sarah Staszak

The Business of America Is Lobbying: How Corporations Became Politicized and Politics Became More Corporate
Lee Drutman

Building a Business of Politics: The Rise of Political Consulting and the Transformation of American Democracy
Adam Sheingate

Prison Break: Why Conservatives Turned Against Mass Incarceration
David Dagan and Steven Teles

The Other Rights Revolution: Conservative Lawyers and the Remaking of American Government
Jefferson Decker

When Bad Policy Makes Good Politics: Running the Numbers on Health Reform
Robert P. Saldin

Citizenship By Degree: U.S. Higher Education Policy and the Changing Gender Dynamics of American Citizenship
Deondra Rose

Politics at Work: How Companies Turn Their Workers into Lobbyists
Alexander Hertel-Fernandez

The Cities on the Hill: How Urban Institutions Transformed National Politics
Thomas K. Ogorzalek

The Cities on the Hill

How Urban Institutions Transformed National Politics

THOMAS K. OGORZALEK

OXFORD
UNIVERSITY PRESS

Oxford University Press is a department of the University of Oxford. It furthers
the University's objective of excellence in research, scholarship, and education
by publishing worldwide. Oxford is a registered trade mark of Oxford University
Press in the UK and certain other countries.

Published in the United States of America by Oxford University Press
198 Madison Avenue, New York, NY 10016, United States of America.

© Oxford University Press 2018

All rights reserved. No part of this publication may be reproduced, stored in
a retrieval system, or transmitted, in any form or by any means, without the
prior permission in writing of Oxford University Press, or as expressly permitted
by law, by license, or under terms agreed with the appropriate reproduction
rights organization. Inquiries concerning reproduction outside the scope of the
above should be sent to the Rights Department, Oxford University Press, at the
address above.

You must not circulate this work in any other form
and you must impose this same condition on any acquirer.

Library of Congress Cataloging-in-Publication Data
Names: Ogorzalek, Thomas K., author.
Title: The cities on the hill : how urban institutions transformed
national politics / Thomas K. Ogorzalek.
Description: New York, NY, United States of America : Oxford University
Press, [2018] | Includes bibliographical references.
Identifiers: LCCN 2017038183 | ISBN 9780190668877 (hardcover) |
ISBN 9780190668884 (pbk.) | ISBN 9780190668891 (updf) | ISBN 9780190668907 (epub)
Subjects: LCSH: Metropolitan government—Social aspects—United States. |
Urban policy—United States. | Liberalism—United States. |
Cultural pluralism—Political aspects—United States. | Federal-city relations—United States.
Classification: LCC JS422 .O36 2018 | DDC 320.8/50973—dc23
LC record available at https://lccn.loc.gov/2017038183

1 3 5 7 9 8 6 4 2

Paperback printed by WebCom, Inc., Canada
Hardback printed by Bridgeport National Bindery, Inc., United States of America

For my parents, Quinn, and my fellow city-zens

CONTENTS

Acknowledgments ix

1. Introduction: One Combined Interest 1
2. Urbanicity, City Delegations, and Two-Dimensional Liberalism 27
3. "A Proper National Policy": The Urban Order and Agenda 65
4. Ties That Bind: City Delegations and Cohesive Representation in Congress 102
5. Antiracism Without Antiracists: City Representation and Racial Realignment 148
6. The Cities on the Hill: Urban Power in Congress 203
7. Conclusion: Notes for a Metropolitan Political Order 230

Appendix A: House CSR Scores 251
Appendix B: City District Demography 265
Appendix C: Urbanicity Regression Results 277
Notes 281
Bibliography 321
Index 331

ACKNOWLEDGMENTS

Many first academic books are simultaneously a sort of summing up and a lurch forward, and this is no exception. In trying to bring together all of the things I am interested in—cities, history, race, geography, power—I have driven myself crazy at times over the past few years, while at others I couldn't imagine doing anything else. It only makes sense when I consider the dear friends with whom I've shared the last ten (!) years, while I found time around the edges to figure out how to turn a title into a dissertation and then into a book.

I could not have sustained this project without the inspiration, guidance, and material support I have received along the way from new colleagues and friends during my time at the New School, Columbia, Syracuse, and Northwestern. My many colleagues at the New School for Social Research, especially Victoria Hattam, David Plotke, Genaro Lozano, Jeffrey Goldfarb, and Columbus Mavhunga, introduced me to the profession and the field, and in their own work and through memories of old conversations I am reminded that it isn't entirely necessary to leave one's normative perspective at the door, no matter what they say, and that research can be for something as much as it can be about something.

I am thankful for the attention and constructive comments given by those generous enough with their resources and time to invite me to present primitive versions of this project without condemning it to the dustbin. These include participants in the Urban Politics Workshop at Columbia; in the Saguaro/Manchester Social Change: A Harvard–Manchester Initiative (SCHMi) Summer Workshop (especially Jane Green, Robert Putnam, Tom Sander, Ed Fieldhouse, Louise Kennedy Converse, and Jenny Birchall); discussants and questioners including McGee Young, Rick Vallely, Richardson Dilworth, Amy Bridges, Steve Erie, Paul Frymer, David Karol, Laura Evans, Eric Schickler, Joel Rast, Devin Caughey, and Andrew Polsky; political science departments at Syracuse University (especially Tom Keck and Kristi Andersen), the Kennedy School (especially Moshik Temkin, Jennifer Hochschild, Alberto Abadie, and

Ryan Enos), the University of California, San Diego (especially Amy Bridges again, Steve Erie, Zoltan Hajnal, Sam Kernell, Gary Jacobson, Thad Kousser, and Peter Gourevitch), Sciences Politiques (especially Patrick Le Galès and Tommaso Vitale), and the Center for the Study of Democratic Politics at Princeton (especially Paul Frymer, Sarah Staszak, and Michele Epstein). Their critiques, suggestions, and encouragement improved the project in many ways.

At Columbia, I became aware of the possibilities for working deeply within a field but also of the importance of maintaining a breadth of interests that can only flourish in a welcoming, friendly community of scholars. I owe the university and the wider community there a great debt. Justin Phillips was a constantly available advisor for a new student trying to gain his feet in the academy. John Huber took many chances on me; the theoretical, technical, and professional insights I gained from working with him are a guide for life. Bob Shapiro, though busier than anyone else, was also the most available for a word of advice or help, even on the simplest matters, and without judgment. He is the kind of colleague we should all be. Rob Lieberman, in addition to writing the essay and collecting the list of cities that gave birth to the ideas I explore here, has been an enthusiastic and welcome presence throughout my time at Columbia, brimming with ideas himself and engaging when we discussed my own. Meredith Sadin and Kate Krimmel were always available for an encouraging word, a conversation to work through a puzzle, or a therapeutic loop through the park. Dorian Warren was an invaluable friend and colleague at Columbia, always generous with time, advice, and attention on any subject, and a perfect companion at the only fancy Manhattan dinners I had in eight years there. Ira Katznelson, beyond the inspiration he has always provided me in his writing and thinking, was a singular advisor and mentor. His wit, insight, work ethic, and genuine care for others have been constant, and his support, in so many ways, has kept me in the game. He will always be my model not only of professional and scholarly life, but of urbanity itself. Would that all students were so lucky.

I could not have had the intuition for this project if New York City (especially Brooklyn, yes) hadn't become a cherished friend during this time. Walking the streets, reading the signs, listening on the subway, running in the park, I learned a perspective on life unavailable anywhere else. I thank Kara Zuaro for making me move there, Tom Herman for getting me acclimated, Joe Napolitano for making me think deeply and for providing a place to schvitz out in the country, K-Ro for making sure I saw all sides of the town, and Brooklyn Heights for giving me a first home with inspirational views and a nice place to read outside.

The project moved from an interesting dissertation to a legible book during my time at Syracuse and then Northwestern. These periods have proved an invaluable time for reflection and autonomous work. Many thanks to my colleagues there in the Departments of Political Science in both places, and the Institute for Policy Research and Center for Civic Engagement at Northwestern for their advice and collegial conviviality, especially Spencer Piston, Abbey Steele, Seiki Tanaka, Shana Garadian, Jim Farr, Tony Chen, Al Tillery, Dan Galvin, Reuel Rogers, and Dan Lewis. I especially thank the department for supporting a manuscript book workshop, from which I was able to get unparalleled, focused advice from two of the scholars whose work I admire most, Eric Schickler and Jessica Trounstine. Their advice made me think more deeply and vastly improved the end product.

Working with Oxford University Press on the project has been a smooth dream. I thank Steve Teles, Dave McBride, three enthusiastic and very constructive reviewers, Emily Mackenzie, Felshiya Samuel, Derek Gottlieb, and Sarah Vogelsong for improving the manuscript immensely and keeping me on track.

I could not have finished this project, or any other, without the love and support over the years from my family. My grandmothers Peg Wade and Florence Ogorzalek, in different ways, are important inspirations for this particular project and for my broader affection for the Long New Deal and city life of a certain character. They each passed away while I was writing this book, but their lifetime of work and love, and the stories and outlook they have passed along, help me make sense of the world.

My brothers, Kevin, Daniel, and Jim, have always been my most stalwart friends; I am the oldest, so I've only recently overcome that hubris and discovered that I have been learning from them forever and should have done so more consciously all along. I appreciate the love, humor, and unwavering fraternity they have offered me over our whole lives, and I hope I can return it.

My parents, Ken and Sharon, instilled in me a love of learning, reading, and travel before I could do anything else. To them I owe my sometimes trivial successes and love of maps, history, and new places. They are the reason I get restless to see something new but also stop to read historic roadside markers and get to know how places used to be. More important, they have always encouraged me to pursue this path but never pressured me to do anything but "have fun." The value of hard work, but not for one's self, that they promote by example is one to which I aspire. I owe them more than I can ever repay, and I hope I make them proud.

Finally, I could not have done much of anything these past few years without the love and support of my partner, Quinn Mulroy. In work, she has been a constant source of moral support, the most challenging and honest interlocutor, a diligent and focused editor, and a role model for careful work. So much more importantly, she has been my companion in life's adventures, the best friend I've always needed, and for that I am so happy and grateful.

The Cities on the Hill

1

Introduction

One Combined Interest

> But why, then, does the city exist? What line separates the inside from the outside, the rumble of wheels from the howl of wolves?
> —Italo Calvino, *Invisible Cities*

> Local experience has taught them that in unity there is power.
> —Leo Snowiss, "Congressional Recruitment and Representation"[1]

In the summer of 1964, rural congressmen were on the defensive. A series of recent Supreme Court cases had enshrined the principle of "one person, one vote."[2] These decisions addressed the fact that, increasingly, representative institutions did not reflect the metropolitan reality of American life. Since the mid-1800s, industrialization had lured new arrivals from the countryside and all over the world into American cities. For much of that time, however, district lines had not been redrawn, so representation at the state and national levels had been frozen and distorted through neglect and intention, privileging townships and territory over people. Because of this lag, rural voters often had about twenty times as much representation per capita as city voters.[3] In essence, an increasingly urban twentieth-century polity was being represented by eighteenth- or nineteenth-century legislatures. The Warren Court waded into this explicitly political thicket and mandated major steps to remedy this imbalance.

Ruralists did not take the Court's changes lying down. They made a case against equal apportionment, even recommending a constitutional amendment against one person, one vote.[4] Attempting to explain the justice of malapportionment favoring rural areas over the city, former representative John Vorys (R-OH) observed that "those of us who have served in the state legislature know of the power that is more than numerical that goes with the organization of the big cities." To buttress this claim, he quoted at length from a 1930 treatise on "The History and Theory of Lawmaking by Representative

Government" by his former House colleague Robert Luce (R-MA), who wrote that

> the great increase of effective force which comes from the election of a large number of representatives of one city—*representatives who represent, not, in fact, their separate districts, but the whole city, representatives who are responsible to the same public opinion, and, in fact represent but one combined interest of the citizens of the city*—the great accumulation of power created by that combination so far outweighed the effective power of a great number of scattered representatives of widely divided centers of population, small centers of population, that a difference in the ratio . . . went but a small way toward equalization.[5]

Testifying before Congress, Vorys argued that rural malapportionment was an important preemptive remedy against better-organized, more united urban forces. To the casual observer's ear, this might have been a curious claim: *united* was probably not a word that applied to most cities in August of 1964. Harlem, Rochester, and Jersey City had already had riots that summer; uprisings in Elizabeth, Chicago, and Philadelphia would occur later that month. If anything, this was an era famous for urban fracture. But while this was a moment of particularly dramatic division, American cities have *always* been the sites of deep cultural pluralism—places where toleration and the political order have been tested to their limits, and where the broader community's interests are not always naturally apparent because so many of its members' interests conflict and clash.[6] Why did places with such obvious divisions inspire in Vorys a concern that, without an institutional distortion, united city delegations would overwhelm rural interests?

An answer to that question comes in part from another speaker at that hearing. Also in the room that day was someone from exactly the kind of urban organization that Vorys and his rural allies feared. Speaking on behalf of the U.S. Conference of Mayors and the city of Chicago was Richard J. Daley. Daley was the kind of boss against which reformers and ruralists railed. Discipline, loyalty, and unity were fundamental principles of the Chicago organization that he led, from the precinct to City Hall to Springfield to Capitol Hill.[7] In state and national politics, Daley famously saw to it that "members of Cook County's uniformly Democratic delegation to the state legislature took their marching orders" from Chicago's City Hall on the issues of the day.[8] As a result of this discipline, Chicago's Democrats were able to punch above their weight in a statehouse where they were typically outnumbered by generally hostile downstate forces and to cohesively push city interests at the national level, even on issues that were controversial at home.

Citing the heightened governance demands being placed on cities, Daley countered that rural areas should not be "given special and disproportionate weight in the legislature because they have special problems. For years, the problems of cities and suburbs—metro areas—and their needs for government aid have been at least as great as those of rural areas."[9] Cities are always high-maintenance places, where statist interventions are more important to maintain social stability and rapid change requires serious policy responses, and Daley argued that since the onset of industrialization and urbanization, the recurrent and urgent governance problems of American cities had been no easier to resolve. Rather, the vulnerability of cities within the national political economy had become even more apparent, and the "special problems" of rural areas paled dramatically in comparison to cities' continual economic upheaval, intermittent violence, and great potential for social ills.[10] Increasingly, America's cities were faced with problems they could not solve on their own, and they sought external aid to shore up finances, deliver services, and keep the social peace. Creating an equitable representational system that would allow cities to adequately represent themselves in the state and nation was an important first step toward addressing these local needs.

In this hearing, Vorys and Daley identified the layered political strategies that the urban political order—a diverse alliance of interest groups, political organizations, and public officials—built and defended with mixed success over the course of the twentieth century, and that will lie at the heart of this book. As the United States moved from a decentralized, agrarian society into the most powerful and prosperous nation in the world, its institutions did not always reflect this reality. As the cities that drove American industrial might grew and grew, they often struggled to manage the long list of challenges that inevitably arise in large, densely populated, heterogeneous, complex, and rapidly changing communities. These problems include pollution, congestion, crime, corruption, fraud, poverty, unemployment, social conflict, and on and on. American cities developed a host of creative local institutions and policies to solve these challenges internally during the Progressive Era, but they also came to see that purely local solutions would be inadequate for problems that went well beyond city borders.

This was especially true during the crisis of the Great Depression, when a vexing paradox of city government—one that has remained true up to today—became crystal clear. On one hand, because cities are large and complex, so they are places where the *demand* for governance is high. On the other hand, the *supply* of governance in cities is constrained by the complexity of interests within them (which can complicate decision making) and—more fundamentally in an age of heightened mobility—by the city's place within a federalist political economy that structures the effective menu of options for local policymakers. Driven by this paradox, both dynamics of which had intensified during the early decades of the twentieth century, city leaders during the Depression turned to higher-level politics, in their states and eventually on Capitol Hill, to seek the policy solutions that would ameliorate city problems and help them manage modern society. In doing so, they patterned their supralocal actions on the lessons they had learned on their own streets and in their own city halls: they promoted policies that might solve some of the recurrent challenges of complex economies, they relied on local bonds to shore up potentially fractious legislative blocs, they built a core coalition of cities seeking solutions to common problems, and they attracted secondary allies from other constituencies in the nation who did not necessarily agree with them or share their primary concerns. And in relatively short order, these cities came to join together in a durable partisan bloc for the first time, making the Democratic Party the party of the cities. In so doing, cities played a remarkable role in the development of national politics.

In the coming chapters, I make three key insights about how cities shaped twentieth-century American politics and the current polarized state of twenty-first-century red and blue America. First, the conditions of urbanicity drove U.S. cities—especially their leaders—to develop a distinctive set of policy commitments and political dispositions that have been invaluable to managing modern urban society that have come to define the two dimensions of progressive liberalism.[11] Cities had already begun to experiment with more statist policies and culturally adaptive policies—a set of commitments I call "double liberalism"—within their borders during the Progressive Era, but as time went by these local solutions proved insufficient. Through new organizations like the U.S. Conference of Mayors, they built official cross-city alliances to develop an urban agenda and pursue these policies in national politics.

But local conditions did more than shape the policy substance of the national agenda. The second theoretical insight of this book is that local institutions also affect the *way* in which cities represent themselves in national politics. Cities that were (and remain) the site of deep contention in the streets and in city hall were nonetheless quite cohesive in their actions on Capitol Hill. Just as Vorys described in the 1964 hearings, congressional representatives from cities often did more than represent their own narrow district constituencies—they often combined their strengths to represent their cities' interests as a whole. Local institutions designed to bridge constituencies and integrate local politics, such as local parties and inclusive municipal boundaries, also had an effect on national representation: they helped hold together city constituencies that might otherwise have broken apart on controversial issues of the day. This was particularly important in how city representatives voiced their position on civil rights issues in the run-up to the 1960s.

Finally, even when they represented what Vorys called "a great accumulation of power," the growth of this cross-city coalition (and the reaction to it) transformed American politics by creating a new urban-rural cleavage that structures ideology and partisanship today. Never a majority in Congress, urban leaders used different strategies in order to work with allies who were far less concerned about policies that would make modern urban society work well. At first, they found a fraught partnership with southerners within the national Democratic Party. Almost from the start of the New Deal, however, the content and character of big-city local politics injected tension into that coalition of strange bedfellows with the country's most rural region. Eventually, that party alliance broke apart in the midcentury racial realignment. Over the second half of the twentieth century, Southern Democrats gradually became Southern Republicans, and a maturing urban–rural divide came to define American partisan politics in both institutions and the electorate. Today, the urban–rural divide is more important than ever before, and only by understanding the relationship between place character, ideology, and changes in partisan alignments can we fully appreciate the dynamics of today's red and blue Americas. American *places*, even more than Americans themselves, are polarized as never before.

This is a study about how local political realities and institutions shape city representation in national politics, ultimately generating a cohesive liberal bloc. That bloc has its roots in cities that anchor one pole of our current national partisan alignment characterized by a significant and increasing urban–rural divide. Key to this story is a puzzle presented by the very conditions that make cities interesting places to study and govern: How do many cities remain unified in politics when they are the sites of so much difference and conflicting interests? Without a "natural" basis for political unity, and under conditions that are believed to *undermine* liberal policies of many kinds, how can we explain the emergence and consolidation of "blue America," a political alignment that is doubly liberal on issues pertaining to the economy and culture?

City institutions have consistently united representatives of many heterogeneous constituencies, many of whom have not gotten along, in support of an overall city position (which has often been identified as the liberal position) on many issues. This cohesion in defense of a distinctive set of policies was what worried Vorys and his rural allies. City institutions foster political cohesion in the face of social division and allow for unified representation of the city in higher levels of government, where policy victories can provide key relief for the challenges of local governance and the everyday problems of city-zens. In telling this tale, the narrative sheds light on several major themes in urban politics and American political development.

1.1 City Organizations and National Alliances

The first theme is a perennial debate in urban political studies, about the effects of "traditional" parties (or machines), and the reformers who were often their staunchest local rivals. Political conflicts like these often make it difficult to achieve policy goals. There is also little consensus as to whether traditional or reform approaches to politics are "better" (or at least less bad, in some sense) for working class or minority group interests. Zooming out to see how city representatives have acted in national politics can help us see around this local tension.

We have a sense that urbanicity and political liberalism go together, but the organizations that run the cities with liberal reputations have not always been obviously liberal. In fact, local party organizations (and the corruption they often spawned) are sometimes thought of as *obstacles* to progressive or liberal politics, but their full story is more complicated. Many of the most ardent programmatic liberals, including government reformers, intellectuals, union leaders, and African American activists, were often at loggerheads with the traditional organizations and their leaders, especially on local issues. As the local center of power, these parties had little interest in radically changing the game so were often reluctant to adopt institutional reforms that might have enhanced local democracy or upended the existing economic order. Sustained by a politics of material exchange and what their critics described as a self-regarding ethos, they were also notorious fonts of corruption.[12] The strongest machines were autonomous organizations, able to play the electoral game so well that their reelection became detached from their responsiveness to their constitutents.[13] On racial issues especially, many of these organizations seemed particularly unresponsive to the needs of African Americans, whose life circumstances rarely improved much under machine rule.[14] From this perspective, getting a lecture on the principles of representative democracy from a leader as notoriously autocratic as Richard J. Daley must have been a surreal experience.

While the machines and traditional parties were assailed from the left, they were also often attacked from the right, and here is where the complexity of these organizations hits home. Despite their notoriety for venality and ideological flexibility (which was often taken for moral vacuity), the urban machine tradition—both its personnel and its mass base—shared much in common with more self-consciously liberal urbanites when it came to national politics. When the time came for counting votes in national politics, urban "liberals" and their more "traditional" local rivals often became indistinguishable. Both groups' shared concerns for their urban constituents and communities and vision for America's urban future (and their own professional interests) made them allies in a nascent urban political order that took shape as the core political change of the New Deal.

Just as the machines and reformers united behind urban policies, over the twentieth century rivalries between cities melt away at the national level. Before the 1930s, city leaders had been focused on local issues and wary of both potentially restrictive outside intervention and competition with other cities. Historians have noted that "united action by the nation's cities to induce the Federal Government to assist cities was still unknown in 1932," but this situation changed quickly as the common experiences of the Depression-era employment crisis and hostility from rural-dominated state legislatures guided cities to become allies in national politics.[15] Over the next three decades, this political order, anchored by the traditional party organizations of major cities such as New York and Chicago, pursued policies that would help manage problems at home, including labor regulation that benefited industrial workers and unions, the provision of aid that cities needed more than other kinds of places, and relief from the foulest racist practices affecting African Americans. Even as they were weakening—and perhaps *because* they were weakening—these anachronistic political institutions and their leaders managed to reshape American politics and played a key role in establishing the content and style of what we call liberalism today.[16]

These positions undermined the cities' national alliance with the South within the Democratic Party. Even before the beginning of the New Deal, the inherent tensions of a relationship between some of the least compatible political forces in the country were evident. Though urban and Southern Democrats both enjoyed the benefits of majority status in the national coalition, they truly agreed on few policy issues. This alliance was held together in part by a pattern of policymaking that encouraged large-scale interventions by the national government but protected many local prerogatives in policy implementation. These interventions were sought especially by urbanites, but they provided desired goods to all coalition members (and in disproportionally large amounts to rural Democratic constituencies) and were tempered by local or partial administration of their programs, a strategy upon which the South relied to protect its white supremacist order.[17]

By the 1960s, however, this alliance was hanging by a thread. Southerners continued to defy (though with less success) civil rights legislation, inching away from the party that had been hegemonic in the region since Reconstruction. This intraparty tension was driven by another paradox of city representation, because national support for civil rights emerged from cities characterized by interpersonal racism and white political dominance. While race was an issue that divided Americans in all kinds of communities, the *representatives* of large cities—whose home districts were the site of violent and destructive racial conflict throughout this era, especially in the 1960s—were not divided. City representatives were united in support of civil rights, despite the division in their streets and city halls, despite the temptation to maintain their dominant national institutional majorities of the past generation, and despite the fact that very few of them had many constituents who were not white.

This urban has come to define our contemporary politics. Many accounts of the midcentury racial realignment point to regional or sectional causes, and are thus content to depict our current political status quo as a contest between red and blue states (clustered in regions). In fact, the map of red and blue states should be discarded in favor of one more like Figure 1.1, which depicts local average support for George W. Bush (lighter shades) and John Kerry (darker shades), respectively, in the 2004 presidential election, and shows dense clusters of very strong Democratic support in major metropolitan areas across all regions, and support for Republicans spread more thinly across the sparsely populated rural areas that make up most of the country. This basic pattern has held, and grown slightly stronger, for several election cycles.

To understand both sides of this polarized urban–rural divide properly, I argue, we must look closely at city representation in national politics, because it was from cities that this transformation initially developed. What does it mean

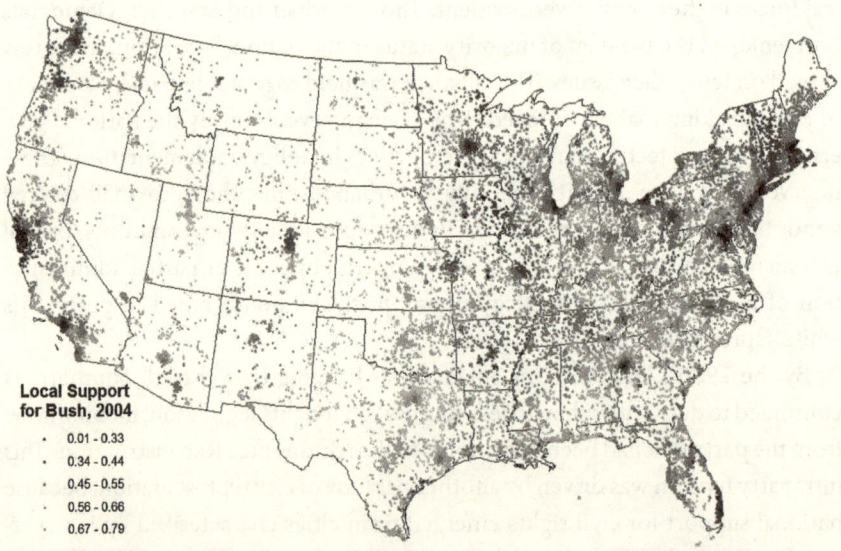

Figure 1.1 **Individual-level Local Support for George W. Bush, 2004.** Each point is a respondent in a 2004 survey, shaded according to the local average probability of saying they would or did vote for Bush in 2004. Darker values indicate LESS probable support for Bush. Probabilities are estimated using a Geographically Weighted Regression (GWR) model of vote choice Esri ArcGIS. Source: 2004 National Annenberg Election Survey.

for one pole of our national alignment to be rooted in cities and the other in more sparsely populated places? And how does our current politics relate to the major partisan developments of the past century? The answers to these questions are vital for leaders and coalition builders who seek to manage the complex challenges of modern democracy as societies around the world simultaneously become more urban and more diverse.

1.2 Cities on the Hill: Reconnecting Local and National Politics

The second theme concerns how geography has driven major changes in American politics. Exponents of American exceptionalism often refer to the United States as a metaphorical "city upon a hill" in describing the country's potentially exemplary place in world history. In this study, I turn to an exceptional period in American history, from the Depression to the Civil Rights Era, and examine the self-presentation of actual cities on "the Hill"—that is, in Congress.[18] While we often think of cities as the *object* of powerful forces—things "happen to" cities—we should remember that the opposite is true as well. People from cities participate in politics, articulating policy positions and political commitments. As in the biblical metaphor of the city on the hill, cities truly "cannot be hid" because of their visibility and centrality in modern society. How cities present themselves, and how they deal with important political issues, inevitably shapes broader conversations and political struggles.

In adopting this perspective, we can see how a distinctive urban vision was communicated through representative institutions on Capitol Hill as city representatives rose to a position of leadership in the New Deal coalition. By turning an analytical spotlight on the relationship between the characteristics of cities and the distinctive way in which these communities represent themselves in national politics, we can better understand the origins of the place-character divide in contemporary American politics.[19]

Cities have not always been associated with one party in national partisan politics, and scholarly attention has focused with only intermittent intensity on cities and their relationship to the broader polity. This is in part the result of disciplinary developments in political science. Once, the city was perhaps *the* central object of study in American political science. Indeed, many of the most eminent political scientists of the twentieth century developed theories and made important contributions to the study of power and democracy by using a local lens, and though they used particular places for data, these works were not in the least theoretically parochial.[20] But this focus has waned for a few lamentable (though understandable) reasons as the subfields of American politics and urban politics have drifted away from each other.

First, analysts of national politics looked away from cities at least partially in response to the American population's shift to the suburbs and the perception that the stakes of city politics were not as high as they once were.[21] As the national government grew and became central to more issue areas, we have also seen some "nationalizing" of both politics and political analyses. Expansion and refinement of surveying techniques have given us many national samples from which to abstract factors that are important in shaping politics but that are typically insensitive to place. Such approaches tend to seek universal, individualist explanations for behavior and employ sophisticated techniques to explain political phenomena without focusing on context or local processes.[22] This abstraction away from place specificity and complexity will inevitably miss important cross-level connections.[23]

On the other side of the coin, when urban political scientists have approached the city, they have typically zoomed in on a city's internal power struggles for insights about those particular places or comparative leverage across cities, or to make more general claims about politics that are not necessarily about local politics at all. The vast majority of urban political studies adopt this "methodological localism," focusing on local causes and effects.[24] This approach is resurgent in our field, and can be repeated to leverage structured comparisons across cities, in either small- or large-N studies, unlocking all manner of insights about local political processes. But digging deep into the details of particular polities can cause a kind of myopia in which analysts lose sight of where cities fit into the bigger picture. The place of American cities within the federal system—within states and within the nation—means that local outcomes are not the results of hermetically sealed processes and "cannot be adequately understood as locally generated or self-contained."[25] To the contrary, the multilayered, overlapping jurisdictions of the federal system mean that politics and policy are generated by interactions between levels, and that local outcomes both influence and are influenced by supralocal factors. Thus this study is not only about city politics, but about how city politics push American political history forward.

There has been a resurgence of scholarly interest in the connection between local and national political life lately. This is a welcome development, because so much politics happens locally, and so many large-scale events have powerful local effects. That outside forces have effects felt within cities is clear. As Bridges (1984) puts it, "Politics in cities is special because cities are not self-contained arenas of political activity.... The dependence and permeability of the urban polity mean that things happen not only *in* cities, but *to* cities."[26] Studies of urban politics often identify constraints on local options in these overarching institutions and examine the things that "happen to" cities and influence local outcomes. Structural economic factors are often identified as the most powerful outside forces, especially the city-crippling forces of deindustrialization and suburbanization. The relationship between these macro-level forces and the "urban crisis" of the 1960s and 1970s is well-chronicled.[27] But technology and modernization are not the only relevant forces. According to Paul Peterson (1981), federalism and easy personal and capital mobility across jurisdictional lines (which are themselves related, but not identical, to technology) structure the kinds of policies that are sustainable at the local level, especially hamstringing local efforts at redistribution. On top of this model of interjurisdictional competition, Hackworth (2007) heaps the power of financial institutions such as bond rating agencies, which discipline local governments bound by budgeting constraints and in need of steady credit on the municipal bond market. Even more explicit institutional limits on city policymaking, such as balanced budget requirements or tax and expenditure limits (TELs), are often imposed at the state level.[28] All of these factors contribute to the fragile position of cities in an age of global capitalism, in which location of production is flexible, capital and residents are mobile, and demand for city services often outstrips the local ability to provide them. This another way of stating the paradox of city governance: cities are high-maintenance places, but there are external constraints on the amount of maintenance they can do.

But while cities are affected by outside forces, they can also affect those apparently external outcomes, like national policies, in their own turn. In fact, a central insight of this book is that creative actors in the constrained city can act in supralocal arenas to shape the broader context in which they operate; the strategic response to Peterson's "city limits" is not to merely surrender to them, but to circumvent those limits. As homes to tens of millions of people in a democratic polity, cities can have and have had significant influence on electoral outcomes. As centers of commerce, industry, culture, and ideas, they also have outsize influence on social norms, the economy, and political conversations. They are not merely buffeted by powerful forces but affect the broader nation and shape the forces at work in it. As we shall see in these pages, and hopefully in the years to come, cities represent themselves in state and national politics and pursue the distinctive kinds of policies that are important for successful governance. By shining the spotlight beyond the city limits and into the halls of national policymaking, this book explores the external effects of cities' internal political processes, which have been important factors in shaping the substance and contending forces of contemporary American politics.

1.3 The Urban Political Order: Nation as City

The third major theme is the urban character of the New Deal alliance. When we look to the halls of national power, we can see that a national political alliance made up largely of city representatives was a key driver of political change in twentieth-century America, and that many of the policies this alliance pursued were prompted by the paradox of city governance described earlier.[29] But the influence of cities on national politics has clearly not been constant over time.[30] The overall share of the national population in large cities grew rapidly in the early twentieth century and has declined slightly since the 1950s as more and more Americans call the suburbs home. Suburbanization itself is a component of the broader demographic trend of metropolitanization, as fewer Americans have remained in purely rural areas. Even though the combined population of central cities never comprised an absolute majority of Americans, it remains a fairly bitter irony that the principle of "one-person, one-vote" was finally established at the same moment that the population of many industrial cities began to decline. In strictly numerical terms, cities were never dominant in the halls of the national legislature.

But the political power of cities predates that moment of representational parity. I deem the key historical moment in a narrative of city-driven political change the "urban interlude," a period during which a city perspective was persuasive in national politics. This period, from the early 1930s to the 1960s, entails a "metonymic moment when the part came to speak for the whole; when a metropolitan vision became appealing to a huge majority of Americans."[31] In contrast to most of our nation's history, when Jefferson's pastoral vision embodied Americanism and cities were considered inimical to democratic-republican self-rule, the political forces of this era were shaped by cities and articulated a vision of American progress that was rooted in the urban experience.[32] This period was also the first time in U.S. history that a national city alliance coalesced within one national alliance. After a long time wandering in the political wilderness, the Democratic Party became the dominant national force during this era, and while its southern wing was its oldest core element, the New Deal alliance owed its national ascendancy to large cities.[33] The Democratic political order that took shape in the 1930s was tempered by the continuation of the conservative Southern bloc, but its "core programs aimed at urban public works investment, urban public employment, direct relief for the urban unemployed, and strengthening the labor market position of the urban working class."[34]

Historians have often characterized the New Deal as eclectic and pragmatic, a temperament more than a coherent ideological program.[35] Compared with the more rigid political-economic worldviews of the age, the New Deal program for crisis remediation certainly seems more plastic and less systematic, but this does not mean it was without guiding principles. More recent treatments have seen elements of a consistent vision in the multifaceted suite of New Deal programs. For Plotke (1996), the ideology of the New Deal Democratic order was characterized by three guiding commitments, which together constitute a "progressive liberalism" that underpinned the alliance's sprawling agenda: a focus on the role of groups in political and economic life; a positive view of the state as a player in social and economic regulation; and governmental responsiveness to the claims of the marginalized, potentially through the expansion of democratic political participation.[36] These principles owed much to lessons that had been learned in urban politics over the previous decades.

Hofstadter and those who characterize the New Deal as nonideological are correct in the sense that this set of programs was not dogmatically derived from and implemented as a complete theoretical worldview, as were its contemporary rivals for the hearts and minds of modern peoples, including programmatic versions of Marxism, fascism, laissez-faire capitalism, and white supremacy. Instead, the New Deal's principles were reflections of actual steps taken in cities by their leaders in response to the suite of challenges posed by modernity: heightened social and economic complexity, the national integration of culture and economy, urbanization, industrialization, and rapid demographic shifts that brought diverse groups of individuals together into a shared social and political space. The New Deal's politics and policies included important elements of both "bread and butter" liberalism of welfare provision and a "politics of amelioration" in which inclusive negotiations and the pursuit of compromise (often through mutual exchange) between groups with deep differences of perspective were privileged over abstract or absolute principles.[37] The Depression exposed the shortcomings of less interventionist models, especially in cities, so these commitments were posed as a solution to the basic problem of providing order and stability while still preserving important elements of liberal capitalism.[38] As such, the New Deal included ideas on different dimensions that didn't obviously or *necessarily* cohere but that worked to alleviate the governance challenges faced by both cities and nation.

The political commitments of progressive liberals were as much about a style and process of politics as a particular set of policies. If there was a patron philosopher of the New Deal's vision of democracy, it would be John Dewey, rather than Karl Marx, Immanuel Kant, or John Locke, because the lessons and principles of the New Deal were derived from action rather than deduced from premises. The new national political order resembled that of the large cities that supported the New Deal. This application of an urban style at higher levels of government is apparent in two ways. First, for nearly a century before the urban interlude, cities had dealt with the tumult of modernity largely on their own, often by developing new institutions or adjusting old ones to deal with new social realities. Recurrent, urgent crisis, which was both more common and costly to resolve in cities, made it necessary for them to develop sustainable routines and practices for maintaining political order in an unpredictable world—what we might think of as flexible or robust governance institutions. Even well before the 1930s, such ideas and commitments were hallmarks of urban politics, and they came to be embraced by the largely urban nonsouthern bloc of Democrats, but they were never the commitments of the mostly rural southern wing. These ideas mirror Plotke's progressive liberalism, and included an innovative approach to economic and social regulation and the inclusion of class-based, ethnic, racial, and religious groups as participants in democracy. Struggle within the national Democratic Party over these principles, which was evident from the start of the Long New Deal and reemerged throughout the marriage of strange bedfellows, presaged the structure of virtually all political conflict within the United States today.

Second, the party used urban strategies to resolve intraparty conflict as well. Cities are the sites of deep pluralism, meaning they are home to divergent interests that may derive from extremely different starting points and therefore be irresolvable; in such circumstances, the "consensus and community" that seems natural in other kinds of places gives way to a "diverse and rather contentious aggregation of interests" whose only shared interest is order and political victory.[39] But because social challenges do not simply wait around for politicians to develop authentic consensus or discover the general will on them—indeed, they may become worse as deliberation is drawn out—action must often be taken, sometimes to perform quotidian housekeeping and sometimes to address disruptive change, even though disagreements may persist. Fundamentally, this perspective entails a belief that even difficult problems really can be managed, mitigated, or resolved, and that informed efforts to address problems are preferable to inaction.

The same tendency became obvious in the tenuous New Deal alliance, which included a cacophony of political voices that were incoherent on their face. Logrolling and the distribution of material goods became the party's *modus operandi*, just as traditional party organizations in cities had built their organizations and dominance on reliable practices of material exchange and avoidance of unprofitably divisive issues. In both cases, the maintenance of such diverse coalitions was predicated upon the urban machine tradition of "making no waves"; that is, the avoidance of potentially irreconcilable moral or cultural issues and a focus on winning key constituencies with material provision.[40] Mayhew (1966) characterizes the Democratic Party of the midcentury as a party of "inclusive compromise," with multiple interested factions held together by the reciprocal distribution of material goods, especially in cities, farm areas, and the South.[41] Thus, the major projects of the New Deal involved the distribution of material goods, especially relief work administered by local officials, and the conceptualization of politics as the exchange of goods and loyalty for the sake of political order. In this approach to politics, a positive view of state activity, especially in policy areas in which credit can be easily taken by incumbents as a sign of a job well done (and as justification of their worthiness to return to office), is more important than rigorous programmatic coherence or the worldview compatibility of allies. The New Deal distribution of goods was about papering over divisive factional conflict and sustaining a tenuous political alliance. This ability to find a way around deep division to establish order is the heart of the urban traditional party, whose bonds were predicated on the pluralist idea that governing coalitions need not hew to a shared conception of the common good.[42] The cities never defected from this alliance, but the rural South, when confronted with the erosion of white supremacy entailed by civil rights legislation, was too rigid and unable to accommodate this change. Rather than bend, as the city organizations were able to do iteratively over decades and generations, the South broke, and broke ranks, to eventually lead today's conservative alignment.

1.4 Analyzing Place and History

A critical piece of this book's analysis is blending a spatial approach to studying politics with an historical one. When we are specifically looking for things that have changed over time, and for the role of geography in politics, new ideas emerge. Such an approach also structures the kinds of claims one can make. Studying an old time in a new way entails a new approach to data, and the empirical chapters of this book combine multiple sources of data, including original data of congressional district urbanicity and demography, the congressional record, and archives of public officials. This book focuses on how institutions that emerged at one level and time (inclusive local jurisdictions and traditional, non-ideological party organizations, from the turn of the twentieth century) addressed sociological conditions (urbanicity, and the crisis of the Depression) and had important effects within another institution during a different time (the national legislature, during the Long New Deal), which slowly led to a new equilibrium in American politics. The claims are not time-invariant or ahistorical; indeed, they rely in part on how institutions characteristic of one era had powerful lingering effects in the next era(s) in American politics. Sequence matters, and the distinctive forms of life across historical eras are important to the story.

I spend much of the book analyzing a pivotal moment in twentieth-century American history that is sometimes called the "Long New Deal," during which this transformation was in process. The era stretches from roughly Franklin D. Roosevelt's first term in 1933 to 1964, when landmark civil rights bills made clear that the tense relationship between the urban and southern wings of the

Democratic Party was about over.[43] This was a moment of gradual but monumental change in American history in several ways. Significantly, the Long New Deal was the era in which central cities peaked as a proportion of the population, meaning city representatives were particularly active, assertive, and persuasive in national politics.[44] If ever there were a time for the urban perspective to gain traction in national politics, this was it, and this fact allowed city representatives to employ several strategies in pursuit of their goals.[45]

Despite strategic obstacles, city representatives during this era found a way to lead a majority coalition and remake national politics.[46] These urbanites, who were mainly Democrats and would find a more secure home in that party over time, combined early in the New Deal to forge an urban political order that was the driving force behind an evolving set of political commitments called liberalism.[47] Never before in national politics had such a distinctively urban bloc taken shape within a single party, and never before had city issues taken such a significant place on the national agenda. In a tenuous alliance with the largely rural and underdeveloped South, which extracted its own share of federal largesse, cities worked to create policies that would alleviate some of the pressure of continual fiscal and social crises at home, which were brought on by such massive external forces as global economic collapse, wartime austerity, immigration, state-imposed budget requirements, economic restructuring, and the automobile, among others. The urban alliance had limited but significant success getting "sympathetic understanding" for "the problems of the urban citizen and community" in national politics, as Daley himself put it in that hearing in 1964.

By then, however, this sympathy was vanishing. Almost from the beginning of the New Deal, a conservative coalition of Republicans and Southern Democrats had been a recurrent feature of national politics, throwing a roadblock in the way of urban Democrats' plans not only to advance any social or civil rights for African Americans (an apparently unacceptable outcome for most southerners), but also to expand national urban policies and continue the national urban growth and redevelopment initiatives that had helped sustain industrial cities through the past three decades.[48] Daley's testimony at the 1964 congressional hearing reveals the urban Democrats' response to the reapportionment mandate in the light of their troublesome coalition dynamics. On this occasion, Judicial Committee Chair Emanuel Celler, a senior Brooklyn Democrat, observed that suburbs might find common cause with the cities:

CELLER: [Maybe if] the suburban areas would have greater representation . . . they might be able to see because of being [in] closer proximity to Chicago the needs of Chicago and might join up with Chicago and therefore give Chicago what it deserves?

DALEY: I think that would be a fair assumption. Not only that, we overlook other facts. There are metropolitan areas downstate who have the same problem. There are metropolitan areas that account for 76 percent of the population... Champaign, Urbana, Davenport, Rock Island, Moline, Peoria, Springfield, East St. Louis.

This exchange by two pillars of the urban political order, one a liberal congressman and the other a big-city machine boss, presaged the new alignment that would take shape as the rural South drifted away from the Democratic Party. Here again, the historical moment of this hearing is important, because the 1960 Census revealed that the large eastern cities that had been the heart of the urban alliance in Congress were no longer growing. The future lay in the rapidly expanding suburbs, which have since absorbed a substantial majority of the nation's population. Throughout the New Deal era, the territory surrounding large cities had been strictly Republican territory, tucked between largely Democratic metropolises and rural regions and small cities of mixed partisanship. As city growth reached increasingly rigid municipal limits, the once-sleepy small towns on the urban fringe became the centerpiece of American growth. As the fastest-growing areas of the country, it was the Republican-dominated suburbs that had the most to gain from the apportionment revolution. This meant that many of the apportionment gains actually accrued to the GOP, despite Daley's hopes of metropolitan unity.

But since the 1960s, there has been a quiet and gradual maturation of national partisan conflict along the urban–rural continuum: large cities have generally remained Democratic (and many have become more so), suburban constituencies have become less uniformly Republican (and many older, inner-ring suburbs in major metropolitan areas have shifted decisively to the Democrats), and rural areas have shifted toward the Republicans. Many smaller cities remain mostly Democratic, as Daley had hoped. No longer do cities leapfrog their suburbs to find allies; their bedfellows are far less strange, in terms of the kinds of places they come from—the "next-most" urban instead of the least urban. The vision of politics that Daley hoped to see realized was based on interests putatively shared by densely settled communities; today's politics, characterized by greater ideological coherence and polarization related to the ways of life and governance more amenable to different kinds of places, was the result.

Because civil rights and the backlash to them were so salient in the 1960s, many conventional accounts look there for the roots of our current politics.[49] But we should look deeper, to the sources of the initial conflict between cities and the South.[50] The creation of an urban political order in the 1930s set in motion the processes that have led us to our current situation of national political division. By bringing two distinctively urban sets of issues rooted in the city experience—statism and group pluralism—to the national agenda, this city bloc wound up setting the terms of debate for the next eighty years, and the urban–rural divide has been maturing ever since. The major glacial changes of the intervening decades—the departure of the white South to the Republican Party and the increasing Republicanism of rural areas even outside the South— have been most obvious since the 1960s, but those dynamics were baked into the cake of the New Deal alliance from the very beginning. This is because when urbanites became a majority of the Democratic alliance in the New Deal, they began to defend their commitments to pluralism, state activism, and new group mobilization. The white South was *always* opposed to these commitments, but it took this group decades to finally change its party allegiance.[51] The intraparty discursive conflict on these issues, and the divergence in roll call behavior, was present early in the New Deal.

This era also provides leverage helpful in analyzing the effects of a key local institution in my account: the "traditional" party organization.[52] During the Long New Deal, there were more members of these local traditional parties in Congress than at any other time in American history, and we now know that this was the high-water point of the institutions' national influence. Thereafter, the traditional party's style of politics would become almost as anachronistic as the feudal system of representation Daley had come to attack. These parties had been the dominant institutional form in late-nineteenth-century city governance, but in most places they had long since passed their prime by the 1960s, and the places where they were still strong were losing people. Population shifts, institutional reforms, and social change had sapped their strength and contributed to their demise.[53] As the urban age gave way to an era of suburban demographic explosion, Daley was the country's most powerful mayor and one of its most powerful Democrats. He was both of these things because he was positioned at a distinctive place in Democratic politics, linking local and national politics.

Like most powerful institutions, the traditional parties were fairly criticized from all sides—for their inefficiency, exclusivity, venality, and democratic shortcomings, as noted above. But the basic function that the most powerful examples of this kind of organization had indisputably served was to integrate politics both horizontally (linking otherwise fractious constituencies across the city) and vertically (linking actors at different levels of government). Anyone who has spent time with those close to such organizations, where they still exist, knows that this kind of professional politics requires a sensitive eye and ear for the detail of local politics—they are about the nuts and bolts of micro-interactions, and they exist and persist as networks that can link politicos up and down the power structure over long periods of time (they also create barriers to entry for those wishing to join the political fray). This integration provided order and unity where the possibilities for each were quite uncertain. Without such binding institutions, Vorys may have had little to worry about—the subdivisions of a city would have had little in common and no more organization than any other collection of districts.[54]

Finally, the timing of the Long New Deal affords analytical leverage in unpacking some tricky issues surrounding spatial demography. On racial issues especially, this was a time before the (mostly inappropriate) conflation of cities with other confounding factors, particularly race. Today, "urban" is often employed as a (benign or insidious) euphemism for "not white," with a particular nod toward African Americans, often because members of racial and ethnic minority groups are disproportionately likely to live in central cities.[55] During the Long New Deal, American cities were places of heightened diversity (as they almost always are), but they were all overwhelmingly white, and their politics were firmly in the hands of white elites. The Great Migrations of African Americans to large industrial cities over several decades did bring another group into these communities, but they did not by themselves utterly transform city demography. A variety of other social, economic, and political processes, stretching over decades, contributed to this change. High levels of local segregation also provide analytical leverage, because throughout this period, most big-city districts included *virtually no* African Americans, so it is difficult to attribute the development of racial liberalism to simple responsiveness to these new constituents. Studying this time period thus helps to limit the explanatory power of the simplest alternative explanations in some of the following analyses, particularly those of patterns of representation on national civil rights issues during this period presented in Chapter 5.

Similarly, the Long New Deal mostly predates the mass migration of whites to the suburbs that also contributed to the distinctive demography of central cities and ultimately to what many call the "Big Sort."[56] American cities in this era were more liberal than rural areas, but they had many, many more conservatives than they do today. When racially driven "uprisings" occurred in these cities during this era, it was typically not minority groups expressing exasperation or frustration; rather, it was usually white Americans rioting against integration. Perhaps more fundamentally, the connection between civil rights and "liberalism" was not really present at the beginning of this era; racial issues were only incorporated into the liberal agenda *during* this time period.[57] As we shall see, it was city representatives, including many from the nonideological traditional organizations, and with very few nonwhite constituents, who helped create and defend this political-ideological link that drove the midcentury realignment.

Thus, timing plays two major roles in this analysis. The broad argument grapples with time and political change: sequences, types, and critical moments. My analyses are developmental in nature because they contend with forces, ideas, alliances, institutions, and models of politics that have changed over time. In particular, the specific timing of the demographic and economic shifts in American cities (the arrival of immigrants, the collapse of local economies in the Depression, the in-migration of African Americans, the dispersion of population within and across metropolitan areas in response to pro-growth policies, white flight), overlaid with the sequence of change in the distinctive local institutions of the era (inclusive municipal borders, traditional party organizations and machines, metropolitan fragmentation, municipal reform), make for the kind of complex, multivariate developmental narrative that is at home within the subfield oeuvre of American political development. The sequence of this process is important and its outcomes are the product of a mix of structure and contingency: it is not clear what would have happened if traditional parties had been fully vanquished in cities with significant African American populations by the 1940s or how important linking institutions have really been in pushing forward civil rights legislation since the maturation of suburban sprawl, white flight, and the relative homogenization of city districts. Alternatively, if partisan rivalries or intracity conflict had kept the U.S. Conference of Mayors from forming a cohesive front, the shape of the urban agenda might have been much different—there might not have been one. The outcomes described here were not the inevitable products of impersonal forces, but rather they constitute a pattern of decisions—ideology-building, coalitional cooperation, and political responses—that were the product of human agency structured but not determined by institutions.

Adopting this long view also aids us in a narrower way: it allows us to rule out some alternative explanations for cities' distinctive politics, especially demography, and to see what happened first in the racial realignment. Even as it was coming together, even *before* FDR's win, the cities and the South were already fighting: over race and immigration, over fiscal policy, and over aid to cities. These changes happened before white flight, and before most city districts had distinctive racial compositions. While the urban–rural divide is still maturing today, it did not begin in 2004 (when pundits started to notice the red–blue states map), or 1964 (when the national parties' positions on civil rights became more clearly opposed), and it did not develop evenly. It began in the New Deal, with the coalescence of a partisan bloc of cities. The rural departure from that coalition took decades.

Geography also plays two roles in the analysis: first, it provides the lens through which the urban–rural divide can be conceptualized, and through which the contours of political ideology can be interpreted as responses, at least in part, to the spatial conditions of the modern city. Second, the key local institutions in the analysis are place-based, and even place-defining in some cases. The place-rooted institutions of horizontal integration (IHIs) theorized in the coming chapters provide a mechanism through which political actors built bridges between constituencies that were not natural allies. Because of shifts in the American population—mainly to the suburbs, where the political fragmentation of territory undermines the possibilities for bridge-building—the Long New Deal is an auspicious time to analyze political geography in this way.

For these substantive and analytical reasons, these analyses deal less with the aftermath of the midcentury realignment and the growth of suburban districts since the 1970s. In part this is to limit the scope of the inquiry to moments of significant change that contribute to our knowledge of American political development. The midcentury Republicanism dominance of suburban voters and government has been widely known and well studied, though the rapid demographic and ongoing political change of that kind of place in the last two decades will surely yield interesting analyses in the near future. While these are very important changes, I want to focus on the "first mover" in the place character divide, the cities.

1.5 Analysis: Data

In analyzing the development of the urban–rural divide and the development of dual liberalism within the city wing of the Democratic Party during the urban interlude, I turn primarily to the congressional record. My primary concern is the character of city representation in national politics, so the national legislature is an important place to look: it is the site at which cities contend most directly with other kinds of constituencies and where decisions about the course of national policy are made. In this focus, I join a tradition of historical political analysis that leverages the wealth of information available for studies of congressional policymaking based on the theoretical idea that representation in the legislature is a central component of liberal democracy.[58] I look mainly to the House of Representatives, rather than the Senate, because this chamber gives us a firmer grasp of the personnel actually representing cities. House districts represent defined territories, often small enough to be located within or roughly coterminous with cities. States have invariably noisier constituencies; while some big-city senators such as Robert F. Wagner, Hubert H. Humphrey, and Paul Douglas were clearly tied to their hometowns and acted as advocates for urban progressivism during this era, analyses of the House are more reliable because its membership more clearly reveals who is actually representing a city (and, just as important, *not* representing other kinds of places) based on district territory. We can also analyze intrastate dynamics within the House, something that is impossible in the Senate.

I examine the historical record in two main ways. As in many political science analyses of Congress, patterns of roll call voting are central to the story. While there have been a few specific previous analyses of urban representatives' behavior in Congress, these have left important questions unanswered because the measures of city districts have been rough, limited, or otherwise incomplete. To remedy this, I created a new dataset that serves as the empirical cornerstone of this book, the CSR (as in "City–Suburban–Rural") dataset. The CSR data, as elaborated in Chapter 6 and Appendix A, include measures of congressional districts' urbanicity and city of origin going back to 1789. Beginning with a list of cities large enough to merit congressional representation and manually coding the congressional districts from those cities and (in the twentieth century) their suburban rings, this dataset includes a series of original qualitative and quantitative measures of districts' place character. By identifying which districts are from large cities and which are from the *same* city, this dataset makes many historical analyses of the role of place character and local institutions in national representation possible for the first time.[59] By analyzing city *delegations* (as well as the whole set of representatives from all cities) in these roll call analyses, we can examine the character of local institutions—not just *whether* a district is from a city, but what *kind of city* it is from.

Knowing about the urbanicity of congressional districts can help support claims about the urban–rural divide, but we need to go further to get a better picture of how different city districts were from each other during this era of growing segregation. Demographic data for big-city districts during much of the Long New Deal were not available when I began this project. Previous studies have relied on congressional district data released by the Census Bureau or estimates based on county-level data, which are too coarse to measure differences between densely packed city districts. For prewar districts, no estimates existed at all. Without good estimates of district-level demography, it is very difficult to systematically assess the effect of local factors on congressional representation, so as an important complement to the CSR data, I have also created original demographic estimates for congressional districts for much of the Long New Deal using an innovative geographic information system (GIS) procedure to calculate these measures from the bottom up rather than estimate from the top down. There is broad agreement that constituency composition matters in shaping member choices, but we can't see the patterns if we don't know the demography. The details and more precise advantages of each of these data collections are described in subsequent chapters and in the appendices.

These original measures of place context are connected to substantive political issues in roll call voting by linking CSR measures with the American Institutions Project (AIP) dataset, which allows some slicing of the data to focus on issues of particular import to cities and to see how the dynamics of policy-making and preferences may differ across policy areas.[60] For analyses of roll calls, I also make substantial use of congressional data from Poole and Rosenthal's voteview.org database, which includes comprehensive information about congressional composition and roll call votes, as well as data from the census. These roll call and district-level analyses are the backbone of the quantitative empirical chapters (4 through 6).

The second main type of primary data upon which I draw is archival. I look mainly in two places. The first is from the beginning of the legislative process: the record of congressional hearings. These records include more nuanced information than a roll call can reveal about how representatives are thinking about these issues (or at least how they want to be *perceived* as thinking about them), how they want others to think about these issues, what their priorities are, and what organized groups in society share their views. Not every issue is discussed in hearings, but many major issues are.[61] And while these hearings include scripted testimony by witnesses, they also frequently include relatively frank, candid conversations between representatives and witnesses and among representatives. Conflicts that may not be apparent in roll calls—because representatives are pressured to conform to a party position or because intraparty compromise has adjusted the content of a bill to reflect a majority-party accord that all factions can live with—may be evident in these conversations, revealing the "truer" preferences of representatives. From these hearings, the subtler elements of city strategies can sometimes be gleaned: pressure to comply with the institutionalized logroll of the Democrats' inclusive exchange, arguments emphasizing the urgency of certain urban issues, the "urbanization" of obviously controversial civil rights policies, and the direction of future alliances.

Second, I draw upon the archival records of the persons who were at the intersection where local and national politics meet: congressional representatives from cities and mayors. In the narratives here, I focus on the biggest cities during this time, New York and Chicago. By looking at the correspondence between these public officials—some locally responsible to an entire city, others ostensibly representing a piece of that city in national politics—we can see some of the contours of these relationships. In particular, we can see that members of Congress (MCs) really did conceive of themselves as members of city delegations, representing a whole city interest, and that their mayors often called on them to do so. We can also trace how this happened at times, following issues as they arose from constituents, passed through city hall, and moved toward action by congresspersons. These interactions are particularly important for Chapters 4 and 5.

From this breadth of sources and range of analyses, we can make a start at understanding how urbanicity—as expressed by city representatives on the national stage—transformed American politics. A note to some readers who might be looking for an even more comprehensive treatment of city policy in America, or findings from other branches and other settings: while I have tried not to be narrow, a book must find a focus. Mine is cities on the Hill, contending with other place character blocs in national politics. For further reading, I encourage readers to visit Biles (2011) for a more detailed chronicle of the rise and fall of a robust urban policy agenda (especially in executive branch politics), and outstanding work of the scholarship I draw upon. And while contemporary politics is evolving quickly in ways obviously relevant to the argument, an historical project simply cannot keep up with the latest news—though I do connect, these analyses to twenty-first century changes in the conclusion. This book should help restart the conversation about cities in American politics, not be anything like a final word.

1.6 Chapter Outline

At its theoretical heart, this book is a syncretistic work combining key insights from the fields of urban politics, the politics of race and ethnicity, political economy, and American political development. The question of how to get diverse majority-rules polities to provide for the preferences of minorities is recurring and vital for those who support both vibrant, sustainable communities and racial justice, but who also understand the resilience of forces that would prefer neither. I hope this book contributes partial answers. At the same time, prompted by Lieberman (2009), Lapinski (2013), and others, much of the data and approach of this book are drawn from historical congressional sources, with the ultimate moving object I am trying to depict being a system-level understanding of American politics that pits cities against other kinds of places in the central ideological struggles of our time.

The briefest possible outline of the book's analytical flow is that at a key moment (the Long New Deal), American cities brought their local approach to governing into national politics in order to help solve some of their local challenges (and because they believed these were the best policies for the nation they wanted to lead). Among these policies were an ever-adaptive set of market interventions that aimed to help manage modern capitalism and an approach to mediating between racial and ethnic groups that sought to prevent rivalries from fatally undermining governance. Among the most important mechanisms for advancing these policies, especially the controversial ones, were local institutions that promoted unity in city representation. The end result was the contemporary urban–rural divide and our current red–blue political alignment. The following chapters elaborate this argument.

In Chapter 2, I outline the city delegation theory, which considers the complex relationship between urbanicity and governance in a modern, representative democracy. This theory begins with a focus on how the distinctive attributes of cities—density, size, and heterogeneity—prompt the formation of a set of policy priorities and foster the development of local IHIs to sustain them by those responsible for a community's well-being. Among these priorities are statism and group pluralism, which, when considered together with the attributes of urbanicity, can help us understand the distinctiveness of cities and the relationship between cities and ideology in modern American politics. These governing commitments, especially statist interventions, are difficult to sustain if enacted only at the local level, so cities must also seek to affect supralocal policies. To do this effectively, a collection of city representatives, who are often rivals in other contexts, must put aside their differences and behave cohesively in support of a citywide interest as a city delegation at a higher level. Cohesive representation is fostered by institutions characteristic of city delegations but not of other collections of representatives. These IHIs bind heterogeneous constituencies together and play a key role in the ability of cities to represent themselves as cohesive units rather than as collections of heterogeneous and separate constituencies.

Chapter 3 tells the tale of the historical moment when urban policy rose to the national agenda, a process initiated not by liberal interest groups but by city leaders in the nascent U.S. Conference of Mayors. Beset by the massive governance challenges of the Great Depression, which were made more intense by the ever-changing nature of the cities, mayors advocated for more connections between the national and local governments and for a national urban policy. For the first time, there was a cohesive set of city leaders who saw each other as allies in a national policy debate and who formed the basis for an urban political order. This political consolidation of the cities was the first "move" in the creation of today's urban–rural divide.

Chapter 4 illustrates how city delegation theory works by showing them in action in national representation. At the national level, were the rural defenders of malapportionment correct in their concern that cities would be more organized or cohesive in representation than we might expect? Is there a difference between cities with different kinds of local institutions? The answer to each question, this chapter shows, is "yes." IHIs—those political institutions spanning multiple constituencies, which are present in cities but not in other areas, and which are stronger in some cities than in others—foster cohesive representation among members of a city's congressional delegation even though those members often represent very different kinds of constituents. In this way, cities foster agreement among representatives. This is especially true in places with traditions of strong local parties. The unit of the city delegation is vital in the maintenance of a progressive, united urban political order, because it is a foundational "building bloc" for such a political force. By overcoming the challenges to political order presented by heterogeneity at home, cities present a cohesive face to the nation in pursuit of national urban policies.

Chapter 5 is the book's pivotal chapter, which explores the role of urbanicity and local IHIs in a crucial policy area: civil rights for African Americans. Throughout the urban interlude, the big-city and southern wings of the Democratic alliance moved further apart on a range of issues, but race was always at the core of their disputes. Eventually, the persistence of city efforts to incorporate African Americans into U.S. politics drove the "solid" South from its place at the heart of the Democratic Party, where it had sat for nearly a century, to gradually become the stronghold of doubly conservative Republicanism that it is today. More than simple sectional conflict rent the fabric of the Democratic national alliance. Urbanicity and the characteristics of local party organization were also important factors in this partisan change. The insights of city delegation theory help explain how local party organizations linking the diverse constituencies of the largest American cities played an important role in fostering national racial liberalism, one that is often overlooked in studies of urban racial politics.

In Chapter 6, I zoom out to broadly describe the development of the urban bloc in Congress after the main events of the previous chapters. The twentieth century saw the birth of a distinct national urban political order, followed by a shift from a "bimodal" coalition of urban and rural representatives to one in which the relationship between urbanicity and partisanship is much more monotonic. Building upon previous analyses, I evaluate the strength of the city bloc over time using measures of institutional strength within Congress. While the Long New Deal was a heyday for the city's place in the national imagination, in some ways the urban political order is potentially more powerful, though also far more vulnerable, today.

Finally, the conclusion takes stock of the urban political order: the maturation of the place-character divide in the contemporary "blue" alignment in the electorate, with its still-strange bedfellows, and the prospects for a regeneration of national urban metonymy. For now, though, let's turn to the relationship between cities, their representatives, and American liberalism.

2

Urbanicity, City Delegations, and Two-Dimensional Liberalism

> When [the American people] get piled upon one another in large cities, as in Europe, they will become corrupt as Europe.
> —Thomas Jefferson[1]
>
> In order for anything to be done under public auspices, the elaborate decentralization of authority... must be overcome or set aside.
> —Edward Banfield and James Wilson, *City Politics*[2]

Among Aesop's fables, there is a tale of a country mouse and a city mouse. The city mouse visits his country cousin and is unimpressed by the rude simplicity of rural life. He invites the country mouse to sample the pleasures of the capital, where the two of them are chased from the refined meal they can find there by a menacing cat. The country mouse returns to his home, reflecting that his cousin "may have luxuries and dainties that I have not, but I prefer my plain food and simple life in the country with the peace and security that go with it."[3] The tale is meant to guide us toward a humble, peaceful life and away from risky plentitude, but it is also a nice way to think about the differences between cities and other kinds of places. Cities are places where conditions change frequently, where social experiences are often more intense than elsewhere, and where highs and lows are juxtaposed in close proximity.[4] Navigating the trade-offs of city life entails constant attention; cities are not always easy places to pursue Aesop's recommended simple life of security. This goes for governing, too: cities and the countryside call for different kinds of policies, and a different approach to politics, than do more bucolic areas.

These differences between places have contributed to the polarization of contemporary American politics; today, the urban–rural partisan divide is larger than it has ever been in our history, with many rural places very Republican and most big cities overwhelmingly Democratic. Some, but not all, of this divide is due to the tastes held by individuals in different kinds of places. Ideologically, though, individuals are far from perfectly sorted; there are lots of liberal ruralites, conservative urbanites, and all the other combinations of ideology and place.[5] On particular policies, the gaps tend to be even smaller, indicating that it is identities, rather than strong policy preferences or even policy-relevant ideologies, that drive the divide within the public.[6] At the mass level, it is very difficult to know whether the urban–rural divide is driven by context or composition—does city living make people more liberal, while the country makes people more conservative? Or do conservatives just prefer to live in the country, and liberals in the city? High levels of mobility make it hard to nail this relationship down, because the dissatisfied can leave rather than adjust. The fact that most Americans actually live in the suburbs—the semi-urban, in-between space where both place character and ideological-partisan composition are even more uneven—complicates the picture even more.

In this book, I argue that the urban–rural divide is not reducible to individuals' preferences about government. Instead, or in addition, it is illuminating to consider how the politics of place comes not only from individuals' differences but from how place and space generate different demands for managing and organizing society, and how political leaders respond to those challenges. The spatial dynamics of these governance demands predate Americans' partisan sorting and can help us explain the content of "liberalism" and "conservativism" in U.S. politics today. The real differences between cities and other kinds of places mean that the *possibility* for political conflict has always been present, but in the United States, that conflict hasn't always been tied to national partisanship. Today, however, this urbanicity divide is the *defining cleavage* in American politics.

The political gap between city and country is associated with sociological factors like density and heterogeneity, but it is not reducible to how the built and social environment shapes individuals' experiences. By virtue of their size, cities combine different areas within space, forcing interactions that more fragmented political spaces do not; thus, a city's politics are distinctive not only because urbanites are different from ruralites, but because urbanites are so different *from each other*. This combination of disparate groups into one common polity creates dynamics that go beyond individual preferences to create a different political culture within cities. It's not *only* the density and diversity of urban areas that matter, but also the *size* of the political communities at their center. This helps explain the real importance of cities in shaping American politics.

In this chapter, I synthesize a set of prominent social science debates that help explain important patterns in American politics. Among these patterns are the "red–blue" divide that has come to define American politics in recent electoral cycles and the formation of a bloc-of-blocs that makes up the blue side of that divide. These theories are not usually considered together in one argument, largely because they were developed by scholars in different subfields, each with their own vital research concerns. By bringing them together, however, we can better see the impulses that link cities together into alliances and the centripetal institutional forces that hold the center together within cities as they participate in the politics of the nation.

At its heart, this chapter explains a paradox of city government: the fact that the conditions of urbanicity in the United States create high demand for relatively active governance (principally because of density and heterogeneity) while simultaneously *inhibiting* the implementation of policies helpful for meeting that demand (principally because of federalism and diversity). City leaders have found some ways—often imperfect, never assured, and in need of continual revision—to address this paradox. These solutions have included both local and national action. While the field of urban politics focuses mostly on the local level, the argument here turns to the national.

2.1 Dimensions of Urbanicity

The United States has always had a love-hate relationship with its cities.[7] Exploring the cultural and sociological dimensions of city life is a fascinating pastime; the priority of this study, however, is to theorize how the specific *political* imperatives of city governance—relative to the other kinds of places that make up the nation—connect to major changes in American politics, which in turn can help shed light on the importance of the city in our common *polis*.[8]

In American politics, there is a recurrent dimension of political tension that we can think of as "place-character conflict," which typically manifests as an urban–rural or urban–suburban divide. Places large and small are wonderfully heterogeneous in their character and particular in their own historical and current experiences, but for the social scientist, it is useful to sort them into three categories: central city, suburban, or rural (nonmetropolitan), with each kind of place having distinctive attributes that sets it apart and creates different political dynamics.[9] To some extent, people choose their surroundings according to their preferences, but these places also shape the kind of politics and policies required to govern them, creating a bigger emphasis on interdependence rather than independence. Simply put, today's city-dwellers and suburban commuters need different policies than Jefferson's independent yeomen did, and they may need an entirely different approach to politics in order to achieve them.

Urbanicity—the condition of being like a city—has many dimensions, but three are particularly important for politics: density, heterogeneity, and size.[10] Studies of urban society tend to focus on density and heterogeneity. At their very essence, cities are densely populated centers of varied, relatively varied social and economic activity.[11] Density is important for economic activity: returns to scale associated with clusters of firms and labor can make production much more efficient, and they can also have powerful side effects that spur further growth.[12] Concentrations of diverse bases of human capital foster interaction, innovation, and growth. In the broad scope of history, the process of urbanization and the development of cities have been powered by commerce and industry, and broad structural economic and geopolitical forces have been determining factors in cities' ascendency, decline, and resurgence; this is especially true in American cities, which have only existed during the industrial age.[13]

Urban life—with its greater density, variety, and anonymity of human interaction; thin ties between actors; specialization of individual roles; and larger institutions—lends itself to a different kind of civil society than do the thicker patterns of traditional social interaction, less specialized or formally codified institutions, and more rigid ties of smaller, more static communities.[14] As a result, the institutionalization, routinization, and depersonalization of many governing practices are both more common and understandable in cities, where authority-wielding personnel are too numerous and too frequently rotated for rules to be enforced based on deep interpersonal knowledge and individuals' personal authority.

This tendency is particularly important in the diverse modern city, because the parties to an activity or dispute are less likely to share the same cultural assumptions or social practices than would be the case in a more homogeneous context. Cities have frequently been points of first contact between members of groups newly arrived from the hinterland and abroad, and this diversity creates challenges for order because preferences and modes of conflict resolution are more likely to differ. In short, density makes all sorts of interactions more frequent, and heterogeneity makes them more uncertain. Managing such a society requires different strategies than are used in smaller communities, where people are better known to each other and where informal codes and norms and shared background experiences provide social organization and control more effectively. In urban, new norms, practices, and institutions need to be developed to make shared life manageable.

Density and heterogeneity thus pose distinctive challenges and opportunities that often make cities fascinating social laboratories. However, cities are also distinctive on another important—and perhaps more definitionally fundamental—dimension that is analytically separable from those characteristics: size.[15] Simply put, cities are *large* local political communities.[16] A city is a container with contents determined by the boundaries on a map, which include residents within a common political community (and exclude others from it). The study of urban politics often focuses on boundaries *within* cities, such as city council districts or less formal neighborhood lines, which can serve as "trenches," reinforcing identities and driving potential allies apart.[17] Today, the more important boundaries are *between* cities, as municipal boundaries bind or divide members of the state or nation on the basis of membership in a local community.[18] Such divisions have consequences for decisions made *within* the city and at higher levels of government.[19]

Taken together, size, heterogeneity, and density constitute the core dimensions of urbanicity and help us understand what a city is.[20] There are other dimensions, but for our present purposes, these three core concepts will suffice, for they have specifically political consequences as well as "merely" social and economic ones. Urbanicity had important effects on American politics in the twentieth century, as cities grew, matured, spread across the nation, and gave way to the suburb as the typical political home of most Americans. Cities have provided national and regional political leadership, given birth to political movements, and served as "laboratories of democracy." They have also provided the basis for the development of progressive, pragmatic liberalism in American politics. These three characteristics of urbanicity have left their mark on how cities and their members have taken part in national politics and changed both the content of the national agenda and the alliances that debate it. In the next section, we will see how urbanicity predisposes elites (and most residents, too) to a suite of political commitments that are sometimes in tension but always distinctive.

2.2 Liberalism as a Response to City Problems

Urbanicity makes cities distinctive places to live, but how might it shape the politics of city residents and leaders? This question is a central investigatory prompt of urban political science, and many urban studies make their contributions to the field by looking at how the dimensions of urbanicity interact at the local level.[21] The urban–rural divide prompts us to examine how place and ideology may be related. We should not assume that cities will have the same effects on all their members, however. Urbanicity may generate different political dispositions for differently situated actors, so in each of the following sections I will consider how everyday individuals (denizens of the city, or city-zens, who are making their way in the world) and elites (those responsible for city governance) may view policies differently when filtered through the lens of urban conditions.[22]

Most viscerally, compared to those who dwell in other kinds of places, city-zens may want different things out of government and may consider a different style of political engagement with others appropriate or desirable. These distinctive individual preferences surely aggregate into distinctive community preferences.[23]

But while cities are collections of individual persons, they are also more than that: they are communities whose situation within society fosters an organic citywide interest—the interest in addressing the paradox of city governance—that may differ at times from the interests of individual city-dwellers (taken separately or even in the aggregate) for the sake of resolving governance crises and maintaining the city's continued sustainability.

This organic interest is more ineffable than a simple aggregation of individual preferences, so it merits brief further explanation. The organic city interest is akin to Rousseau's general will in its essential unknowability (as opposed to the aggregate "will of all," which we might discover from elections or polling).[24] A prominent articulation of the city interest is that described by Peterson (1981) in his landmark analysis of the "limited" policy role of local governments in a federal system. Peterson identifies the key organic interest of the city as its health, which he narrowly operationalizes as the maintenance of a tax base and the retention or attraction of above-median taxpayers. The organic interest of a city may be more nebulous and harder to conceptualize or measure than that, but the insight remains that the maintenance of community order may be derived from different principles than a simple aggregation of individuals' preferences or actions. Peterson's minimal operationalization can lead us toward an organic interest in some policy areas, but not in others—for instance, the proper way to handle race relations cannot obviously be deduced from the pursuit of above-average taxpayers. The vast number of perspectives and interests expressed (or invisible but normatively relevant) in contentious city politics means that no solution to any problem is likely to coincide with the preferences of all members of the community, or even a majority.[25] While most individual residents likely consider only their own preferences, city leaders (including representatives at all levels of government) are likely to be particularly sensitive to this organic interest (or at least their perception of it), because their careers and livelihood often depend on the overall health of the city, however defined; unlike the typical resident, they cannot usually decamp to another place and maintain their same status as leader, so they will take steps to perceive and defend a city interest.[26] Attempts to define the city position are often revealed in city policy, as well as in how cities represent themselves at higher levels of politics, when a city interacts with other political communities and interests.

It is at that higher level of politics that the connection between a city's interest and ideology begins to make sense. A nation as large as the United States has countless potential and actual cleavages. The nation's geographic size, political constitution, population diversity, and geopolitical importance have led to innumerable divides, but scholars have observed that a great deal of the political conflict in American national politics in the twentieth century can be described as fitting within two dimensions of substantive disagreement, which today are often folded into the ideological systems of liberalism and conservatism. The first dimension is related to the role of government in the economy, or statism, while the second dimension has to do with race, region, and culture.[27] Positions, or at least the observable congressional alliances, on a host of issues are explicable in terms of these dimensions. Each dimension has a liberal and a conservative pole, and one of the central questions of American political science is how these two dimensions—once ostensibly separable—increasingly overlap or coincide, and thereby deepen polarization.

There is a logical *city* position on the two primary dimensions of conflict in American politics, and this city position (again, the city's organic interest, though not necessarily the aggregate preferences of city-dwellers, and almost certainly not the preferences of all important *subsets* of a city's dwellers) informs what we call the liberal position on issues in these dimensions. Particularly in the Long New Deal era, when cities were both coalescing as a political bloc, and pursuing national urban policies for the first time, political ideologies came to reflect the governance demands prompted by urbanicity.[28] Attention to place character and space can help us understand this polarization better because the liberal position on each of these dimensions is related to the political management of large, dense, heterogeneous communities.

2.3 Cities and Statism

In this section, I consider the relationship between urbanicity and the primary dimension of twentieth-century American political conflict, statism.[29] It is not surprising that politics involves disputes about the role of the state in the economy, because much modern government activity at any level and at any time, even in a market society, is devoted to economic management. In the modern United States, government interventions in the economy most often take three forms: regulation, public goods provision, and redistribution.[30] Urbanicity creates relatively high demand for each of these classes of policies because of the nature of participation in a large, dense, heterogeneous market. This demand seems likely to be felt by both leaders and citizens. Part of the paradox of urbanicity, however, is that because of federalism, cities may not be able to promote these policies locally. As a solution, they can turn to complementary action at higher levels.

Economic regulation, the making and enforcement of rules about behavior, is more important in a city than in other kinds of places for several reasons. First, increased density makes the value of coordination and routinization more important. It is a simple thing to traverse a rural crossroads with little traffic. At a major city intersection, that task is more complicated, even dangerous: regulations like street lights and roundabouts make traffic flow more efficient in the aggregate, even though from the perspective of any individual they may appear to slow things down. Such a basic truth made the urbanist Louis Wirth observe that "the clock and the traffic signal are symbolic of the basis of our social order in the urban world."[31] Similar observations for other forms of regulation can be made: given a density and volume of interactions of any kind, regulation can improve efficiency simply through coordination, especially when participants in the activity may be of uneven skill, experience, or benignity.

Second, production and commerce often generate negative externalities such as pollution or congestion, which are more serious in densely inhabited communities because they can accumulate more quickly and affect more persons when they do. Regulation of these externality-generating processes can mitigate their effects. For instance, if there are no rules about how one disposes of garbage in a rural space, it may be no big deal—nature will dispose of it (at least its organic components) before it can accumulate. In a city, such anarchy leads to health crises quite quickly, as we have seen during garbage strikes or disease outbreaks in big cities. The same argument can be made about other kinds of pollution or other externality-generating behaviors.

Third, because cities are more fluid and anonymous environments, with thinner ties between members, we may see frequent attempts at what Wirth described as "mutual exploitation" and irresponsibility.[32] In such places, regulation provides valuable information for and constraints on economic actors, reassuring them that the other participants in the marketplace have cleared at least some minimal bar for entry and continued participation of a certain kind. The clear, obvious posting of health inspection grades in the windows of New York City restaurants is an example of this; in a place with only a few restaurants, where potential customers would know quickly which ones tended to make their patrons sick, large letters would be less necessary and reputation alone might keep would-be diners healthy. In a city with over 23,000 restaurants and rapid turnover, neither word of mouth nor personal experience can suffice.[33] Effective regulation thus ameliorates information problems that are more severe in cities.[34] City residents, even those who are themselves regulated, thus tend to be more accepting of heightened regulation than their counterparts in less dense places. For leaders and policymakers concerned with creating and enforcing such measures, regulation can also be done more efficiently in large communities than elsewhere, because the size of the community allows for more specialization and professionalization of regulatory functions and therefore more expertise among local city regulators. For these reasons, relatively more regulation is in the interests of both cities and their city-zens.

The second major form of governmental intervention in the market is the provision of common or public goods.[35] While some goods, like clean air, are obviously valuable across all spatial contexts, many are *more* valuable in a city than in another setting.[36] Goods that must be located in a particular place and the use of which is related to proximity to that good are more valuable in a densely populated area than in more sparsely populated places.[37] For instance, to the extent that people prefer to walk to a park in order to use it, having a park within walking distance of lots of residences increases the use value of that park. In a city like New York, where many thousands of people can walk to Central Park in a few minutes, this is particularly clear.[38] In a less densely populated area, fewer people would live within walking distance to the park, and its use value would be less.[39] Similar arguments can be made about museums or other cultural institutions, as well as public transit infrastructure: these goods can be valued more, by more people, in densely populated areas. As in the regulatory logic outlined previously, there are returns to scale available in large, dense communities for the provision of goods that do not exist in less densely populated communities. In the nineteenth century, this reality was clear for both city boosters and residents seeking services. For instance, several large cities, with their greater and/or established access to significant water sources, virtually held adjoining areas hostage, demanding annexation in exchange for access.[40] This logic also plays out in practice: large and dense communities do tend to provide more public goods than other kinds of localities.[41]

Finally, the third major category of state intervention in the economy is redistribution. Government often actively adjusts economic outcomes through policy. Among individuals, attitudes toward redistribution are likely to be related to the *character* of redistribution (we usually think of redistribution as moving resources from rich to poor, but other patterns are certainly possible and have different implications) and one's place in the income distribution.[42] For instance, a person at the less affluent end of the income distribution seems more likely to favor a progressive redistribution regime, as they would likely gain a net benefit from it. A rich person would be more likely to oppose such a regime, because they would experience a net cost from it. From this basic claim, Meltzer and Richard (1981) predict that aggregate preferences for redistribution will be stronger in unequal electorates.[43] Cities—as a consequence of their economic heterogeneity—tend to be more unequal than other political communities, so on average, demand for redistribution should be higher in cities than in more economically homogeneous communities (to the extent that preferences for redistribution are based on local information about inequality). Moreover, in densely populated places, we might expect residents to have more information about inequality because they are likely to encounter their neighbors more, giving them a better picture of the income distribution. This should in turn inform their preferences for redistribution.[44] Finally, the traditional means of revolt against conditions of inequality has often been the riot.[45] In densely built areas with heavy investment, such conflagrations are exponentially more costly than analogous uprisings in sparsely populated areas (and may also be more difficult to defeat). Thus, even the rich in very heterogeneous places may have an incentive to support moderate redistribution.[46]

In cities, then, regulation, public goods, and redistribution are very likely to be more popular or valuable than they will be in other places. Such are the governance demands of complex, high-maintenance places.[47] Thus, for each of these important types of state intervention in the economy, we expect the preferences of urbanites and their representatives to favor statism more because of the characteristics of their communities.[48] A review of the historical record provides empirical support for this theoretical claim at the local level. Conflict over statism came early to cities, and the interventionists tended to win. In New York City, for instance, the Democrats came to represent "a kind of primitive social welfare state" against proponents of "small, efficient government; individualism; and laissez-faire" as early as the 1850s, and that argument would be "at the heart of local politics for the rest of the nineteenth century and well into the twentieth."[49] Other cities' later experiences were similar. Primitive social welfare policies, regulation, and public goods provision were hallmarks of nineteenth-century city parties and governments.[50] The Progressive movement of the early twentieth century, especially its urban component, promoted many forms of economic regulation and reforms at the local and higher levels, including those concerned with food safety, labor regulation, municipal zoning, and the redistributive income tax.[51] Today, density and community size are associated with increased public goods provision.[52]

The other side of the urbanicity paradox is that despite a city's organic interest and urbanites' ostensible *preferences* for these interventions, cities face many formal and informal constraints that can make significant market interventions very difficult at the local level. Almost all states impose debt limits on their local governments, a legacy of nineteenth-century municipal debt crises. Many states cap the actual amount that localities can spend or tax with explicit tax and expenditure limits (TELs), and some municipalities have self-imposed TELs as well.[53] Informal constraints exist, too, in the market for municipal bond debt, which can discipline municipalities that stray from policies preferred by lenders concerned about a city's ability to repay.[54] Sitting behind or alongside all of those constraints is the pervasive logic of interjurisdictional competition, which predisposes cities to pursue developmental policies and avoid local redistribution.[55]

According to this public choice logic, above-median taxpayers (often businesses, but also rich individuals) are likely to relocate to avoid paying for policies that disproportionately benefit others if such movement is feasible. Under such conditions, significant market interventions may be unsustainable if applied unilaterally at the local level. Peterson (1981) makes this argument about redistributive programs such as welfare, but it applies to other kinds of market intervention policies that might disproportionately displease the rich as well. High levels of public goods provision (at least those that are not self-financing or that provide benefits that may not be apparent to the above-median taxpayer) may be difficult to sustain under this logic, as business interests seek to keep their tax bill down. This was a common justification for many of the business-related municipal reforms of the Progressive Era.[56] Heavy regulation, too, may encourage businesses to seek to relocate, if feasible, to laxer environments. The most powerful such regulations have historically had to do with labor: this is a major reason why so many manufacturers have moved from the union-friendly North to the open-shop South (where wages have tended to be much lower) and the threat of such moves help explain why organized business interests are sometimes able to keep democracies from raising the local minimum wage, even when they are far outnumbered by low wage-earners.

This logic applies even more powerfully today than in previous eras because mobility has increased with technology, and in some markets the effective competition is not just suburbs or other American cities, but the entire world. Thus, city leaders are often faced with a dilemma: the conditions of urbanicity make market interventions important for the maintenance of their communities (and perhaps for their political careers, because the citizens may demand such interventions), but if such interventions are adopted unilaterally, they may undermine the city's resource base. This is a key area in which the aggregate citizens' interests and the organic city interests may be in tension.

For instance, according to Meltzer and Richard's (1981) logic, we should expect very unequal cities to have high demand for redistribution. Their representatives, elected by the median voter(s), should also ostensibly share this preference. But if city hall unilaterally imposes a progressive local income tax, while other nearby jurisdictions do not, high earners—who would provide most of the revenue for the tax—can leave, dodging the tax but still enjoying the other benefits of city life. Even the most active, well-meaning, and responsive local government may be overwhelmed by the governance challenges presented by powerful forces well beyond local control if it tries to intervene too much.[57]

However, if the progressive tax is imposed at a *higher* level of government, such that it would be very difficult or costly for the high taxpayers to move away (say, to another country instead of a neighboring city), then the preferences of the voters (and officials) can be met without undermining the organic health of the city. Those who seek such interventions may therefore do better to pursue supralocal policies—to shape outcomes at higher levels.[58] By pursuing interventionist policies particularly beneficial to high-maintenance places but imposed across all local polities, city representatives can weaken the power of interjurisdictional competition and circumvent the constraints that keep them from engaging in such policies. Since roughly the 1930s, when the effects of both formal and informal constraints began to bite sharply as a result of the Great Depression and creeping suburbanization, this is what cities have sought to do in national politics.

It is this turn to higher-level government, especially at the national level, that is the key insight of this book. Local politics remains highly contentious and fascinating for many reasons, but it is vital that we understand how cities participate in national politics to *create* the context in which they can pursue policies to manage their communities without undermining them. Of course, cities do not exist in a vacuum, and they must often contend with other kinds of communities where demand for statism is not as great. Because cities seldom constitute a majority in state or national politics, they must pursue strategies for political success at those higher levels. These strategies will be explored in greater detail later in this chapter.

2.4 Cities and Group Pluralism

On the first dimension of national political conflict, there is a clear logical connection between urbanicity and preferences for statism, with the main challenge being *how* to provide the demanded interventions in a manner that balances democratic preferences with organic interests in light of institutional constraints. The second major dimension of national political conflict, having to do with racial and cultural issues, is even more complex.[59] Because cities are heterogeneous, they experience heightened levels of intergroup contact and potential for conflict. The city's interest in maintaining social peace is often in tension with the preferences of city-zens, who are often deeply socially divided—at times, to such a degree that they may no longer agree on statism.[60] City leaders, however, can and do develop institutions for mitigating this tension and addressing the city's perennial governance challenges.

It is not clear how urbanicity influences individuals' views about other groups and cultures; rather, this question is the subject of a half-century's scholarly controversy. There are two broad schools of thought on the relationship between diversity and intergroup relations. The first is contact theory, which holds that an individual's exposure to (and especially intimate contact with) persons from groups different from one's own will erode stereotypes and diminish intergroup hostility based on those stereotypes.[61] Most versions of contact theory identify conditions under which such stereotype erosion is more likely, including equality of status, pursuit of a common goal, and repeated interactions that enable individuals to build trust and get to know group members that they otherwise might not have. In an America both highly segregated and profoundly stratified by race and class, it is unclear whether these conditions hold very often for many people. But in spaces where those conditions do sometimes hold (such as in the military, the schools, or the workplace), there does seem to be evidence of this process as people from different backgrounds come into intimate contact with one another.

On the other hand, the bulk of political evidence has supported the group threat hypothesis, which holds that tensions between groups are likely to grow when levels of diversity are high or increasing. This more pessimistic theory predicts that competition over material resources, status, culture, or other valued goods leads to the increased salience of one's own group identity (as opposed to the obliteration of preconceived bias), heightened tension or conflicts between groups, and negative affect toward members of other groups.[62] To the extent that the group threat hypothesis holds, American cities—the sites of tremendous diversity and frequent inflows of new groups—should be hotbeds of intergroup conflict. Historically, it is not difficult to find examples to fit this account. Indeed, much of the evidence on which this theory was originally based is drawn from attitudes among white Americans toward African Americans, which is precisely the racial conflict that drives the second dimension in national politics and was the most visible manifestation of intergroup conflict in most American cities during the twentieth century. The preponderance of evidence supports the argument that demographic change, especially African American arrivals, fostered racist views among and actions by white Americans, even outside the South.[63] Race riots and smaller-scale racial violence were chronic realities in many cities over the entire twentieth century.[64] Most survey evidence tends to support this perspective as well.[65] At the community level, the evidence suggests that diversity typically makes people from different groups *less* likely to get along.

The implications of diversity are different for elected officials and other elites than they are for individuals, however. Should we expect these urban elites to be liberal, conservative, or mixed on racial issues? Certainly we could find examples of officials with each of these positions, but which more broadly reflects the city's interest? Democratically *responsive* officials ought to translate their constituents' preferences and interests into action, a normative position that is theoretically enforced by electoral considerations.[66] When it comes to racial issues in heterogeneous constituencies, however, it is difficult to know what this responsiveness would look like. It may be that representatives with more minority constituents will be more attentive to their concerns, a tendency that should be reflected in their taking racially liberal positions. Conversely, representatives with small but significant numbers of minority constituents may be more likely to attend to the heightened sense of threat that may be held by many of their majority-group constituents. The relationship may change with the size of the groups. In fact, scholarship does indicate that representation of minority positions on racial issues may be nonlinear: areas with small but significant nonwhite populations are likely to be more conservative than areas with none, but once these populations exceed some (relatively high) threshold, elites are very likely to represent minority communities, both descriptively and substantively.[67] This relationship is basically consistent with the group threat hypothesis, and it is also consistent with what we have seen in American cities over time: recurrent flares of racial tension and strife, group-based politics, and the ascension to power of coalitions led by minority politicians in sync with demographic change (both the continued influx of new groups and the exodus of those intolerant of diversity).

Cities as a whole tend to be pretty diverse, but twentieth-century American cities were often composed of segregated, fairly homogeneous subconstituencies.[68] While the expected representation of *diverse* constituencies is difficult to predict, the responsive representation of homogeneous constituencies near large populations of groups *perceived* as threatening is clearer. Because such representatives need only respond to members of their own particular geographically based constituency, group threat theory leads us to expect representatives from all-white constituencies near nonwhite constituencies to be relatively conservative on racial issues.[69] The representatives of nonwhite constituents, who are often spatially concentrated within districts because of segregated settlement patterns and voting rights legislation, are likely to be from minority communities themselves and to substantively represent those communities' concerns. Given segregated settlement patterns and responsive representatives, then, we might expect cities to be *divided* on racial issues, with some threatened constituencies and some minority-majority districts.

A different model of representation may lead us to have different expectations for city representation, however. City elites, who are typically not from minority communities themselves, may nonetheless have an interest in acceding to demands for justice and civil rights for marginalized groups. Most obviously, some local officials may be reliant (at least in part) on minority votes for continuation in office. Given segregation, this pressure would be most likely to be felt by a citywide official like a mayor, but not by a representative from a smaller geographic constituency, like a member of Congress. There is some evidence that such electoral pressures were important in the midcentury American city, even when white voters remained a vast majority of the electorate.[70] Beyond electoral pressure (since not all city elites face citywide election or are elected officials), city leaders may support civil rights and inclusive politics because they believe such an approach will maintain the social peace. However one actually feels about racial harmony or members of other groups, as long as physical entry into a community is relatively easy (and as long as overt apartheid-style repression by force is ruled out as morally repulsive, inefficient, or impracticable), then finding a way for groups to get along—rather than explode—must be a priority in governing a heterogeneous community. Potentially explosive group divisions are against a city's organic interest.[71]

This concern for maintaining the social peace has been reflected in the actions taken by cities when racial strife has been evident. New York City mayor John Lindsay famously took to the streets in the wake of Martin Luther King's assassination, seeking peace to avoid the riots that broke out in so many other cities. Since the early twentieth century, many cities have established official commissions to mitigate, resolve, and prevent such conflict. With names such as the Mayor's Committee on Human Relations, the Commission on Human Relations of Los Angeles County, or the New York City Commission on Human Rights, these committees were established with a mission of easing group tensions within their communities. Today, for instance, the New York City Commission on Human Rights is charged not only with "enforcement of Human Rights Law," but also with "educating the public and encouraging positive community relations."[72] These commissions, and those who share their goals, have identified the city interest of racial liberalism in service of intergroup comity. Less formally, the group of local leaders that served as an informal regime in twentieth-century Atlanta and promoted a vision of the city as "too busy to hate" self-consciously sought to strengthen intergroup comity and minimize potential disruption to business activities.[73] In many instances, the principal function of this kind of organization is to provide a space in which the concerns of marginalized groups are recognized and specific instances of conflict are resolved. In essence, they provide a forum for group pluralism, which has emerged as the guiding framework for managing intergroup relations in cities.[74] To be sure, these kinds of institutions have often left minority groups dissatisfied, or been accused of merely paying lip service to underlying issues. The fact remains, however, that such moves, even if merely symbolic, are far more liberal than the frequent elite response to demands made by racial minorities in American *rural* contexts—there, violent repression has been much more common. In cities, imperfect, halting, aspirational amelioration in the name of social peace has emerged across many contexts. But how can the individual and aggregate tendency toward *conflict* be overcome in the name of the organic interest in peace?

2.5 Second-Dimension Conflict and First-Dimension Liberalism

The prior sections have outlined two tensions in the relationship between urbanicity and the two dimensions of liberalism. On the first dimension, citizens and elites are generally in agreement on what to do (make some statist interventions), but not necessarily on how to do it (city-zens will just tend to want such interventions, while constrained elites often prefer them to be provided at higher levels). On the second dimension, city-zens are generally divided, while elites tend to support group pluralism and the accommodation (though probably not the prioritization) of minority demands in order to preserve the social peace.

The story is even more complex, however. While it is sometimes helpful to see these issue areas as analytically separable dimensions,[75] there are theoretical reasons to believe that they are deeply intertwined. This is because of the many findings related to the group threat hypothesis that indicate that diversity tends to undermine not only intergroup relations (i.e., second-dimension liberalism) but *first*-dimension liberalism as well. Studies in this vein suggest that there is reason to expect racial and ethnic heterogeneity to undermine statism, even as density promotes it, prompting us to think twice about how we might expect heterogeneous cities to represent themselves on "first-dimension" issues like regulation, redistribution, and public goods provision.[76] These key findings suggest that diversity may present challenges for proponents of *both* dimensions of liberalism, deepening the paradox of city government described earlier. And yet, experience indicates that the most diverse places in the United States—the nation's cities—have been the *most* liberal places on both of these dimensions, both locally and in representation for a very long time (as we shall see in the upcoming chapters). Thus, a key insight of this book is that we can understand this puzzle only if we remember that cities do not operate in a vacuum, and that they are led by human agents seeking to address this very problem. City leaders can act creatively to leverage local institutions and use national policy to help govern locally. Crucially, they can develop strategies and patterns of politics that are able to keep second-dimension conflict from crippling first-dimension governance.

It is impossible to really know if American cities of the mid-twentieth century would have been *more* statist if they had been less diverse. But we do know that those "doubly liberal" city leaders of the Long New Deal developed tools to keep the potential challenges of diversity from undermining the promises of modern life. And when we look closely at how cities represent themselves in national politics, the pessimistic expectation that diversity engenders racial division and fiscal conservatism—that is, that diversity contributes to two-dimensional conservatism—has emphatically not been borne out. Rather, while cities in the twentieth century were often the site of internal racial hostility and domination, they were also the home of modern racial liberalism, incorporating many disparate ethnic and racial minorities, even if very imperfectly, into a broader political community. The second major round of immigration-driven American diversity (from roughly 1890 to 1920) eventually gave rise to the initial articulation and promotion of both dimensions of liberalism at the national level, producing a set of ideas that was resilient to the challenges to governance posed by diversity.[77]

How, then, are we to understand the complex relationship between liberalism and urbanicity in national politics? A piece of the puzzle lies in city delegation theory, a theory of city representation that proposes a mechanism by which one element of urbanicity (size) can help mitigate the challenges of another (heterogeneity) to achieve the urgent interventions required for successful city management. We can only see this clearly if we turn our lens away from local action and analyze the patterns of urban representation in national politics.

2.6 Cities and Representation

Most urban politics research focuses on the local level, because that is where a city's formal power lies. However, the paradox of city governance means that we should expect city-friendly policies to be pursued at higher levels (as well as locally), so analysts should look there as well. But how can cities overcome their deep internal divisions—which are, after all, often based on the same geography as representative institutions—to coherently represent an urban interest? An answer may lie in the pattern of city representation about which John Vorys worried in 1964 (see Chapter 1), in which city representatives are responsive not only to their particular constituencies, but to a broader city interest as well. It is not obvious how this dual responsiveness happens, however, because even though some legislators have city constituencies, cities themselves do not have formal standing in national politics. The several House members from a territory within a big city are elected by their *districts*, not their cities. There is no representative of "Chicago" or "New York City" in either the statehouse or Congress. The shorthand "D-LA" would be interpreted as "Democrat from Louisiana," not "Democrat from Los Angeles." Instead, these large, heterogeneous communities are represented by a collection of representatives, each with his or her own separate geographically based constituency, which may include a subsection of the city as well as some part of the surrounding area.[78] These collections of representatives, which together make up a city's delegation to a legislature, often represent very different kinds of constituencies: neighborhoods with different class or ethnic compositions, with different business interests, and so forth.[79] Beyond proximity, they often share very little, and their residents may see themselves less as natural allies than as cross-town rivals, creating an environment in which organic citywide or otherwise broad interests may lose out to parochialism.[80] But in reality, American cities have come to represent themselves quite cohesively in Congress.

When scholars have considered the role of cities in the national legislature, the typical approach has been to identify "urban" districts, aggregate them, and study how representatives from urban districts behave in Congress: how numerous or powerful they are, their partisan distribution, and their potentially distinctive behavior on urban issues.[81] This typical approach basically assumes that districts from large central cities, wherever they are, have similar interests and will pursue those interests in concert. For some analyses, this is a good framework.[82] In many cases, however, we should examine this assumption more closely for two important reasons.

First, while cities may resemble each other as urban agglomerations and often face similar challenges, particularly in the wake of the industrial age, it is also true that cities, states, and regions can and do organize as rivals rather than allies. Gelfand (1975) pointedly observes that "rivalry, not cooperation, marked most inter-city relations" for most of American history.[83] The American system of cities, which does not give primacy to one central metropole that is central to culture, economy, and politics, contributes to these rivalries.[84] Particular development strategies have favored one region or group of cities over another. This was certainly true in the nineteenth century, and it is true at times today as well. In the early days of the republic, New York and Philadelphia vied for supremacy. Half a century later, Chicago and St. Louis competed to be the preeminent gateway to the West, and Chicago even made a brief bid to usurp New York's place at the top of the city hierarchy (five-borough consolidation saved the day). As California grew, rivalries between Los Angeles, San Francisco, and San Diego often made the cities rivals rather than allies.[85] At a regional level, Republican urban policy in the middle of the twentieth century tended to favor the rapidly growing Sun Belt cities, while Democratic eras have tended to be more beneficial for the older cities of the Northeast and Midwest.[86] Thus, the creation and construction of an urban bloc and the partisan place-character divide was not inevitable or natural; rather, it was a political project that involved interactions between national elites, urban constituencies, and city elites.[87]

Second, the assumption that each city district will identify a common interest, line up, and coalesce into an urban coalition underestimates the plurality of interests not only across cities, but also *within* them. Perhaps the central insight (or premise) of the study of urban politics since the field's birth is that cities are the site of diverse and plural interests, heterogeneous constituencies, and deeply contested politics.[88] Not only should we not assume that a cross-city urban coalition will endure, but we should not even assume that a "Los Angeles" or "Chicago" position on contentious issues will arise, because local politics is as likely to be conflictual as it is to be consensual, and there are likely to be winners and losers within cities even on issues of supralocal importance. Urbanicity may foster some predispositions, but a city's organic interest (or citywide accord) may not "naturally" coincide with the aggregate positions of its several districts, especially because those with different interests and perspectives are likely to be separated into different constituencies. Thus, the key attribute of the contemporary urban political order—increasing unity and cohesion in representation as the base of a major party—is remarkable precisely because rivalries both among and within cities have been overcome to create such a stable urban alignment in national politics. And the basic building block of this alignment, in which cities' propensity for insoluble conflict is overcome in the name of national coalition, is the cohesive city delegation.

For the rest of this chapter, I will outline the city delegation theory, an explanation of how city interests are clarified and pursued in the national legislature that focuses on the middle level of politics—not the person on the street or the national party leaders, but the local parties and representatives in between. This model of supralocal city politics draws on the study of local politics to help identify key local institutions that both provide local political order and contribute to the formation and maintenance of a cohesive urban bloc in Congress.

2.7 City Delegation Theory: Unity Despite Diversity

Earlier in this chapter, I theorized how statist interventions and pluralist politics are relatively important for city governance and are combined today as key elements of "dual liberalism." That set of ideas was concerned with a *direction* of politics compatible with a city interest: to the left, on most issues. For the rest of the chapter, I offer a theory on a *quality* of politics—cohesion—fostered by certain local institutions. Such cohesion is important because of the constant challenge to city governance presented by urbanicity itself. Cities—like other places, only more so—are home to a multiplicity of voices and political perspectives and are often deeply divided. Given such divisions, how can a city represent itself cohesively in higher levels of government in pursuit of policies that help make city governance easier?

Maintaining order in the context of difference is what city politics is all about, so while most of this book examines how cities represent themselves elsewhere, it is important to see how they overcome analogous challenges at home by examining how cities establish and sustain *internal* political order. This will help us understand how the national urban order sustained itself through most of the twentieth century.

Because of their high levels of social conflict and vulnerability within the federal order, cities are prone to political chaos and sometimes appear to be "ungovernable."[89] Capital flight, crime, congestion, labor and social unrest, pollution, and even weather all present recurrent, powerful governance challenges to American cities compounded by severe resource constraints. Overlaying these chronic governance problems is the high level of ethnoracial diversity present in many cities, which can complicate or intensify those challenges or create conflict in its own right. The result of these many cleavages and constrained resources can often resemble irresolvable "hyperpluralism," resulting in fragility, chaos, and the constant danger of civic crisis.[90] With all of these complications—which are challenges everywhere, but especially so in densely populated communities—it is no wonder that we seem to be in a perpetual "urban crisis," prompting many residents to leave the city, which further compounds these challenges.

For political *elites* within the city, however, exit is *not* an option. For this group, which is concerned with managing the city and solving governance problems, the establishment of political order and the pursuit of some approximation of an organic city interest are priorities. Those who represent or govern a city composed of heterogeneous building blocks need to seek a common basis, or at least a shared forum, for political action. About the only thing that members of a city *do* share is membership in a common local political community, their city.

City unity is not naturally occurring, but several important institutional arrangements that are distinctive to cities foster the creation of civic political order from social disorder. These institutions integrate politics "horizontally," across the geographic extent of the city, by including different constituencies and their representatives in common forums. Inclusion in these common settings forces negotiation, and fosters common interests and perspectives among their participants and serve to smooth (even if only a little) the rough edges of city politics.[91]

Under the model of city delegation theory, there are two main categories of institutions of horizontal integration (IHIs): jurisdictional and organizational. The chief jurisdictional institutions are simply the city boundary and the central city government that oversees governance of the territory within that boundary. This kind of horizontal integration is common to all cities and is what makes size such an important characteristic of urbanicity. We often take the city boundary for granted, but this invisible line is one of our most important political institutions. The larger the city, the more likely that different kinds of areas will share some civic and political connections. For instance, membership in the large political community of New York City means that residents of all five boroughs may live very different from one another—the quotidian experiences of people in the Queens Village neighborhood (on the outer edge of the borough of Queens) may be much like those of residents of Elmont, the Long Island suburb right across the street, and much less like those of citizens in the South Bronx, Midtown Manhattan, Annadale (on Staten Island), or Park Slope (in Brooklyn)—but still have the same mayor and share membership in the same city. Imagine a parallel world in which the five boroughs had not consolidated but instead had fragmented even more, such that the units we now call neighborhoods had continued as self-governing municipalities all on their own, of a size comparable to that of other nearby towns. The politics and settlement patterns of those five counties would surely be quite different from those of New York City today. Smaller communities, such as suburbs and unincorporated hamlets, do not have the same dynamics in their local politics, because they tend not to include such disparate elements. As American political communities get "fenced off" into smaller and often more homogeneous units (often suburbs), this atomization shapes politics in a way that creates divisions between communities and undermines the possibility for political integration of any kind.[92] Connecting very different lived environments in a common local political community means a greater capacity for action by the city government, as well as a greater need for constructive conflict resolution between the disparate parts.

A basic example of a jurisdictional IHI is shown in Figure 2.1, which shows the city of Chicago surrounded by its suburbs.[93] Within the suburbs, there are scores of small, relatively internally homogeneous villages, each with its own internal politics. Most of the time, in part because they are smaller and less diverse than their more urban counterparts, suburban politics are less contentious and involve fewer people.[94] There are heterogeneous pockets scattered throughout the metropolitan area today, but the sheer size of Chicago (and its high relative population density) means that its municipal boundary brings many different kinds of people (and neighborhoods) into one common political community. In the figure, the shading reflects local levels of income inequality in 2010; we can see that Chicago is more unequal than most of the suburbs around it. It includes different kinds of people, while most of the suburbs are more internally homogeneous, walling off difference with municipal boundaries.[95]

This simple fact of a common *polis* is important. When heterogeneous collections of residents, constituencies, and representatives are forced to come together in a central place for municipal matters, they may conflict, but they will at least interact. More, they will have a shared stake in the organic health of the city and a chance to take part in the creation of a citywide negotiation or accord. This is the heart of the ideal-type political pluralism described by Dahl (1961) and others. It is unlikely that power in cities is as dispersed as the pluralists believed, but membership in a democratic local community, even if imperfect,

Figure 2.1 **Jurisdictional IHI: A Large City.** Each city (Census Place) in the Chicago metropolitan area is shaded according to the local level of inequality, with darker shades meaning more inequality. Though about the same number of people live in Chicago as its outlying area, the inclusive borders of the central city integrate politics across a relatively heterogeneous social space. Source: 2010 U.S. Census.

allows for different views and interests to contend in a common political space. Such processes are the sources of binding legislative or administrative decisions. Even though decisions made in one place can have effects elsewhere, persons and representatives from outside the border tend not to have a seat at the table where authoritative decisions are made—about the allocation of goods and services over space within the city, about the kinds of social provisions and public goods the city will provide, about economic development policies, or about what kinds of people will be welcomed or served by the city. These policy decisions are made centrally, so access to and participation in these centralized city decision-making processes is important, both for residents who want access to city services and public goods, and for elites who want to take credit for their provision or direct them in particular ways for some reason or other. As we will see in Chapter 4, membership in such a shared community itself makes representatives more cohesive in national politics, even though congressional districts are not formally associated with citywide governance and their constituencies are often very different.[96]

While jurisdictional IHIs formally combine or divide social spaces into political communities by drawing lines between places, there is another type of institution that can also integrate heterogeneous constituencies. Sometimes overlapping with jurisdictional IHIs, *organizational* IHIs include the many more visible institutions that have been created to help provide political order in cities, from parties and machines to informal regimes. Made up of groups of persons, usually elites, concerned with promoting some vision of a city's organic interest, these institutions have been the focus of much of the field of urban political science, especially the study of local political parties.[97] Unlike jurisdictional IHIs, the strength of organizational IHIs varies widely across cities: their influence is pervasive in some places, while in others it is virtually absent. Where these institutions are strong, ties between the center and periphery within a city, or between far-flung and very different parts of a city, may be stronger than we would otherwise expect. Where a single boss or small group controls access to offices and resources, as in the strongest machines, that boss has many resources with which to enforce political discipline and order across the city; not only will candidates be selected partly based on their loyalty to the organization, but elected officials dependent on that central decision maker for (re)nomination and material delivery of goods and services to their constituencies will be more likely to attend to the will of the center. The dynamics of such organizations are complex, and certainly they often stray very far from the ideal of inclusive, participatory democracy. But they do serve as a kind of political glue binding together areas that would otherwise share even less. These connections provide an avenue for strong demands from some part of the city to reach the citywide agenda and become part of the citywide accord, even though they may be parochial, minority concerns to which most citizens may be indifferent or even hostile.

While the map of Chicagoland shows how a territorially inclusive boundary includes more people in a common polis than most local governments, Figure 2.2 depicts a concrete example of an organizational IHI. Published in the *Chicago Tribune* in 1955, this image shows the most powerful political leaders from that city during the Long New Deal. They are gathered as a party slating committee to negotiate and make decisions, in this case on who their organization is going

Slate making committee of Democratic party meeting yesterday in the Morrison hotel. Left to right: Seated—Rep. Dawson, Ald. Weber, Ald. Bieszcat, William Milota, Municipal court bailiff; Mayor Daley, and Chairman Joseph Gill. Standing—Ald. D'Arco, Ald. Keane, State Sen. Donald O'Brien, City Clerk Marcin, Ald. Murphy, Thomas C. Bradley, Maine township; Frank Broucek, Berwyn township; County Recorder Ropa, John J. Touhy, Roy D. Petersen, Leyden township; Arthur X. Elrod, Richard J. Fitzgerald, Thornton township, and Barnet Hodes. [TRIBUNE Photo]

Figure 2.2 **Organizational IHI: Chicago's Cook County Democratic Party Slating Committee, 1955.** Party leaders from all around the city meet in a single political organization to select candidates for nomination and govern their territory.
Source: Chicago Tribune, December 21, 1955.

to support in the upcoming elections. In the previous year, a similar group had chosen not to endorse the incumbent Democratic mayor, Martin Kennelly; the committee's chair, Richard J. Daley, became mayor instead. Daley himself (seated second from right) selected many of those committee members pictured here, and he assured reporters that they would in turn select a "blue ribbon ticket." The members of this powerful, centralized decision-making organization may have been Democrats, but the machine was not particularly democratic in its internal operations.

Two important things stand out in this image to remind us of the integrative power of these organizations, which includes representatives from the many township subdivisions of Cook County. First, seated at the far left is not just a ward committeeman or alderman but a member of the U.S. House of Representatives, William L. Dawson. He served as both the leader of a submachine on the South Side and as a member of Congress for nearly four decades. His membership in the slating committee not only linked the black South Side to the hegemonic force within local politics (i.e., the Cook County Democratic Party) but also directly linked the local organization to national representation. Second, a close look at the names of the committee's members (who represented geographic territories in the city) reveals something about the character of the group. Irish Americans—Daley, Keane, O'Brien, Touhy, and Fitzgerald—are probably overrepresented in the group's ranks and were closest to the center of power. But given the famously group-based politics of this city of neighborhoods, it matters that other groups are also represented in the larger committee, which reflects the waves of immigrant arrivals to America and Chicago: in addition to Dawson, we have Leyden, Weber, Petersen, D'Arco, Bieszcat, and Milota. Any white Chicagoan who has been asked, "What are you?" knows that these men represented ethnic communities that were meaningfully different, especially during the Long New Deal.[98] To be joined together in a cohesive organization, and to achieve political order, even one that was not based on anything approximating equal terms, was an important step toward city governance in mid-twentieth-century America.

Integrative institutions like this one, formally or informally, have the important effect of channeling or limiting the potentially infinitely varied content of public participation in policymaking toward some ultimate decision, enacted and enforced by an established authority. While they been often—and often fairly—criticized as undemocratic, these criticisms are oblique to the deepest crisis of the twentieth-century American city, beset as it was on all sides by both demands for action and constraints on resources and authority. In such a context, representation and responsiveness to public opinion on particular issues are important but must coexist with, and at times accede to, the primary goods of political order and a city's organic interests; when disorder is pervasive, social justice and democratic responsiveness are difficult to sustain in any case.[99] IHIs enhance the ability of local leaders to achieve a citywide accord and establish political order.[100] These IHIs, which have been developed in cities but generally not in other social spaces of comparable population size (like highly fragmented suburban areas), force plural interests into resolution and allow cities to create unity from such disparate elements. Their chief effect is not the creation of some particular set of policies or ideologies, but simply *unity*.

This outcome is very important for managing the tendency of second-dimension conflict to undermine first-dimension liberalism. Political scientists have glimpsed IHIs' effects in analyses of strategies that city leaders employ to overcome diversity's challenges, establish political order, pursue a city agenda, and meet urgent governance requirements. Such dealmaking practices of local parties have been studied for more than a century, and important findings continue to emerge when scholars look for them. Trounstine and Rugh (2011) find that agenda setters in diverse cities tend to combine bond issues into larger packages and procedurally link them more closely to more salient elections; these choices by local elites reveal their mediating function in local politics, which generates governing coalitions in a kind of cooperative logroll. Similarly, Berry (2009) finds that strong local parties can help bridge different local governments' ability to manage the commons of the local tax base by using an informal organizational IHI to overcome a fragmented geography of policy implementation.

Such IHIs are developed locally, and their main effects are local—or, at least, most studies focus on their local effects. City delegation theory argues that their effects are not *merely* local, but that they influence the way cities represent themselves in higher levels of political decision making, especially by making them more cohesive in their representation of a putative city interest. This is how IHIs coordinate action by the representatives of cities in Congress.

2.8 Local IHIs in National Representation

The local IHIs described in the previous section serve to structure local decision making in city policy. When cities move beyond their borders, to the state and national capital, however, the object of analysis becomes the city delegation—the collection of representatives working on behalf of the city (and/or its subdivisions) to pursue city interests and build a city-friendly supralocal policy context. Local IHIs affect how these collections of representatives operate, translating solutions for local order into tools for supralocal cohesion and building cohesive representation out of a set of heterogeneous districts.

Many factors influence legislative decision making, and the composition of a constituency is frequently employed to explain legislator behavior.[101] Much of the study of Congress and lawmaking is devoted to determining how much these factors matter—the relative influence of legislative parties or precameral "preferences" (of constituencies or legislators themselves) in shaping legislative behavior.[102] City delegation theory complicates traditional models of representation by adding an extracameral intermediary between constituency and legislative behavior. IHIs can smooth out heterogeneous preferences into more cohesive blocs, just as they can create political order in a fractious local environment. Consider the abstract model of representation in Figure 2.3. At left, there are four hypothetical districts to be represented in a legislature. District-level characteristics, abstracted as different patterns at left, are reflected in representation at right.[103]

In such a model, the atomistic districts are unlinked, and representation is largely determined by district-level characteristics. When districts share district-level characteristics (like demography, political traditions, region, economic structure and production profile, and so on), they are likely to "agree" (in broad terms) on a particular policy, and this agreement should be reflected in their representatives' behavior. When such districts are very different on demographic or other fundamentals, however, it may be harder to coordinate action, even when the districts are part of the same legislative party. This is a particularly relevant

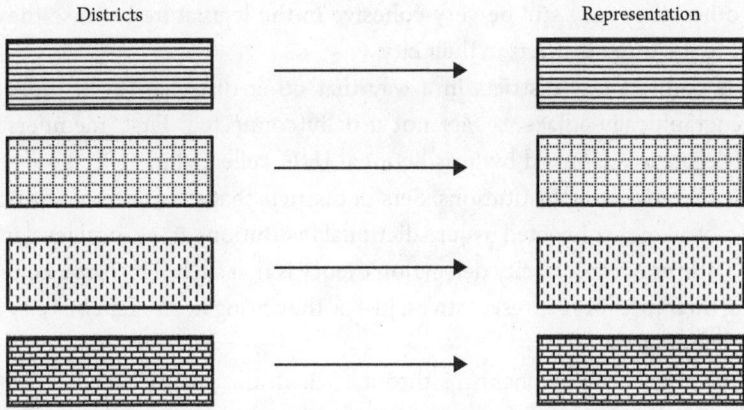

Figure 2.3 **A Model of Atomistic, Responsive Representation.** Diverse preferences and interests at left are mirrored by representatives at right.

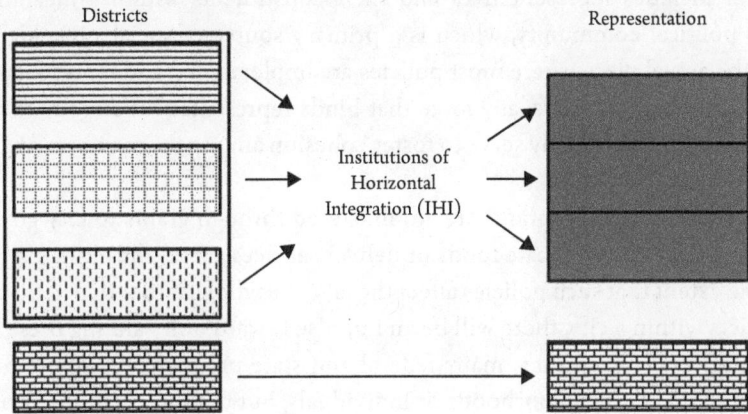

Figure 2.4 **Model of a City Delegation.** Diverse preferences and interests, at left, are smoothed into a more cohesive bloc, at right, as they are filtered through the intermediate institutions of the city.

consideration in the historically relatively weak congressional party system of the United States, and a big part of the meaning behind former Speaker of the House Tip O'Neill's famous aphorism that "all politics is local."

In city delegations, however, IHIs mediate the relationship between district and representative. Figure 2.4 depicts this change. Here, the abstracted districts are just as different from each other, but they are no longer atomistic; rather, they are connected as part of a broader citywide "molecule," as indicated by the rectangle that lies around the districts. Inclusion within this group means that the constituencies and representatives share some common political identity, and their diverse preferences are at least somewhat filtered through the intermediate city institutions. The result is that even when districts are very different from each other, they may still be very cohesive in the legislature because they are linked to the other districts in their city.

IHIs connect city districts in a way that other districts—even those that are geographically adjacent—are not usually connected. First, members of a city delegation are linked by jurisdictional IHIs, reflected in a city border and formal city governing institutions. Sets of districts that are not from within the same city are not connected by jurisdictional institutions at the local level in this way.[104] The basic logic of city delegation theory is that such IHIs foster cohesion among their member representatives, just as they bring heterogeneous city constituencies together.

There are several mechanisms through which the jurisdictional IHI of the city boundary can bind representatives and make representatives sensitive to governance demands and preferences not merely within their district but in their city as a whole. These mechanisms are rooted in the fact that the city border includes representatives and their constituents within a meaningful local political community, which is a primary source of social/civic identity and the actual place where most policies are implemented and representatives build their careers. Thus, any force that binds representatives directly to each other or to City Hall may serve to foster cohesion among the members of a city delegation.

First, many city programs are administered through grants to city governments, which then allocate funds or deliver services across the city's districts. To the extent that such policies affect the city as a whole, rather than particular districts within a city, there will be an impulse toward unity among these representatives. For instance, many federal and state programs distribute funds not to particular neighborhoods or individuals, but to municipalities or other political subdivisions for final expenditure. This has been true of all major housing and redevelopment programs, both before and since the creation of the Department of Housing and Urban Development, including urban renewal initiatives and today's Community Development Block Grant program, which are implemented locally by delivering funding to local housing agencies that are granted a fairly large degree of discretion. It was also true of relief programs during the Works Progress Administration (WPA), when local governments selected and oversaw many of the projects chosen, and it continues to be true for most major infrastructure programs.[105] Even when such programs are intended to be locally allocated entirely based on need and merit, differential allocations inevitably occur. Need typically outstrips funding, so choices have to be made, and when they are, politics is inevitably involved. In local development decisions, local institutions influence the location and character of public goods distributed, discretionary funds spent, economic development pursued, and constituency services provided.[106] In a city with several congressional districts, a mayor, city council, or central administrative office often has great discretion over how funds are distributed across districts, effectively centralizing power in the city's center and enhancing the bonds shared by the city delegation. Because in a large city a congressional district is just a piece of the city, maintaining a close and positive relationship with city officials and agencies gives a representative a better chance to increase his or her share of any discretionary allocation. This relationship essentially functions as a form of constituency service, wherein the representative tries to deliver goods to his or her district but has to convince local rather than federal officials to do so.

Second, because of the density of cities and the contiguity of their districts, the overall well-being of one city district may depend to a great extent on the well-being of the wider city. Many externalities of city life do not stop at legislative boundaries, so working as a city delegation to maintain or improve the health of the city—mitigating pollution, preventing crime, providing housing, spurring economic development, and many other issues—is likely to benefit all participants. A representative who would typically be against environmental regulations on business in his district may sing a different tune if the closely neighboring district is full of polluting factories. In that example, all residents of both districts might support pollution mitigation policies in a way that would not occur if the districts were more sprawling and less likely to impact one another. The dynamics may be different in suburban or rural districts, each of which may contain many local governments without much overlap in day-to-day governance. The sparser populations of such districts are also less likely to interact with or affect outcomes in other districts, so there is less impetus for coordination across constituencies. If these ideas are true, then we should expect representatives from the same city to coordinate their behavior on policies that affect the city they share.

Third, while members of the public often identify strongly with their neighborhood, city, or state, there is little indication that constituents identify strongly as members of their congressional district. We don't often see people walking around in hats declaring their allegiance to the "New York Tenth District"—rather, they bear a simple "NY." This identity as New Yorkers, or Chicagoans, or Los Angelenos means that constituents sometimes turn even to members of their city delegation who are not their own representatives for assistance with all kinds of issues, both local and supralocal. As we shall see in Chapter 5, groups and individuals from all over Chicago wrote to the South Side congressman Barratt O'Hara (D-Chicago) to share their opinions and urge him to act in one way or another, even though he only represented some of them. The same was true of New Yorkers writing to John Rooney (D-Brooklyn), whom they saw as an advocate not only in Washington, but also in City Hall.[107] Many voters, even in cities defined by turf-defending, locally oriented political organizations, have seen the city delegation as a set of representatives who will be responsive to residents of the entire city.

But why would representatives pay attention to constituents from outside their district? In part, because the city itself is a more meaningful community than a congressional district, these letters from nonconstituents probably did share useful information about what many of their actual constituents were thinking. For a certain set of representatives, though, these letters from other parts of the city were also important information from potential *future* constituents. The power and resources available in cities often means that city representatives want to pursue higher office not necessarily in Washington, but as mayor of their hometown. Such progressive ambitions and aspiration to higher office are common among all politicians, but their implications are different in big cities, because moving up might mean moving home, rather than into the Senate or state capital. Not all mayors have served in Congress, but many have. Notably, each of New York's most politically successful twentieth-century mayors—Fiorello La Guardia, Robert F. Wagner, John Lindsay, and Ed Koch—had previously served in Congress. Thus, when the representative makes decisions in Washington to represent the city as a whole, he or she is staking a claim to have the community's interest at heart, not just that of his or her narrower district constituency.

Organizational IHIs are more plural, variant, and powerful than jurisdictional IHIs. While the city boundary includes several districts' territories into one city whole, organizational IHIs strengthen delegation cohesion in more obvious human ways. The most important organizational IHI in American cities, and the focus of the analyses to follow, has been the local traditional party.[108] A traditional party is an autonomous organization that can successfully control access to nominations to office and therefore serves as a very important institutional site for shaping political outcomes. In the nineteenth and twentieth centuries, these organizations served (and in some places still serve) broad integrative functions in local politics.[109] Urban machines are particularly powerful species of this kind of organization—they not only control nominations, but are very successful at winning office as well.

Controlling access to nominations and office is the key lever for the local party organization to exert power over city delegations. This power can create cohesive delegations in a number of ways, either by selecting agents whom the party is confident will be reliable and loyal or by threatening a rogue candidate for the next election through strategies such as removal from the ballot or the withholding of resources for reelection. Watching a local party in action reveals that many of the most successful city congressmen (such as Adolph Sabath, Emanuel Celler, John Rooney, and Dan Rostenkowski) operate as both conscientious advocates for their constituents *and* loyal partisans without much cognitive dissonance.[110] They are able not only to reliably regain office but also (in part because of their seniority) to gain better access to policy positions and goods that further their districts' and cities' interests. Local organizations can also serve powerful agenda-setting functions, shaping the realm of the "possible" or acceptable in politics and providing a durable forum in which potentially rival leaders or constituencies can become partners in stable logrolls and other forms of cooperation. Even more basically, local parties can play an informational role, helping to clearly articulate the city position on an issue that may be confusing or controversial for a representative.[111] In these organizations, "unity and hierarchy" make "organization decision-making relatively impervious to the influences of rival non-party groups, associations, and elites in the primary electorate."[112] This power to effectively choose candidates and officeholders, extends not just to local or state office, but often to congressional office as well.[113] Even in places or historical eras without parties, other organizational IHIs, such as the elite coalitions known as "regimes" or labor unions, still rely on longstanding relationships that develop norms of loyalty and reciprocity to maintain partnerships in city governance, though these levers of influence may be less powerful or durable.[114]

An important difference between jurisdictional and organizational IHIs is that the strength of the latter vary much more over space and time. City boundaries shift somewhat over time, but rarely does the *meaning* of a city boundary change much, and the Los Angeles boundary has consequences similar to those of the New York or Chicago boundary. Conversely, while some cities have a tradition of very strong local parties (especially at some historical moments), others have virtually none. If city delegation theory is correct, this variation means that different cities will likely show different patterns of representation at higher levels—stronger-party cities will be more integrated than weaker ones. We will find this to be the case in the empirical analyses in later chapters.

Thus, a representative from a city with strong IHIs, especially of the organizational type, must attend not only to the preferences of his or her own constituents, but also to the citywide accord manifest in the integrative institutions—and the stronger these institutions, the greater the cohesive effect the IHI can have on the representative's primary goal as a Mayhewian "single-minded seeker of reelection." A city without such strong IHIs will be less effective at achieving this goal, and its city delegation will be less cohesive.

2.9 Cities in Nation: Strategic Concerns

IHIs foster cohesive city delegations, which is important because cities must be united to advance many of their urgent priorities in higher-level politics.

Scholars of supralocal urban politics at the state level have found that city delegation cohesion is a major contributor—perhaps even a necessary precondition—for legislative success.[115] But in national politics, internal cohesion alone is not enough to create a national urban political order. Regional or intercity rivalries must also be overcome to create a cohesive national urban political alliance. This first occurred nationally during the Great Depression, when a group of city leaders came together to forge a cross-city alliance to advocate for city-friendly policies.[116]

Scholars have noted that uniting and maintaining the loyalty of these large cities into one national bloc of blocs was a major political project of the New Deal and the key to Democratic control during that time.[117] This creative act required the articulation of a national agenda that could address the urgent governance requirements common to all cities and regions. Far from assured, this project was always in jeopardy, and the obstacles it faced within cities and from the conservative coalition have been chronicled in several notable studies[118]; I describe the actual consolidation of city representatives in one party and the maturation of the urbanicity divide over the course of the twentieth century in Chapters 2 and 6. Assuming for the moment that an urban position can be identified and defended by such a wildly heterogeneous coalition, such cohesion creates the possibility of concerted strategic action by cities in national politics. Even when the urban bloc-of-blocs is in complete agreement, however, legislative victory is still far from assured, because city representatives have never made up a majority of the legislature. It is helpful to consider the strategic considerations the leaders of the urban political order have faced and how these considerations have shaped their behavior and pursuit of allies over time; these strategies, many of which have been identified in studies of city delegations at the state level, will appear in the book's subsequent analyses of how cities represent themselves in national politics so previewing them now will help make the argument clearer.

2.9.1 Strategic Position: Marginal Urgency

One major challenge for urbanites derives from the conditions of city life within a national political context that is not generally friendly to cities. Bloc unity is most strategically effective when the bloc can realistically claim to constitute a majority or hold the balance of power. City districts have never been close to a majority in the House, so claiming pivotality would be the next best thing. Such a claim is most credible when a bloc is near the center of the preference distribution, making it more likely to include the pivotal vote (in the House, the median voter). If a bloc includes the median voter, then its members' decision to stick together to shape policy places them in a situation of "pivotal cohesion."[119]

But once a city–country divide has emerged, cities' claims to being pivotal are quite weak. For one thing, as we shall see, during the Long New Deal it was the city representatives who were doing much of the proposing and pushing on issues; threatening to "switch" to the other side as a pivotal voter would make little sense in this context. Second, cities may frequently find themselves at the margins (as opposed to the pivot), because on urban–rural issues they have relatively extreme preferences and thus little real leverage based on cohesion alone—even the most cohesive minority will lose every time without allies. But the quickly changing conditions of urbanicity also mean that it is often necessary to actively adjust the policy status quo to meet concrete governance challenges and maintain social order; thus, the obstructionist tools often used by minorities in American politics may be less useful to cities. This "marginal urgency" means that further steps are needed to achieve policy success on urban issues.

Political scientists have occasionally investigated how city blocs deal with the strategic challenge of marginal urgency by examining state politics. While the urban–rural divide is *relatively* new and complex at the national level (because there are also important racial, regional, and sectional divides, as well as rivalries between cities), it has long been clearer and more enduring as the central cleavage structuring politics within many states with large cities. In some states (such as Illinois, New York, and Michigan), a major city (e.g., Chicago, New York City, and Detroit) is often pitted against suburban and rural constituencies in partisan and ideological struggle. In many cases, the main thing that noncity constituencies hold in common is antipathy toward (or at least mistrust of) the metropolis; when this antipathy is strong, it may be extremely difficult to rally allies for a city position, no matter what it is.[120] Regardless, the city is faced with we might label the marginal urgency problem: city representatives constitute a nonpivotal minority bloc that must attract allies to an agenda that usually demands adjustment of the status quo.[121] The strategic situation is similar in national politics.

2.9.2 Strategic Tool: Agenda Control

Several tools are important for advancing the city agenda, and each is important (and was at different historical moments) for the subsequent empirical chapters in this study. For each of these tools, bloc unity is a necessary precondition.[122] As complementary preconditions for legislative success, majority status and leadership positions can also be pursued by the city bloc. In both chambers, but especially in the House, majority status confers special power for advancing or defending a policy agenda.[123] Control of committees and the floor agenda allows the majority to dictate much of the action of the legislature. Thus, membership in the majority coalition is vital for a bloc, such as the urban political order, that seeks to create national policies to meet important local governance needs. Additionally, membership in the party's chamber leadership (or "cartel," consisting of the Speaker, floor leadership, committee chairs, and membership on "prestige" committees such as Rules, Ways and Means, and Appropriations) is especially desirable for shaping the agenda.[124] Given that these leadership positions are largely a function of seniority, city representatives could take steps to enhance their own prospects for return to office, in both absolute terms (indeed, this is a primary goal of most ambitious politicians, but easier said than done) and *relative to other members of their party.* This strategy requires a difficult balancing act by the bloc, potentially trading off between its policy priorities and party success in order to hit the sweet spot of leadership-in-majority. If there is another firmly entrenched (and therefore electorally "safe") bloc within the party that is a threat or obstacle to the urban bloc's policy goals (Southern Democrats in the case of urban interlude city Democrats), then majority status alone may not be enough to satisfy a bloc that cares about more than retaining office, so complementary strategies or coalitional shake-ups may be strategic imperatives. As the parties have polarized and conservative southerners have left the Democratic fold, city Democrats have had some success in achieving leadership positions, but these political shifts have also left them in the minority for most of the last two decades.

In pursuit of long-run majorities in support of its desired policies, the national urban political order has pursued partisan allies using several strategies that are also apparent among city delegations in other contexts: mutual exchange,[125] urbanizing,[126] and affinity.[127] Each of these strategies have been apparent in different eras or areas of policy.

2.9.3 Strategy: Mutual Exchange

In the search for elusive majorities, a nonpivotal minority like the urban political order can pursue a strategy of inclusive exchange, or logrolling, in which it may be able to institutionalize legislative success in conjunction with allies with whom it shares little in common.[128] This is a useful strategy when some groups of legislators have intense preferences about some issues but are relatively indifferent about others and can thus exchange support to meet their goals. Throughout the Long New Deal, city representatives were never a majority of the Democratic Party (see Figure 6.4), and most of their copartisans may have been unconcerned with the distinctive pressures of city governance. In many cases, these rural allies, especially southerners, grew (or were always) wary of centralized statism.[129] To get the interventions its cities needed, the New Deal city bloc held its coalition together with the distribution of material benefits.[130] In keeping with the urban politics tradition of material exchange and distributive politics, city representatives were the most avid and consistent logrollers on distributive issues in Congress during this period; that is, they were just as supportive of many rural projects and programs (from which their constituents gained little) as they were of programs targeted at the cities. The same was not true of rural representatives, even Democrats, who increasingly defected from this intraparty arrangement, in part on ideological grounds.[131] Intense ideological conflicts that are more difficult to resolve with the exchange of material goods, such as those about race and culture, are particularly dangerous for such alliances. This city–southern partnership was fraught from the beginning, though city representatives worked hard to establish and maintain it from early in the 1930s.[132]

Over time, however, the urban bloc's main partners in this distributive politics (the South) became increasingly unreliable on a range of issues of critical importance to cities.[133] This was especially true on nationalized urban issues such as labor organization, public housing, and fair employment, in which policies were being pursued that would apply to all cities, including those in the South, and that southerners saw as endangering the regional Jim Crow order. City representatives therefore turned to alternative or complementary strategies to pursue their city agenda.

2.9.4 Strategy: Urbanizing

The second strategy, "urbanizing," is a strategy cities employ in state legislatures to address their urgent needs in the face of potentially hostile outstate forces.[134] Urbanizing consists of a three-step process. First, a city bloc defines a problem as distinctively urban. Second, it articulates an urban consensus position on the issue (and demonstrates that consensus by voting cohesively). Finally, city members urge outstate copartisans, who know little about the issue and should therefore have weak prior commitments on it, to defer to the wisdom of the city delegation and support the urban position.[135] This strategy is attractive because, if successful, it leads to the adoption of the city bloc's preferred position without much compromise. However, it is also a risky strategy for two reasons. First, it is premised on city cohesion. As Burns et al. (2009) note, when the city bloc is divided, the noncity representatives do not have a powerful cue to defer to it and may make up their own minds on the issue. Thus, developing a cohesive city delegation (or nationally, a cohesive urban political order) is a necessary condition for this strategy and without IHIs is more difficult. Second, the strategy relies on the persuasive power of the city bloc to bring the noncity votes to the table. Those noncity voters may not be persuadable, depending on the strength of the urban–rural divide. They may, on a range of issues, choose not to defer to the city bloc's position precisely *because* they find urban positions anathema, leaving the urbanites without sufficient support for their policy. Nevertheless, city Democrats used this strategy to build support for civil rights issues during the Long New Deal.

2.9.5 Strategy: Affinity Coalition

Even more straightforward than urbanizing is an affinity strategy, in which a city bloc forges an alliance with the next-most-urban constituencies, essentially emphasizing the urban–rural continuum. This is what Daley seemed to propose in his exchange with Rep. Celler in 1964 (in Chapter 1) when he proposed an alliance with suburbs and smaller cities. To pursue this strategy at the state level, the big-city bloc pursues allies among suburban constituencies, especially those with important links to cities (the first ring of suburban communities in a metropolitan area, which are often older and increasingly face some of the same governance challenges as central cities). Theoretically, the alliance is *almost* natural, with cooperation desirable because interventions vital for big-city governance are only a little less important for the next-most-urban environments. For most of the twentieth century, however, city–suburban relations were acrimonious at best; suburbs formed with the express purpose of political separation from the city, with cultural, economic, racial, and other divides leading to political differences that only strengthened during the postwar decades.[136] Many years later, however, things are changing quickly. Weir, Wolman, and Swanstrom (2005) identified such an emerging alliance between city constituencies and inner-ring suburbs in contemporary Illinois politics.[137] On a national scale, the city bloc can build alliances with these older suburbs, as well as with districts that are not in large metropolitan areas but may include one or more smaller cities that are facing similar governance challenges. Surveying the contemporary political landscape, these districts make up much of the composition of "blue" America today.

Pursuing an affinity strategy may reduce the material costs of maintaining a more diverse coalition with logrolls, because the preferences of marginal members of the alliance (suburbs or small cities, in this case) are closer to the preferences of the city bloc, so they should be cheaper to pay off. In circumstances in which ideology or other factors make exchange or compromise very difficult, logrolls may be impossible in any case. An alliance based on affinity also makes it more likely that city representatives will hold important leadership positions, and thus agenda power, because as the urban–rural divide is emphasized, the least safe members of the coalition may face the most competition from the opposition, be more likely to have partisan turnover in office, and therefore be junior members of the coalition. On the other hand, this situation may contribute to further polarization, as relatively extreme coalition members will be safest. The affinity strategy also gives some leverage to the marginal additions to the city bloc, because it is essentially a median-voter, minimum-winning coalition strategy, and important policy outcomes may thus reflect those members' preferences more than those of the "core" members of the city bloc. This leverage may restrict the range of policies the city bloc may successfully pursue, or simply shape the content of what policies will ultimately succeed, because of the character of suburban politics.[138]

2.10 Urban Politics in National Institutions

Beginning with the partisan consolidation of the nation's large cities in the New Deal, urbanites in Congress pursued or employed each of these tools (bloc cohesion, agenda control, logroll, urbanizing, and affinity), sometimes in combination, and instances of each are observed in the following chapters. A fundamental dysfunction ran through the New Deal Democratic Party, which had as its key elements a rural remnant bloc from the "Solid South" that was deeply conservative on *both* fiscal and (especially) racial issues and a city bloc that was driven by the logic of federalism to pursue a suite of progressive liberal, especially statist, policies at the national level in order to prevent (or even just manage) catastrophe at home.

The strategies pursued by city representatives, and the character of their behavior in Congress, were mimetic of the character and values of the city representatives and the political traditions from which they emerged. Many of these representatives came from the "traditional party organizations," common in northern cities but rare elsewhere, that emphasized a politics of party discipline, unity, local orientation, a preference for mutual exchange involving materially distributive politics for core members, and largely symbolic recognition of peripheral members.[139]

Along with these well-known qualities, however, the importance of these organizations' inclusive traditions of cultural pluralism (values shared by the more "programmatic" liberals with whom they increasingly came to be allied in national affairs) should not be underestimated and became crucial in the area of civil rights. Uncontested white supremacy was not a necessary condition for politics urbanites would support, as it was for southerners. For Southern Democrats, the pursuit of electoral success was related (or secondary) to the maintenance of white supremacy. In the city organizations, the realities were more complicated. City organizations were not paragons of racial harmony, and there is little evidence that the inclusion of marginal groups was an ideological priority for them.[140] But they *had* incorporated other "suspect" groups in the past (notably the Irish) and often actively sought black support at home when it suited their political needs (these new constituencies were urbanites, after all). The result was support of a transformative egalitarian agenda by organizations that were racially conservative themselves, but which prioritized governance over white supremacy. These efforts permanently alienated their national southern allies, but they also drove the most important political change of the twentieth century and helped clarify the two dimensions of the urbanicity cleavage for generations to come.

3

"A Proper National Policy"

The Urban Order and Agenda

> It is incumbent upon us to let the American nation know that our city governments today are sincere and honest men who are laboring to solve the problems of urbanization—men who have given up partisan and political connections and methods for a truer and surer attack upon them, and that these men believe that they can help the state or national government to an understanding of the life and the future of urban population.
> —C. A. Dykstra, City Manager of Cincinnati[1]

> Perhaps they might still continue as municipal functions, but they are no longer local problems.... We are woven into one unit. I do not know what would have happened to this country if the Federal Government had not provided relief.
> —Fiorello La Guardia, Mayor of New York City[2]

In the early years of the Depression, it became clear to mayors and other urban elites throughout the country that their cities shared many experiences and interests. Rather than continue as rivals for economic development and federal favor, these leaders became allies in creating a new federal urban policy portfolio that would ease the demands and challenges of city governance. This chapter traces the beginnings of the urban political order. While urban forces have never been hegemonic within U.S. national politics, city officials were particularly active, salient, and successful during the Long New Deal. Their efforts meant that urban issues would gain a foothold on the national agenda, where they had not been before, and that city officials would establish direct connections to national agencies from which they could seek help in solving their urgent governance challenges. The symbolic and institutional culmination of these efforts was the establishment of a cabinet-level Department of Housing and Urban Development (HUD) in 1965.

Prior to the 1930s, there was basically no national urban agenda. Mayors rarely, if ever, appeared before Congress to give advice or seek resources. The

American Municipal Association and some similar groups connected cities to each other, but not to national politics.[3] And there were no policies that regularly delivered aid to cities for infrastructure or other programs. From the 1930s on, however, mayors and their representatives increasingly appeared on Capitol Hill to articulate the urban position on a range of issues. In 1932, leaders of the nation's big cities forged a common voice through the creation of the U.S. Conference of Mayors (USCM). At the outset, this group focused on a relatively narrow but very significant range of concerns directly related to the key areas of statism outlined in the previous chapter: redistribution, in the form of food relief and relief work to alleviate the effects of unemployment; regulation, in the form of housing programs that altered the dynamics of urban housing markets to make housing more affordable for members of the poor and working classes; and public goods provision, in the form of major infrastructure construction projects. By the end of the Long New Deal, these big-city leaders had become a permanent voice in designing and implementing urban policy, helping to establish a new relationship between nation and city.[4]

Most studies of national urban policy focus on the postwar period and the struggle to establish HUD or on the federal government's retreat from channeling aid to large cities in the 1970s and 1980s.[5] The massive urban renewal programs of the postwar era, which so visibly (and for many, tragically) reshaped the physical space of the central city, also "solidif[ied] a new system of alignments in American politics."[6] But it was not war or the growing urban crisis of the 1960s but rather the emergency of the Depression that first prompted the cities to leave their wariness of outsiders behind and seek direct links with the national administration.[7] This chapter will focus on crucial moments in that decade, when that alignment was being forged and a suite of factors led to a durable shift in the relationship between local governments and the American state that was linked to a new vision of American society.

The new actions by the urban order created new policies, but they also created a new politics. Over time, mayors and their allies voiced distinctive positions not only on vital economic interventions but on a range of potentially divisive cultural issues as well. How much to intervene, how to solve the governance problems created by urbanicity, and how to hold together a kaleidoscopic bloc-of-blocs alliance remain the primary challenges for the Democratic Party today. This chapter chronicles the disjuncture of the 1930s when this shift occurred and identifies instances of the different strategies urbanites employed to pursue their legislative agenda. At times they engaged in logrolls with rural members, reminding them of the development funds and stability-enhancing features of programs, such as the Agricultural Adjustment Act (AAA), that were supported by the urban order but did not directly benefit urbanites. At other times they used an urbanizing strategy, emphasizing their specialized experience with city problems and their status as elected officials to characterize ostensibly national programs as distinctively urban areas of policy in which urban positions should hold sway for the sake of both the cities themselves and the nation as a whole. Each of these strategies had sometimes been used to good effect in state legislatures before (and continue to be used today), and the city forces employed them again to mixed effect in national policymaking.[8] They would also employ such strategies in the promotion of civil rights liberalism, which would divide the nation, the Democratic Party, and cities' residents—but not their representatives in Congress. That particular case of city representation is the subject of Chapter 5.

3.1 Emergency in the Depression

Before the 1930s, the shape of the American state had failed to keep pace with the development of its increasingly urban society. The maturing industrial revolution and the resulting waves of domestic and foreign immigrants arriving in the cities to staff factories and keep up with demand for production meant that American cities were booming. During the second half of the nineteenth century, from the Civil War to 1900, all of the largest cities in the United States grew rapidly, both in raw numbers and in terms of their share of the national population. New York grew from 813,000 to 3.4 million and Chicago from 112,000 to 1.7 million, while Philadelphia "merely" doubled from 565,000 to 1.3 million. In 1860, large cities made up 11 percent of the nation's population. By 1910, that figure had doubled to 22 percent, and it would increase to a peak of about 27 percent by the 1930s. The world had not seen such massive, compact populations of humans before.[9]

The new arrivals came from all over to meet the unprecedented demand for industrial labor in these rapidly growing places: from the hinterland surrounding the cities (though flows also continued out *from* the cities to the West and began to trickle into developing streetcar suburbs during this period as well), from southern and eastern Europe, and from the American South (when harshening Jim Crow conditions combined with several periods of slowed immigration from abroad during the First World War to prompt the beginning of what we call the Great Migrations). Newcomers arrived by the thousands, and developers could scarcely keep up with demand for housing as the cities burst at their seams.

Cities were booming, but they were not being governed well. They were legendarily unhealthy and dangerous, often led by corrupt politicians who sought self-enrichment as much as civic improvement. The venality of these men (they were almost exclusively men in this era before full adult suffrage) intermittently endangered the fiscal health of the city, while the physical health and lives of its city-zens were more routinely placed at risk. In response, a host of local reformers of various stripes arose and became known as the Progressives. The movement's energy was drawn from a range of visions for better municipal governance.[10] Some social reformers, like Jane Addams, sought to reform cities by working directly with the newcomers to create better citizens. Others, such as the leaders of the National Municipal League, took a more structural approach, focusing on changing local institutions, especially the political parties.

One solution for these structurally minded Progressives was to disconnect higher-level politics from city affairs, and to run cities as supposedly apolitical businesses.[11] Seeing national and state parties as nefarious rent-seekers either indifferent or genuinely hostile to the common good of the city, movement leaders sought to insulate local city politics from higher levels of governance. Given the tremendous wealth being generated by these urban agglomerations, reformers believed that the right local institutions and personnel—implementing up-to-date policies for mitigating the various and evident social ills of the metropolis—were all that were required for the betterment of the city and its city-zens.

Although some reformers created cross-city or national organizations to share insights, and despite the fact that most city parties were connected to state and national political organizations, the running battles between partisan machines and reformers were mostly parochial fights within their hometowns. City issues might rise to the statehouses, where Progressives could often team up with noncity allies to beat the machines, but they were curiously absent from the national agenda. To be sure, individual cities sought assistance from the federal government at times, especially for financing and technical support for major infrastructure projects or the repression of labor unrest. But there was no urban agenda in the sense of a unified set of policies advocated by cities across the nation, because cities saw each other as rivals, not allies. When city and national politics did intersect, it was often the case that some particular "distribution of federal largesse figured in the outcome of these inter-city competitions."[12]

The crash of 1929 and the long Depression that followed changed that pattern. The depth and breadth of the downturn made a national solution, built on links between local and national politics, extremely compelling. The effects of the Depression were felt most immediately in industrial centers, as production plummeted and expectations for continued growth were dashed. Employment in the industrial cities of the era was wholly dependent on the business cycle, drawing firms and workers into an interdependent web. Drops in production and capital availability immediately led to cascading layoffs and wage cuts—quickly producing a lack of both food and money. In those cities that were most dependent on industry, the effects of decreased production were particularly severe, with unemployment rates well above the national average of 25 percent. Chicago saw its unemployment rate rise to 40 percent. In Philadelphia, manufacturing fell by half, factory payrolls fell by 60 percent, and unemployment also reached 40 percent. Industrial centers across the (not-yet rusty) Rust Belt saw their overall economies more than decimated.[13]

Cities, which had grown so quickly in the previous decades, were suddenly cash-strapped and faced a major crisis of governance. Residents were destitute and in need of greater services and relief, but there was no clear path to meet these needs. Private charities lacked the capacity to feed half a city for long, and the laissez-faire ideology ascendant in the past half-century similarly meant that few cities had sufficient means to provide relief. More, because residents could not even afford to pay their property taxes (the main source of city revenues), cities were suddenly without the resources they had come to rely upon to provide even the basic housekeeping functions that are so important under conditions of urbanicity at any time. Since the nineteenth century, cities in most states had been constrained by balanced budget requirements and municipal debt limits, typically based on the valuation of taxable property within the city's limits. Such policies, often put in place by Progressives in order to prevent Boss Tweed–style corruption and inefficiency, may work well in times of economic growth but are deeply insufficient in times of contraction because they prohibit countercyclical measures that can mitigate or alleviate hardship (an idea that would be the central insight of Keynesian economic policymaking, a set of ideas not developed or embraced anywhere until this crisis).

The city's vulnerable place in the federal hierarchy was also recognized as a cause of this crisis. As C. A. Dykstra, the city manager of Cincinnati, argued before the USCM in 1933, "Both state and Federal governments have invaded most of the areas of possible revenues and have thus cut down the opportunities of local areas to finance themselves adequately" through the typical means of the property tax. Available property tax revenues were often curbed legally by state constitutional "tax limitation provisions," procedurally by state appraisal boards that reduced the appraised value of property, and practically by homeowners' inability to pay, reducing by half the available property tax revenues in some cases.[14]

In addition to these formal constraints, city officials were becoming aware of the logic of interjurisdictional competition as a powerful force for limiting the size of the local fisc. While cities had always seen each other as rivals in the matter of attracting business and sought to promote themselves as appealing places to live, they had often done this by *providing* services that other cities did not, such as professional policing, water, and services for the indigent, rather than limiting them.[15] By the 1930s, however, this attitude seemed to have changed, and local government expense was sometimes seen as a "millstone around the neck of business . . . in spite of the retrenchment programs of American cities."[16]

New York mayor Fiorello La Guardia warned his fellow mayors not to be blind to the threat of flight to outlying "satellite" areas:

> Industry will go to these new community centers, if they are built, for one purpose alone. Surely, they are not going to get away from the center of industry, they are not going to pay additional charges for freight, just to go and put up a factory in a new rural community. They go there for one purpose only, and that is to get cheaper labor. And the minute that industry seeks to break away from cities for that purpose it will bring our whole standard down, and no city can afford to meet that kind of competition.[17]

For the times, this was a rare, prescient accounting of the vulnerability of central cities to surrounding areas, which can benefit from their proximity to the city's agglomeration of benefits without paying the costs of membership. La Guardia continued to comment on these surrounding areas:

> Surely, taxes are less now [in these areas], because if you take a tract of land you have no taxes there for pavement or sidewalk upkeep. You have no taxes for sewerage and sewage disposal. You have no taxes for schools, fire and police protection. . . . We as cities ought to take some action in advising the Administration that their plan should be very carefully watched lest it may do more harm than good.[18]

Constrained and desperate, the only plan available to these cities was austerity budgeting, which in times of hardship is a recipe for ineffective urban governance and a spiraling tendency toward social neglect and disintegration. These constraints, generated by outside forces (either legal, economic, or a combination of the two) can prevent cities from performing the basic functions required to preserve social order, including maintenance of infrastructure, policing, and sanitation.

This is what occurred in American cities during the early years of the Depression, as laid-off workers increasingly could not pay their rent or property taxes. Some went to live with relatives, some became homeless or moved to the growing Hooverville camps, and some stayed and took a radical stand against eviction or foreclosure at a time of crisis. The dire times faced by individual households were eventually reflected in the fiscal state of their communities. Municipal tax receipts plummeted as local unemployment rates rose. In Chicago, attempts to increase revenues by taxing different kinds of properties at different rates were met by a tax strike by wealthy and commercial property owners. Within three years, the city was unable to meet its payroll. When it turned to the state for relief and for a reassessment of local property values, it was met with downstate resistance and legislative obstruction.[19] In Boston, Mayor James Curley estimated that in 1932, "only" 20 percent of local property taxes went uncollected, but his counterpart from Milwaukee, Mayor Daniel Hoan, estimated that even with a six-month grace period, 40 percent of his city's residents would be delinquent in their taxes, a figure he considered "average" among cities and that coincides with the estimates of unemployment that have been made for these hard-hit industrial areas.[20] Desperate to keep up with the mounting problems within their jurisdictions, city leaders turned to the banks for short-term loans, but with such low revenue streams, and with banks failing nationwide, they could not gain access to credit markets either. This is why the cities first turned to the federal government for assistance, approaching the Reconstruction Finance Corporation for access to increased government credit to augment local revenues and even out the budget crises of municipal governance. With no credit available elsewhere, the cities sought relief from the ultimate lender of last resort. To do so, city representatives banded together for the first time in a cohesive unit to advance pro-city policies, to share information, and to create a political alliance and advocacy organization that endures to this day: the U.S. Conference of Mayors.

The crisis of the Depression prompted city leaders to coalesce into a unified group seeking aid to meet their urgent governance needs. The USCM became the unified voice of the urban agenda in the 1930s, an instrument through which intercity rivalries could be subordinated to the broader goals of the urban political order. In establishing the group, city elites forged an interest group that sought to identify and pursue policy goals that would benefit all cities and was capable of battling for goods within the evolving pluralist group politics of the age. Their basic goal was simple: to shore up the fiscal health of the cities in order to meet the governance needs cities were often too constrained to achieve individually.

3.2 The Urban Political Order

The Depression was a worldwide crisis for industrial capitalism and liberal democracy. While some other nations turned to less democratic regimes as a solution, American politics evolved its system of national interest-group pluralism.[21] As the 1930s wore on, the debates over policies designed to manage the industrial order and save the cities came to include a hodgepodge of advocacy groups representing diverse constituencies who were not natural allies. These groups were part of an assertively group-based politics that was becoming more common in the modern era, a politics that resembled city politics for the plurality of voices involved. National union organizations were the most powerful of these groups, led by the American Federation of Labor (AFL) and the Congress of Industrial Unions (CIO), organizations that vied for leadership within the union movement and held different ideological dispositions and member profiles but clearly landed on the same side of most major debates of the era, especially those concerning the relationship between capital and labor and the establishment of the national welfare state. The Urban League, the National Association for the Advancement of Colored People (NAACP), and A. Philip Randolph's Brotherhood of Sleeping Car Porters (a union that straddled the border between civil rights and labor advocacy) were also gaining a national voice on civil rights issues of the day, and the partisan transformation of the 1930s would give them new coalition partners open to supporting racial liberalism. Religious groups, especially Jewish and Roman Catholic organizations, were also constant participants in urban policy conversations and invariably espoused liberal positions.[22]

But the urban order also included groups we would not identify as liberal. The associative impulse of the Progressive Era and the 1920s gave birth to many federations of corporate and business interests as well—and these interests were, after all, based in the cities that were the home of capital, labor, and finance. The U.S. Chamber of Commerce and its local branches sought to shape urban policies in a broadly business-friendly way, as did many industry-specific trade associations. Real estate interests coalesced in the National Association of Real Estate Boards, which was especially active in debates surrounding housing policy and sought to limit state interventions in local housing markets except where they would increase land values. Finance found a voice through the Mortgage Bankers Association.[23] With so much value and potential profit at stake within the booming cities of the age (fallow though they might be during the slowdown of the Depression), urban elites were a significant and powerful pressure group for urban policymaking.

Each of these groups and their leaders shaped the arc of American political history in the twentieth century. But they were also just interest groups in the traditional sense: civil society membership organizations rooted in prepolitical identities and with relatively narrow policy agendas focused on the issue areas relevant to the shared identities and interests of their members. They also represented groups that were often at odds with each other and that had their own particular interests, which political and ideological rivals could use to advantage. The tension between labor and capital was obvious and had been ongoing for decades. The racial strife within labor was often violent, and divergent positions on the issue between labor leaders and their rank and file nearly destroyed the movement.[24] Even the closest of allies were not above significant conflict. Despite their growing ranks in the wake of the Wagner Act of

1935 and the Fair Labor Standards Act of 1937, the AFL and CIO fought highly visible national battles over membership drives and the broader vision for the labor movement. The *Chicago Tribune* reported that a "large proportion" of the membership of AFL unions was "plumping" for Republicans in the Democratic intraparty struggles of 1938, and Southern Democrats would use AFL resentment of CIO gains to undermine the National Labor Relations Board itself.[25]

What, then, served to bind this fragile urban coalition together? Even with their particular interests, these groups nonetheless all had a shared stake in the development and maintenance of the cities where most of their members lived and worked. Within those cities, local democratic politics—always contentious, never resolved—provided political order. City officials, particularly those responsible to citywide constituencies and organizations, represented this political order and distilled the infinite perspectives of the city into one voice. Mayors and other local political leaders sat at the hubs of interlocking networks that bound all of these heterogeneous constituencies to politics and tied local politics to the national level as well, typically through a connection to party organizations. For the cities to create a cohesive national voice—a voice that was derived not from a particular group interest but from the position of speaking for the "city interest," accountable to all those plural interests and responsible for local governance but not thoroughly identified with any one of them—in the form of a national advocacy organization like the USCM was a turning point.

The USCM was not the first cross-city association, but it was the first to take on the specific mission of advocating for city positions in national politics and to seek aid from the federal government in the form of enduring programs to help cities meet their urgent governance needs. Other cross-city organizations served not as advocates, but as resources for would-be city leaders. The National Municipal League (NML; today it is called the National Civic League) had been founded in 1894 by prominent Progressives seeking to promote the reformist model charter for city governance. In keeping with the Progressive desire to separate local politics from the partisan fights on the state and national levels, the NML was not very active in national politics. The group sent only four witnesses to Congress before 1933: each argued on behalf of reforming Prohibition in order to make it more effective.[26] The National League of Cities (NLC) coalesced as a confederation of state municipal associations in the 1920s.[27] A traditional, bottom-up membership organization with a decentralized federal structure, it was primarily concerned with building cross-city networks rather than affecting national policies.[28]

The USCM, by contrast, was organized specifically by highly visible local officials as a response to the national economic collapse of the 1930s. In 1932, Detroit mayor Frank Murphy invited the chief executives of thirty-two large cities for an "unprecedented" conference to develop a unified voice calling for assistance from the federal government; the initial meeting passed resolutions in favor of emergency policies to ease the relief crisis in cities, and the mayors also voted to "perfect a permanent national organization," a move that became official in February of the following year when the mayors reconvened in Washington.[29] There, they dispatched to Capitol Hill Boston's mayor, James Michael Curley, who declared that "unless action is taken at an early date, the welfare of the people is not only in jeopardy, but the continued existence of our nation is problematical."[30]

The USCM has had a permanent presence in Washington ever since. Because this was an advocacy organization that was "post-political"—that is, because the mayors were as much the product of democratic politics as participants in it—they could bring a unique and persuasive perspective to policy debates on the Hill. While some characterized the cities as "mendicants" in asking for supplementary funds for purposes that had been handled traditionally by states or not at all, it did not take much fiscal detective work to see that industrial centers generated most national income, that their relief requests were indeed urgent, and that access to credit and help with alleviating the national unemployment situation were at least partial remedies to the local crises.[31] Claims made by mayors were not made on behalf of narrow interests within the city, but in the name of the city itself. And when regional, sectional, and intercity rivalries were subordinated to broader goals, these leaders' status as public officials organized and united in favor of an urban position boosted the legitimacy of their claims and calls to action. This was an important mechanism for distilling the polyvocality of city interests into a clearer signal. USCM participants consciously pursued this strategy.[32] Their position as local political and administrative executives meant that they brought on-the-ground expertise to issues, deep familiarity with local conditions, and a pragmatic approach to solving particular problems with action. By organizing local governments, not only social interests, the USCM allowed for a new perspective to be voiced in national politics, one that would not fade away and would keep national urban policy on the permanent agenda beginning in the 1930s.

The USCM developed a network through which the leaders of large cities, regardless of their partisan disposition, built relationships with the New Deal administration in Washington. This network utilized the mutually beneficial particularistic exchange idiom of traditional local party politics—services and jobs down, votes and political support up—to build both literally (infrastructure) and metaphorically (local organizations and the national Democratic Party). Roosevelt made allies with local leaders that would help him achieve his political goals, and the locals in turn benefited by taking credit for projects that visibly addressed the crisis.

Flanagan (1999) argues that "Roosevelt chose the USCM as the conduit to the urban bloc of voters."[33] Because he was a Roosevelt, and because he had made his name by attacking the Tammany machine, forging direct links with the heads of local organizations may have seemed a strange move for the new president. Seen from Washington, however, in practice, "there is often strikingly little difference between so-called bosses and so-called reformers"; both are local leaders who can help solve problems and serve as political allies.[34] Roosevelt's New Deal framework for urban policy also helped to build the politics of the pro-growth coalitions that would dominate the urban agenda throughout the rest of the twentieth century.[35]

The new direct relationships between national and local leaders that Roosevelt cultivated were vital precisely because he (like subsequent Democratic candidates) became so reliant on the huge majorities provided by city organizations in presidential elections.[36] This reality made alliances with the leaders of these complicated local polities central to Roosevelt's reelection aspirations and to the implementation of the initial New Deal policies, which were based on a sort of federated corporatism that differed from the unmediated transfers to individuals that would become another hallmark of the welfare state over the long run. Thus, in building strong ties to the major cities of the nascent urban political order, Roosevelt could simultaneously pursue political and policy goals.

New York was distinctive among these cities for several reasons. Even more than today, New York was unrivaled among American cities. More than twice as large as any other city, it was represented by twenty-three members of the House in 1933. New York was the nation's leader in finance, industry, and cultural production. It was also the most urban place in the country: large, densely populated, and extremely heterogeneous. But perhaps even more important than these characteristics, New York held a distinctive place within the Democratic Party. Outside the South, the Democratic Party had been dominated by the Republicans for decades. William Jennings Bryan's Populist insurgency from the West failed in the 1890s, and only an intraparty fight between GOP titans Theodore Roosevelt and William Howard Taft allowed Woodrow Wilson to gain the Oval Office in 1912. As the party of Reedemer southerners in the wake of Reconstruction, Democrats were tied to that section's Civil War legacy. But there was a tenacious city organization outside the South that also held national import for the Democrats. New York's Tammany Hall had been the strongest single force in city politics since before the Civil War, combining the seemingly inchoate and colorful elements of staggering venality, significant immigrant incorporation, alternating periods of working-class representation and domination, and impressive local development initiatives that kept New York far ahead of its rivals for national economic pre-eminence.[37]

Tammany was a powerful force within New York City politics, but it also faced many rivals both near and far. Tammany leader Al Smith's 1928 nomination for President by the Democrats exposed the national intraparty tension on the grand stage of the Electoral College. Urban bosses in the North supported Smith (especially his commitment to ending Prohibition, a position quite popular among big-city and immigrant groups), but his nomination was too much for many southerners to take, and the defection of all but the deepest South to Hoover—even as many large cities and new white ethnic populations were brought into the Democratic fold for the first time—presaged later Dixiecrat revolts. Closer to home, Tammany also faced serious rivalries with reformers and Democratic organizations in the outer boroughs.[38] Chief among these were Ed Flynn, boss of the Bronx Democrats and leader of outer-borough Democrats who sought to defend their own organizational prerogatives from Tammany's control in the consolidated city.[39] Roosevelt made his name fighting the party regulars, and party loyalty typically gave way to political expediency in his calculations. His decades-long feud with Tammany meant that he embraced Flynn and his allies (including Joseph McKee, an insurgent Democrat who ran for mayor in 1933) at some moments and left them in the lurch at others.[40]

Perhaps because of this fraught relationship with New York City's Democrats, Roosevelt's administration worked most closely with Fiorello La Guardia on projects in the Big Apple. Affiliated with local Republicans, La Guardia had earlier served in Congress. There, he was an early and ardent supporter of urban liberalism, known especially for his opposition to the immigration quotas enacted by the Republican Congresses of the 1920s and for the labor-friendly Norris–La Guardia Act of 1932. It was as the longest-serving mayor in New York City history, however, that he achieved his iconic status as an advocate for the nation's largest city and for cities across the nation. Despite the fact that he was never elected as a Democrat—or perhaps because of it—his ties with Roosevelt reinforced the "most important political alliance of the New Deal."[41]

La Guardia was a perfect ally and booster for the New Deal program. A quintessential New Yorker with a dominating personality—garrulous, charismatic, tireless, and pugnacious—he was a crusading reformer for many causes, untainted by Tammany association because of his previous affiliation with the Republicans, but a resolute liberal and unapologetic big-city booster (and therefore a link to important liberal groups as well). Roosevelt ultimately maneuvered to support La Guardia's election on the Republican–Fusion line in 1933, one last jab at his Tammany rivals after besting Smith for the 1932 presidential nomination.[42] As Roosevelt's special relationship with La Guardia strengthened, the mayor built his own powerful base without the benefit of a major party machine by leveraging WPA projects and the patronage they entailed. La Guardia was stalwart in support of the president and his New Deal programs, and FDR returned the compliment, stating that "Mayor La Guardia and his Administration have given to the City the most honest and most efficient municipal government of any within my recollection."[43] Simultaneously, Roosevelt also threw some support to outer-borough Democrats fighting their own intraparty battles with Tammany.[44]

Tammany had kept New York Democratic for generations, but several other cities that had tended toward the GOP joined the urban political alliance in the 1930s. Chicago was chief among these; generally led by Republicans since the days of Lincoln, Chicago swung firmly to the Democrats in the early 1930s as Anton Cermak consolidated the party's factions within one "house for all peoples." Cermak was suddenly killed in early 1933, and Edward Kelly rose to fill his place.

Kelly, with his mentor Patrick Nash, built what would become a Democratic stronghold in Cook County that has survived to today: since 1933, Chicago and Cook County have consistently provided huge majorities for Democratic presidential candidates, Chicago has had only Democratic mayors, and 300 of the 330 cumulative House seats representing Chicago have been occupied by Democrats.[45] Perhaps even more importantly, Chicago's Democratic organization has been remarkably stable and unified since 1933. While New York was riven by internal rivalries between professionals and viable reformers, and between Manhattan and the outer boroughs, Chicago's centralized party institutions helped make it a cohesive political organization that has endured for the last eight decades.[46] The Kelly–Nash organization proved an able partner for the national administration, turning out huge majorities in Chicago for Roosevelt and helping get a recalcitrant governor (a downstate Democrat who saw Kelly as a rival) to raise state matching for WPA projects. Like New York, Chicago encountered controversy over who should administer, and thus receive the credit for, work relief programs in Illinois. Kelly's enthusiasm for the New Deal meant that Harry Hopkins, one of the New Deal's administrative leaders, funneled the money through the Chicago organization and turned a blind eye when workers were pressured to make campaign contributions to and vote for organization candidates. Such "party-building" activities were obviously corrupt, but they were a longstanding practice of machine-style city politics.[47] Roosevelt and his allies again showed their pragmatic flexibility in gaining and holding valuable political allies in the cities, and the cities gained the relief funds they so sorely needed. Kelly and Richard J. Daley, his even more powerful successor as head of the Cook County organization, were figures who served as important party power brokers and links between local and national politics throughout the midtwentieth century. Chapter 4 illustrates how these local bosses helped provide the organizational glue to bind together their otherwise heterogeneous constituencies during this time, providing support for liberal positions, especially on civil rights.[48]

New York and Chicago were the anchors and leaders of the urban political order, but the rest of the nation's cities increasingly joined the Democrats from 1932 on. This shift is illustrated by the overall trend in Figure 6.2. Formerly Republican bastions in Philadelphia and Pittsburgh made halting moves toward the Democrats in the 1930s, and more permanently in the 1950s.[49] Boston, a smaller city that had been strongly Irish Democratic for a while, remained so even as Roosevelt built one of his closest political relationships with Sen. David Walsh, a party rival of Mayor Curley. Detroit, with its weaker traditional party organizations, eventually established political order and Democratic dominance through the leadership of the local industrial unions, especially the United Auto Workers. Milwaukee's Socialist mayor Daniel Hoan was an active founding member of the USCM, and that city's liberal Progressive leadership increasingly joined, and eventually merged with, the Democratic Party. In the West, where cities were smaller and local parties less important, local leadership nonetheless saw the importance of federal–local links and cross-city alliances, priorities often voiced by veteran liberal New Deal representatives such as Helen Douglas and James Roosevelt. Perhaps because of the difficulty of transcontinental travel, or perhaps because they did not share close organizational links with national politics, mayors of western metropolises like Los Angeles and San Francisco were less vocal in national affairs. These cities, where institutions to bind heterogeneous groups and demands together were weak, were also more divided than their counterparts in the East, as shown in Chapter 4.[50] Not until after the 1960s did these cities become reliably unanimous supporters of the urban agenda.

Many of the relationships among mayors and between mayors and national officials were quiet and formed outside the public eye. There are ways that we can see that the relationship between city halls across the country and Capitol Hill strengthened over time, however. One place to look is the forum in which the cities can formally speak "on the Hill": congressional hearings. Under the auspices of the USCM, big-city mayors began to appear before Congress more regularly. Before 1930, it was a rare event for a mayor to appear before Congress to make a case for policy or to provide information. With the creation of the USCM, such appearances became key elements of hearings on urban issues, and far less rare.

Figure 3.1 illustrates this point. It depicts the number of appearances in congressional hearings by the mayors of the ten biggest cities every year from the Civil War's conclusion to the present. The pattern is impressively clear and reflects the growing importance of interaction between local and federal officials during the mid-twentieth century. Before 1930, the line is flat and low: on average, there was only one mayoral appearance per year during this period, and often none at all. During the post-Reconstruction period of 1872–1885, not a single big-city mayor testified before Congress. In the early 1910s, appearances became somewhat less infrequent. In 1914, there were more than five appearances by mayors for the first time; a handful were by a single mayor, and all were regarding local construction

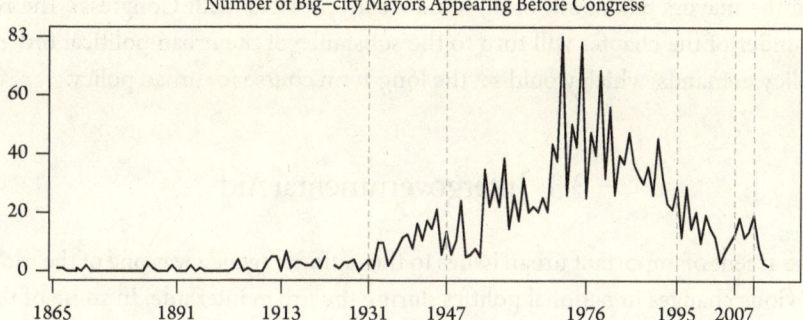

Figure 3.1 **Total Annual Appearances by Big-City Mayors.** Total number of congressional hearing appearances by big-city mayors over time. Before the 1930s, mayors seldom appeared before congressional committees to provide testimony but visited Washington with increasing frequency from the New Deal through the fiscal crises of the 1970s. Their presence has diminished but leveled off at a rate much higher than that seen before the 1930s. Sources: ProQuest Congressional; CSR Dataset.

projects such as canals and historical monuments. Indeed, particular water engineering projects and World's Fair expositions were the most common subjects of mayoral testimony. Though very important for a local economy, such programs should not be seen as a matter of national urban policy. The only issue of national urban concern to rise to the national agenda more than once was labor unrest, which was a matter of great discussion in the early 1890s.

After 1932, however, there was a marked shift. An average of twenty-three big-city mayoral appearances per year since then has strengthened the link between Congress and cities and has developed into a constant conversation calling attention to city concerns and potential policy fixes in which the national government could play a key role. The era from 1932 to 1970 shows a clear trend of increasingly common mayoral appearances, peaking at eighty-three appearances in 1971. Many of these mayors appeared as representatives of the USCM, a role in which they articulated the organization's perspective while also clarifying how their own particular experiences on a given issue gave them special insight into the matter. In readings of these testimonies, however, it is notable how tightly these politicians—gregarious, outspoken, skilled practitioners of verbal retail politics—stick to the unified line of the urban order.

Certainly the most important voice in this conversation was, again, La Guardia, who neatly bridged the federal–local divide and "absolutely dominated" the USCM while serving as its president from 1935 to 1945.[51] During his twelve years as mayor of New York, La Guardia appeared sixty-five times before congressional committees, frequently on behalf of the USCM. "Whatever rivalry there might have been between cities heretofore I can tell you we are bound together today through a common misery and misfortune," he told Congress in 1934. "The problem of every large city is very much the same."[52] But what did the mayors talk about in these new conversations with Congress? The remainder of the chapter will turn to the substance of the urban political order's policy demands, which would set the long-term course for urban policy.

3.3 Intergovernmental Aid

The ascent of important urban issues to the national agenda was one of the most obvious changes in national politics during the urban interlude. In some of the most famous national policy innovations of the New Deal, the federal government did most of the heavy lifting. For instance, the Social Security Act changed the conditions of individuals' lives by providing more robust safety net provisions, and the National Labor Relations Act leveled the terrain of combat between labor and capital by allowing for collective bargaining and providing an administrative court to act as a neutral referee. In these areas, subnational units were involved mainly as deliverers of services—often with foreseeable discriminatory results that were cooked into the bills themselves as necessary conditions for passage.[53] But there were also major changes in the way the national government related to cities themselves: it engaged in more financial exchanges, sponsored more local programs, and created new areas of policy that cities would come to depend upon for governing their local polities and maintaining political order. This orientation was something new in American politics, and it would have a profound effect on twentieth-century urban governance. Representatives of the local government and their agents in Congress sought good outcomes not only for their own narrow constituencies, but also for their city and ultimately for all of the cities in the urban order. In pivoting toward national policy programs, local officials came to act simultaneously as local sovereigns and subnational policy demanders, and the enduring questions of twentieth-century national urban policy were first asked in the 1930s.[54]

Representatives from cities that were (now more obviously) vulnerable to sudden collapse under conditions of capitalism and federalism began to support a program of national economic regulation, but more strikingly, the national government showed itself willing to channel aid of all sorts to urban centers. Over the course of the 1930s, city representatives made federal aid to cities a major element of national policy, and as time went by, it would become an increasingly important source of overall revenue for cities themselves.[55]

Before 1930, when the federal government considered the provision of aid to local governments, it was almost exclusively intended for rural areas in response to natural disasters or other accidents. After 1930, aid was increasingly thought of as a response to market conditions, to help cities weather economic storms and structural adjustment.[56] We can see this shift in Table 3.1, which is a list of

Table 3.1 **Hearings About Federal Aid to Local Governments, 1900–1940**

Hearing title	Year
Agricultural Education and . . . the Oleomargarine Law	1908
Sites and Plans for Public Buildings	1910
Compensation for Use of Highways	1912
Good Roads.	1913
Urgent Deficiency Bill, 1915	1914
Donation of Land, Malden, Mass.	1914
Flood Control at Pittsburgh, Pa.	1918
Farm Organizations	1921
Umpqua River, Bar, and Entrance, Oregon	1922
Forestry	1922
Aswell Agricultural Extension Bill	1924
County Agents in Flood-Stricken Areas . . . for South Carolina	1927
Flood Control. Part 1: Mississippi River and Its Tributaries	1927
Flood Control. Part 3: Mississippi River and Its Tributaries	1927
Cooperative Agricultural Extension Work	1927
Flood Control. Part 4: Mississippi River and Its Tributaries	1928
Flood Control. Part 5: Mississippi River and Its Tributaries	1928
Loans for Relief of Drainage Districts	1930
River and Harbor Bill	1930
Unemployment Relief	1931
Nontaxable Indian Lands	1931
Emergency Appropriation . . . in Rural Sanitation, etc.	1931
Flood Control, Drainage, Levee Districts	1931
Unemployment Relief	1932
Roads	1932
Rehabilitation of Storm-Stricken Areas	1932
Establishment of Administration of Public Works	1932
Roads	1932
Boston Harbor, Mass.	1932
Federal Aid Highway Legislation	1932
Drainage, Levee, Irrigation and Similar Districts	1932
Loans for Relief of Drainage Districts	1932

(*Continued*)

Table 3.1 **Continued**

Hearing title	Year
Relief to Municipalities	1933
National Industrial Recovery	1933
To Amend the Emergency and Construction Act of 1932	1933
Surplus Navy Coal for Distribution to Needy at Nominal Prices	1933
Hearing on H.R. 13026, to Amend Section 546, Title 34, of the U.S. Code	1933
Further Unemployment Relief Through the RFC	1933
Loans by the RFC to Aid Public Schools	1933
Additional Public Works Appropriations	1934
Roads	1934
To Provide Loans Through RFC	1934
Revision of Laws Concerning Bankruptcy of Drainage Districts	1935
Revision of Municipal Districts Bankruptcy Filing Procedures	1935
Revision of Municipal Districts Bankruptcy Filing Procedures	1935
Payments in Lieu of Taxes on Resettlement Projects	1936
RFC Aid to Refinance Indebtedness . . . in Conservation Areas	1936
Service Charges on Federal Slum Clearance Projects	1936
RFC and Federal Housing Loans for Municipal and Flood Relief	1936
U.S. Housing Act of 1936	1936
Stream Pollution	1936
To Create a U.S. Housing Authority	1937
Comprehensive Flood Control Plan for Ohio and Lower Mississippi Rivers	1937
River and Harbor Bill	1937
Amendments to U.S. Housing Act of 1937	1938
Loans to Public Agencies and Business Enterprises by RFC	1938
Public Buildings and Grounds	1938
Rehabilitation of Drainage Works . . . Ottawa National Forest	1939
To Amend the U.S. Housing Act of 1937	1939
Federal Cooperation in Development of Airports	1940
Construction of Hospitals	1940

Note: Hearings primarily about national, rather than city-specific, aid programs to cities highlighted in gray.

Source: ProQuest Congressional Hearings database.

all hearings that relate to federal aid to local governments from 1900 to 1940.[57] In this table, the gray rows indicate those that are primarily about city or urban issues.[58] Early in the century, federal aid was considered for many particular agricultural and hydrological purposes. Flood control was a primary concern—indeed, before 1930, the only hearing that was primarily relevant to a city was about flood control in Pittsburgh.

This changed between 1930 and 1934, when a *wendepunkt* occurred in the relationship between cities and the nation. Particular projects, like the aforementioned flood control in Pittsburgh, had long been within the purview of the federal government, typically through the activities of the Army Corps of Engineers, but there was an abrupt change in the discourse surrounding these projects over time. In March of 1932, a proposal to dredge Boston Harbor was debated before the House Committee on Rivers and Harbors. The witnesses, all New Englanders, were supportive of the project as a boon to Boston and the region. A young John McCormack (D-MA) testified to the importance of Boston Harbor as a "principal seaport for New England" and a "conduit through which the business life of that great section flows."[59] His colleague William Connery (D-MA) agreed that "everyone in northern New England looks to the city of Boston for everything," and rural representative Joseph Martin (R-MA) agreed that "all of us in Massachusetts and New England are vitally interested in this development."[60] These kinds of arguments, about the appropriateness of the particular project and the economic effects that might redound from it, were longstanding and had been made by potential beneficiaries from other places as well. The new argument, articulated most clearly by McCormack, who would go on to be Speaker of the House during the 1960s, was not about Boston Harbor itself, but about building intercity alliances to pursue what he called "a proper national policy":

> Money expended by the federal government, when spent with a regard for the future welfare and development of our country, and to the immediate advantage of the various sections thereof, is capital investment well made. We, of New England, indorse and support the development of the ports and the waterways of the various sections of our country. We have unselfishly supported other improvements, and we are now asking for the same consideration for Boston.[61]

In this speech, McCormack argued for the Boston project, but more important, he argued for federally funded local improvements more generally, as an effective way of maintaining the economic infrastructure of the nation. Such developmental activities had been part of federal policy in the early republic but had fallen off the docket in the era of laissez-faire hegemony.[62] Now nationwide patterns of robust intervention were returning to the agenda, and city representatives were finding the language to support them. Simultaneously, they were seeking to develop the political alliances, built on mutual exchange in the classic urban tradition, necessary to uphold and sustain such policies. One-off bills like the dredging of Boston Harbor can be quickly identified as particularistic pet projects—earmarks, in today's language. Under the system produced by the older urban strategy, if Boston fell out of favor, or if a different regional alliance took control of national politics, Boston could see its harbor intentionally neglected and be forced to pay for all improvements locally, a project that might be impossible for a constrained local polity. But in supporting a "proper national policy" in which cities across the nation could benefit from federal contributions of funding and expertise to their infrastructure development, McCormack could argue, without jealousy or provincialism, for Boston to receive such developmental support along with all other major port cities. Such a nationally distributive development policy would be the new hallmark of urban policy in the coming decades.

As the Depression set in and hit the industrial cities of the North particularly hard, federal aid was considered for a much larger portfolio of policies, most of them primarily targeting urban areas. Unemployment relief, road building, and public works were frequently considered as candidates for federal aid, and funds were ultimately appropriated for these purposes, marking a shift in the target and scope of federal aid to local governments. As Fiorello La Guardia put it in a 1937 hearing on housing, "If anyone had suggested ... 10 years ago that mayors would come to Washington to talk about housing with the congress it would seem so extreme and so far-fetched as to receive no serious consideration."[63] Aid in these areas was adjusted to help cities more than it had before, and while these kinds of policies could ostensibly benefit all kinds of communities, city leaders and representatives staunchly supported these programs, and cities certainly gained great benefits from them.[64]

Urban issues, especially programs that would help cities *qua* cities, came to the national agenda to stay during the urban interlude. The constraints faced by cities were severe, and local governments increasingly sought urgent help from on high. But the use of the federal government for such purposes remained controversial. Even in the Depression years before Roosevelt's election, a difference in attitude toward federal aid to cash-strapped local polities was apparent among Democrats from different kinds of districts. In 1932, several bills for unemployment relief were considered in a Senate hearing. The bills were written by senators from the urban industrial states (Democrats Robert Wagner from New York and Robert Bulkley from Ohio, as well as Republicans William Barbour from New Jersey and James Davis from Pennsylvania). At this hearing, the three perspectives on government activity that would persist throughout the Long

New Deal were already in evidence. Wagner, who was already the face of urban liberalism in the Senate, advocated for large-scale unemployment relief in the form of public works construction financed by a combination of grants, loans, and bonds by the national government to the states through the Reconstruction Finance Corporation.[65] He was supported by a bipartisan group of senators with close ties to industrial cities: Bulkley, who had formerly represented Cleveland in the House; Davis, a former union official and civic organizer from Pittsburgh; and James Couzens (R-MI), a former mayor of Detroit.

Wagner and his allies met with resistance from Secretary of the Treasury Ogden Mills, who voiced the administration's chief concerns of maintaining a balanced budget (the bond issue would effectively constitute deficit spending) and the efficiency of government-financed public works as a means for relieving unemployment. Mills objected to the measure on the grounds

> that it unbalances the budget; that it resorts to the unsound device of an extraordinary budget, that it breaks down a sound financial policy pursued since the beginning of the government.... These figures prove beyond question that this method of attack is wholly ineffective in solving the unemployment problem.... It becomes all the more necessary when you consider that an unbalanced budget and the abandonment of sound financial practices will cause a further shock to public confidence, tend to retard business recovery, and so not only prevent re-employment on a large scale, but very possibly add to the number of those already unemployed.[66]

While Mills supported emergency grants to states and small loans to businesses in an effort to jump-start production, he voiced the concern that the program as designed would allocate funds to all states, including large, relatively wealthy ones, which he argued should be able to fund these projects themselves:

> I know of no conceivable reason why great, rich states like New York and Pennsylvania should receive a grant from the federal treasury or be invited to accept one. They are well able to take care of their own. The bill should be so drafted as to provide for an emergency fund for the states that need it; not for a gratuitous distribution to all states on a per capita basis irrespective of need or resources.[67]

This perspective ignored the intrastate urban–rural divides that cities like New York faced, which made it difficult for New York City to get much help from Albany. It also ignored the broader constraints inherent in the logic of federalism (i.e., interjurisdictional competition), which provided a "conceivable reason" why even relatively wealthy states would be smart to pursue such essentially redistributive interventions through national policy rather than autonomously; because of their place within the federal system, the effects of market interventions and tax increases undertaken by subnational units will likely not be contained within those places.

In the hearing, city senators from both parties attacked Mills for his contention that public works were not effective or efficient means of providing unemployment relief and spurring other industries, but their main contention was that under the urgent conditions of the Depression, massive action must be taken by the national government. Mills's main support came from a pair of conservative Southern Democrats on the committee, Carter Glass of Virginia and Thomas Gore of Oklahoma. These two represented the older strain of the Democratic Party, having been in the chamber for over a decade each (of the aforementioned "urban" senators, only Couzens had arrived in the chamber before the late 1920s). While Mills was chiefly concerned with maintaining a balanced budget and was generally supportive of emergency aid to states in principle, Glass and Gore went further, emphasizing the principle of state self-reliance. Glass stated plainly that he was "opposed to the whole business. I don't think a state has a right to exist that can not take care of its own interests."[68]

Wagner responded that his bill had a purpose of "giving relief to the destitute where the facts justify it . . . and that is where we are working toward opposite objectives." For him, action by the national government was the appropriate response to the nationwide economic crisis.[69] With New Yorkers Roosevelt and Smith again preparing bids for the Democratic presidential nomination, Mills argued that the appropriate source of funds for relief of unemployment in New York was the state of New York:

> The question is, whether they are going to get those funds from their own people, or are going to the federal government for them. New York . . . need[s] funds for relief work today. But the question is whether the governor of the State of New York is going to call the state legislature into session and ask additional income taxes let us say, for relief purposes; whether he would call upon the great wealth of New York to meet the situation, or whether he will avoid that responsibility and come to Washington to get it.[70]

Glass agreed, calling "so-called federal aid the biggest humbug on earth. You get money from the states and bring it on here and land it in the treasury, and then you dole it back to them."[71] This conservative southern position was close to agreement with that of the administration and emphatically opposed to the bipartisan city position. Later in the hearing, Gore also took this stance, arguing that increased aid to states would lead to a state "ceas[ing] to be a body sovereign and becom[ing] a department like the departments of France."[72]

But the southerners did not agree with Mills on everything. Glass and Gore also criticized government intervention on behalf of businesses, which was the core of Mills's position. Glass cantankerously lamented that "ordinarily when private industry no longer has any credit it closes up, and it ought to close up.... I am old fashioned. I do not understand these modern devices,"[73] while Gore wondered:

> What is the difference between government ownership and government wet-nursing? ... The contention is that there should not be government ownership. A large group of people look upon it with bitter criticism and horror and yet it is proposed that the government shall set up a wet-nursing establishment—the RFC—and collect taxes from the people and loan money to public utilities and everything else that comes along.[74]

Gore also saw some hypocrisy on the part of businesses calling for state intervention in crises, declaring, "In normal times whenever mention is made of the government engaging in private business, a chorus is raised against it, but in hard times they raise a chorus in favor of it. 'Come over and help us,' they cry."[75]

On distributive matters, Glass and Gore agreed that "the government ought not to go into your pocket to furnish me funds," and that schemes to "tax the people of Oklahoma to fix a roof in New York" were unacceptable (even as they agreed that relatively wealthy New York paid more in taxes than Virginia or Oklahoma, both overall and per capita). They were joined by Duncan Fletcher (D-FL), who wondered if "the people who pay taxes are now beginning to realize that in order to decrease taxes they must decrease this demand for appropriations?"[76] In this hearing, at least, the rhetoric of these (noncity) Southern Democrats was even more fiscally conservative than that of the Republicans, expressing a deep skepticism of any national plan to manage the economy or deal with the current economic crisis.

After the landslide elections of 1932, the conflict within the Democratic Party over aid to local governments did not disappear, but the terrain on which it was fought changed: now, city advocates of robust, national intervention were clearly on the higher ground. This shift was apparent during a 1933 appearance by Boston mayor James Curley before the Senate Banking and Currency Committee, during which Curley gave the city perspective on another Wagner bill that would allow cities to borrow against anticipated tax receipts to cover current shortfalls. Since the previous year's RFC bill, the aid proposal had shifted its target from the state to the local level. In this hearing about "Relief to Municipalities," Gore sought to preemptively admonish cities for seeking aid from the national government:

> If [witnesses] are here to make a statement concerning the state of the union or matters of interest to the public generally, of course, we greet them with courtesy and are glad to hear the suggestions. If they have come here to seek money out of the Treasury of the United States and out of the pockets of the taxpayers of the United States, I want to enter a protest against hearing them.[77]

Speaking as "Ambassador from the American cities to the Congress," Curley quickly replied that he could not imagine

> anything that would be more in the nature of an innovation than some representative of any of the various units that go to make up the government of the United States or the states of the union appearing in Washington *for any other purpose than endeavoring to seek some money out of the Treasury*. So far as I have been able to ascertain, following the press, that has been about the purpose of the visit of every one that has come to Washington.[78]

Gore, in response, urged local fiscal self-reliance:

> I feel that when they come here, these towns and cities, to ask money at the hands of the federal government it is just a deadly blow to the system. Not only that—it is an admission that they are dead, and they will never rise, and I am going to bid you good day.[79]

Gore's frustrated, rather stormy exit from this exchange marked a moment when the coalescing urban political order, represented by Curley, confronted the previous heart of the Democratic Party and forced it into a both symbolic and literal retreat. A new pattern of distributive politics that would benefit a wide range of constituencies would be established, allowing for the "inclusive exchange" of goods throughout the New Deal era.[80] But city representatives needed to continually remind their partners of their obligations in this deal and had to make concessions to keep it alive. In 1933, for instance, the National Industrial Recovery Act formula for allocating road construction and maintenance funding was adjusted to increase the importance of population (and decrease the importance of a state's geographic area). When Rep. Claude Fuller (D-AR) objected to this change, John McCormack (D-MA) testily rebuked the Arkansan for not being "big-hearted" enough approve of the shift of funds to states with large populations.[81]

While transportation and infrastructure policies could be subtly adjusted, housing policy was a new realm of massive activity for the national government in the 1930s. Early housing and slum clearance programs were clearly designed with cities in mind, taking into account as they did the relative scarcity of city land and high costs of construction in metropolises. In keeping with the party's principle of inclusive exchange, however, benefits were also extended to rural areas. Urban liberals (mainly Democrats in Congress and the administration) were careful to characterize the nascent housing programs as unbiased and inclusive with regard to urbanicity; thus, in addition to support for programs that benefited urban areas, city representatives also included in housing legislation benefits for rural areas, sweetening the deal for their rural colleagues. In the hearing on the initial approval of the U.S. Housing Authority (USHA), when Sen. Franklin Hancock (D-NC) expressed skepticism that the program would actually make an impact outside the cities, Fiorello La Guardia (appearing on behalf of the USCM and New York City), was barely able to disagree:

HANCOCK: Why was the word "rural" inserted [into the bill describing slum conditions]? . . . I am in favor of aiding slum people whenever they exist and naturally some of the advocates want to leave that word in, but I do not want to fool my people. You must know why it was put there. You know the practical philosophy of this bill makes it unsuited to rural communities as well as I do. . . .
LA GUARDIA: Don't you think that the American farmer would like to have a nice cheerful place to live in, just as much as the unskilled laborer of a city would?
HANCOCK: Of course, but who would buy it for him? He couldn't participate under this bill.
LA GUARDIA: Some sort of arrangement could be made, the same as in the city.
HANCOCK: Does this bill contemplate the purchase of farm lands? . . . Why make a gesture in this bill in that direction? Let us make this an urban bill and work out a companion measure for the rural communities.
LA GUARDIA: Will you vote for it?

Later, in 1939, USHA administrator Nathan Straus insisted that his agency did not subscribe to

> the principle that slum conditions and the ill-housed poor are phenomena existing only in large metropolitan areas. Our assistance in attacking the low-rent housing problem is based, not on the population, not on the urban or rural character of the applicant, but on the demonstrated need for slum clearance and rehousing.[82]

This insistence that housing policy (and other city-centric New Deal policies) would also benefit rural communities was no doubt attractive for noncity legislators who might not have supported such expensive programs otherwise. Rep. James Meeks, a downstate Democrat from Illinois, inquired of Straus in 1938 how he could gain benefits for his district, which included no large population centers, saying, "I see that you earmarked nothing under 100,000 population there [in Illinois]. I would like to get what the local difficulty is in Illinois, because if we are going to pass a nice fat pie around, I want our State to get some of it."[83] Illinois did indeed get some, though maybe less than it "should" have.[84]

While the housing program was mostly targeted at larger cities, as seems to have been intended by its authors and proponents, the partisan distribution of the program's early funds is apparent. The 1937 Congress was the most lopsided in modern history: Democrats held 75 of 96 seats in the Senate and 333 of 435 seats in the House. Even so, the initial allocations of USHA funds were somehow even *more* disproportionately sent to districts represented by Democrats. Ninety-two percent of over $600 million in first-wave USHA funding for housing went to localities (mainly cities, but also small towns and counties) represented by Democrats in the House. Most of the money went to major Democratic cities: New York City received $53 million, Chicago $16 million (Illinois got a late start in the program), and Philadelphia $32 million.[85] None of the members of these large cities' delegations were Republicans. Smaller Republican cities in some of these states did receive grants as well: Syracuse, Peoria, and Worcester all sent Republicans to the House, but they were also real industrial cities with demonstrable need of redevelopment. It is the smaller allocations that reveal partisan allocation of funds. Such poetically small towns as Paducah (Kentucky), Muncie (Indiana), Norwalk (Connecticut), and Laurel (Mississippi) also were among the recipients of these initial grants. The sums they received were fairly trivial in the grand scope of the program—typically less than $1 million. But of the forty "small-town" allocations made by the USHA, thirty-eight (95 percent) were to places represented by Democrats. Most of these small-town grants were made in the South, despite the very low costs of labor, construction, and land in that region (the high costs of these factors in cities were what had been cited as making government intervention in the housing market necessary in the first place). It seems unlikely that 95 percent of the low-income housing needs outside of the cities just happened to be in these particular districts; clearly, this was a strategy of distributive politics intended to woo rural representatives into signing on to the city-centric housing program.

All of these observations are consistent with the cities' primary strategy of addressing marginal urgency by inclusive exchange. The large cities in the Democratic fold (as well as some, like San Francisco, that had not yet entered it) received much-needed funds to implement low-income housing and slum clearance programs, but the cost of the urban program was that a small allocation (about 5 percent of the total funding) went to small-town Democratic constituencies where the demand for such subsidies could not have been as strong.

Nonetheless, this urban–rural mutual exchange program had begun to fray by the end of the decade. While rural areas and states with small populations received greater largesse as measured per capita from New Deal programs, these same places ultimately joined a conservative coalition less than enthusiastic about supporting programs (notably housing) that primarily benefited cities.[86] Frustrated with the perceived disloyalty of such defection from the inclusive bargain, city representatives Raymond McKeough (D-Chicago) and Henry Ellenbogen (D-Pittsburgh) engaged in the following pedagogical exchange for the benefit of their rural colleagues in 1937:

MCKEOUGH: Do you think that the requirements of this [housing] bill are to cover a parochial problem, or a national problem?
ELLENBOGEN: National.
MCKEOUGH: Is there any more reason why the municipalities that have got to cure this condition should be penalized, as against the farmer that receives his soil-erosion contribution from the federal government?
ELLENBOGEN: I agree. . . . [Cities] contribute millions and millions of dollars more in Federal taxes than the Federal government pays in servicing that area. The money goes somewhere else.
MCKEOUGH: May I ask if any of those dollars that Pittsburgh paid in were earmarked so that none of them might reach the rural settlements in the payment of gratuities to the farmers?[87]

Ultimately, city representatives were successful in getting city issues onto the permanent national agenda. At the final stages of representation—roll call voting—this achievement has been lasting. Figure 3.2 shows the trend over time in the number of roll call votes having to do with explicitly urban issues during the twentieth century.[88] These votes were about three distinctively city-centric policy areas: urban and regional development, public works employment, and housing.

Previously absent from the congressional agenda, these issues began to appear during the urban interlude. In Figure 3.2, the solid line indicates the number of votes on city issues, while the dashed line indicates the proportion of all votes in these four city categories, revealing that the urban interlude saw an increase in the salience of the urban agenda in roll call voting. The general trend in overall urban votes is an increase since about the early 1930s, with an outlying peak during the urban fiscal crises of the mid-1970s. As a proportion of the overall

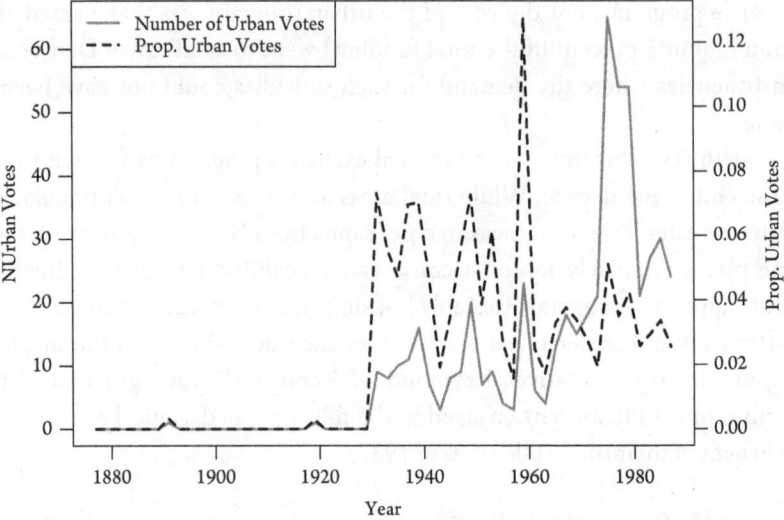

Figure 3.2 **Total Urban Roll Call Votes and Urban Votes as a Proportion of All Roll Call Votes, 45th–100th Congresses.** The solid line indicates the total number of votes on urban issues and the dashed line shows the proportion of urban votes as a share of all votes. The number of votes about urban issues has increased since the beginning of the urban interlude. The proportion of the overall agenda taken up by urban issues was generally high throughout the period and peaked in the 88th Congress (1959–1961).
Sources: Voteview; AIP.

House voting agenda, urban issues rose with the new Democratic majority in 1931 and reached their highest levels over the period lasting from the 1930s to the 1950s (the extremity of the 1959 peak is due to a series of bills with several quick procedural votes). Simply counting roll calls on a topic does not provide detail about political outcomes (and these city issues did not *dominate* the national agenda in any case, usually making up about 5 percent of roll calls, as we shall see in Chapter 6). But reaching the agenda, and changing the conversation, signifies the clearance of the first hurdle, and these figures also reconfirm the findings of historical treatments of urban policy and coincide with the content of the hearing agenda examined previously.[89] In the next section, I turn briefly to accounts of the development of the two specific components of the urban agenda that took center stage in the 1930s, providing the impetus for the USCM and congressional urbanites to spur action on big-city policies.

3.4 Relief

The most urgent, novel crisis facing the United States during the Depression was industrial unemployment: while the United States had grown to become the world's manufacturing titan during previous decades, rapid spiraling decreases in demand had led to approximately one in four workers being laid off, firms failing, and diminished overall production. As the crisis dragged on, those workers and their families became not just unemployed but destitute. Millions lost their savings and their homes. A crisis of national scope was met with merely local efforts at amelioration, however. A long tradition of Anglo-Saxon-style welfare and charity services placed the burden of poor relief upon local governments. The federal effort was meager at best. From the cities' point of view, there was no single federal point of contact to administer or coordinate urban relief, and the "latest news out of Washington" a year and a half into the Depression was that "cities can best handle their own industrial crisis problems."[90] Developed over the centuries, the existing system was no longer adequate for the industrial city or for the business cycle of the modern economy. The first line of aid to the poor, local charities, certainly meant well, but they were quickly overwhelmed by the scale and duration of need. Local governments, historically more attuned to local development policies and the provision of basic services than to poverty alleviation, stepped in valiantly. They borrowed money, raised taxes, and cut municipal salaries to increase local appropriations for relief, but their coffers, too, quickly ran dry as emergency measures were required to provide food relief for over 4.8 million families in early 1933.[91]

Throughout Hoover's term in office, as the Depression deepened, the essentially hands-off approach of the national government allowed urban unemployment to give way to urban insecurity, with desperation making genuine social unrest seem more likely. The Bonus Army of veterans marched on Washington and camped there, demanding payment from the federal government until clashes with General Douglas MacArthur's forces dislodged them. Vast Hoovervilles sprang up in Central Park in New York, in Grant Park in Chicago, and along the Schuylkill River in central Philadelphia, each with thousands of semipermanent residents pushed to the brink by prolonged deprivation. For city leaders, the exhaustion of food aid was not a viable option; cutting off relief would compel people "to choose between starvation on the one hand or lawless search for food on the other. To present such a choice is not to promote law and order; it is to foment anarchy."[92] Recognizing a national crisis, local officials turned to the national level but found little assistance there—federal officials lacked even basic information upon which they might act, given the will and the means. In 1932, it was still safe to say that "there has never sat in Washington an urban-minded administration."[93] This changed immediately after that year's elections. The establishment of the Federal Emergency Relief Administration marked a disjuncture from the previous national approach to dealing with the Depression, and active bureaucracies started to collect and disseminate information on the state of cities in America. The Roosevelt administration came into office determined to establish a significant federal role in solving the problem, and both the mayors and their allies in Congress became more assertive and united in their lobbying to grow and shape the urban agenda.[94]

The work relief programs of the New Deal, most famously the Public Works Administration (PWA) and its successor (and rival) agency the Works Progress Administration, were a mixed form of redistribution. The PWA made loans to cities for infrastructure development projects, while the WPA made grants for a wider range of projects, typically administered by local officials. Both were national programs that targeted cities for the lion's share of their investment. They functioned in part as jobs programs to alleviate poverty, but unlike pure food or cash relief, they were designed to exchange benefits for labor with some public purpose. At the same time, these programs were clearly aimed toward the unemployed and not meant to be equivalent to typical government work or government contracting, and many of them would not have been undertaken if there hadn't been such a gap between industrial demand and the surplus availability of laborers. As such, these programs represented "the greatest opportunity for municipal improvements in the history of any country."[95] The initial administration of the PWA was accomplished through grants to localities for particular projects. This system proved too slow in distributing funds to the cities because outlays were determined by plans that were often slow to be drawn up. The cities advocated for, and eventually received, the more decentralized framework of the WPA; from the city perspective, the ideal framework for aid has always been centralized funding and decentralized administration. During the Depression, this approach allowed local governments to determine the character of projects undertaken as well as achieve the primary purpose of accelerating relief spending for the unemployed.

This decentralized framework also allowed local officials important political leverage: not only did they have an increased bounty of resources for which they might claim credit, but they enjoyed a fair amount of discretion over how those resources were distributed. By 1932, Roosevelt and his innermost circle of allies, especially WPA chief Harry Hopkins and patronage chief James Farley, were developing a program that aimed to simultaneously address the great need for poverty relief and consolidate the massive political gains that Democrats had made in cities over the past three election cycles.

The numbers on WPA construction are fairly staggering: over 124,000 bridges, 650,000 miles of roads, and 125,000 buildings were built or improved, and myriad other improvement projects, affecting airports to shipyards to streetlights, were undertaken.[96] Initially treated as a side effect to boosting income and resuscitating local economies, such public works and infrastructure developments proved durable achievements and continue to serve important functions in many aging cities today. They also helped build political connections between national agencies and city leaders. Later in the decade, the major welfare state programs of the Social Security Act became the main source of federal action to alleviate poverty for individuals. Federal programs for cities continued, but their primary purpose was not to provide cash help to needy individuals, but rather to help needy communities by providing a framework for large-scale "maintenance" projects, such as urban renewal, public housing, and a broad portfolio of community development programs run through HUD. These policies helped cities intervene in densely populated housing markets and overcome perennial fiscal challenges.

3.5 Housing

Relief programs provided stopgaps to alleviate some of the most crippling and urgent problems of the Depression, but housing issues moved to the center of the national urban agenda because of their ability to simultaneously boost economic activity and alleviate a market shortfall common in dense cities. Housing markets are distinctive because they are rooted in place; real estate values are determined at least as much by relative position and proximity to other places as by the contents within or improvements made upon the land. Once a city center has been established, nearby area values are structured by ease of interaction with that center. Technologies that increase density, like the elevator, or overcome the effects of distance, like the train or automobile, can have massive effects on land values.

In the 1930s, city leaders faced a serious dilemma. Their communities had grown quickly during the previous decades, incorporating new members from all over the world who came to work in their factories. These newcomers had often arrived to find substandard living conditions: hastily constructed, antiquated, and run-down structures; insufficient infrastructure to support large numbers of residents; and high living costs as the demand for housing outstripped supply. Over the early decades of the twentieth century, the nation's urban housing stock deteriorated to the point that U.S. cities were observed to have "the worst slums in the civilized world."[97] The slowdown of the early 1930s meant that maintenance was deferred further, accelerating cities' physical decay.

City leaders in the public and private sectors knew that this industrial working class (as well as the large segment of the population just below it socioeconomically) needed improved places to live, but the "natural" functioning of the private sector housing market did not serve this group well. Housing reformers had advocated for alleviation of the worst slum conditions for decades, but only the crisis of the 1930s prompted action.[98]

The initial New Deal programs, including the National Industrial Recovery Act and the PWA, included substantial public housing construction, but these were quickly nullified by the Supreme Court's laissez-faire rearguard actions.[99] In their place, Congress passed the Housing Act of 1934, which took a different tack in seeking to reinvigorate urban housing markets. The act created the Federal Housing Administration, which built upon the efforts of the Home Owners' Loan Act of 1933 and would become the forerunner of the cabinet-level Department of Housing and Urban Development. Framed first as an employment bill by its authors, who estimated that a 90 percent drop in residential construction activity had created 5 million unemployed construction workers, the bill sought to thaw "frozen and inoperative" mortgage markets to stimulate construction work.

The bill folded several policies into what amounted to a bold, comprehensive approach to regulating the home lending market. First, it sought to provide urgent relief to the unemployed by seeking to "revive the building trades and to bring them again to a point where they can be an assisting factor rather than a retarding factor in the recovery program." The bill's logic was founded on the belief that "sizable relieving of the unemployment situation can be accomplished over the summer months by a nationwide program of home modernization and repair" made possible by the extension of small loans to existing homeowners. Beyond this temporary measure, the bill sought to "permanently provide employment for all of those normally engaged in the building trades and associated activities" by creating the government-guaranteed national secondary mortgage market that has continued to this day.[100] This move fundamentally altered the incentives for home purchase for acceptable buyers, simultaneously boosting homeownership rates across the United States and (because the definitions of acceptability reflected and reinforced the prevailing prejudices of the day) generating the increasingly segregated, unequal racial settlement patterns that came to characterize the midcentury U.S. metropolis.[101] The act also provided incentives for slum clearance, which would become a hallmark of later urban renewal and public housing programs. Aimed as it was at the lending industry, the act's proponents in congressional debate were largely bankers and builders, not representatives of the working class or liberal interest groups. The sole advocate from outside that industry was Benjamin Marsh, representing the People's Lobby, a pioneering public interest advocacy group, who argued that "to meet this housing situation, you will have to create a government housing corporation with the right of eminent domain to go into every city of the nation and condemn property" for redevelopment. His arguments were not taken seriously by the Senate committee that heard them and were soon overruled by the Supreme Court in any case.[102]

These new programs were targeted at the private sector, which did a poor job of providing suitable housing to marginalized groups. As the first federal housing administrator, Nathan Straus, would later reflect, "Practically all of the [private sector] construction was to meet the needs of the [wealthy]. It is evident that private enterprise has not and cannot provide safe and sanitary homes for the third of the nation who are ill-housed."[103] Over time, the Federal Housing Administration (FHA) developed a two-tiered housing program that would endure for many decades. The first tier, aimed at those equipped and allowed to participate in the market (i.e., middle-class, white, "native stock," male-headed households), sought to encourage middle-class homeownership, unfreeze mortgage lending, and provide economic stimulus through the construction trades by regulating and subsidizing mortgage lending as described previously. Programs of this sort, which helped boost homeownership rates from 44 to 63 percent in three decades, descended from the Home Owners' Loan Corporation (HOLC) and the National Housing Act of 1934. The second tier was aimed at those particularly "ill-housed" persons excluded from the primary housing market. These policies created subsidized housing, often in the form of housing owned and administered by local housing authorities or agencies (today, this tier consists mostly of vouchers for use on the private market). The second-tier programs are largely descended from the Housing Act of 1937 (often referred to as the Wagner-Steagall Act), passage of which was "a key victory for the USCM and other urban interest groups" and which provided federal funds to localities to subsidize slum clearance and construction of low-income residences and established the USHA to help administer these programs.[104] Together, these two tiers of housing policy have helped stabilize the kind of heterogeneous housing market that can sustain class diversity in relatively small spaces.

From the very start, private builders and lenders were staunchly opposed to the second-tier programs and organized repeatedly to oppose them. In this effort Southern Democrats teamed up with Republicans, who were critical of basically any interventions, but this was one area in which the urban order was successful in articulating a distinctively urban problem and defending it. The USCM and its urban allies had mobilized a massive campaign on behalf of a similar bill the year before but had been let down by tepid Roosevelt support behind the scenes, leading that act to die in the House. In 1937, Wagner and his allies from around the country again brought pressure to bear on behalf of the public housing program, which they portrayed as crucial social legislation for cities and their residents.[105] La Guardia was particularly adamant and eloquent in his justification for the program, which he argued was a positive panacea for urban malaise:

> Private capital cannot build, operate, and maintain these buildings at a rental rate that a large group of our citizens can afford to pay.... We ask the Federal Government to provide "sunshine and air"... the difference

in the cost of construction between a modern, sanitary, building, and the old-type railroad-box form of building of the tenement house type.... [With such a change] there is a transformation not only in the buildings, not only in the neighborhood, but, gentlemen, there is a transformation in the tenants themselves.... [T]hey live right up to their new apartments. Their children are healthy and attractive. The death rate has gone right down. Their homes are immaculately clean. There is cheer and the morale and cheerfulness has gone right up.[106]

Subsequent arguments that state housing was tantamount to socialism in the midst of a Red Scare in the late 1930s were turned on their heads by Detroit mayor John W. Smith, who argued that decrepit housing conditions "breed sociological problems that ultimately burden the taxpayer more heavily than if the conditions were met and solved now. Too, Communist agitators are sowing fertile seed right now among the dispossessed."[107] Asked if by perhaps the bill went too far and spent too much, La Guardia simply replied, "No. The Republic is worth saving."[108] This provision of housing, he believed, would mitigate the allure of communism, saving the republic by making people more generally cheerful.

Revealingly, mayors and city representatives at the 1937 hearing emphasized that rural-dwellers were eligible for the housing program, but that it was principally an urban program, justifiable at least in part because rural areas had already received substantial aid from the federal government to alleviate the problems distinctive to their environments. Housing regulation and market interventions were necessary for maintaining urban communities, and the solution proposed was the correct way to manage the policy area, in their perspective. Income thresholds for participation were to be set locally and adjusted for local conditions, meaning that a working-class family in a major city (which might earn substantially more than most rural households) would still be eligible for subsidized housing if the local market was not providing a suitable place for them to live.

La Guardia was successful in his push for the Housing Act of 1937, but his fears of national policy subsidizing suburb satellite cities and sapping the larger cities of strength were well-founded. The two-tiered housing system was not "carefully watched" in the postwar era. The top tier, targeted at building the pool of middle-class homeowners, provided the financial underpinnings of the suburban rings that would slowly strangle their cities in a decades-long chokehold. The lower tier developed the massive modernist public works projects of the postwar era that were meant to provide the city with much-needed maintenance but had unexpected effects: the creation of notorious islands of segregated poverty abandoned by authorities, the razing (rather than renovation) of historic residential neighborhoods deemed blighted (according to perspectives we now consider benighted) to create downtown development projects that sucked the life from the street, and the construction of eight-lane highways through residential neighborhoods to central business districts that were meant to ease access to downtown but wound up allowing those who would flee the city to do so at a higher speed. The shortcomings and pathologies of the urban crisis are well-known. To the prewar mayors, however, these problems were fairly unimaginable as they sought to solve their current crises from their constrained position.

3.6 Conclusion

Over the course of the 1930s, the mayors provided concrete, authoritative perspectives that came from local experience, and they were frank in their pursuit of federal programs that would allow them to manage the problems that their cities increasingly shared. They also were firmly in favor of establishing permanent policies for dealing with what they saw as a new chronic condition facing their local polities. As Richard Flanagan has noted in his close history of the organization, "The USCM was the first group of notables to argue that the Depression was a permanent condition, not a temporary emergency . . . [requiring] permanent plans" for solution.[109] La Guardia observed as early as 1937 that "technological displacement, with labor-saving devices in agriculture as well as in industry," meant that unemployment was not only cyclical, but structural: "a new normal" to which the nation must adjust.[110] Such permanence would require a more elaborate federal administrative apparatus and institutionalized links between the national and local governments. Though the USCM advocated for such reorganization, it never came, and even since HUD was established in 1966, this framework for national urban policy has remained largely weak, fragmented, underfunded, and directionless (as well as under constant existential threat from Republicans).

This weakness reflects a paradox of the cities' position in the federal system: from the start, even as they seek federal aid, cities have jealously guarded their autonomy and been wary of interventions from above. When it became undeniable that their challenges were no longer local problems, they turned to the federal government for aid. The patchwork solution to the emergency of the Depression established a fairly ad hoc system in which relief and housing were used to boost the economy quickly, using the administrative capacities of the cities themselves. City leaders took credit for these projects and programs and again became used to the autonomy; the USCM argued from its first year that the national relief program "should be centralized without question, but there must be more administrative decentralization if local governments are to participate in Federal activities."[111] Most city leaders have not wavered from this view, seeking increased budgetary authority as well as increased flexibility for solving local problems. One price of this flexibility has been vulnerability. The adoption of general revenue-sharing and formula-based block grants in the 1970s allowed more communities to receive aid and to apply it to specific local needs. This approach spread the wealth and provided almost perfect flexibility but also diverted some funding from the neediest communities. It also allowed these programs to be cut more quietly over the 1980s and 1990s: because allocations were more liquid, cuts to each locality were smaller, and the effects less noticeable. This reality of slashed federal transfers led some observers to note that Washington had "abandoned the cities."[112]

But the crisis of the 1930s produced two major lasting developments for cities. The first was the USCM, a new organization that overcame intercity rivalries, united and led a "diverse coalition of urban interest groups," and regularized the practice of intergovernmental lobbying during the New Deal.[113] Over time, the USCM has remained active, lobbying the national government to shape policy on an ever-widening suite of issues: housing, community development, and welfare are still on the legislative agenda, but so are civil rights, employment training, energy policy, the environment, transportation, and international affairs.[114] The organization has grown to include the leaders of smaller cities and provide member services, but it continues to operate as a "peak" advocacy group representing a big-city perspective; though nonpartisan, the mayors remain advocates of federal interventions to ease local governance challenges. Such an entity did not exist before the 1930s.

Ultimately, however, such lobbying by local officials cannot get very far without reliable, well-placed allies. This leads us to the second lasting development from this time: the urban political order's incorporation into the national Democratic Party. The cities, having identified and argued for city-friendly policies to become part of the national agenda, needed to act politically to pursue these goals. They didn't necessarily have to do it in the Democratic Party, though—it is conceivable that they could have done this under the Republican umbrella. After all, local leaders were not overwhelmingly Democratic leading up to this time. La Guardia was a Republican; Chicago, Philadelphia, and Pittsburgh were run by Republican machines throughout the 1920s. Though the Great Migrations stalled a bit during the Depression, these cities had significant African American blocs that were still loyal Republicans. In the previous massive urban–rural national fight, the election of 1896, the city side had been decisively Republican, and many of the Progressives from the previous decades had been Republicans as well.

Two major elements made the urban–Democratic order more likely, however. First, the Republican schism of 1912 and the party's subsequent hegemony during the 1920s made it clear that the party's core would remain its business bloc, which had chosen small-tax laissez-faire over the Progressive wing's experiments in scientific-informed, pragmatic good governance as its preferred guideline for governing. The party was more chamber of commerce than pragmatic reformer, and Hoover's anemic response to the crisis of the Depression hammered this realization home. Active response to urgent governance crises was not part of its preferred repertoire, so the energetic problem solvers (like the mayors who founded the USCM) increasingly sought a new home—La Guardia himself would abandon the label of Republican by the time of his run for reelection.

Second, in addition to economic conservatism, the Party of Lincoln by the 1920s had also sent clear messages that it was *not* the party of inclusion. Reformers may have sought pragmatic solutions to new problems during the Progressive Era, but many of them also privileged assimilation over other, softer forms of new-group incorporation. This, too, marked a split within the movement and its potentially Republican elements. The Immigration Act of 1924 codified the idea that the American character was racial, was chiefly Anglo-British, and ought to be preserved in the country's makeup through reduced entry and a period of assimilation. Many new Americans who arrived in (or were the offspring of) the second wave of mass immigration around the turn of the century rejected this xenophobia and embraced the much more multicultural and pluralist idiom of their local big-city Democrats, many of whom were themselves members of the classes despised and disadvantaged by the 1924 act—Al Smith and Robert Wagner in New York and Anton Cermak in Chicago are notable examples. Republicans were slow to recognize or pursue the latent political might of these white ethnics, who would very shortly mobilize and coalesce into perhaps the dominant force in American elections.[115] Democrats were well-positioned to make a play for these groups, and the GOP's inept response to crisis only drove more voters away. Thus did progressive liberalism—the mix of savvy political inclusion and pragmatism that defined city governance across the local machine–reform dichotomy—rise behind a city-led coalition into the core of the Democratic governing approach during the Long New Deal.

But this urban order was terrifically diverse, and its mass elements were absolutely divisible. Holding together the individual building blocks of the cross-city coalition was not a foregone conclusion, and just because mayors had identified some of their cities' interests and articulated them through the USCM didn't mean that the representatives of smaller pieces of the city would cohesively agree with that position. For that, institutions of horizontal integration were key in binding city delegations together in pursuit of higher policy. The next two chapters analyze the mechanics of those institutions and how they mattered for defining twentieth-century American politics.

4

Ties That Bind

City Delegations and Cohesive Representation in Congress

> In order for anything to be done under public auspices, the elaborate decentralization of authority... must be overcome or set aside.
> —Edward Banfield and James Wilson, *City Politics*[1]
>
> Local experience has taught them that in unity there is power.
> —Leo Snowiss, "Congressional Recruitment and Representation"[2]

In Chapter 1, John Vorys gave voice to a certain wariness felt by rural representatives when they eyed their rivals from central cities. While ruralites have long worried about the alleged corruption and venality of cities, the cohesion of a city bloc is what made it formidable in legislative politics. In Congress, only since the 1930s has there been a united political bloc in support of an urban agenda. As described in Chapters 3 and 6, this bloc has articulated and defended a distinctive liberal agenda over time.

But before there can be a meaningful urban political order in the nation, it helps if there is political order within the cities themselves. The imperative of bloc cohesion means that in order to effectively pursue policy goals at the national level, cities must reach an internal accord about what policies best address governance challenges associated with urbanicity. But this unity will never naturally rise out of the city, because urbanicity presents *political* challenges as well: heterogeneity of all kinds creates a famously fractious politics. These divisions can themselves undermine civic unity as well as support for the statist interventions in the market discussed in the previous chapter. At times, the most salient social characteristic of city politics is the presence of deep *divisions*, not unity. This was most obvious in the 1960s, when racial and class tensions collided with fiscal shortfalls and bubbled over into an urban crisis that left an indelible mark on the face of many cities' geography, politics, and residents.[3]

But even in less extraordinary times, social conflict seems sewn into the very fabric of city life. Groups and individuals compete for scarce resources, workers and bosses clash, business leaders and neighborhoods fight over development patterns, and so on. Residential segregation by class and race means that representative institutions may reinforce rivalries and identities by linking them to the distribution of benefits, further deepening the potential for divisions along group lines.[4] Given the wide range of complex issues cities face, fragmented politics and their simultaneous, conflicting demands can lead to "hyperpluralism" and make a city "ungovernable."[5] Such deep pluralism means that articulating a singular city interest may be impossible or a contradiction in terms—the interests of a city's residents and groups are too varied and numerous, and too much in conflict, to be easily aggregated into a single position capable of being articulated. How, then, can a city pursue its interests at higher levels of government?

One answer to that question is that disparate elements can be held together in a cohesive whole in part by institutions of horizontal integration—local institutions that provide political order as well as connections between representatives in a common local *polis* or organization. The study of the development and effects of such institutions in binding together disparate parts of a city is a major literature in urban political science, but the field's analytical lens has been almost entirely focused on local dynamics. In this chapter, I use evidence from congressional roll calls to argue that IHIs developed at the local level do indeed foster cohesion among the representatives of cities. Consistent with city delegation theory, I find that city delegations are more cohesive than other collections of representatives from similarly proximate districts, and that city delegations from places with stronger IHIs are more cohesive than those from places with weaker ones. Looking more closely, I find that members of a city delegation are more likely to agree on roll call votes than representatives *not* from the same city, even when we account for other measures of plausible legislative affinity, such as congressional party, geographic proximity, and district-level characteristics (including urbanicity). These results buttress the claim that city institutions contribute to greater unity in legislative behavior, helping to make the city delegation the building block of the larger urban political order in national politics.

4.1 Local IHIs in National Politics

As argued in Chapter 2, institutions of horizontal integration foster cohesion among representatives of different constituencies across a city and are generally not present among other collections of representatives. The two main IHIs I will analyze here are the *jurisdictional* IHI of the city boundary, which includes or excludes constituencies and representatives from a local political community, and the *organizational* IHI of the traditional party, which moves an important locus of political influence outside of particular districts and into a citywide party or party committee, centralizing politics within a city and providing institutional linkages between particular constituencies and the city as a whole.

New York and Chicago were the most important Democratic cities during the urban interlude and set the tone for the rest of the urban order. These cities were also the homes of effective traditional party organizations, which controlled access to nominations throughout the Long New Deal; similar local political conditions were present in many of the other, smaller, cities of the New Deal coalition.[6] Wilson (1962), in his close study of intraparty dynamics in three large cities, observed that the Chicago organization was "virtually unbeatable" in primaries even when the offices were statewide, and that in the (then) thirty years since the establishment of a citywide Democratic organization, "only one Democrat . . . has won nomination to an important office without regular organization backing."[7] In New York, the organization's dominance was challenged more effectively within the party, but even as late as 1960, almost all New York City Democrats in Congress "owed at least their initial victories to organization slating."[8]

In the next sections, I turn to the historical archival record for some examples of city delegations in action; after that, I use statistical analysis of roll call votes to demonstrate that strong local institutions were associated with greater cohesion during the urban interlude. It is somewhat difficult to observe archival instances of this kind of interaction between elites, in part because of the general partiality of the record, but also because of the actors' observance of Lomasney's Law of political communication.[9] However, if we know where to look, we can see instances of city delegation theory at work, and what we do find supports the central tenets of city delegation theory. In both New York and Chicago, a mix of informal party relationships and formal city positions helped shape the contours of the city delegation. In each case, however, it bears mentioning that these groups of representatives saw themselves, and were seen by local officials, as a meaningful collectivity. Both they themselves and their mayors very frequently referred to the bloc of representatives from the city as a "delegation"; moreover, they took stands on issues together, and the mayors wrote to them collectively. Thus, the key logical starting point for city delegation theory is the recognition that these representatives are not disconnected atoms, responsive only to the part of the city that is their formal constituency, but rather parts of a citywide molecule. They are conscious of their membership in this delegation. As we shall see, during the Long New Deal, these individuals viewed themselves as members of a group of persons representing the entire city and were responsive to appeals made on that basis. Often, this meant voting as a bloc based on a city interest (as expressed by a mayor or other local official). At other times, it meant performing constituent services or intervening on behalf of the city, at times even when the matter at hand was specific to *another* congressional district—albeit one within the representative's home city. This kind of cross-district service provision (along with unified roll call representation despite an uneven preference distribution) is strong evidence that the city delegation is useful for understanding city representation.

4.2 New York's Delegation: Big-City Interests

New York City's complexity is reflected in its congressional politics in several ways. First, because New York is the biggest city in the nation, its mayor and delegation have a huge portfolio of concerns to attend to. It is also the most urban city: larger, more dense, and more diverse than any other. This means that New York often encounters particular challenges of urbanicity earlier, and more urgently, than other places and consequently has also been a place for early policy solutions and a source of basic information and governing advice for federal officials, as well as officials of other cities. And its size and diversity also mean it is the home to many, many distinct communities of interest on many dimensions: race, ethnicity, class, economic sector, religion, ideology, and more. New York is a microcosm of contentious interests.

Second, New York's institutional politics are as complex as its prepolitical building blocks. The city itself is composed of five counties, each with its own party organizations. Since the Democrats' rise to local preeminence in the mid- to late nineteenth century, Tammany Hall and the other regular Democratic organizations have been the most powerful forces in town, but they have been far from hegemonic.[10] The Tammany-led Democrats had an (earned) reputation for venality and were less than inclusive, so they generated significant opposition not only from Republicans but from other parties of varying success and significance, including the American Labor Party, Fusion groups, liberals, Progressives, Communists, and more; reform-oriented suborganizations also emerged periodically within the local Democratic Party itself. Unique local institutions, including the fusion ballot and a decade of proportional representation, helped foster this diversity of party organizations, which continues to powerfully shape the city's local politics.[11] This complexity is revealed in the colorful historical record of interactions between city leaders, in which we can observe all manner of exchanges. The complexity of the city's political arrangements is visible even in its succession of mayors. The two most powerful New York politicians during the 1930s, Franklin Roosevelt and Fiorello La Guardia, shared an antipathy toward the regular party organizations and frequently worked together to weaken them. The postwar mayors varied in their relationships to the organizations— William O'Dwyer's administration imploded over corruption scandals, leading to his resignation; Vincent Impellitteri, who succeeded O'Dwyer after his resignation, had previously enjoyed support from Tammany but was passed over for the nomination and won reelection in a 1950 special election with only a plurality victory on the Experience Party line. Impellitteri was then defeated in the 1953 Democratic primary by the organization's nominee, Robert F. Wagner, Jr. (the eldest son of the famous Progressive senator). Wagner himself ultimately broke with the regular organizations in his successful bid for a third term in 1961. This historical progression shows that city government was not closely tied to organizational prerogatives throughout this era, and that recurrent waves of reform led to a weakening of politically defined personnel and policy decisions. On the other hand, the regular Democratic organization was not completely toothless. For instance, Rep. Eugene Keogh (D-Manhattan) was a member of its inner circle, and Tammany boss Carmine DeSapio successfully purged a rogue Democrat from the city's congressional caucus in 1949.[12]

Thus, though the regular Democratic organization was very powerful, especially at the city council level, throughout the twentieth century, its efforts to install its choices in the top leadership position were decidedly less successful. Throughout this era, the city's congressional delegation was predominantly, but not entirely, Democratic. The collection of New York City representatives ranged from twenty-three Democrats out of twenty-three representatives in 1933–1935 to fifteen out of twenty-four representatives in 1947–1949. This medium-strength party organization is reflected in the city's medium-strength congressional cohesion, revealed in the analyses later in this chapter.

New York's twentieth-century mayors were in frequent contact with the city delegation on matters low and high. The archival record of mayor–congressional correspondence shows that members of Congress requested favors or relief on behalf of their constituents, kept the mayor apprised of legislation relevant to the city, and sent congratulations on occasions such as the mayor's birthday or reelection. Mayors asked for information, called MCs to intercede on behalf of the city (either formally or informally), and sent congratulations on the MC's birthday or reelection. Some of these relationships were warm, some less so. A few brief examples from the Long New Deal can show the typical kinds of exchanges, and then three closer looks at city delegation mechanics will explain how information and action travel through these networks.

In the 1930s, Fiorello La Guardia was a man without a party—a nominal Republican, he was also probably one of the most liberal figures in national politics (in every sense: he was helping to define urban liberalism during this time, in an ongoing partnership with Sen. Robert F. Wagner, Sr.), and by the end of the decade he was affiliated mainly with the American Labor Party. He was a very busy person: fighting the Depression in the world's largest city, building a national network of mayors to pursue the burgeoning urban agenda, and building his own political organization to vie with Tammany and its sister organizations in local elections. What he did *not* do much of was make strong organizational connections with most New York MCs.[13] La Guardia was forthright in refusing to provide the nepotism, favors, and city jobs that many MCs assumed would be available for the asking, at least to most Democrats. La Guardia did have a close relationship with his protégé and congressional successor, Vito Marcantonio; Marcantonio, too, was elected on the American Labor Party ticket and certainly was among the most outspoken antiracist and pro-labor MCs.[14] La Guardia built his own political organization by securing allocational authority over much of the city's WPA relief funding.[15]

While La Guardia was not particularly chummy with New York's largely machine-controlled Democratic delegation, he did communicate the city's interests to its members and on its behalf at times (as a national figure and former MC, his correspondence, while fairly limited in volume, is actually quite balanced and national in reach). Emanuel Celler (D-Brooklyn) had been a liberal ally during his days in Washington, especially in battles over immigration policy, and the two continued their connection when La Guardia moved back to New York. Their interactions were friendly—La Guardia referred to Celler as "Mannies"—and they habitually requested mild favors from each other.[16] Only rarely did they correspond about legislative matters in Congress, however. In one instance late in January 1935, Celler and La Guardia tried to rally support for an amendment that would provide relief through the Reconstruction Finance Corporation (RFC) to municipalities faced with a high number of delinquent taxpayers; such an amendment would ostensibly help all cities, including New York. (The RFC had been a key piece of the city relief package proposed by the USCM, described in Chapter 3.) On January 29, Celler sent La Guardia a list of the members of the conference committee for the RFC bill, advising him "to urge conferees to hold section 12A in bill as helpful to municipalities. Expeditious action necessary since RFC expires 2/1."[17] Later that day, La Guardia dashed off a telegram to Henry Steagall (D-AL), the chair of the House Banking Committee, stating that he "believe[d] that the Celler amendment (now section 12A of bill) . . . will be beneficial to many municipalities. Hope the amendment will remain in bill."[18] The next day, however, the mayor received bad news from Celler: "Conferees turned down my amendment . . . will give more details later."[19] The next day USCM executive director Paul Betters informed La Guardia that he "firmly believe[d] attitude [of RFC director] Jesse Jones caused Senate's yesterday not to accept House Celler amendment. Celler will either attach again to omnibus measure or introduce as individual bill."[20] La Guardia responded by sending a perhaps passive aggressive telegram to Jones offering assistance in pursuing the matter further.[21] The effort was unsuccessful in this case, but one mechanism of the city delegation was at work: a representative pursuing a city-friendly policy alerted his mayor of the development and asked him to lend his national profile in support of the measure. La Guardia responded by articulating the position of New York and many other municipalities and liaising with the director of the U.S. Conference of Mayors, the organization connecting cities to each other. Generally, however, La Guardia did not frequently interact with the New York City delegation as a whole, in large part because it was mostly composed of local political opponents. In their correspondence with him, New York's Democratic MCs sometimes went so far as to argue against themselves by reminding him that they had "no right to make any appeal to you [because] I did not vote for you," as Rep. William Sirovich (D-Bronx) did in 1934.[22] Though La Guardia was a charismatic figure, an ally of Roosevelt, and leader of the national urban order, he was not trying to build a cohesive political bloc to represent the city.

Among New York mayors during the Long New Deal, it was Robert F. Wagner, Jr., who kept up the steadiest stream of correspondence with his delegation in Washington. One of four New York mayors to serve three terms in the modern era, Wagner was the son of the famous liberal Democratic senator. Like his father, he was a product of New York organization politics who also paid close heed to national affairs and policy details, with a disposition toward technocratic progressive liberalism rather than rapacious opportunism.[23] Though less obviously charismatic than La Guardia, Wagner was an outspoken booster of the city and sought to promote its interests and the urban perspective both locally and in national politics.

Three anecdotes, of increasing controversy and consequence, from the Wagner era can illustrate some of the concrete interactions of city delegation politics, which embodied a mix of party action and city interest pursuit. The first occurred in May 1954 when the U.S. Army posted a relatively banal notice that within sixty days, it would be relocating the office of the New York Quartermaster Procurement Agency (NYQMPA) to Philadelphia. The office, which was charged with finding and contracting goods for military use, had been located in New York for a decade and employed about 1,600 people. The office was located just east of Union Square, in Republican Frederic Coudert's district, but its employees resided throughout the city, and most did not want to take the offered relocation. Army officials stated that the move was being made for budgetary and strategic reasons, but the employees swiftly petitioned the mayor to halt the action, arguing that the move was motivated by "political chicanery" to "satisfy the ambitions of Philadelphia congressmen."[24] Dozens of telegrams and letters were sent to the mayor's office by NYQMPA staff in the first week of May. In a joint telegram, dozens of the NYQMPA's civilian employees complained that the move represented a vital blow being struck against textile and clothing industry, which is heart and soul of New York and the bread and butter of hundreds of thousands of its residents. There is no question but that the congressmen from the state of New York have been asleep at the switch and that the Philadelphia and Pennsylvania congressmen have plucked a ripe plum to the detriment of the city and state of New York.[25]

New Yorkers noted that "whenever this move was mentioned in the papers, it was always stated that the Philadelphia Congressmen were behind the move and it was always stated that the New York representatives had made no comment."[26] Obviously, they argued, this was a political move because when "the procurement of textiles and related items were moved from Philadelphia to New York in 1945 it was because it was determined it was more economical to procure these items in this city."[27] Seeing a pattern of such departures in other divisions of the federal government, the employees argued that the "political leaders of other States have been quite successful . . . in bringing employment and all benefits connected therewith into their states at the expense of the residents of New York,"[28] and they urged Wagner to take action to stop the move. As one employee put it, "I helped you in my small way with my vote, let's see what you can do in this crisis."[29]

This Wagner did, writing a letter to all members of the New York congressional delegation on May 15, urging them to take action to keep the office open. Wagner argued that "there will be no saving for the taxpayer in this move" and offered to house the agency's operations in city-owned facilities to reduce the costs of staying. He observed that the NYQMPA was created in the first place in 1944 "because New York was the center of the world's textile and clothing manufacture, and still is," and noted that both New York City and the state would suffer from the loss of the agency's $8 million payroll.[30]

MCs from both parties in the city responded to the mayor's entreaties. Many indicated that they had been involved in efforts to keep the office in New York even before the announcement. The mayor's closest political allies, eleven members of the New York City Democratic delegation, visited the Army's decision makers as a group on May 18 to argue the city's case for keeping the agency in New York. They described the encounter as deeply unsatisfying in a joint press release (written by Reps. Charles Buckley, Isidore Dollinger, and Sidney Fine and signed by eleven more New York City Democrats) on May 20, in which they warned that the Army had not "heard the last from the New York Delegation" on the matter.[31]

Having failed to move the Army in that meeting, the city delegation turned to its own arena of power, the legislature. In the House, Louis Heller (D-Brooklyn) took the floor to argue against the move on May 20. His floor speech included a brief rebuke of the Army's logic of expenditure savings, as well as a verbatim repetition of Mayor Wagner's awkwardly phrased suggestion that city-owned property could be used to rehouse the agency at significant saving, and argument that the agency had initially been located there in 1945 because New York was "the center of textile and clothing manufacturing, and still is." But Heller spent the bulk of his time arguing parochially for New York's city interest and wondering aloud whether his congressional colleagues were "determined to transform the great City of New York into a ghost city" by repeatedly relocating federal agencies away from the nation's hub of commerce and industry.[32]

Sen. Herbert Lehman (D-NY) took up the fight on the floor of the Senate, where he argued first for a delay in the move so that the newly established Commission on Organization of the Executive Branch of the Government could evaluate the budgetary and practical considerations of the relocation. Lehman gathered allies in this proposal, including his fellow New Yorker Irving Ives (R-NY), Sen. John F. Kennedy (D-MA), and Rep. Herbert Bonner (D-NC), who had developed the plan for the commission, which was supposed to promote efficiency and oversight of the growing executive branch. Beyond this apparently efficiency- and knowledge-based argument for delaying the move, Lehman further asserted that

> Congress has a right and duty to consider other effects of such a move. The representatives in Congress of the area in question have a right to be satisfied that the transfer is truly in the national interest and is not unduly prejudicial to the local interest.... [T]he Members of the Congress from New York City [have not] been afforded an opportunity to consult [on the matter].[33]

Pennsylvania Senators Edward Martin and James Duff (both Republicans) objected that such a delay was unnecessary, impractical, and inefficient. They took special issue with Lehman's demand that the proposed move "be cleared with the New York delegation first," rather than simply decided by the bureaucracy's bean counters.[34] The New York delegation's perspective, reflected in all of the correspondence leading up to the members' efforts to save the NYQMPA, indicates that they saw location of the office not so much as an administrative decision as a political one, a piece of pork and the outcome of a struggle between two city delegations.

Frederic Coudert was a Republican, and the NYQMPA was located at the downtown end of his district (which ran up the East Side and included Central Park). But it was to the Democratic mayor that the NYQMPA employees petitioned (though they may have written to Coudert directly as well). There is no mention in any of the letters circulated of the damage this move might do to the Seventeenth Congressional District, or even to Rep. Coudert. The mayor's letter opposing the move, which was sent to all New York representatives, references the city's and state's interests, but not those of the district. And Wagner was able to mobilize more than a dozen congressmen to his position, rather than just work with the one whose district was directly affected. Rather than Coudert's copartisans, it was the New York City *Democrats*, especially Buckley (D-Bronx), Dollinger (D-Bronx), and Fine (D-Bronx), who responded to Wagner's letter and paid a group visit to the Pentagon, and it was Heller who repeated the mayor's positions on the House floor. Coudert himself did not sign onto the joint press release calling the decision into question and advocating for the city's interest in retaining the NYQMPA; nor did he join the statement when Rep. Celler (D-Brooklyn) had it included in the *Congressional Record*.[35] Indeed, Rep. James Donovan (D-Manhattan), whose district neighbored Coudert's, may have been complaining about his colleague's lack of action when he responded to Wagner's note with the observation that New York's efforts "might get somewhere if it were not for the fact that the *whole* Pennsylvania delegation in Congress is pulling for Philadelphia."[36] On the other hand, one New York Republican who *was* joining in the fight was Jacob Javits (R-Upper West Side), who knew he expressed

> the views of the many Members from New York on the Republican side of the aisle and on the Democratic side who are urging the Department of Defense not to make this transfer which I understand is in the works at this time.... [I] am in favor of New York City having a common front and including all the five boroughs.

Significantly, Javits's point was rebutted immediately on the floor by a phalanx of Philadelphians: Reps. James Byrne of Philadelphia, Hugh Scott of the Philadelphia suburbs, and Leon Gavin of northern Pennsylvania rose to the defense of the decision, expressing their "full faith" in the Army's "careful research and survey" that led to the relocation.[37] These Pennsylvanians even gained an ally in New Jersey Rep. Charles Wolverton, whose district was centered on Camden, just across the river from the Philadelphia Depot.

In the end, the New York delegation's efforts came to naught, and the office was moved in July of 1954.[38] Nonetheless, the episode illustrates the New York City delegation in action. The understanding of the decision as a fight between two cities' interests runs throughout the discussion of the move and emerges most intensely in the letters from those closest to the employees and supervisors of the NYQMPA. The delegation essentially analyzed the decision by the Army as the outcome of a struggle between two city delegations to host the agency, a struggle that Philadelphia won. Crucially, it was the city *delegation* that was involved and in play in this fight, not just the representative of the actual location of the agency. These representatives expressed the *city* interest. And the interests expressed and rhetoric deployed in the representation of that interest traveled from citizens, to the mayor, to Congress and were heightened by party ties, as demonstrated by the intensity of representatives' involvement in the discussions.

The NYQMPA episode illustrates a pitched battle between two city delegations for a piece of juicy federal pork, which was going to be located somewhere—the agency's presence was interpreted by all actors as beneficial to whichever city it ended up in. In a second instance, city government provided information to help members learn what the city position was and then strengthen their support for it. In 1964, a mass transportation bill was making its way through Congress, and House Speaker John McCormack was seeking to count and rally support for a June vote.[39] By May, however, success was far from assured. In a May 22 letter to New York City Transit Authority (NYCTA) Chairman Joseph O'Grady in support of the bill, administration insider Stuart Rothman reported on a recent meeting of the White House team led by adviser Larry O'Brien charged with steering the bill through Congress. In the letter, Rothman outlines O'Brien's prioritization of the bill as "the major program at hand" but states that the legislation was still lacking forty to fifty votes needed for passage. Specifically, Rothman asked O'Grady to reach out to members of the New York delegation to "make local contact ... and secure the kind of commitment that will stand up in a hard headcount." Rothman reported that several MCs had recently been equivocal in their support for the bill.[40]

O'Grady took this charge to the mayor's office. New York City stood to benefit substantially from the bill, which would provide a regularized funding stream for programs to alleviate the chronic urban problem of congestion.[41] On June 4, Assistant to the Mayor Bernard Ruggieri reported to Wagner that he had communicated with several congressmen to nail down their votes for the act. Rothman's letter had included a list of equivocators: Hugh Carey, Edna Kelly, Leo O'Brien, John Murphy, Otis Pike, Adam Clayton Powell, Sam Stratton, John Lindsay, Paul Fino, Ogden Reid, James Grover, Seymour Halpern, and Frank Horton. Ruggieri subsequently received explicit "will vote for the bill" statements from Carey, Murphy, O'Brien, Pike, and Kelly. Stratton (an upstate Democrat) reported that he was undecided, being under the impression that "New York City would not get any money under the bill." Ruggieri looped in the city's transit authority to provide Stratton with information "to the contrary." He was unable to reach Powell.[42]

Such efforts continued, and on June 12, Wagner was able to report back to McCormack that it was his "understanding that H.R. 3881 has strong bipartisan support and can pass the House at this time. This program is vital to urban America and should be enacted without undue delay."[43] As the bill neared the floor, however, the tone became more urgent. Wagner sent a final telegram to the city's delegation stating that "Speaker McCormack advises me that HR3881, Mass Transportation Bill, will come to a vote Thursday and that such vote may be close in spite of bipartisan support. I hope that you will do all that you can to effect passage of this long overdue and urgent legislation."[44] He was sure to let McCormack know that he had sent the note, and the order in which its recipients were listed on the Western Union receipt is telling, for it reveals that the theoretical power of the local institutions outlined earlier in this chapter map onto the closeness with which Wagner identified with New York MCs. Rather than simply list all of the MCs in order of their district, or alphabetically as they might appear in a directory, he listed first New York City's Democratic delegation, then other upstate Democrats, and finally three city Republicans. Upstate Republicans didn't get the message, because, well, maybe they wouldn't have gotten the message. In the end, the New York delegation acted with great cohesion in favor of the bill. The only Democrat in the state not to vote for it was Powell, who did not cast a vote. Stratton apparently took stock of the information from the transit authority and supported the bill (even though it didn't really touch his district). All of the city Republicans that Wagner telegrammed voted in favor of the act, while nearly all those he ignored voted against it (although four Long Island and Westchester Republicans supported it). This was an instance in which the city's interest was clear, but for some reason city representatives were not initially sure how to vote, even when communicating behind closed doors with the party vote counters. The national party leadership and administration therefore turned to local leaders to connect with them personally and provide information about how the proposal would benefit their city; ultimately, those conversations yielded firmer commitments and votes on the floor. With the Republican leadership and dozens of (especially rural) Southern Democrats opposing the bill, those persuasive efforts to gain the marginal urbanite and Republican votes were crucial. The bill passed 212–189, meaning that only 12 changed votes could have swung the balance in the House. Ninety-eight percent of nonsouthern Democrats voted in the legislation's favor, as did twelve urban Republicans.[45]

Finally, we can see the city delegation come to a consensus on the very divisive issue of trade policy. In 1958, the Reciprocal Trade Agreements Act (RTAA) was up for a five-year extension.[46] In the postwar era, when U.S. industry was preeminent in virtually every field and most other industrialized nations were still reeling from the wartime devastation, the low barriers to trade supported by the RTAA were generally seen as a boon to U.S. exporters and industry generally. By the mid-1950s, however, the winners and losers of the emergent framework for global trade were becoming clearer and more controversial. In a series of congressional hearings on the RTAA's renewal, which was supported by the administration, many witnesses and representatives voiced deep concerns about the churn generated by liberalized trade, especially in lower-value-added areas of production. These witnesses questioned the conventional wisdom of the day, arguing that competition from abroad was hurting American businesses and workers. This critical view of trade cut across party and regional lines. John Taber (R-NY) argued that "industries in this country are very much upset. We must keep the wheels of industry turning and avoid the things that creep up on us."[47] William Jennings Bryan Dorn (D-SC) asked whether the RTAA was not "undermining union labor in this country if the big powerful corporations of this country can go abroad and put up plants, use this slave labor, and bring the goods back in this country? I do not see how that is mutually advantageous."[48] Arch Moore (R-WV) said that while he generally supported the administration's policies, in this case it was not "possible to go along with programs which are detrimental to the economy of a particular state or area or repugnant to the best interests of the nation and its people."[49] Moore's fellow West Virginian (but not copartisan) Cleveland Bailey declared that the current administration's actions were at odds with previous assurances by "every President since 1934" and both parties' platforms that "domestic industries were not to be seriously injured" by trade agreements, and that the reason American firms were unable to compete with foreign concerns was largely the result of "obligations in the form of minimum wages, shorter hours, social security, and collective bargaining," which made "our producers more vulnerable to import competition."[50] And William A. Dawson (R-UT) melodramatically wondered: "How can I close my eyes to what I have seen when one of our trade agreements backfires, bringing a prosperous American industry to its knees and throwing its workers into the worried ranks of the unemployed?"[51]

Despite the structural unemployment caused in some areas by low-wage foreign competition, and the clear potential for such unemployment to increase, organized labor was generally supportive of the measure to extend the RTAA. Andrew Biemiller, director of the AFL-CIO legislative department, testified to his organization's "unanimous support" for the administration's position and its support for the "basic goal of . . . the gradual reduction of barriers to trade without undue hardship to American industries or American workers." The actual justification for his position was more qualified, however—he did not dispute the "hardships which an increasing flow of goods to the United States [can inflict] on American business firms and American workers." Rather, he argued less on behalf of the material interests of workers than on behalf of the moral interest of the nation during the Cold War: "It would be to the detriment of the entire free world if the United States should choose the course of economic isolation," Biemiller declared. "The interests of the free world, both economic and political, will be enhanced by the development of more prosperous and stronger nations in Western Europe," an area that was emerging as a manufacturing rival for many industries. Biemiller then argued at length that the RTAA should include a "trade-adjustment program" with a wish list of measures to mitigate the disruptive effects of free trade, including an escape clause for certain industries harmed by trade, unemployment and early access to retirement benefits for the long-term laid off, and massive funding for the retraining of laborers and programs and transportation of entire families to new areas of employment.

Biemiller spoke on behalf of a massive national labor federation, but the concentrated effects of open trade policies were certainly felt in some sectors more strongly than others, and labor was (quite reasonably) divided on this issue. While industries and areas that were dependent on extractive work—coal in West Virginia, timber for plywood in Michigan, tin in Washington—were the most likely to see job and firm losses related to the RTAA, other relatively low-skill sectors were suffering as well. Chief among threatened manufacturing sectors with a large presence in New York, at least in the hearings, was the textile industry, which was under threat from many emerging economies, especially Japan. The previous time hearings had been held on reciprocal trade, in 1956, many representatives of particular industry groups as well as labor unions had appeared to take a stance against free trade and the downward trajectory of many tariffs, including the United Mine Workers, the National Brotherhood of Packinghouse Workers, and the United Hatters, Cap, and Millinery Workers International. Of particular relevance to New York, the Textile Workers Union of America (a CIO union) had submitted a brief protesting the lowering of tariffs, which it claimed "add to the workers' dislocations and anxieties by threatening the continued existence of those branches of the industry ... seriously affected by foreign competition."[52] As in the rest of the United States, textile manufacturing was under threat in New York. Testimony from the 1956 hearings showed that while the nation was still a net exporter, its trade surplus had shrunk dramatically, and that the United States had lost over 300,000 textile manufacturing jobs since 1950.[53] Tens of thousands of these losses had come from New York City: in 1950 (the most recent census before these discussions took place), textile manufacture was still the city's biggest single manufacturing sector, with about 350,000 New Yorkers working in this area; however, this number was falling rapidly.[54] Moreover, these losses were spread unevenly, with a greater concentration of Brooklyn and Bronx residents involved in the industry and a smaller concentration of Queens and Staten Island residents.[55]

Given these broad and uneven objective interests, what did the city's delegation do in 1958? Trade is exactly the kind of issue in which special interests and parochialism are likely to prevail in legislative politics, because the costs and benefits are not distributed in a balanced way. Indeed, it was precisely that insight that made the switch to executive-negotiated reciprocal trade such a transformative moment in U.S. policy.[56] So at this decision point, we might expect strong contention from all kinds of interests, including those within cities that would foreseeably be hurt or helped by renewal. We might expect protectionism, uneven pressure from places suffering uneven consequences, or other signs of division. Although leadership in both parties supported the extension, and a majority of each party ultimately voted for that position, more than a quarter of Democrats and over 40 percent of Republicans opposed the reapproval. What did the cities do?

On April 1, 1958, Mayor Wagner wrote a telegram to each member of the New York delegation urging support for the bill, making it clear that there was a city position on this issue, and that it was the prompt extension of the RTAA. Not every representative responded, and there were some variations among those who did. The elder statesman of the group, Emanuel Celler (who had been Senator Wagner's partner in numerous pieces of liberal legislation in the House throughout the 1920s and 1930s and now worked closely and frequently with his son as mayor), reiterated his internationalist credentials, noting that he had "been an ardent supporter of such legislation throughout my legislative career.... We are not, as a nation, self-sufficient.... New York, of course, a fine maritime port, plays a highly important part in this international trade."[57] Much of that fine maritime port was located on the waterfront in John Rooney's Brooklyn district. Rooney was always a strong supporter of labor, and his secretary also replied that he considered the RTAA "highly important to the economy of the City of New York and of great benefit to all those people whose income depends upon foreign trade and activity along the waterfront."[58] Not all of the letters showed such automatic support, though. Eugene Keogh, who was a Tammany point man and the "key power broker" in the New York delegation before all else, showed general support for the bill during the hearings but assured Wagner that "having your expression of opinion strengthens me" in support of the bill.[59] Republican Albert Bosch replied rather ambiguously that "it has been my endeavor to bring about constructive legislation which has as its purpose the *protection of American labor and American industry*. I intend to continue that policy in the best interests of the progress of management and labor in this great country of ours."[60] Most of the letters in reply were brief statements of agreement.

The actual effects of relaxed trade barriers on a place like New York in the 1950s were varied and difficult to parse or aggregate. Many firms and workers suffered from this relaxation, and while the general economic dynamism of the place certainly mitigated some of the effects of dislocation, that was surely poor consolation for laid-off workers or failed firms. The city's major nonmanufacturing sectors, including shipping and finance, almost certainly tilted the city's overall interest in favor of trade promotion. But its variegated economic geography meant that there were many different reactions to the RTAA, and this controversy was reflected by the witnesses from New York and other cities in the hearings that took place before the votes.

For New York and other big cities, however, locally disparate attitudes toward trade were not reflected in congressional representation, as was the case for the rest of the country. When the RTAA extension of 1958 hit the House floor for a vote, parties, regions, and other place types were all internally divided, as Table 4.1 shows. There were two votes on the bill: the first, to recommit it to the Ways and Means Committee for amendment (vote 140 in the table), was opposed by party leaders and failed; the second, to actually pass the bill (vote 141 in the table), was supported by party leaders and passed. Support for the bill as it stood ("RTAA support") was the most common position and was signified by voting "No" on vote 140 and "Yes" on vote 141. Sixty-eight percent of Democrats and fifty-four percent of Republicans took this set of positions. Consistent opposition to trade was signified by the opposite set of positions: "Yes" to a return to committee and "No" on passage. A third set of representatives ("trade reformers"), intending to amend the agreement to include more protections for particularly vulnerable industries and places, as Biemiller had proposed, included about 10 percent of each party—these members voted "Yes" to amend but chose not to throw the baby out with the bathwater and ultimately supported the legislation.[61] Overall, Democrats were more likely to support the bill, but urbanicity mattered more. Region and party were filtered through place character: for example, southerners were

Table 4.1 **Support for RTTA, 1958**

	All	Non-city	Non-city NE	All City	NYC
(Vote 140)					
All	64	55	52	88	90
GOP	56	50	54	77	60
Dem	72	61	47	95	100
(Vote 141)					
All	76	69	60	94	100
GOP	69	63	62	91	100
Dem	82	75	53	96	100

Note: Cell entries are percent from each group voting for Eisenhower administration's (pro-trade) position on two votes related to the Reciprocal Trade Agreements Act of 1958.

Sources: Voteview; AIP; CSR.

most likely to take the protectionist position, but noncity northeasterners were just as divided.

But in New York (and other big cities), support for the administration's position was virtually unanimous. Even Rep. Bosch, who had cryptically voiced support for protectionism in his reply to Wagner, took the moderate position and ultimately supported the extension. Despite different positions voiced by New Yorkers in the hearings, and the uneven effects of trade liberalism already being felt in the 1950s, the city delegation strongly supported the city position, as articulated by Wagner in his letter to them, on this vote. The New York City delegation unanimously supported final passage of the extension. Such unity was *not* automatic when it came to trade issues: on the fifty-three other votes having to do with trade and tariffs between 1947 and 1967 (i.e., a decade before and after the 1958 RTAA reapproval), the New York delegation only voted unanimously four other times and was divided 40 percent of the time.[62] The attention given to this bill and the clear signal of a city position—Wagner did not write letters to the delegation on all trade votes, and based on the archival record, both his predecessor Impellitteri and successor Lindsay were far less likely to take this approach—helped drive the result.

This case also provides a small window into what happened during the Long New Deal in the fairly rare instances in which leading unions and big cities had divergent preferences. These two constituencies overlapped considerably, but also embodied slightly different interests at times. For many, organized labor movement was the beating heart of the New Deal.[63] I do not have a deep disagreement with this position in principle, but it seems clear that city positions taken by leaders were not just epiphenomena of pro-labor ideology, or beholden to labor's political muscle. When they wanted to be, cities took positions orthogonal to, or opposed to, organized labor's preferences, and staked out autonomous space in articulating a vision for governing American society.

In each of these three cases, the city delegation cohesively represented a city interest—against another city, in cooperation with other cities, and on behalf of the broad (but not hegemonic) midcentury pro-trade alliance, respectively. These cases show that congressional city delegations are subjectively real. Their members conceive of and refer to them as such; they are sensitive to the interests of the city, not just their home districts; and local officials both know this and act on it, reaching out to legislators with instructions and requests on behalf of a clearly articulated and unitary city interest. Several mechanisms are also on display in these examples, each ostensibly contributing to delegation cohesion: constituent complaints, aggregated in the mayor's mailbox and then circulated to call MCs to action; requests by national partisan leadership for local officials to intervene on the city's behalf to gather and persuade votes in both parties; and the distillation of diverse organizational interests, expressed by businesses, experts, representatives, and labor unions in public hearings, into a city-wide position expressed by the mayor and ultimately supported by the entire city delegation.

The examples in this section focused on the city delegation as a whole, emphasizing the importance of the jurisdictional IHI in defining the contours of delegation contacts. Though we shall see that the organizational IHI of the local party was more important in Chicago, it should not be inferred that this type of IHI was not important to New York's operations. Cooperation could be more difficult for nonpartisans to obtain in New York as well as elsewhere. For instance, in early 1965, Rep. Paul Fino (R-Bronx) wrote repeatedly to the mayor "on behalf of [his] Northeast Bronx constituency" to protest the construction of working-class multifamily housing in his district.[64] At first his letter was ignored, and then Wagner responded that Fino's protestations indicated "an unawareness of the facts and circumstances surrounding this project," arguing that the proposed project was in fact a "distinct asset to the community and the City."[65] The project continued as planned. When up-and-coming congressman John Lindsay (R-Upper East Side) made similar entreaties, they were sometimes greeted with mayoral silence or condescension.[66]

Local party bonds played a role in navigating federal bureaucracy as well. When the city was seeking permission to develop the Manhattan waterfront along a stretch of the East River for a park and school, it needed a congressional bill to declare that section of the river "non-navigable." The section of riverfront, from 17th to 30th Streets, fell within Lindsay's Seventeenth District, but Wagner wrote to Emanuel Celler (whose Tenth District, in Brooklyn, did not border the river) for help. At Wagner's request, Celler "proposed [the matter] on behalf of the city ... and consulted with the appropriate committee chairmen and members, who were persuaded that the project had such outstanding merit."[67] Celler's bill was subsumed within an omnibus appropriations bill, and after passage Wagner thanked Celler: "Your presentation ... was, I know, important and decisive. ... This development would not have been possible without your assistance."[68] Celler was not on the relevant committee and had no formal connection to the site. Yet he was the key actor in this decision, and there is no mention of Lindsay anywhere in this conversation, even though it was his district under consideration. Perhaps Wagner pursued this strategy because Lindsay was a budding and slightly annoying rival, preparing to run for mayor against him. Perhaps he did it because Celler was a forty-year veteran of Congress and knew the tricks of the legislative trade. But most basically, these exchanges and actions should be interpreted as a city delegation in action, in which a member of Congress pursues policy to benefit another district within a city where the mayor is a political partner tying the member to the other districts.

Later in this chapter, I build on these concrete instances of city delegations in action through a bird's-eye quantitative analysis of patterns in roll call voting.

In each of these analyses, the data reveal similar patterns to those seen in the New York examples: local institutions—the city community and the local party—are independently and additively related to cohesive representation in Congress and are key to the representation of a city interest and to the construction of an urban bloc in Congress.

4.3 Chicago's Delegation: Loyalty and Party

In Chicago, unlike in New York, local party power strengthened during the Long New Deal, making the midcentury Chicago Democrats an archetypal case of a strong organizational IHI. Chicago's delegation behavior is almost completely described by party relationships. After Daley's rise to the mayoralty in 1955, which fused party and city leadership in his own person, Chicago was extremely cohesive in congressional action, even through the tumult of the urban crisis.[69] This cohesion could arise naturally from social conditions, but such a view trivializes the clustered diversity within and across city districts and the intensity of the rivalries felt between groups. Chicago is less kaleidoscopically diverse than New York, but its congressional geography is perhaps more heterogeneous, because of its greater sprawl and segregation by class and race. Chicago's disparate peoples during this time were separated into territories that were local rivals. This situation made a strong organization all the more necessary, and its ability to hold itself together as long as it did (even though its distribution of local power and resources was simultaneously unjust), well into decades when its peers had lost control even over their own local internal nominating processes, is impressive.[70] In the Windy City, the usefulness of strategic action at higher levels has always been readily apparent, and for decades the Chicago Democrats have been the most powerful actor in the state party, if not the state government itself.

In everyday communications between City Hall and Congress, the Chicago delegation never strayed far from its dual operations as party and government. This was true even (or perhaps especially) when performing low-level constituent services. When a group of women visited Washington and wanted to visit John F. Kennedy's grave, Daley mentioned that they were Democrats in requesting that Rep. Roman Pucinski escort them on the visit, and Pucinski pointedly acknowledged their partisan affiliation in his affirmative reply.[71] In 1966, when Pucinski wanted to inform his constituents about how they could benefit from Social Security and Medicare, he distributed informational packets created by the Department of Health, Education, and Welfare and the Social Security Administration to his precinct captains and recommended to Daley that they be sent to all captains in the city as well as to all clergymen (not only because there was a change in the law relevant to clergy, but also because of their status as important community figures).[72] Appointments and nominations to even federal administrative positions frequently included a reference to local political or faction affiliation and were directed through Daley, despite the fact that he held no national position. When Rep. William Dawson (D-South Side) wrote to Daley to recommend the appointment of a constituent to the Interstate Commerce Commission, he included the constituent's home precinct and ward, as well as references to his party service.[73] Similarly, when Thomas McKenna needed a recommendation from his congressman to get a position with the Postal Service, he did not write directly to Rostenkowski but asked Raymond Krier, his local party committeeman, to intercede on his behalf. Krier then wrote to Daley of McKenna's long membership in two local Democratic suborganizations, assuring the congressman that "the McKenna family have been staunch supporters of the Democratic Party," and that the appointment would be a good one. Daley then wrote to Rostenkowski that he would "appreciate it if you would do everything you possibly can to be of help to this man."[74] This type of reference chain recurs frequently in Daley's correspondence record, indicating that it was a common procedure for making personnel decisions. In this way references for federal appointments flowed through local organizations.

Some of the party's power flowed through its slating committee, which chose candidates and exerted discipline over them. During those decades, the head of the Cook County Democratic organization (first Mayor Kelly's mentor Patrick Nash, and then Mayor Daley himself) routinely slated loyal long-time party stalwarts for congressional seats and structured statewide tickets to provide maximum benefits for the county organization.[75] The powerful county slating committee was the ultimate authority in such matters; at its head invariably sat a member who was dedicated to loyal service to the organization.[76] The slating committee typically supported incumbents, but not always; probably the most famous instance of such a refusal was when it rejected Mayor Martin Kennelly's bid for reelection in 1955, instead choosing the slating committee's chair—Daley himself.[77]

Beyond using conventional incentives such as career advancement and renomination for office as disciplinary tools, the traditional organizations were often able to rely on their agents in Congress, because they were creatures of habit. These men (and they were invariably men) had all risen through the disciplined and unified local party organization and were well aware of the virtues of party unity. As the political scientist Leo Snowiss observed in his close study of their work routines and decision making, "Chicago Democratic congressmen . . . value party cohesion as a positive good in need of little or no justification."[78]

As Daley rose through the ranks as a Kelly lieutenant, he witnessed and experienced the power of loyalty in an organization, and he was frank about the value of this character trait in politics. In a conversation with Lyndon Johnson in the 1960s, Johnson asked Daley what he thought of replacing Democratic National Committee Chair John Bailey, a long-time traditional party operative from Connecticut, with Larry O'Brien, a member of the Kennedy political team who had remained on Johnson's staff. Daley's advice was to keep Bailey, based on his firm belief that the first principle of selection for such a position should be "loyalty to the fellow they're with. Many of these fellas haven't the fundamental principal of loyalty.... Bailey is a dedicated, loyal Johnson man."[79]

The most routine evidence of the importance of loyalty for Chicago Democrats comes from first-person observations of communications between Daley and representatives in Springfield and Washington. The local organization's wishes for legislative action were communicated in the famous "idiot lists" that Daley sent to Democratic representatives in Springfield. MCs had higher independent profiles than their colleagues in the state legislature and were probably treated with more respect, but even they knew that loyalty to local prerogatives and organizations was paramount for both legislative success and continued personal privileges. These principles and everyday practices shaped the kinds of persons who achieved office (via party nomination processes and very high rates of electoral success) and the actions they took once there (operating through those same mechanisms, as well as through authentic representation of district and city interests).[80]

In practice, the relationships between Chicago and its delegations in Springfield and Washington appear to have been similar. For much of Daley's administration, Raymond Simon served as an intermediary between the city and its legislative representatives. Simon was a young lawyer and Daley protegé who grew up on the same street that Daley lived on as an adult and who was initiated into city politics by his father, a precinct captain on the South Side. By his own account, Simon did "a multiplicity of jobs," including "dealing with the general assembly and with the Congress." While most of his time was spent transmitting the mayor's guidance to state legislative leadership, he also developed a "very significant relationship" with Rostenkowski, the second-generation member of the Cook County Democrats who led the city delegation and acted as City Hall's point person in Congress.[81] The delegation's leaders frequently visited Daley to, as Simon put it, "review pending legislation." At such meetings, Simon (and either downstate delegation leader John Touhy or DC delegation leader Rostenkowski) would bring a list of pending bills and legislative matters relevant to Chicago and take away notes and an understanding of "what [Daley's] position is on bills that affect the City."[82] Rostenkowski was a frequent private guest of the mayor, preferring his Chicago turf to Washington, DC, when he could. He visited the mayor often to discuss strategy, though they rarely made notes for the record during these conversations.[83]

The selection of quietly loyal agents was a conscious strategy by Daley. In the same call between Daley and Johnson mentioned earlier, Johnson referenced the retirement of Roland Libonati, a Democratic congressman from Chicago's West Side. "Did you know he had the best voting record of any congressman, as far as I'm concerned? 98 percent," said Johnson, referring to the frequency with which Libonati had voted with the party position; three of the Democrats' top ten scorers on this measure were from Chicago. Daley's response is revealing:

DALEY: Well, the fella we'll send down there will have 99.
JOHNSON: Did you bump Libonati off, or did he quit?
DALEY: He quit himself.

Johnson's casual reference to the possibility that Libonati had been "bumped off" by his mayor reveals the power of candidate selection that rested in Daley's hands, as does Daley's confidence that the newest member of the Chicago delegation would be a reliably loyal Democratic vote.[84] This confidence was borne out: Libonati's successor in Illinois's Seventh District, Frank Annunzio, took the party line in all 187 party-line votes in the next Congress.[85] Clearly, Daley's power over Chicago politics extended not only to the city borders, but to Springfield and Washington as well.

Another picturesque episode of Daley using his position as head of a local organization to effect outcomes far beyond the city limits is the sequence of conversations leading to the election of Texas Rep. Jim Wright as House Majority Leader in 1976, which he won in a tight three-way race. Daley and Rostenkowski talked Wright into running in the first place, because he had been a good ally to Chicago as head of the Public Works Committee; they then changed the votes of the other Chicago Democrats, who were the only nonsoutherners to support Wright's bid, which succeeded over a more liberal candidate by a single vote. To justify their backroom dealing and support for a southerner over California Rep. Phil Burton, Rostenkowski explained: "[Burton] was too liberal for me. I really am not a liberal. I am a Daley Democrat—liberal only when cities are getting screwed and they're entitled to more money." Asked why the Chicago delegation had built such a tight bond with the Texas Democrats, rather than the liberal Californians with whom they shared more urban affinities, Rostenkowski went straight to the value of loyalty and bonds built through adversity over time and party autonomy. "Burton was totally tied up to labor, out of San Francisco. I just never felt comfortable in the company of those people," he said. "Nobody like Dick Daley had better allies than Texans." Rostenkowski, whose father had been a machine alderman and close Daley ally in his early years, was never shy about how important organizational prerogatives were and was a perfect exemplar of the local-loyalty-first ethos of the organization (and of the material venality that has long been associated with it and that eventually led to his conviction for abusing his congressional mail privileges).[86]

For Chicago's Democrats, unity and cohesion were themselves valued goods, the product of socialization and habit as much as of continuous monitoring or oversight. On domestic issues in particular, such representatives—members from traditional parties with localist backgrounds and orientations—were extremely cohesive and loyal as a bloc to the city position. This loyalty was given to both the local and national parties (the positions of the two typically overlapped), but if forced to choose, the local organization seems to have been the primary home for many of these representatives.[87]

Among New York City's Democrats bonds of friendship were frequently referenced in communications. But loyalty to the party was not a central feature of the ongoing correspondence between local and national officials. There was also more than one game in town in New York—not everyone was part of the same political organization, so civic spirit was more important than organizational loyalty (even if party wasn't irrelevant). In Los Angeles, by contrast, a large city with no traditional party organization, contemporary analysts observed that party-like activity during this era was limited to clubs that were both weaker and more parochial than the citywide organizations present in Chicago and New York.[88] Without a citywide political "umbrella," political integration was much weaker. As we shall see in the following section, the Los Angeles delegation was less cohesive down the line in representation.

4.4 Cohesion from Diversity

For the remainder of this chapter, I will share some statistical tests derived from the basic implications of the city delegation theory. In short, the logic of the theory is that city IHIs—developed to provide political order at home—foster cohesive representation in national politics, even though cities are more heterogeneous than comparable collections of representatives.[89] Before testing these claims, I will define a few terms I will use in the analysis more precisely.

First, in this analysis and in other chapters, a *city district* is a congressional district that is entirely or almost entirely within a large, central city, as identified by the CSR dataset developed for this project.[90] A *city representative* is the House member from a city district. A *city delegation* is a collection of city representatives in the House of Representatives from the same city. Thus the Chicago city delegation is the set of representatives from Chicago districts at any given time. Over the course of the twentieth century, the Chicago city delegation ranged in size from six to twelve representatives. A *suburban district* is a district wholly or mostly within the developed area surrounding a large city,[91] and a *suburban delegation* is a collection of representatives from such districts within the same city's metropolitan area. A *metropolitan delegation* encompasses both the city delegation and the suburban delegation from a given metropolitan area. *Cohesion* is the tendency to agree on roll call voting; the more likely the members of some pair or set of representatives are to agree, the more cohesive they are. Cohesion will be measured slightly differently in the upcoming analyses.

Empirically, the main argument of city delegation theory is that collections of representatives that are bound by common local IHIs will be more cohesive than we might otherwise expect.[92] This thesis can be tested by examining the relationship between IHI, diversity, and cohesion among different groups of legislators in the House of Representatives. Two basic hypotheses about city delegations should be true if local institutions play a role in fostering cohesion in representation. First, city delegations should be more cohesive than collections of districts that do not share a common local political community but are otherwise comparable. This indicates the effect of the city boundary (the primary jurisdictional institution of horizontal integration) on legislative cohesion. To evaluate this hypothesis, we can compare the cohesion of city delegations with that of like delegations-of-interest, such as their suburban rings and their metropolitan area. Formally, this hypothesis is

$$H_{Jurisdictional} : C_{City} > C_{Metro, Suburbs} \qquad (4.1)$$

where C is cohesion of the subscripted delegations. Second, we can compare cohesion across cities, because cities vary in the strength of their organizational IHIs. Cities with strong IHIs should be more cohesive than cities with weak ones. Formally, this hypothesis is

$$H_{Organizational} : C_{StrongIHI} > C_{WeakIHI} \qquad (4.2)$$

I will test these hypotheses on representatives' behavior at the group and individual levels.

First, we can compare city delegations to suburban and metropolitan delegations, with the expectation, drawn from the jurisdictional hypothesis, that cities will be more cohesive.[93] Comparing cities to their suburban rings is useful because they often have comparable numbers of representatives, because state and local politics are often characterized by a strong city–suburb rivalry (an indication that suburban districts do share some political affinity in common, just as city districts do), and because using these groups allows us to automatically "control" for factors related to region, geographic proximity, and urbanicity.[94]

4.4.1 Heterogeneity, Not Just Diversity

Before making direct comparisons between delegations, it is important to note that city delegations are typically more heterogeneous than other collections of districts. This is different than saying a city is more diverse than its suburbs, though this statement is also usually true. Diversity is non-uniformity in observable traits, something that is indeed more common in cities. For instance, New York City is considered to be very diverse because it has lots of persons who are different on dimensions considered to be important: several large racial groups, roughly at numerical parity; many immigrants but also many native-born persons; many millionaires and many poor persons; thousands of Ivy League graduates, many with postgraduate degrees, and many more without much formal education at all. Economic specialization is greater in cities as well, so people have different occupational and class identities; such comparisons can continue. This is less true in the smaller, less diverse communities that are common in the suburbs or rural places. If you were to pick two New Yorkers at random, it is more likely that they would be different on whatever important dimensions you chose than if you picked two persons from a less diverse place. This is what we typically mean by *diversity*, and the most common measures of the concept employ similar logic.[95]

This mass diversity is a necessary precondition for delegation heterogeneity, but one other thing must be true for *districts* to be different from each other: the different sorts of people who make a place diverse must also be unevenly grouped in the political geography of the city. For instance, class heterogeneity requires that richer people be separated from the poorer ones, instead of sprinkled evenly across the city; racial heterogeneity requires that racial groups be separated from each other; citizenship heterogeneity requires that immigrants be separated from natives; and so on. If this kind of separation does not exist, then the districts are actually quite alike, despite the fact that their internal elements may not be. For various historical and economic reasons, including a mix of market forces, public policy, and historic racism that generated very high levels of racial segregation in particular (but also class segregation), this is usually the case in American cities.[96] Because the diversity within a city is often "lumpy," with concentrations of different groups rather than even spacing across the city, city districts (not just city *residents*) tend to be quite different from each other, on average. This is an important point because with different kinds of constituencies, we would expect the pressures on representatives to be different; in a city delegation, therefore, we should not assume that agreement among representatives of such different districts will occur "naturally," not only because of divergent preferences but also because of competition over resources.

First, to show that city delegations are made up of districts that are different from each other, and thus lack the basis for "natural" cohesion, it is helpful to see that the constituencies within city districts are indeed different from each other; this will make the ensuing analyses more powerful. To illustrate this point, consider Figure 4.1, which shows demographic district heterogeneity of congressional delegations in four metro areas. More precisely, this figure shows a summary measure of how different the districts in a given city or suburban delegation are from each other on two major dimensions of American political conflict: race and class.

For each of these cities, in each congress, I calculated a city delegation two-dimensional cross-district heterogeneity score that estimates how different from each other (as opposed to how internally diverse) the districts of the city delegation are, using some complicated but intuitive math.[97] For each delegation (city and suburban, for cities big enough to have meaningful delegations), I calculate a two-dimensional score of class and racial heterogeneity across districts within a given bloc of districts. As a rough measure of class, I use the median family income.[98] As a measure of district-level racial diversity, I use the percent identified or identifying as "not white" in the district.[99] I then add together the differences between districts within a delegation to make a class-and-race heterogeneity score.

A discrete example may clarify the intuition of this measure, showing how city and suburban delegations compare on these dimensions. Consider Figure 4.1, which plots the median income against the percent nonwhite residents for those districts in Philadelphia in 1975 (the 94th Congress). What we can see conforms to our expectations about cities and their suburbs during this era. All of the suburban districts are richer than the city districts, and they are all racially homogeneous, more than 90 percent white. Most important for our purposes, they are very alike, clustered together on the graph. The city districts, on the other hand, are much more spread out: one is close to the suburban districts on both dimensions, while the others have lower median incomes (similar to each other). The range of racial diversity is stark and typical for a city delegation: one district has a minority majority, while one is over 90 percent white, and the others are in between. The two-dimensional scale is essentially the total of the average distance between these points on each dimension.

The key point here is that the city districts are very different from each other, while the suburban districts are quite alike. This is generally true of city delegations over time. Figure 4.2 shows the outcome when we process the measures analogous to Figure 4.1 (but for each congress and delegation) to show how the two-dimensional heterogeneity of city delegations in the four main twentieth-century metropolitan areas compare to their suburban rings.

Although city delegations are not uniformly more heterogeneous than their suburban ring delegations (for some cities, especially in more recent decades, the two blocs are actually comparably heterogeneous, especially on the economic

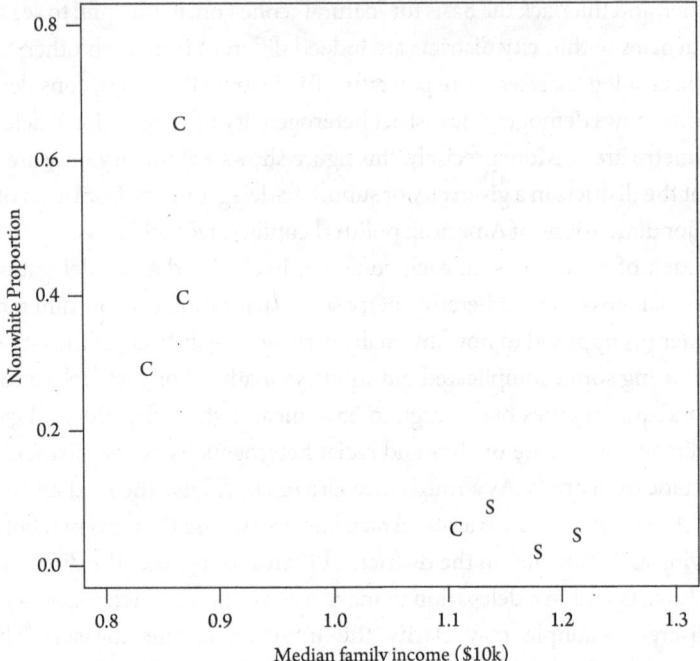

Figure 4.1 **Heterogeneity in Philadelphia Districts, 94th Congress.** City (C) and suburban (S) district measures on race (proportion nonwhite) and class (family median income) dimensions from 94th Congress. Sources: CSR data; Lublin (1997a).

dimension), this measure does confirm that there is almost always more heterogeneity among city delegations than among suburban delegations, and that this was especially true in the mid-twentieth century. This demographic analysis provides clear evidence of what all urbanists know to be true: cities are not sites of easy consensus building: they are deeply divided. This division is reflected in the political geography of the city, as it is in the streets. On these two important dimensions, at least, in almost every instance the city delegation is much more heterogeneous than the suburban, so the rawest social building blocks of congressional affinity might be expected to be weak. If city delegations are more cohesive *despite* being more heterogeneous, this would support the argument that IHIs have some influence and make the alternative explanation of cohesion based in "natural," prepolitical similarity less persuasive. This was certainly the case in the mid-twentieth century, as we shall see.

4.4.2 City Delegation Cohesion

City districts are often so different from each other on politically relevant measures that we might not expect city *delegations* to be very cohesive in how

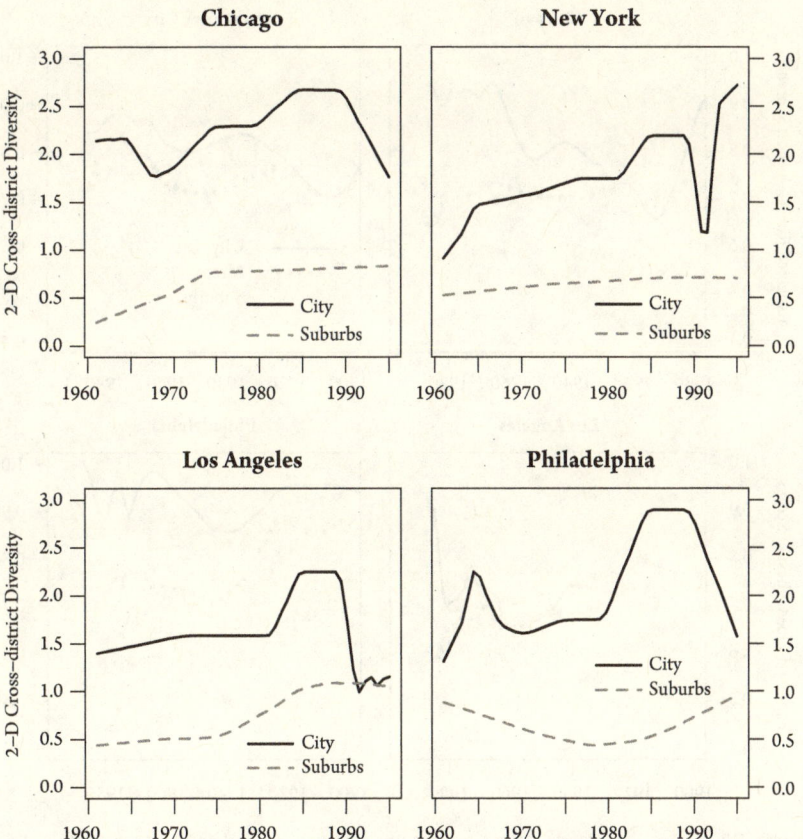

Figure 4.2 **Cross-District Heterogeneity Among Congressional Delegations (1960–2000).** Each line shows the summed two-dimensional heterogeneity of a city or suburban delegation over time. Higher levels indicate districts in a delegation are more different from each other. In each case, the city delegation is generally more heterogeneous than its suburban ring delegation. Sources: CSR data; Lublin (1997a).

they represent themselves in national politics. However, there seems to be a general impression, articulated by John Vorys and other observers of city delegations, that city representatives are more "organized" than other sets of constituencies. We can test this impression more rigorously with cohesion scores, which measure the extent to which a group of voters agree with each other.[100] If city delegations foster cohesion, the expected cohesion of city delegations should be higher than that of suburban rings, even though the constituencies of those other places are similarly contiguous and more demographically similar. Over time, this has indeed been the case. Figure 4.3 shows the average expected cohesion on all roll call votes for the four largest cities' city delegation (solid line), suburban delegation (dashed line), and metropolitan area delegation (dotted line). As a benchmark of "high" cohesion, the horizontal

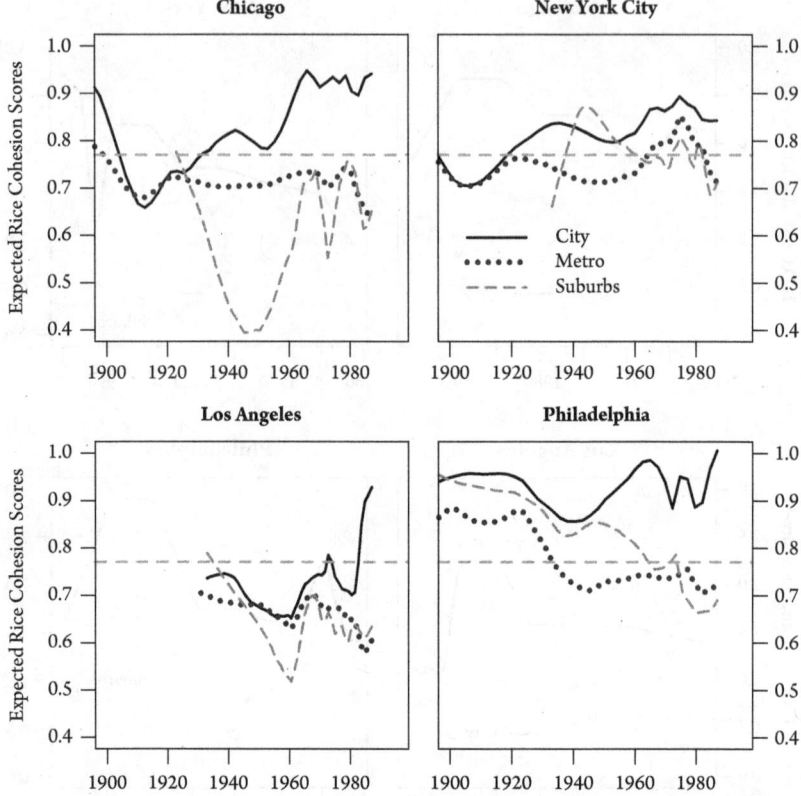

Figure 4.3 **Average Cohesion Scores for City, Suburban, and Metro Delegations in Four Major Cities.** Each line represents the average annual expected cohesion score for each delegation on all roll call votes, smoothed over time for better visibility. The horizontal line is the average of the two parties over all roll calls over all Congresses. Sources: CSR data; Voteview.

gray dashed line represents the global mean of the two congressional parties on this measure over time, y = .77.[101]

In each case, the city delegation is generally more cohesive than the delegations of its suburban hinterland and the metropolitan area that encompasses both blocs, despite the high levels of cross-district heterogeneity that exist within the city delegations. The only time the suburban delegation's cohesion exceeds that of the city is for New York during a brief time in the 1940s. The city delegations from Chicago, New York, and Philadelphia are particularly cohesive (as evaluated against the standard of a national party), while the other blocs are not, being much closer to or even below the average for a congressional party, even though they share important baseline affinities such as geographic proximity. But even fragmented Los Angeles is more cohesive than its neighbors from the suburban delegation. This first-cut analysis provides support for the power of jurisdictional institutions of horizontal integration in contributing to representational cohesion.

There is also variation among cities. If the effects of local political organizations matter for the character of city representation at higher levels, we should see the cohesiveness of city delegations vary with the strength of local organizational IHIs. While all cities have jurisdictional boundaries that serve a centripetal function, not all cities have had the same intensity of organizational political centralization over the course of the twentieth century. Among the four large cities included in this analysis, there was great variation in the strength of these organizational institutions, as described in many studies. Philadelphia and Chicago had very strong organizations that unified local politics. For Banfield and Wilson (1963), Chicago was characterized by an "extreme centralization of power" in the machine leadership, especially under Kelly and Daley.[102] Philadelphia had a similarly powerful machine organization, though the mayor was typically not a part of it.[103] New York's local pattern of influence was "halfway" centralized; Democratic leaders there were strong but far from hegemonic. County divisions within the city and struggles between party factions made New York City's local politics less integrated.[104] Los Angeles's local nonpartisan rules and traditions made it virtually impossible to integrate politics citywide; power there was decentralized, and no significant citywide organizations existed.[105] In each of these cities, the strength and coherence of organizational integration has varied over time, but the general fact of the institution's existence, and the culture of city politics it creates, has not.

Figure 4.4 takes the cohesion scores from the city delegations presented in Figure 4.3 and superimposes them on the same graph for ease of comparison. Consistent with the expectations of city delegation theory, city delegation cohesion is correlated with local institutional strength. Cities with traditions of powerful parties that largely control a city's politics should have more cohesive delegations than cities without such strong organizations. From this graph, we can add to the observation that city delegations are more cohesive than suburban delegations the further observation that some city delegations tend to be more cohesive than others.

A similar observation can be made about the frequency with which the cities were perfectly cohesive—that is, unanimous on a roll call vote. Table 4.2 shows that the relationship between local institutions and city delegation unanimity is present for all roll calls, for all domestic roll calls, and for substantive issues most obviously relevant to cities: housing, infrastructure and public works, transportation, and urban/regional development.[106] In each of these categories, the cities with strong IHIs were much more likely to be unanimous in representation than were the cities with weaker IHIs. Again, the figures for the congressional parties are presented, though they are not very informative because American congressional parties are so infrequently unanimous on roll calls.

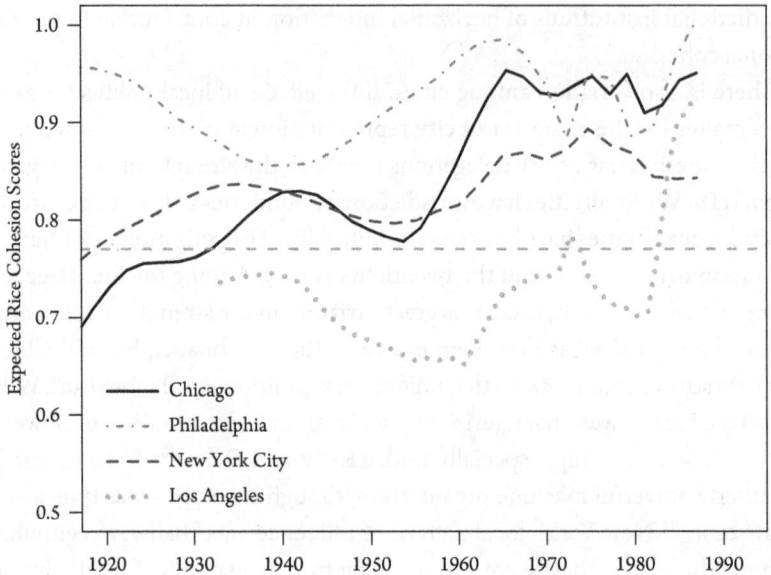

Figure 4.4 **Average Cohesion Scores for Four Major City Delegations.** As in Figure 4.3, these lines represent the average annual expected cohesion score for each delegation on all roll call votes, smoothed over time for better visibility. City delegations with stronger organizational institutions of horizontal integration have been more cohesive than those with weaker ones. Sources: CSR data; Voteview.

Table 4.2 **Unanimity Among City Delegations**

City	IHI Strength	All Votes	Domestic Votes	City Votes	IR Votes
Philadelphia	Strong	0.76	0.59	0.77	0.59
Chicago	Strong	0.67	0.53	0.64	0.72
New York City	Halfway	0.48	0.38	0.47	0.38
Los Angeles	Weak	0.46	0.34	0.40	0.45
All Democrats		0.10	0.07	0.06	0.11
All Republicans		0.11	0.07	0.06	0.14
Total votes		13,962	10,185	1,099	2,814

Note: Cell entries are the proportion of votes (in the categories across the top) on which city delegations and congressional parties were unanimous over the 70th to 100th Congress.

Sources: CSR Data; AIP; Voteview.

The relationship between IHIs and voting unanimity holds particularly well for domestic votes and city votes.[107] Unlike in the measure of overall cohesion, this analysis does not account for delegation size, and larger delegations are less likely to be unanimous. This helps to explain why New York is as infrequently unanimous as Los Angeles, but it cannot explain the overall difference; for most of this time period, Los Angeles was about as large as Chicago or Philadelphia, but it was unanimous far less often. Interestingly, the pattern is not as strong in international relations votes. The IHIs may not exert the same pressures on votes that are not as obviously relevant to cities themselves. This is an area for further investigation.

Of course, because congressional voting is closely related to a member's party, we can attribute much of a city's cohesion to the partisan makeup of a city's delegation—or, more plainly, the results of elections, when districts select their representatives. Winning seats in elections is a primary mission of a traditional party, and this is reflected in the partisan homogeneity of the strong-party cities. The most cohesive city delegations, Chicago and Philadelphia, have often had essentially one-party delegations, while New York and Los Angeles have had more partisan division; this fact is itself related to the strength of local IHIs. Chicago's citywide Democratic machine was consolidated in the early 1930s and matured as a local hegemon in the mid-1950s when Daley assumed office, linking the formal heads of the local government and local party in the same person.[108] In Philadelphia, local party chiefs, who held grassroots mobilization power, converted *en masse* to the Democratic Party in the 1930s.[109] These cities were unified in their partisan mobilization, and their organizations were strong enough to elect a predictably cohesive bloc. Struggles within the Democratic Party in New York (between reformers and regulars in Manhattan, and between Manhattan and the other boroughs) left that city more open to Republican inroads at the congressional and even mayoral level. Los Angeles enjoyed no local organization that included the entire city,[110] so the personnel of the city delegation seems more closely related to district-level characteristics, rather than a citywide political order. Los Angeles's city delegation wound up being far less cohesive than that of the other cities, despite having generally lower levels of cross-district heterogeneity.

4.5 Pairwise Cohesion and Two-Stage Representation

Figures 4.3 and 4.4 show the aggregate patterns of delegation cohesion for the four largest cities of the Long New Deal and fit the expectations of city delegation theory. These patterns are easily visualized, illustrative findings, but they are not particularly rigorous tests of IHI effects because cohesion scores are inescapably noisy. The analyses in this section extend the same logic but look more closely at the data in three ways. First, they expand the universe of districts to make the tests of city delegation theory's key hypotheses more generalizable. Second, they disaggregate the process of representation into its two stages—the selection of representatives and roll call voting—to see if delegation cohesion is attributable to events at one stage rather than the other. Finally, they employ a smaller unit of analysis, the dyadic pair of MCs, to allow a multivariate regression framework and more precisely account for alternative explanations of legislative cohesion. Together, these analyses serve as both a robustness check and a deepening of the broader observational analyses conducted earlier. As we shall see, this closer look supports the main observable implication of city delegation theory: local IHIs are associated with greater cohesion in both party affinity and roll call voting.

City delegation theory complicates traditional models of congressional representation by considering an extracameral institution outside the district—the IHI—as a factor that shapes congressional representation.[111] But it is not clear at what stage of representation those effects might take place. Strong local IHIs could foster unity among representatives by creating city delegations that are more homogeneous in party affiliation. This is what the traditional party at its strongest—the machine—was particularly good at: winning elections across a city regardless of the actual differences between constituencies. Alternatively, or as a complement to creating a partisan delegation, IHIs could also influence roll call voting, making city delegation members more likely to agree either by sending particularly loyal partisans to the chamber or by using their leverage to monitor and discipline delegation members. The analysis of four large cities in the previous section indicates that IHIs might have effects at both levels. For instance, Chicago's and Philadelphia's congressional delegations were so cohesive in part because they leaned so heavily to one party, while New York and Los Angeles had less monolithic delegations, in partisan terms.[112] On the other hand, partisan affiliation alone cannot explain all of the cohesion we observe in city delegations, because city delegations are typically more cohesive than the congressional *parties*, as we can see from the gray lines in Figures 4.3 and 4.4.[113] Furthermore, the cohesion of city districts at both stages of representation might be attributable to basic district characteristics—class or racial composition, state or region, urbanicity itself—rather than shared local institutions, but we cannot tell from the previous analysis.[114] We need to use a different approach to be more confident of the role of local institutions while accounting for these alternative explanations.

To evaluate the independent roles of city institutions, constituency-level factors, and congressional parties in shaping representation, we can use a statistical model of similarity in representation among congressional dyads to test which factors are associated with two representatives sharing party affiliation or voting alike on a given proposal. This approach is akin to breaking up the aggregate cohesion analysis in the previous section into micro-units. The difference is that while cohesion scores measure agreement among members of a group, dyadic analysis estimates factors associated with agreement between any two legislators.

If IHIs foster cohesion, then city institutions—membership in the same city delegation and/or traditional party organization at home—should be independently associated with congressional partisanship and roll call agreement, even when we account for other important factors. The following analyses support these hypotheses estimating positive associations between local institutions and congressional cohesion at both stages of representation. The rest of the chapter will look at each of these stages in turn, estimating dyad-level models of the relationships between similarity and agreement by congressional representation at each of the phases of selection and roll call voting.

4.5.1 Selecting City Delegations

First, I consider the role of city institutions in creating a city delegation that shares partisan affiliation. Despite the existence of heterogeneous building blocks that are often oriented as rivals in local politics, sending members from the same party to the delegation is probably the most reliable way to foster agreement. These dyadic models are slightly unusual and merit fuller explanation. Because the unit of analysis is the dyad (a pair, whether of legislators or votes), and we are interested in cohesion as an outcome, all of the variables in the model are measures of *similarity* on a given indicator, not *levels* of that indicator.[115] For instance, if two MCs are in the same party, then the measure for party equals 1 and is 0 otherwise. If the two members' districts have similar class compositions, then the dyad's "Class Similarity" measure is high, and so on. The underlying logic behind the model is the same as that often employed in congressional studies: that similar inputs, such as constituency pressures, will lead to similar outputs, such as roll call vote decisions. Here, the inputs and outputs from two MCs are combined into single observations.[116]

The key observable implications of the jurisdictional hypothesis at this phase is that being from the same city should be associated with congressional party affinity. Because many factors may be relevant in determining congressional agreement, I include several other explanatory variables in the model. First, there are several measures of geographic proximity. These categorical spatial variables are dichotomous indicators of agreement: 1 if from the same city, region, section, or state, and 0 otherwise.

Urbanicity measures are drawn from the CSR dataset developed for this project. In the regression, the difference between the dyad members' scores on the seven-category ordinal CSR measure (ranging from a rural 0 to a core city 6) is subtracted from six to give a measure of similarity on this dimension of demography and district character.[117] Thus, a pair of core city districts would have a score of 6 and a pair of rural districts a 6, but a pair made up of a city district and a suburban district might have a score of 3.[118]

The demographic measures for dyadic similarity along ethnoracial diversity and class lines were developed using a procedure as follows. "Race" is an estimate of similarity of the proportion of the electorate identified or identifying as "native white" in each congressional district. From the 73rd through 89th Congresses, this is the total population minus the proportion of the voting-eligible population that is black/African American or foreign born.[119] For later years, data on racial identities including Hispanic and Asian are available from a combination of Lublin (1999) and Adler (2012). Once each district's percentage of native white residents has been estimated, I calculate the difference between the dyad members' native-born white populations and subtract that value from 1 for use as a measure of ethnoracial similarity. For class similarity, I use the same procedure, using percent blue-collar from Adler (2012) as the initial measure. For both class similarity and racial similarity, demography for districts within a single county (for which Adler does not have precise measures) in early congresses is estimated using the procedure described in Appendix B. Finally, more direct measures of districts' mass ideology are helpful to account for possible clusters of liberalism in the population. Two different measures attempt to account for this. The first is union membership, as seen in Model 2 of Tables 4.3–4.5; however, in Adler (2012), this variable is measured at the state level and therefore is not quite appropriate for a district-level analysis; in any case, it appears to play a role similar to blue-collar population. More important are district-level measures of electoral partisanship or ideology, drawn from electoral results. To this end, I include the similarity in the percent of voters in the districts casting their votes for parties to the left of the Democrats, such as the American Labor Party, the Farmer-Labor Party, the Socialist Party, or the Communist Party, in the race for that seat. These give a sense of whether a Democratic representative might feel major pressure from such an outspokenly ideological and often quite antiracist, at least by contemporary standards, political force.[120]

The model includes four measures of geographic similarity (the primary explanatory variable of interest, City; and three secondary explanatory variables, State, Region, and Section) and four measures of district-level similarity on urbanicity, ethnoracial composition, class, and ideology. I estimate logit models with Congress-level fixed effects to account for shifts in the overall partisan balance of the chamber (which would affect the baseline probability of two members being from the same party).[121] The models include seats from the 78th to 105th Congresses (1943–1997 seatings, those for which all the measures were available); Models 1 and 2 include all seats, and Model 3 includes only seats from cities, a tougher test of the theory because it removes the potentially confounding effects of the emerging urban–rural divide.

City delegation theory produces several key expectations for this model. First, the jurisdictional hypothesis holds that city boundaries should be related to the partisan composition of city delegations. This means that a pair of legislators from the same city should be more likely to be from the same party than an otherwise similar pair that is not from the same city, even when we account for other factors on which representatives' districts may be similar. If this is true, the coefficient on "SameCity," the indicator that representatives represent the same local political community, should be positive in Models 1, 2, and 3.

Second, members of strong local political organizations should be even more likely to be co-partisans. Model 4 in Tables 4.3–4.6 tests the organizational hypothesis, according to which strong local IHIs should foster additional partisan cohesion among representatives from the same city. Cities with strong IHIs (like Chicago and Philadelphia) should have more partisan-monolithic city delegations, because they are better able to resolve local conflict. Cities with weak IHIs will be relatively disorganized, and their districts should be less likely to cohere within one party because district-level forces will be more powerful, relative to citywide factors, in determining the representative from that place. This expectation would be supported if we observed that the relationship between membership in the same city and same national party was stronger in cities with strong IHIs than cities with weak IHIs. To test this organizational hypothesis, I add a measure of local party strength, David Mayhew's traditional party organization (TPO) scores, to the model, but only test it on a subset of the dyads: those from the same city.[122]

4.5.2 Discussion: Homogeneous Delegations from Heterogeneous Constituencies

Tables 4.3 and 4.4 show the results from estimating these models of congressional party affinity, listing the regression coefficients and marginal effects, respectively. The coefficients of primary interest, those having to do with the

Table 4.3 **Probit Regression Results: Congressional Party Affinity. City Delegation Models with Different Samples of Congressional Dyads**

Model (District Dyads Included)	1 All	2 All	3 City Only	4 Same City
Same City	0.79** (0.03)	0.49** (0.02)	0.78** (0.08)	
High TPO				0.68** (0.18)
Same State	−0.21** (0.01)	−0.11** (0.00)	−0.45** (0.06)	
Same Section	0.14** (0.00)	0.11** (0.00)	0.06* (0.03)	
Same Region	0.30** (0.00)	0.19** (0.00)	0.05 (0.03)	
Urbanicity Similarity (7 category)	0.03** (0.01)	0.02** (0.00)	2.26** (0.24)	−0.90 (2.11)
Similarity in FarLeft %	−1.52** (0.11)	−0.93** (0.06)	−0.58 (0.32)	−8.69** (1.44)
Race (Similarity in % Non-native-white)	0.85** (0.02)	0.53** (0.01)	−1.02** (0.15)	−1.63* (0.81)
Class (Similarity in % Blue collar)	0.13 (0.10)		5.98** (1.00)	38.60** (6.15)
Union (Similarity in % in state)		−0.54** (0.03)		
Adjusted R^2	.01	.01	.02	.085
N	2,171,755	2,171,755	158,504	6,851

Note: Dependent variable is membership in same congressional party. Independent variables are measures of similarity on the variable listed at left. Cell entries are probit regression coefficients with robust standard errors, clustered by dyad. Significance levels for all key explanatory variables of interest (identified in grey) verified using nonparametric simulation technique in Rader, Pinto, and Erikson (2014). Estimated with constant term and Congress-fixed effects not listed here. * $p < .05$, ** $p < .01$.

Sources: Voteview; CSR data; Adler (2012); Lublin (1997a).

IHIs of city co-membership and local institutions, are highlighted in gray in the tables. In short, the results and substantive interpretations are broadly consistent across the models and subsets and consistent with the expectations of city delegation theory. There is a positive association between sharing

Table 4.4 **Marginal Effects: Congressional Party Affinity. City Delegation Models with Different Samples of Congressional Dyads**

Model (Dyads Included)	1 All	2 All	3 City Only	4 Same City
Same City	.20	.19	.18	
High TPO				.12
State	−.05	−.04	−.10	
Section	.034	.044	.01	
Region	.075	.07	NA	
Urbanicity	.0082	.01	.51	NA
Far Left	−.37	−.37	NA	−1.56
Race	.21	.21	−.23	−.29
Class	NA		1.35	6.9
Union		−.21		

Note: Cell entries are the marginal effects of similarity on dimensions at left on dyad co-membership in congressional party. Estimated with covariates held at appropriate levels. Estimates based on coefficients that were not estimated to be significant at $p < .05$ in Table 4.3 marked NA.

*$p <.05$, **$p <.01$.

these local institutions and membership in the same congressional party, even when we account for other likely factors such as geography and demography. In Models 1 through 3, which test the jurisdictional hypothesis, the positive, significant coefficient on SameCity is consistent with the theory that membership in the same local community is associated with sharing a national political party as well. From Table 4.4, we can see that membership in the same city is associated with a nearly 20 percent increase in the chance of being in the same party, though the precise magnitude of the effect is sensitive to other specifications of the model.

The city boundary itself is not doing all of the work, however. Model 4's test of the organizational hypothesis (the TPO measure) indicates that two MCs from a strong-party city are about 12 percent more likely to be in the same party than their counterpart duo from a weak-party city. This coefficient is positive and precisely measured, providing support for the idea that strong organizational IHIs are associated with citywide agreement. As we shall see in the next section, these copartisans from strong local parties are also more likely to vote together.

These results, incorporating data from most of the twentieth century, provide support for the role of both jurisdictional and organizational IHIs in fostering unity within a city delegation through common congressional affiliation—that is, as the result of one party winning the city's elections for Congress.[123] These results focus on the first phase of congressional representation, the selection of partisan representatives. Other results of the models are worth noting: being from the same region and section is positively associated with membership in the same party, but dyads from the same state are *less* likely to represent the same party, all else being equal. This may reflect intrastate rivalries of various sorts. District-level characteristics include some surprises: while being similar in place character makes districts more likely to come from the same party (reflecting the urban–rural divide), class and race seem far less important in this respect, and similarity on race in particular does not reveal a clear pattern. Ideological similarity also yields an unexpected result that merits further investigation elsewhere. If anything, similarity on these dimensions makes districts *less* likely to share a party. Finally, the low pseudo-R-squared measure across all models indicates that even these measures of "prepolitical" geographic and demographic similarity do not account for much of the variation in the outcome variable. Electoral politics is obviously complex, and simple similarity between districts tells us less only a small part of the story.

4.5.3 Cohesive Voting

The results of the previous analysis indicate that local IHIs are associated with the partisan unity of their cities' delegations. This is obviously important, as congressional party is almost certainly the strongest predictor of how a member will ultimately vote in the halls of Congress. But it is not the whole story. According to city delegation theory, in addition to fostering city delegations with unified party membership, IHIs will be associated with cohesion in final voting—a particularly important point for votes that divide the parties themselves. Some of the IHI's work moves indirectly through partisanship, but because national American congressional parties are not strong or disciplined themselves, we should also estimate a direct relationship between IHIs and actual legislative agreement.

The analysis in this section builds on the previous analysis to show that membership in common IHIs fostered agreement in roll call voting in the twentieth century. The basic framework is the same (a dyadic measure of agreement, regressed on measures of similarity), with two key differences. Now, the dependent variable is agreement on final roll call votes, and their partisan affinity becomes one of the right-hand-side explanatory covariates. Membership in the same city delegation (and the strength of that party delegation) are still the explanatory variables of interest. The analyses will show that city delegation theory still seems to have explanatory power at this level: local IHIs are associated with agreement on final roll call votes, all else being equal.

In the previous section's analyses of dyadic partisan affinity, there was just one observation per dyad per Congress, and the dependent variable measured whether the seats were held by members of the same party. To analyze agreement on roll calls, the dependent variable becomes a dichotomous indicator of whether the *votes* of the two representatives were the same, with one observation per complete dyad on a vote. The dyad is coded 1 if the two members of the dyad cast the same vote and 0 if they disagreed.[124] I then regress this agreement indicator on several covariates of similarity between the dyad elements. As in the analysis of party affinity, the explanatory variables are all measures of similarity—members' similarity in party and districts' similarity in urbanicity, traditional party organization, racial (percent native white) and class (blue collar and union) composition (where available), region, section, and state—and values are the same for all roll calls in a given Congress.

The basic observable implications of city delegation theory are analogous to those seen in the previous sections (both the regression and aggregate cohesion analyses). For the jurisdictional hypothesis, membership in the same city should be independently associated with roll call agreement; for the organizational hypothesis, the theory predicts that copartisans from the strong-organization cities will be more likely to agree than copartisans from weak-party cities.

While the seats analysis included the universe of cases, the much larger number of possible observations on votes means we must be selective. The following analyses test the two hypotheses associated with city delegation theory using roll calls from the 73rd through 90th Congresses (roughly spanning the Long New Deal).[125] Multiple results are presented here both to illustrate robustness across slightly different subsamples of the data (given limited availability of class variables) and because the different models illustrate slightly different aspects of the patterns in the data. First, for Models 1 through 3, I test a sample of all roll calls identified by the American Institutions Project dataset as having to do with domestic policy from the urban interlude.[126] There are about 1,700 such votes and about 90,000 voting dyads associated with each of them, making analysis of the whole universe computationally unwieldy. For the results presented here, I sampled 10 percent of those votes from each Congress and dropped uncontested votes from that sample.[127] After sampling, the dataset for analysis included 9,014,495 total observations on seventy-two roll calls.[128] In Table 4.5, these analyses of a random draw of all votes are indicated by the label "All" in the top row. In all of these models, the key variable of interest is "City," the indicator of whether a dyad consists of two members from the same local *polis*, and, to a lesser extent, "Urbanicity," to keep an eye on the urban–rural divide. Finally,

Table 4.5 **Probit Regression Results: Vote Agreement. City Delegation Models with Different Samples of Congressional Dyads**

Model Dyads Included	1 All	2 City Pairs	3 Same City & Party
Same City	0.14** (0.01)	0.09** (0.01)	
TPO			0.17** (0.03)
Same Party	.76** (.00)	.88** (.004)	
Same State	0.03** (0.00)	0.01 (0.01)	
Same Section	0.02** (0.00)	0.17** (0.00)	
Same Region	0.05** (0.00)	0.03** (0.01)	
Urbanicity Similarity (7 category)	0.04** (0.00)	0.12** (0.01)	−0.05 (0.08)
Similarity in FarLeft %	1.11** (0.04)	0.64** (0.08)	0.88** (0.25)
Race (Similarity in % Non-native-white)	0.10** (0.01)	0.04 (0.03)	0.05 (0.12)
Class (Similarity in % Blue collar)	0.20** (0.04)	−0.88** (0.18)	4.56** (1.24)
Adjusted R^2	.07	.12	.14
N	9,014,495	676,426	21,106

Note: Dependent variable is agreement on a roll call vote. Independent variables are measures of similarity on the variable listed at left. Estimated with a constant term and Congress- and vote-level fixed effects (not presented here). Cell entries are probit regression coefficients with robust standard errors, clustered by dyad following Green, Kim, and Yoon (2001). Shaded rows are coefficients of interest, with significance for these coefficients retested with a more demanding nonparametric simulation technique following Rader, Pinto, and Erikson (2014). Total pool of observations include dyad-pairs from a random sample of contested votes in the 78th to 105th Congresses. All models include (unlisted) Congress- and vote-specific fixed effects. *$p < .05$. **$p < .01$.

Sources: Voteview; CSR data; Adler (2012); Lublin (1997a).

Model 3 provides a test of the organizational hypothesis by including only dyads from the same city and same party. The key variable of interest is the indicator for local party strength, TPO, with the expectation that dyads from strong-party cities will be more likely to agree than those from weak-party cities.[129] Measures of partisan, regional, sectional, and state similarity are dropped in Model 3 because all representatives from the same city necessarily share those higher levels of geographic affinity. All models presented were estimated with a constant term and Congress- and vote-level fixed effects to account for dynamics that might make agreement more or less likely during a Congress or on a particular vote.[130] Table 4.5 lists the results of these three models evaluating the relationships predicted by city delegation theory and IHIs. Cells of primary interest for tests of city delegation theory are highlighted in gray.

Again, the predictions of city delegation theory are supported by the data. Table 4.6 lists the marginal effects associated with a one-unit change in each measure, calculated while holding the other variables constant at appropriate values.[131] Being from the same city is associated with about a 5 percent

Table 4.6 **Marginal Effects: Vote Agreement. City Delegation Models with Different Samples of Congressional Dyads**

Model	1	2	3
Dyads	All	City Pairs	Same City & Party
Same City	0.05**	0.03**	
TPO			0.05**
Party	0.26**	0.30**	
State	0.01**	NA	
Section	0.01**	0.058**	
Region	0.02**	0.011**	
Urbanicity	0.02**	0.042**	NA
% Far Left	0.41**	0.22**	0.26**
% Dem	−.04**	0.14**	0.36**
Race	0.03**	NA	NA
Class	0.07**	−0.31**	1.3**

Note: Cell entries are the marginal effects of similarity on dimensions at left on dyad agreement in roll call votes. Estimated with covariates held at appropriate levels. Estimates based on coefficients that were not estimated significant at $p < .05$ in Table 4.5 marked NA.

increased probability of roll call agreement. When we restrict the sample to only those dyads that include two city districts, being from the same city makes the pair about 3 percent more likely to agree. As expected, there is a strong relationship between party and agreement: across these models, copartisans were about 26–30 percent more likely to agree than members from different parties.

Finally, the test of the organizational hypothesis on the subset of dyads whose members were from the same city and party also provides support for city delegation theory. Local copartisans who were from places with strong local parties, which provide stronger links between representatives from different parts of a city, were about 5 percent more likely to agree than local copartisans from places with weak local institutions.[132] Not only are pairs from cities with strong organizational IHIs more likely to share party affiliation, but they are also more likely to agree more when it comes time to vote. These local party organizations provide strong glue holding representatives of sometimes very different constituencies together in the final phase of representation. In additional analyses restricted to the kinds of "City Votes" on the vote categories of Housing, Public Works and Infrastructure, Urban and Regional Development, and Public Works Employment, the marginal effect of sharing membership in a city delegation appears to be even larger, around 12 percent, though it is measured less precisely.[133] Sharing a city may matter more on issues that matter more for cities.

Overall, the results of these dyad-level regressions support the main hypotheses of city delegation theory at both levels of representation: sharing common local institutional and political roots makes representatives more cohesive. Pairs of representatives who come from the same city are more likely to agree on roll call votes than pairs who do not, and this is especially true for those pairs in which both representatives come from cities with strong organizational IHIs. Moreover, pairs of representatives from cities with such institutions (the most important of which are the traditional party organizations tested here) are more likely to come from the same party than those pairs who do not. Since partisan affiliation is an especially strong force for congressional behavioral agreement (that's what these parties are *for*, more than anything else), creating a city delegation that is monolithic in its partisan identity is also an important means by which local parties operate. There is still much work that remains to fully understand the precise mechanisms that foster cohesion. The models in this chapter still do not account for much of the overall variation in whether or not members of dyads ultimately agree. But this is not an issue unique to the questions at hand—after all, I include what is thought to be the main determinant of voting behavior (national party) as an explanation in the model.

4.6 Conclusion: National Effects of Local Institutions

The streams of evidence in this chapter provide concrete examples of how city delegations operated during the Long New Deal and statistical evidence of the general association between extracameral IHIs and legislative cohesion predicted by city delegation theory. Officials in city hall and on Capitol Hill work together to articulate the city interest and to cooperate in making the city work. The representatives from the city conceive of themselves as a delegation, and the mayor reaches out to them as a group with instructions or requests. Sometimes the relationship goes the other way, but from the record it appears that this occurs less often. There are lots of ways these bonds are reinforced, but membership in a common local polity and political organization are among the most important.

In the aggregate, we can see that cities are more cohesive in their legislative behavior than are other collections of legislators, and cities with strong IHIs are more cohesive than cities with weak IHIs. This cohesion is partly attributable to partisanship; dyads from the same city are more likely to be affiliated with the same party than those from different cities, and this relationship is even stronger in cities with strong traditional parties. But even beyond party membership, city delegations foster cohesion in roll call voting on domestic policy issues. Representatives from the same city are more likely to agree with each other, even across party lines, an indication that something like a city interest is being represented.

Finally, among city representatives, those from the same local party are extremely cohesive. Qualitatively, they do favors for each other and effectively lobby each other to take positions and defend a city interest. More quantitatively, they vote together. This relationship is estimated precisely in the regressions carried out in the previous sections, but it is also clear in the actual outcomes on the chamber floor. During the urban interlude Chicago Democrats were unanimous on 85 percent of votes; New York Democrats were unanimous on 75 percent. These percentages increased to 90 percent (for each city) on key votes on which the national parties disagreed.[134] Despite the fact that these cities' constituencies were often quite different on important dimensions like race and class, these blocs of legislators consistently spoke with one voice for a city position and were particularly cohesive when their votes were most valuable. Whether this pattern of relationships holds for all substantive policy areas or only those most relevant to cities (like city-centric or domestic roll calls) is an area for further investigation.

The broader theoretical aim of this analysis is to draw attention to a set of institutions that are external to formal models of representation that focus on factors internal to the Congress (like national party affiliation) or to a particular constituency (like one shaped by demographics). According to such models, the city and related institutions are typically seen as irrelevant to national representation, but something about cities fosters cohesion among their representatives to an extent the analytical usual suspects cannot fully explain. Such institutions link constituencies with something in common at the local level (membership in a common political community and/or in a local political organization whose primary aims are focused at the local level) despite sometimes vast differences in the building blocks of politics.

The large cities upon which the urban political order was built were famous for fractious (and recurrently violent) politics at home, but they are notable for the cohesive way they represent themselves in national politics, and on domestic issues in particular. Moreover, differences in overall cohesion among city delegations are related to the institutional configuration of the cities themselves: cities with traditional party organizations are also more cohesive in national politics, in part because they elect more members from the same party. Crucially, these bonds were not just artifacts of ideological or demographic similarity, as some would contend—politics is as much about allies and teams as it is about preferences, policies, and ideologies. By creating such cohesive representative units, IHIs foster *vertical* integration as well: they transmit a disciplined, cohesive style of city politics into the higher legislature, making the effects of their local institutions felt in national legislative politics.

The mechanisms for city delegations and cohesion examined in this chapter and Chapter 2 are surely not exhaustive. Further possibilities for organizational IHIs are particularly intriguing, because human ingenuity can invent countless forms of them. Beyond the parties themselves, it is certainly possible that other informal, extracameral local institutions serve similar functions in places where traditional parties were not (or are no longer) present. In midcentury Detroit, for instance, the nominally nonpartisan local politics was often dominated by CIO unions, notably the United Automobile Workers.[135] In many formally nonpartisan cities, reform-style regimes integrated politics into government at the times when they held political "monopolies" (as described in Trounstine 2008), though the foregoing analysis indicates that nonpartisan cities tended to be more divided than those with partisan institutions; by eliminating the party from local politics, reformers may have undermined the possibility of supralocal delegation unity.[136] The precise institutions that shape politics and cohesion can change or adapt over time as well. In contemporary Chicago, for instance, local mayoral politics have been formally nonpartisan since the mid-1990s (Richard M. Daley ran on ballots without party labels, though the city council remains partisan), but there has been little experiential doubt of the continued power of the machine there, or of its sustained organizational ties up and down the chain of political authority.

Because this analysis is most concerned with the growth and consolidation of the urban political order, it concludes with the 105th Congress. In today's hyperpartisan environment, however, independent associations may be tougher to find, because both parties have become more cohesive and more associated with certain prepolitical attributes (especially urbanicity and race), and because geographical sorting according to these lines has matured. We should still be able to find evidence of the day-to-day cooperation within city delegations, however, even if such ties are less determinative or mathematically isolable in roll call outcomes than they were at midcentury. This analysis shows in part how the bloc-of-blocs was built, but other factors may hold it together after construction.

The cohesive force of city delegations complicates Tip O'Neill's famous observation that "all politics is local." We usually understand this statement to mean that a politician will be responsive to his or her constituency's interests and potentially resistant to a national party line when it conflicts with the local position. This is true to a point, but we must be careful about how we understand *local*, at least for city politicians. The cohesion of big-city delegations indicates that city representatives are responsive to the *city*, including the part that they do not formally represent, as well as to their own particular district within the city. In each case, from the seeming abstraction of jurisdictional integration to the stronger human bonds of organizational linkages, the ultimate point is that for city representatives, important local politics can happen outside a representative's district. These facts—that cities foster cohesion even though their component parts are very different from each other, and that particular constellations of local institutions, especially parties, amplify cohesion—present both a puzzle and a key insight for understanding the role of cities in national political institutions. These city delegations, made up of heterogeneous rivals at home but united on the Hill, form the backbone of the "blue" alignment of the Democratic Party today, making up the cross-city alliance described in the previous chapter. The next chapter addresses a policy area in which the cohesive forces of IHIs were particularly important: the advancement of civil rights for African Americans during the urban interlude. This development, shaped by local institutions, restructured American partisan politics and reinforced the place of cities within the Democratic Party.

5

Antiracism Without Antiracists
City Representation and Racial Realignment

> Lynching is called an American institution.... They protected life and property, at least in a way, and made those sections of the country, where there was no organized government, very safe sections in which to live.
> —Rep. Hatton Sumners (D-TX), 1934[1]

> The frontier days are gone, and few of us familiar with the rigors of living in that era are likely to bewail its departure.
> —Rep. John Rooney (D-NY), 1949[2]

> The only genuine difference between a southern white and a Chicago white was in their accent.
> —Mike Royko, *Boss*[3]

In previous chapters, we have seen that the consolidation of the urban political order during the New Deal provided a base of support for national interventions in the economy. Cities' representatives on Capitol Hill were notable for their economic liberalism and for their cohesion, which was rooted in local IHIs that fostered unified blocs representing otherwise heterogeneous and fractious parts. In this chapter, civil rights and race take center stage as drivers of American politics and conflict. Race is a perennial source of fracture in American politics—both nationally and locally. Throughout the Long New Deal, conflicts within the parties over these issues created a second dimension in American politics, one on which the usual alignments did not hold.[4] This second dimension split both parties, but it was far more dramatic on the Democratic side. Urban Democrats began to defend a new, pluralist vision of America that sought (and for decades failed) to advance national civil rights for African Americans specifically and cultural inclusion of ethnic minorities generally. This push by liberal Democrats flew in the face of their southern copartisans, who recommitted themselves to white supremacy. It also presented a paradox of representation, because even though the urban base and local government elites were typically less aggressive in defense of white racial prerogatives than their counterparts in the South, these groups were overwhelmingly white and most were not antiracist ideologues. Despite the manifest racial conflict present in city streets, neighborhoods, and city halls, big-city representatives did not reflect this tension in the national conversation. In congressional settings, urban leaders presented the inclusive racial liberalism that came to be identified as the city position on these issues, even if it was not the position of all city-zens. This paradox may have contributed to the backlash politics of the 1960s and later decades, but it also paved the way for the United States to make a major step toward fuller democratic incorporation of all its citizens.

On the Republican side, there was a milder split between rural Republicans who generally eschewed the blunt racism of the South but were uncomfortable with difference (whether in the form of African Americans or immigrants) and some very liberal urban Republicans who were old rivals of the conservative big-city machines and generally supported civil rights. These urban Republicans were a dwindling breed even by the 1940s, though their remnants would ultimately be pivotal for the passage of civil rights legislation in the 1960s. There are very few such Republicans among elected officials today. Today's red–blue political alignment reflects the parties' resolution of civil rights debates, such that the opposing sides overlap (rather than cut across each other) in arguments over the role of government in the economy and race. Neither of these dimensions of conflict has disappeared; rather, the two reinforce each other. This chapter considers how place character and local institutions shaped the congressional politics of race during this time and how cities provided surprisingly strong support for racial liberalism during the urban interlude.

5.1 Racial Realignment

The New Deal realignment was marked by a major, lasting shift of city districts to the Democratic Party, forming a bloc that supported an agenda generally congenial to big-city interests (and other liberal goals). In other words, the Democrats quickly became the "party of the cities."[5] This bloc-of-blocs, however, did not enter a void. Democrats had dominated politics in the southern states since the region's reentry to the union after Reconstruction, and white southerners had long been the core of the national Democratic Party. Deeply conservative on racial and cultural matters, and wary of any centralization of power that might threaten their regional racial order and political economy, representatives from the South made it clear early on that race would be a central dimension of conflict in the expanded New Deal coalition.

This tension between city and Southern Democrats constantly simmered and periodically boiled over. Eventually the ties that bound the alliance frayed and came undone. In the end, the sectional wings parted ways, and after a long process of sorting (which also entailed a long period of party building by Republicans in the South), our contemporary partisan divide—with the white South as the red base of the GOP and the multicultural cities as the heart of blue Democratic support—represents the full flowering of the seeds sown in the New Deal realignment of 1928–1936.

The analysis in this chapter joins recent scholarship on this intraparty conflict by shifting the analytical lens away from the South and to a period well before the 1960s, when the most visible turbulence occurred, looking for causes of the change rather than providing a description of continued southern racial conservatism. Most accounts of this partisan change focus on the migration of conservative white Southern Democrats, the most estranged of the strange bedfellows coalition of the New Deal, to the Republican fold.[6] Southern elites were infamously racist, and the reemergence of racial civil rights on the national agenda understandably alienated them from the party of white supremacy they had built in the decades after the Civil War. Less attention has been paid to the other wing of the party—cities outside the South—for which race was also a deeply divisive issue and the source of great contention, but which had been shaped by local circumstances and institutions that fostered durable support for racial liberalism in national politics.

Because the midcentury partisan realignment unfolded slowly and unevenly across decades, it is not entirely clear precisely when the critical elections were, and scholars are still debating its mechanics.[7] There is considerable scholarly consensus as to *why* this change occurred, however: race. The conflicts in America and within the Democratic Party over the civil rights movement made obvious the incoherence of a political alliance that included both the most recalcitrant supporters of the southern racial order and its most strident critics. Many authors have identified the 1960s as the key moment of partisan political change on race because of the landmark legislation of the time and the reaction by Republicans (Barry Goldwater's presidential campaign pioneered the conservative positions on civil rights that the national GOP has taken since) and white Southern Democrats (who left the Democratic Party over the course of several decades).[8] A more durable departure by southerners from the Democratic Party took place in the 1960s, as the heart of the South went for Goldwater, and then for Wallace, Nixon, and Reagan. In recent electoral cycles, the South has been the core of the Republican strategy to win the White House. One classic narrative of how race undid the previous national alignment focuses on key visible moments that have occurred since 1960. In their account of "issue evolution" and partisan realignment, Carmines and Stimson (1989) focus on the role of contingency and elite political choice in describing how Republicans came to embrace racial conservatism. In this telling, the critical moment was the Republicans' presidential nomination of Sen. Barry Goldwater (R-AZ), whose opposition to the Civil Rights Act of 1964 was articulated in terms of a racial conservatism based on noninterference by federal authorities in local matters. Goldwater wooed the South (if no other states besides his home Arizona) with this appeal, and subsequent Republican presidential candidates have had national success building on it.[9] Carmines and Stimson identify this move by the GOP as a reversal—prior to this moment, they contend, the Republicans were still the Party of Lincoln and on aggregate the more racially liberal of the two parties. With this in mind, the issue evolution account of political change focuses chiefly on strategic decisions made at that historical moment by Republican leaders seeking to escape permanent minority status by driving a racial wedge into the Democratic Party.

The ensuing southern transition to the GOP happened at different moments in different institutions. Democratic presidential candidates generally have not done well in the South since 1964. In Congress, some erosion of southern solidity took place in the 1960s, but it was not until the 1990s that a majority of southern members of Congress were Republicans (see Figure 5.1). Today, there are fewer southern Democrats in the House than at any point since the end of Reconstruction.[10]

The transformation of the southern white electorate and its chosen representatives from Democrat to Republican was a major change in partisan politics, but in other ways it represented continuity. After all, the contemporary southern Republican parties are composed largely of white conservatives, just as their Dixiecrat forebears were. Southern whites remain more racially conservative than

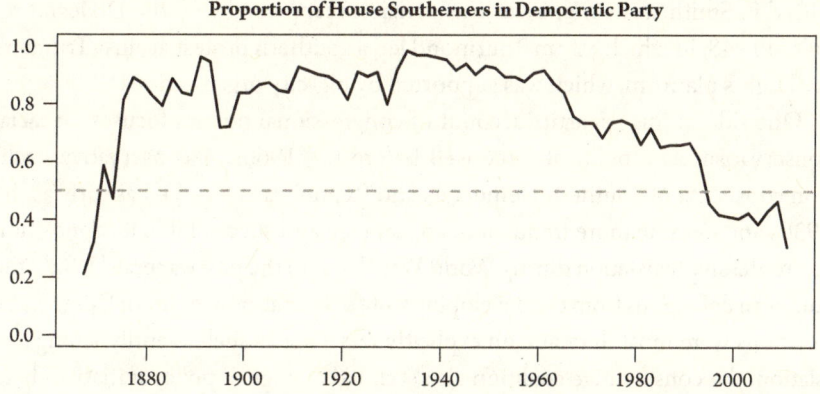

Figure 5.1 **Share of Southern House Seats Held by Democrats, post–Civil War Congresses.** While an overwhelming majority of Southern Representatives were Democrats for most of the twentieth century, that proportion has declined gradually but steadily since the 1960s.

their counterparts in other sections or groups, and they often put racial issues at the heart of their political appeals. The partisan conversion of leaders like Strom Thurmond and Jesse Helms illustrates this idea and focuses attention on how elite positions on racial policy filtered their way down to the other levels of politics.

But describing how southerners became Republicans blinds us to important changes that drove that process itself—after all, why didn't they just remain Democrats? A recent literature has more closely investigated the intraparty dynamics that led to the Democratic schism and complicated the story of how the parties oriented themselves toward controversial racial issues during this epoch.[11] While Carmines and Stimson focus on the two parties in the aggregate to find evidence of realignment and party positioning on race and see the events of the 1960s as highly contingent, the alternative approach disaggregates the Democratic Party during the Long New Deal and sees more long-term forces at work, shaping party decisions and dispositions well before 1964. Scholarship employing this lens helps us see an essentially tripartite system throughout the era, with southern and nonsouthern Democrats deeply divided and operating as separate blocs on many important issues.[12]

With this tripartite model in mind, it is better to consider the 1960s as more of a midpoint, because the process of Democratic dissolution took place over decades. The southern and urban wings of the party were never natural ideological allies, on race or much else, and signs of southern frustration with urban Democrats were apparent even before the New Deal elections of the 1930s consolidated Democratic strength in the cities. This was a conflict as much over city–country differences as about section or religion.[13] In 1928, several southern states left the Democratic presidential coalition for the first time since the Civil War when the party chose an urbanite, the Catholic former New York mayor Alfred E. Smith, as its nominee. This division reappeared with the Dixiecrat revolt of 1948, in which Strom Thurmond led a southern protest against Truman's civil rights platform, which was supported by big-city organizations.

One side of this tripartite account of congressional politics focuses on racial conservatism as a political force well before the 1960s. A conservative coalition consisting of Southern Democrats and Republicans emerged as early as the 1930s and became more frequent in appearance and successful in its opposition to progressive legislation during World War II and in the postwar era.[14] While the southern defections from the developing suite of liberal, nonsouthern Democratic positions were most dramatic on explicitly racial issues such as antilynching legislation, the conservative coalition also stymied a range of policy initiatives held dear by the urban wing of the party, including those having to do with housing, urban redevelopment, labor conflict, and political economy.[15] Racial conflict and the divergence of the partisan wings were present and important much earlier and subsequently spread to a broadening set of ostensibly nonracial policy areas.[16].

This alternative tripartite account provides a richer context for Carmines and Stimson's critical moment. When we place race at the roots of the recurrent conservative coalition, it changes our understanding of the apparently dramatic reversals of the 1960s. The proper evolutionary metaphor for the racial realignment may not be punctuated equilibrium (with its emphasis on rapid, unpredictable bursts of change) but rather more gradual, less dramatic Darwinian change. Examining race as a driver of realignment over the Long New Deal era leaves a far less important role for contingency and elite strategy in the 1960s.[17]

The recurrent conservative coalition in Congress was a leading indicator for the later national partisan realignment, but a focus on southern racial pathology only goes halfway toward explaining how race transformed American politics during this era. After all, the importance of the existing racial order to southern whites was no secret, and throughout the Long New Deal Southern Democrats openly viewed many issues through a racial lens, aggressively opposing any measures that even hinted at a threat to their regional racial order, and national party elites worked hard to keep race from collapsing the coalition.[18] This racial conservatism was not a change—Southern Democrats had worked (often with many powerful allies from other regions) since the Revolutionary War to strengthen white supremacy and to insulate its southern version from federal intervention or even expand its territorial reach, and they had been particularly successful in these efforts in the late nineteenth and early twentieth centuries. After Reconstruction, race and civil rights were remade into a regional issue and were basically absent from the congressional agenda for the first three decades of the twentieth century, when the general national trend was to reinforce white supremacy, or at least ignore its ugliest manifestations.[19]

For national Democratic elites, then, the political embrace of racial liberalism was far from automatic or hasty. The position southerners held within the Democratic Party, especially in Congress, and their intransigence on race made any policies or agenda that would undermine white supremacy both difficult to enact and politically risky. The push for change that demands explanation is how the proponents of racial egalitarianism could become a compelling enough political force that the northern wing of the Democratic Party (sometimes in ad hoc alliances with a dwindling group of moderate and liberal Republicans) embarked down the road to civil rights, consciously and conspicuously alienating a large part of their governing coalition in a strategic move that they recognized as risky, if not fatal, in the U.S. majoritarian system. The change that demands explanation, then, is why the nonsoutherners pushed for civil rights, and that question becomes even more of a puzzle when we actually look closely at the elements that made up the Democratic coalition outside the South as well.

5.1.1 *Urban* Strange Bedfellows

The existence of the sectional intraparty cleavage is famous, but the party's internal conflicts were not only sectional—the New Deal coalition included some of the strangest bedfellows imaginable. In the Democratic electoral base, white southerners were joined by polyphonous industrial cities, where organized labor, African Americans, and newly mobilized ethnic whites were enmeshed in deeply felt conflicts of their own at the mass level. Among urban Democratic elites, the decades-long rivalry between machine-style party organizations and their local opponents (often self-described reformers) continued, with the conflict sometimes manifest at the national level, as in the 1932 nomination battle between New Yorkers Franklin Roosevelt and Al Smith.[20] None of these groups got along particularly well, jostling for position and power in local politics. Significantly, most of the powerful and numerous groups in this hodge-podge are often characterized as forces of resistance *against* racial egalitarianism, not as actors who would risk the national power of the New Deal coalition on behalf of civil rights.

The rise of racial liberalism during this time has been understood mainly as a function of dedicated activists and partisan constituents fighting for antiracist goals against long odds.[21] The early work by these actors gets too little attention in histories that focus on civil rights protests and activities in the South and in later decades; many crucial actions were taken and ideas worked out in the cities of the North as organized labor and civil rights activists sometimes found common cause in organizations or coalitions. While "union leaders, African Americans, ADA [Americans for Democratic Action] liberals, and Jews" were important members of the coalition, however, it is not obvious that this collection of liberal ideologues is the group that "northern Democrats most depended upon for votes and activist support" in the party's key urban strongholds.[22] Thus, the strategic moves to embrace racial liberalism in national legislative politics (and foreseeably alienate the South) should not be viewed so simply, as a function of constituency pressure, because, as another main thread of political science engaged with local urban politics has noted, even outside the South the core elements of the Democratic alliance were hardly what we would call antiracist. These very same cities, and the most important Democratic organizations within them, were often the site of strong racial hierarchies themselves and usually approached politics from a professional rather than ideological angle. New York and Chicago, preeminent within the national hierarchy of cities and Democratic organizations during this era for their importance in winning seats in Congress and their position as vital swing states, were places where such "programmatic liberals" were important members of the Democratic Party but hardly dominant in the local organizations essential to electoral victory.[23]

At the mass level, there were other important (i.e., numerous and/or organizationally powerful) members of the coalition, even outside the South, who were not natural members of a pro–civil rights coalition. Their racial opinions ran the gamut from comity to apathy to antipathy. It is very easy to find instances of strong racial antipathy by northern urban whites during this period (and continuing beyond it). The most important of these fraught blocs was organized labor, a large sector of society that often combined broad ideological movement politics with narrower concerns about collective bargaining. Though labor leaders were often outspoken proponents of inclusion and racial justice, rank-and-file union members themselves were less so, and throughout the midcentury era the weight of the evidence is that they were at least split on race, if not generally hostile to racial egalitarianism.[24]

Overlapping significantly with, but not identical to, union members in northern cities were the legions of ethnic whites, a massive group that probably made up a plurality of the nonsouthern urban Democratic electorate and was the *most* important constituency mobilized for the massive Democratic gains of 1932–1936.[25] Despite their mobilization for the Democrats, these groups were never noted for their racial progressivism, as veteran Chicago reporter Mike Royko observes poetically in the quote at the beginning of this chapter. Indeed, to the extent that ethnic whites shared a common identity, it was often articulated in the claim that they were *not* black and were newly eligible for the privileges of white status in the United States at that time.[26] It is between ironic and tragic that the white identity of these descendants of new-stock immigrants was itself forged at least in part by the ambitious statism of New Deal programs, filtered through a racialized southern lens. In countless instances, members or subsets of this heterogeneous group—including some leaders of prominent Democratic Party organizations—became the antagonists in the racial conflict that periodically beset almost all cities throughout this era. In the post–civil rights era, this bloc's loyalty to the Democrats has eroded, not least because of the less ambiguous liberal positions eventually embraced by prominent national Democrats on civil rights.[27]

If the urban Democratic mass base was split over racial issues, not all nonsouthern Democratic elites should be counted as staunch ideological supporters of racial comity, either. At the intersection between the electorate and institutional politics in many important Democratic cities sat traditional party organizations, the bosses and their political kith. While they may have been past their Tweed-style wheeling-and-dealing prime in most places, these urban traditional party organizations were still in the midst of their national heyday: never before or since have so many city representatives come from such organizations.[28] These autonomous organizational leaders, famous for being almost *by definition* nonprogrammatic about much of anything, were not typically dependent on African Americans or ideological racial liberals for their electoral success; their relationships with such groups were consequently varied and complex.[29] By their liberal contemporaries and in hindsight, the traditional parties have often been judged conservative, corrupt, and unresponsive.[30] While some of these party chieftains reached out to African Americans as they arrived in massive numbers during the waves of the Great Migration, these moves were usually interpreted as pragmatic political gestures—not as part of an antiracist ideological agenda. The often-tribal nature of big-city politics did not leave much room or resources for new coalition members, and politicians accustomed to trading in material goods were understandably averse to wading into divisive cultural issues like race, which cannot be quite as easily negotiated or apportioned as city jobs or similarly material benefits.[31] These local partisans frequently practiced politics with "a sharp racial edge,"[32] and African Americans were subordinated within or excluded from local political organizations, a major exception to the tradition of new-group incorporation chronicled by optimistic pluralist urbanists such as Dahl (1961).[33] In their strongest form, machines became the only game in town, tended to bias entire local political systems away from ideal forms of electorally driven democratic responsiveness, and delivered valued policy goods only to their core members. In such cases minority constituents had even less leverage than usual, and the end result was typically further marginalization of already peripheral African American communities.[34]

All of this racial conflict is in keeping with the prevalent theory of racial "threat," which holds that relations between groups will tend to get worse when a new group arrives, grows, and competes for status or resources with previous residents.[35] Given this tendency toward division and racial conflict on the streets and in city hall, the decision to support racial liberalism in national politics was not an obvious one, and we might expect city Democrats to have been as likely to oppose racial liberalism as to support it.

The potential foundations of support for racially liberal policies by nonsouthern Democrats in Congress were further complicated by urban spatial demography. The most straightforward explanation for nonsouthern Democrats' resilient support for civil rights legislation might be a direct electoral connection running from black constituents to racial liberalism. On controversial issues, when legislative parties are split, constituent pressure and the pursuit of reelection are often cited as important predictors of a representative's behavior.[36] Race was one of those issues during the Long New Deal, so we might expect civil rights liberalism by nonsouthern representatives to have emerged as a response to African American constituents. The Great Migration meant that black populations in northern cities did increase quickly, and areas like the South Side of Chicago and Harlem eventually gained black representatives in

Congress who became leaders in bringing civil rights issues to the fore. Other black representatives followed in the early 1960s.

But this constituent pressure explanation cannot easily explain much of the support for civil rights because of the extremely segregated patterns of residence of the time. Today we think of urban districts generally as naturally sympathetic to minority groups' concerns because these districts usually include disproportionate numbers of minority voters; this demography is mostly a product of white flight, immigration, and the Voting Rights Act of 1965, which sought to ensure minority group representation in the face of white-dominated organizations—North and South—that often drew district lines and oversaw elections in ways that minimized minority representation. City district demography was different before the 1960s. Throughout the eras of the Great Migration (and after), exclusionary and discriminatory housing policies, realty practices, and social pressure created high levels of residential segregation, concentrating almost all the new black arrivals in particular neighborhoods, usually the places with the oldest and worst housing stock.[37] These patterns of racial separation meant that most city congressional districts—even in those cities with relatively large, rapidly growing African American populations—remained almost entirely white. For representatives of these districts, whose constituents had little reason to clamor for racial justice, the electoral connection was not so clear.[38]

To better understand this pattern, consider the stark and very important example of Chicago in 1940, just as fair employment was about to appear on the national racial agenda. Chicago had been the first 20th century city to send an African American to Congress, the Republican Oscar De Priest in 1927. By the 1940s, Chicago's black South Side had become a Democratic stronghold in local and national politics. William L. Dawson, himself a convert to the party of Roosevelt, was the only black member of Congress and sat at the head of a strong local suborganization, holding senior positions in the local party leadership and eventually in Congress.[39] Migration, policy, and practice made Chicago the most segregated large city in America, and almost all of the city's black residents lived in or near Dawson's First Congressional District.[40] The rest of Chicago's districts were almost entirely white, ostensibly making the pressure for civil rights quite uneven across districts. To analyze how these segregated residential patterns influenced legislative behavior, I created a new dataset of congressional district demography for city districts based on historical census data and a geographic information system procedure that spatially maps census tracts onto congressional districts and adds them up to create new district-level estimates. This procedure is detailed in Appendix B. Previous estimates used in such historical analyses imputed city district demography from above, assuming that every district within a single county shared that county's demography equally. Because of segregation, however, this assumption was not correct, and taking segregation seriously means seeing these districts for what they were—racially homogeneous pieces of a diverse whole, as shown in Figure 5.2a and 5.2b as well as the analysis of cross-district heterogeneity in Chapter 4.

Figure 5.2a shows the percent black population at the census-tract level in 1940 in Chicago.[41] The dark area on the map just south of downtown represents an area of extreme concentration of African Americans: though only

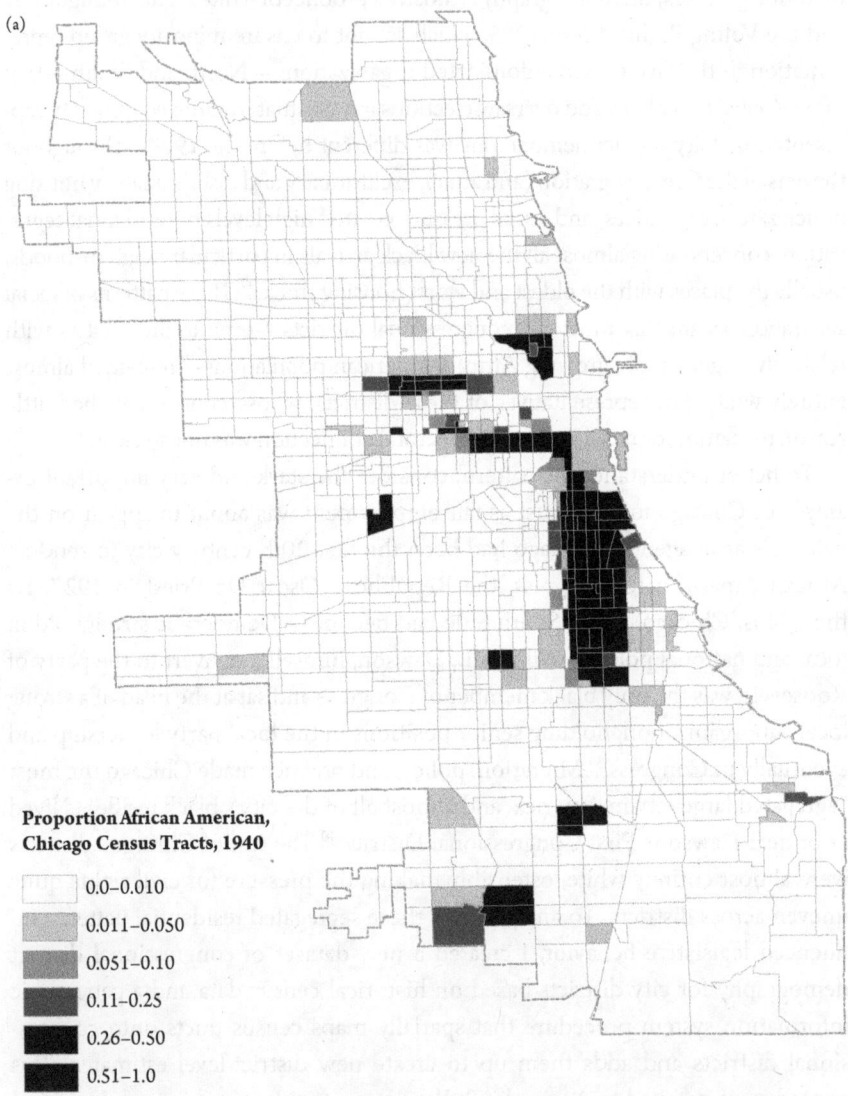

Figure 5.2 **Concentration of African Americans in Chicago.** (a) Percent black in Chicago census tracts, 1940 Census. African Americans were heavily concentrated within all American cities like Chicago. (b) Percent black in Chicago congressional districts, 76th Congress (1939–1941). Because of residential segregation, most representatives had very few black constituents.

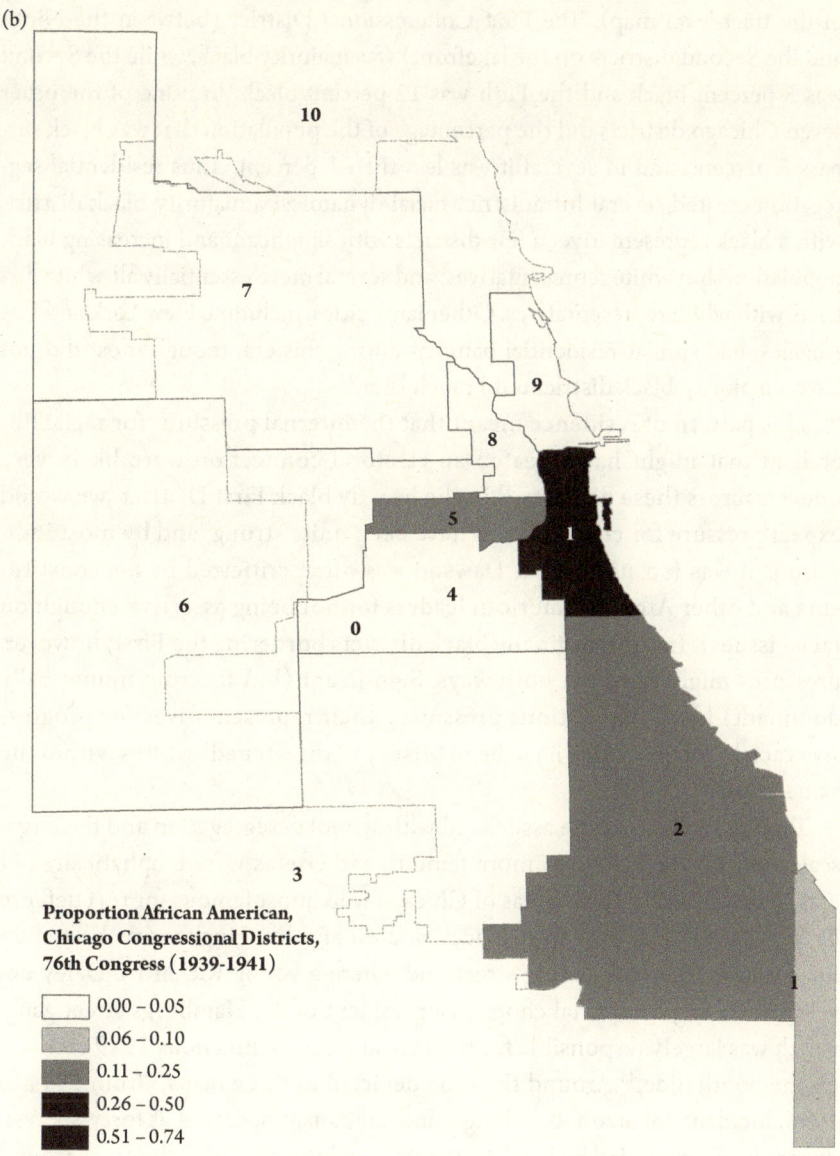

Figure 5.2 Continued.

about 11 percent of all Chicagoans were black, more than three out of four in this area were. In most of the rest of the city, where this map shows white, the local population was less than 1 percent black. This residential concentration was transmitted to the political system, as we can see in Figure 5.2b. When we aggregate from the tract level to the congressional district level, we can see that Chicago was as starkly divided in its political representation as it was in its social demographics (note that the color scale of this map is slightly different than that of the tract-level map). The First Congressional District (between the Ninth and the Second districts on the lakefront) was majority black, while the Second was 5 percent black and the Fifth was 12 percent black. In none of the other seven Chicago districts did the percentage of the population that was black surpass 5 percent, and in several it was less than 1 percent. Thus residential segregation created several intradistrict racial dynamics: a majority-black district, with a black representative; a few districts with significant and increasing black populations but white representatives; and several more essentially all-white districts with white representatives. Other large cities, including New York and Los Angeles, had similar residential patterns during this era, though most did not have a majority-black district until much later.[42]

This pattern of residence meant that the internal pressures for racial liberalism that might have created an electoral connection were likely very uneven across these districts.[43] In the heavily black First District, we would expect pressure for civil rights to have been quite strong, and by most indications it was (so strong that Dawson was often criticized by his constituents and other African American leaders for not being assertive enough on racial issues). In the marginally black districts bordering the First, however, pressures might have cut both ways. Significant (but far from numerically dominant) black populations pressuring their representatives for progressive racial policies might have been offset by "threatened" whites within the same areas.[44]

Though the racial strife associated with school desegregation and the large-scale riots of the 1960s are more famous, earlier eras were emphatically not eras of racial peace. These areas of Chicago were most famous for turf defense by white residents; they were places where Langston Hughes was beaten up for walking down the wrong street and where a young Richard J. Daley developed his organizational chops as a president of the Hamburgs street gang, which was largely responsible for the escalation of an infamous 1919 race riot on the South Side.[45] Around the time depicted in these maps, "from 1944 to 1946, incidents of arson, bombings, and vandalism occurred at forty-six residences newly occupied by black residents" as whites defended the areas around Chicago's "Black Belt."[46] Quasi-legal strategies of exclusion like restrictive covenants were particularly common in these areas as well.[47] In the all-white districts of the North Side, there was certainly little evident grassroots pressure for racial liberalism. Representatives of these white areas did not have any black constituents to respond to, and the best evidence (along with conventional wisdom and later experience) indicates that their white ethnic constituents were not particularly liberal on matters of race (though, again, support for most civil rights measures was probably higher among whites in these areas than among southern whites). Publicly, strident and violent racist antipathy was continually on display over the decades as African Americans moved into new neighborhoods or made other gains in the face of a resistant white majority.[48] Throughout the decades of the Great Migrations, white urbanites (and suburbanites) employed a veritable arsenal of exclusionary tactics: legal and illegal, personal and impersonal, violent and merely discriminatory.[49]

Of course, the most dramatic actions can be misleading indicators of how most people feel about issues, so we should dig deeper than the headlines. Contemporary opinion polls are the best way to rigorously assess the attitudes of nonsouthern white city-dwellers during this time, though the analysis of their findings is difficult because early polls did not always use appropriate sampling techniques. The best opinion data available from this time are mixed when it comes to race, showing a strengthening relationship between economic and racial liberalism in the electorate but little overwhelming support among city residents for liberalism on the most contentious racial issues of the day.[50] Outside the South, majorities were for antilynching legislation, but nonsouthern white Democrats were split on fair employment and other issues more directly relevant to northern communities; furthermore, these groups expressed frankly racist views about social contact with African Americans.[51] Schickler (2012) does find stronger support for civil rights among Democratic voters than among Republicans and perceives that this relationship grew during this period. Big-city whites were almost certainly *more* racially liberal than noncity residents, and as the time period went on, racial liberalism became associated with other dimensions of liberalism. However, this *relationship* does not mean that *levels* of support for civil rights were overwhelming in these cities, and it is unclear how important civil rights were to these individuals.

For instance, in the 1952 American National Elections Study, a representative sample of Americans was asked about whether Congress should pass a national fair employment law (as opposed to passage of a state law, some other action outside official channels, or government noninterference). Fair employment was the salient civil rights issue most relevant to life outside the Jim Crow South, and civil rights groups and liberal activists had been pushing for a permanent national law for at least a decade, with little concrete success to show for it. In the survey, only 29 percent of white, nonsouthern Democratic identifiers from union households (a group that was roughly one in eighteen respondents in the survey) supported federal fair employment legislation, and about 32 percent of that same group preferred that the government do nothing at all.[52] If union activism was the spur behind civil rights liberalism, this is perhaps the group of whites *most* likely to have supported fair employment practice (FEP), but they were nevertheless divided. Closer analysis shows that while Democratic identification and central-city residence were positively *associated* with support for federal FEP protections, on average, white nonsouthern urbanites (who made up about one in five respondents) were probably about 27 percent likely to support national FEP in that survey. This percentage is roughly consistent with (though a bit lower than) Schickler's analyses of polling from a decade earlier, when white nonsouthern FDR supporters were split on federal fair employment (41 percent in favor, 39 percent opposed) while white nonsouthern Republicans were strongly opposed to such a measure (27 percent in favor, 59 percent opposed).[53]

Generally, white opinion across specific issues within the broad topic of race and civil rights varied considerably. Policies that would alleviate the most obvious injustices of Jim Crow repression, such as antilynching laws and the abolition of poll taxes, enjoyed greater support across the North. Laws against subtler and more personal forms of discrimination that were also prevalent in the North, such as employment and housing discrimination, were supported by fewer northern whites.

In short, ethnic white urbanites were not particularly devoted to racial egalitarianism, a fact that local politicians were aware of and which the GOP would later exploit.[54] Even among local liberal activists within the local Democratic parties at the time, racial justice does not seem to have been a priority according to contemporaneous accounts, as they preferred to focus on less divisive issues and attack the machine's organizational structure.[55]

In such an opinion context, the political geography of the urban bloc reveals a puzzle of representation. While the Chicago pattern of racial segregation shown earlier was particularly stark, concentrating a very large black electorate into relatively few districts, the same general pattern was present at the congressional district level in most large cities in the 1940s. In New York City, only seven out of twenty-eight districts were more than 5 percent black, and none became majority black until the mid-1940s; the other three-quarters of districts were less than 5 percent black. In Philadelphia and Detroit, the pattern was less stark, but black populations were still concentrated. Four out of six Philadelphia districts had populations that were between 10 and 25 percent black, though in none were blacks a majority; the other two were less than 5 percent black. Detroit's distribution was more even, with three districts (out of six total) with populations that were more than 5 percent black and none that were more than 25 percent black, but the other three were less than 5 percent black. This pattern was recurrent in the large cities that made up the liberal heart of the New Deal coalition: even in cities with a relatively large citywide black population, racial residential segregation meant that most city congressional districts were essentially all-white.

5.1.2 Urbanicity, City Delegations, and Cohesive Racial Liberalism

Given the different patterns of likely constituent pressure from urban districts, we might expect some division in the way cities were represented in national politics. To the contrary, however, these cities, so obviously divided on race at home, represented themselves as cohesively liberal on race in national politics and were *more* liberal than other nonsouthern Democrats.[56] Perhaps most importantly, the racial conservatism evident in local city politics was not present in city representation in national politics.

Rather than (or alongside) a straightforward electoral connection, the bases of which are elusive, the distinctive character of cities and their political institutions may have been an important factor in encouraging the growth of racial liberalism during this era, fostering unity in political representation despite division in social relations. One dimension of urbanicity, heterogeneity, has in the American experience entailed a constantly refreshed diversity of groups from all over the country and world within the dense political space of our cities. Our cities have never been free from racial or ethnic strife, but the simple fact of diversity within a common political community has meant that cities have been forced to find ways to deal with racial heterogeneity, and in that task IHIs have been important vehicles for mediating and mitigating group conflict. During the half century before and including the New Deal, traditional party organizations served the important political functions of incorporating new groups into a citywide order and creating a political space, flawed though it may have been, in which conflicts might be resolved.[57]

By the time of the Long New Deal, in almost all cities the Democrats had become the party in which such culturally pluralist political group incorporation took place (if it took place at all), while the Republicans had reinforced their ties to supporters of Anglo-Saxon homogeneity and dominant-culture assimilation, a division showcased in showdowns over temperance and immigration in the 1920s.[58] Leaders and members of these local Democratic parties, who were often members of the same white ethnic groups frequently noted for their racial *conservatism*, played key roles in promoting racial liberalism in national debate and were resolute in their behavioral support for national civil rights during this era. In doing so, they seemed to be not so much promoting the perspective of their districts (where support for racial liberalism was rather weak and viewed as not worth the sacrifices it would entail) but rather attending to a citywide position (in which African Americans were often indispensable coalitional partners in citywide politics and norms of pluralism helped sustain social order in a dense, heterogeneous local society). By again disaggregating the Democratic Party—first by section, as the revisionists of the racial realignment have done, and then again by place character—we can gain insights into not only the dynamics of this political change, but also the effects of cities and their institutions on national politics.

5.2 "Urbanizing" Race

Urban Democrats' support for racial liberalism, and their apparent strategy to pursue it in national politics, resembled the "urbanizing" strategy theorized by Burns et al. (2009) in their study of how city delegations operate in supralocal politics. Knowing they would be opposed by their copartisans from the South on an issue that divided the party, they needed to persuade their disinterested sectional allies—those with few if any nonwhite constituents and without strong prior positions on racial issues—that race was an urban issue, that there was an urban position on this issue, and that nonurban representatives should defer to that urban perspective. This section illustrates how they pursued that strategy.

The support for racial liberalism among urban representatives, especially urban Democrats, during this era is evident on multiple fronts, including roll call behavior and discourse. First, the expressed justifications for racial liberalism—for supporting issues of central importance to African Americans, but not to other key elements of the Democratic coalition—took on an urban tone during this era. This rhetorical shift promoted a distinctive vision of American society and politics that was pluralist and multicultural and was rooted in the urban experience, characterized as it was by high levels of group heterogeneity. As such, racial liberalism was framed as an issue relevant for many groups (not just African Americans) who were themselves largely city-dwellers. State action and regulation of behavior, again an urban disposition, was proposed as an important spur to progress in this area. Second, urban representatives, especially those from places with the kinds of party organizations that had commonly served as the vehicle for groups' political incorporation, were more likely to vote in support of these racially liberal policies throughout the Long New Deal. Even though race was controversial at home, these places—especially those with strong organizational IHIs—represented themselves as unified, making racial liberalism an urban position in national politics.

5.2.1 Urban Conceptions of Racial Liberalism, 1920–1963

Over the course of the urban interlude, race became associated with cities in political discourse. That racial issues were not particularly urban before the 1920s is understandable, because until this historical era African Americans and indigenous Americans (the typical referent groups for national racial questions) lived mainly on the rural periphery. With the arrival of millions of African Americans to cities outside the South in the first half of the twentieth century, however, binary racial conflict took on local importance in these places as well, even though African Americans still constituted a relatively small proportion of the local population in most cities. As black Americans became a significant presence in urban places, the arguments made in defense of racial liberalism took on an urban character that was not present in earlier discussions of the issue. To illustrate the new urban character of this civil rights rhetoric, we can turn to the record of congressional hearings on race during the urban interlude, with attention to statements made by members of Congress—especially those from cities. These hearings can provide richer context for the ideas underlying more discrete actions such as roll call votes. Because participation in hearings requires extra effort (not only to appear, but also typically to prepare a statement), the record can reveal members' priorities; appearances do away with the ambiguity sustained by silence. Furthermore, the give-and-take structure of these meetings can reveal attitudes by congresspersons toward others who hold views with which they agree or disagree and can afford opportunities for candid, spontaneous exchange. Unlike floor debate, hearings also include participants from civil society (representatives of various groups or private citizens), and this adds further information about allies, rivals, and foes.

There were many hearings on explicitly racial issues and policy proposals during this era, an indication that they were salient enough to draw national attention. At first, civil rights hearings focused on antilynching legislation; later they expanded to the poll tax, fair employment, and broader civil rights legislation as well. With increasing force and in increasing numbers, urban representatives articulated support for the racially liberal position on proposed legislation rooted in urban concerns and urban experience.

At a glance, we can see that participation in these hearings during the New Deal was often the domain of Southern Democrats and city Democrats. Participation in the early hearings seems to have been particularly meaningful (i.e., not routine), as relatively few representatives chose to participate in them.[59] In these hearings, members expressed their support for or opposition to civil rights legislation in prepared or spontaneous statements. Members appearing before the committee typically made their position quite explicit; those not interested in taking a position could choose not to appear. Table 5.1 tallies hearing testimonies for or against civil rights legislation by members of the House over the period 1926–1949, well before the alleged evolution identified by Carmines and Stimson (1989).[60] We can see that the conservative position was almost invariably taken by southerners (almost all of whom were Democrats). The liberal position on these issues was disproportionately taken by urban representatives (who constituted a majority

Table 5.1 **Number of MCs Testifying in Hearings About Race, 1926–1949**

	FEP	Polltax	Lynching	Overall
Conservative position	6	13	12	31
Southern Dem	5	13	12	30
Liberal position	19	11	24	54
City	16	8	15	39
City Dem	15	6	12	33

Note: Cell entries are counts of representatives from groups at left testifying at House hearings on the civil rights subjects at top of the columns. Indented subcategories are subsets of nonindented categories. Highlighted cells call attention to tripartite split on civil rights. Substance of testimonies typically split along sectional lines. Nearly all noncongressional testimonies were made by urbanites.

Source: CSR data; Proquest Congressional.

in each category of speaker, despite the fact that city representatives were never a majority of chamber members overall, even outside the South) and city Democrats during this era. This is consistent with the observation by Feinstein and Schickler (2008) that the conversation on race seems to have been between two factions within the Democratic Party, with the Republicans more apt to maintain silence. Although this table includes only members of the House and how they represented their districts, the hearings also included many more witnesses who were not members of Congress. Especially on fair employment, the issue that most directly affected places outside the South and that had the longest list of total witnesses, the overwhelming majority of witnesses were liberal urbanites.

A closer reading reveals that even these numbers mask the extent to which urban New Dealers assertively engaged with southerners on these issues. The modern thread of national race and civil rights legislation began with antilynching legislation that was repeatedly proposed but never passed into law over the ensuing decades. The original bill was introduced by Leonidas Dyer, a St. Louis Republican whose district included many African Americans and was the site of an antiblack riot in 1919. In the 1920s, several members of Congress appeared before hearings in support of antilynching legislation. Most were from cities outside the South, and they were mostly Republicans: their ranks included Dyer, from St. Louis; Frederick Dallinger and Peter Tague, from Boston/Cambridge; and Merrill Moores, from Indianapolis. Most support for antilynching legislation at this point was articulated in terms of a (belated) universalist understanding of African Americans' worthiness of full citizenship rights. In a typical argument in favor of the antilynching law, Sen. William B. McKinley (R-IL)[61] argued in 1926 that

> although he [the African American] has been in possession of [political and civil rights] for relatively so short a time he has shown himself to be worthy of them. As a free man he has always been amenable to reason and persuasion; as a citizen he has uniformly been a patriot, and as a voter he has consistently aligned himself with the intelligence, the efficiency, the administrative ability, and the forces that stand for order and property. What can be said of any other group of our fellow citizens?[62]

This argument, which appealed to abstract principles of citizenship in defense of African American rights and full protection by the state, did not make reference to a lived environment or social context in which rights or citizenship might be exercised. Similarly, at a 1921 hearing about the Ku Klux Klan, Bostonian Peter Tague argued (after a trip through the South) that "the rights of citizens throughout that section of the country . . . had been violated, and they had not been protected in those rights which are allowed and given to them under the Constitution of the United States."[63] Again, this was an abstract argument about rights, citizenship, and the Constitution, made without reference to place. These arguments are liberal in the classic sense—affirming an (imaginary and abstract) individual's worthiness and competence for democratic citizenship, a basis upon which he could merit full inclusion in the polity. In this light, the "African American" McKinley envisages is worthy of support not because of his membership in a marginalized group but because he has overcome previous obstacles to competently participate (almost invariably as a Republican) in politics. This individual competence merits protection from the violent violation of civil rights that lynching entailed.

Another set of arguments was developing in parallel, however, that included several elements rooted in the experiences of city life and likely would have resonated more powerfully with audiences in cities. These arguments focused on group-based pluralism, government as a regulator of social forces, and the relationship between social peace and economic production. By making arguments that employed distinctly urban frames, these speakers staked out racial liberalism as *the* urban position on an urban issue. City representatives were pursuing an urbanizing strategy for convincing copartisans to come along with them on a potentially divisive issue.[64] The racial division present in the streets at home was referenced but never reproduced in the way cities represented themselves in Congress, and a set of urban justifications for racial liberalism were made.

First, this perspective entailed recognition of the plurality of groups and the importance of group identity as opposed to a strictly liberal individualism of rights. Rather than propose the ungrouped worthiness of an imaginary individual, this argument involved the use of analogies to other groups that, despite not being the central target of the legislation under consideration, had experiences in common with African Americans. This approach adopted a *group* basis for political incorporation. Thus, attacks on lynching and the southern racial order referenced groups—particularly religious minorities such as Jews and Catholics—who were generally less exposed to (though not perfectly safe from) lynching, but who might find common cause with African Americans because they faced similar prejudices from the white Anglo-Saxon Protestant mainstream. Thus, as early as 1921, Rep. Thomas Ryan (R-New York City, later a Democrat) argued against the Klan that "any organization that is anti-Catholic, anti-Negro, anti-Jew, and against the foreign element in this country, which comprises over 25 per cent of the voting strength of the country, is really a menace to the community."[65] Ryan included Catholics and Jews in the same list as African Americans, even though at this point these groups shared little besides their relatively marginal social status within American society. While Tague's argument might have resonated with a conservative because of its reverence for the Constitution and individual rights, Ryan's would have been more controversial outside of the polyglot cities. After all, for those who were (successfully) seeking to restrict immigration from Southern and Eastern Europe (and elsewhere) at exactly this time, a group that included the Klan itself, the transformation of American demography afoot through immigration was itself a primary "menace to the community." Ryan was thus articulating a particular vision of community, ostensibly one that included distinct groups. It is to this kind of argument that Plotke (1996) refers in arguing that the mobilization of previously disadvantaged groups into politics was a core tenet of the emerging progressive liberalism. Significantly, all of these groups were more numerous, and just beginning to flex political power, in cities.

Reference to other "different" groups would later become a theme of the urban argument for fair employment in the 1940s. Arguing for FEP legislation, Adolph Sabath (D-Chicago) noted that "while the Jews, colored, and foreign born are the most numerous, minority groups in wide variety exist in sections, states and cities throughout the country. All are the victims of unjustified local prejudice, oftentimes of actual discrimination."[66] Thomas Scanlon (D-Pittsburgh), a career union official, had earlier introduced FEP legislation by declaring that "bad as it is, discrimination against a man because he belongs to a union is not nearly as evil as discrimination because a man is a Negro, a Jew, a Catholic, or because his ancestors came from another country."[67] Later in that hearing, Arthur Klein (D-Manhattan) had the following friendly exchange with

William L. Dawson (D-Chicago), who had co-authored the bill with Scanlon, which helps to clarify the real purpose of the legislation (to alleviate discrimination against African Americans) while stepping out of the way to draw in other groups as well.

KLEIN: I agree that the Negroes today are the outstanding victims of economic persecution, but you will admit ... there are other minorities as well who are also subjected to the same sort of thing.
DAWSON: I do, but I feel that when the day comes that we are broad enough to encompass the Negro within the confines of the Constitution all other minority problems will be solved.
KLEIN: I agree with you wholeheartedly. I simply wanted to point out that all other minorities would probably gain from an act such as this.[68]

A decade later, Victor Anfuso (D-Brooklyn) also emphasized pluralism (as opposed to straightforward racial justice for individual citizens) as Americanism when defending broad civil rights legislation.

Our country is comprised of people who come from all races, religious beliefs, and national origins. All of them have made important contributions toward the development of the US as a great Nation and toward shaping its destiny. . . . I do not believe in the superiority of one race or one nationality group over another. As soon as we encourage second-class citizenship, we open the door for discrimination and bigotry.[69]

Each of these city representatives, coming from a local traditional party organization and having local black allies (but very few black constituents themselves), articulated a view of racial liberalism that was multicultural, inclusive, and tied to the experiences of nonblack marginalized groups concentrated in the cities. These statements seem to have been aimed at audiences who were ambivalent about racial equality but who might have identified themselves as the object of similar discrimination. Of course, a permanent national Fair Employment Practices Committee was not instituted despite these urbanites' efforts, so in the 1960s, as omnibus civil rights bills were under consideration, Chicago represented itself in Congress in much the same way it had when Rep. Sabath and Mayor Kelly headed up the local Democrats. At a hearing held in Chicago on discrimination in employment, Mayor Daley appeared to support civil rights law under consideration, arguing that

Chicago is a melting pot city, as you know. Chicago was built by the people of many lands, of every race, creed, color, and ethnic origin. . . . Negroes are not the only segment of our population that has benefited from the city's [fair employment] policy, for nationality and religious groups benefit when the employer adopts fair employment practices.[70]

Roman Pucinski (D-Chicago) added that in Chicago, "8 out of 10 workers suffer some form of discrimination.... [T]herefore this committee is trying to look at this problem along a four-front approach, rather than just the one area of racial discrimination, tragic and lamentable as racial discrimination may be."[71] In this articulation of the issue, potentially controversial legislation benefiting African Americans was again presented as beneficial to religious and national-origin minorities as well. Daley further expanded the class of potential beneficiaries of such a policy by including workers over forty. This pluralist, urban understanding of difference, in which almost everyone is importantly different, when combined with the cities' historical experiences in dealing with new groups, made racial liberalism the city position on these issues and softened the potential downside of taking what might have been riskier positions if articulated as strictly black–white racial issues. Even the fundamental impulse to embrace groups, rather than individuals, as the building blocks of political life is a hallmark of urban pluralism rooted in places where we see ourselves and encounter anonymous others as members of groups. For politicos like these, the ability to identify and negotiate with the leaders of such groups—whether labor groups, ethnic or racial groups, business leaders, activists, or others—as power brokers was a basic tool for governing the metropolis that was, again, different from the personalism and solitary individualism more likely in less densely settled places.

In addition to highlighting their cities' experiences with diversity, urban representatives cited previous successful experiences with federal intervention as evidence that such intervention was desirable and could be effective in areas where local officials were unable or unwilling to act. Prohibition aside, support for social regulation was a distinctly urban position; ruralites and southerners were wary of such adventures, but analogies to other areas of regulatory intervention and the power of legislation to shape behavior and change minds were often made by city representatives, ostensibly because they found them persuasive. Dyer argued in 1920 that

> Congress has exercised its rights in enacting legislation with reference to child labor in the various states [and] intoxicating liquors. If congress has felt its duty to do these things, why should it not also assume jurisdiction and enact laws to protect the lives of citizens of the United States against lynch law and mob violence? Are the right of property, or what a citizen shall drink, or the ages and conditions under which children shall work, any more important to the Nation than life itself?[72]

For Dyer, federal passage and enforcement of lynching laws was appropriate because corrupt or inept local and state officials were either unable or unwilling to enact such laws, just as federal intervention to regulate other social practices had been important in the past.[73] Similar arguments were made by later urbanites on the efficacy of government action to reduce prejudice itself.

By 1934, Leonidas Dyer was gone from Congress and antilynching legislation had become the provenance of congressional Democrats: that year, Sens. Robert Wagner (D-NY) and Edward Costigan (D-CO) introduced legislation similar to Dyer's earlier bill. These progressive urbanites held that taking an official national position against lynching to help establish new norms on race was just as important as taking specific actions against the practice. Wagner argued that

> legislation alone cannot quench the fires of intolerance and hate. But the speedy passage of the federal antilynching bill will rally and sustain all the forces of enlightenment in the US and nowhere more than in the areas where right-thinking people have been hoping and pleading for reinforcement in their courageous battle against the scourge of lynching in their midst.[74]

A similar argument was later extended from lynching to employment discrimination. In 1949, Sabath argued that the conservative argument that education could serve as a substitute for FEP laws was "fallacious":

> Prejudice of course cannot be eliminated by legislative act or edict, but discrimination—the outward social manifestation of prejudice—can be corrected by legislation and perhaps only by legislation.... Although a constantly increasing percentage of the adult population is the product of [education], both prejudice and discrimination are very much in evidence. FEP legislation does work.[75]

Five years later, the young Peter Rodino (D-Newark) made a similar case for omnibus civil rights legislation:

> It has been argued that civil rights cannot be legislated, that their preservation and extension are essentially a moral problem that only education, not law, can cope with. This can hardly satisfy the many thousands, even millions, of Americans who live in the shadows of second-class citizenship.... [F]or example, it is certainly true that many people find their rights sharply curtailed by laws. There is surely no reason why we cannot do something by law to combat these evils. Secondly, civil rights are often infringed upon or jeopardized by antisocial actions which can

be curbed by law. Finally, the enactment of civil-rights legislation can engender the idea and atmosphere of freedom in which the rights of men can grow and prosper.[76]

His colleague from across the Hudson, Victor Anfuso (D-Brooklyn), added an argument focusing on the power of legislation to change social norms and ratify social practice:

> Law is an effective instrument for changing social conditions and law acts as a powerful factor in preventing discrimination. It fosters the conviction that discrimination is wrong by fixing standards which are respected by the majority of the people. Because people as a rule are law-abiding, their behavior tends to create customs which are in harmony with the law.[77]

Again, city representatives, coming from traditional party organizations and representing cities (but not districts) with sizable black populations, voiced faith in the power of state interventions to alter norms about racial discrimination. These arguments also explicitly added to the earlier emphasis on universal rights, but the link to changing norms in society was equally important.

Most southerners, in arguing against civil rights legislation, said they were wary of such legislation generally and preferred to rely on education as the key to the gradual elimination of prejudice and racial conflict. But this was not an exclusively southern position; it was also a rural one. Clare Hoffman (R-MI), representing a largely rural district in the west of that state, was a rare Republican participant in civil rights conversations and less than sanguine about the prospects for legislation as a social transformer—not only because he doubted the power of the legislation, but because he opposed its goals as well.

> In truth and in fact, while the avowed purpose of the [FEP] bill is to end discrimination, give equality of opportunity in employment, another objective is to bring about, though Federal legislation, a social intermingling (and some advocate intermarriage) among the races.... Everyone should be treated fairly and equally and have equal opportunity. But I do not believe in agitators or self-appointed apostles of righteousness . . . taking over the proposition. I have seen so little discrimination in my community that it is difficult for me to realize that some of the statements made by advocates of this sort of legislation are factual.[78]

Hoffman went on to call for stricter oversight of segregation. These positions by a rural northerner are particularly striking because of the reversal they entail—Hoffman himself had introduced FEP legislation during the war, but now in 1955 he declared that such a law could not be effective. Discussions of this issue reveal important differences (or at least professed differences; we should always be wary of inferring actual attitudes from politicians' speech acts) between the city Democrats' and the conservative coalition's attitudes toward the possibility of social change through legislation. The urban approach to bringing about such change was active and involved, while opponents of the legislation, whether cynically or not, argued that lawmaking was an inappropriate tool for changing social attitudes.[79]

Finally, the urban perspective on the relationship between racial liberalism (or at least nondiscrimination) and the basic good of public order was different from that voiced by southerners and ruralists. Hoffman was worried that "indiscriminate bathing" on Michigan beaches by black visitors from Chicago would lead to trouble[80] and used this as an argument against broader reforms of race relations such as FEP laws. Southerners emphasized the importance of segregation for maintaining social peace, as Charles Bennett (D-FL) argued in 1949:

> They are not perfect, but I personally feel that race relationships are better in the South than they are anywhere else in the country. I believe that the people get along better there. You will find a lesser percentage of race riots, less hard feeling, and less misunderstanding in the section of the country where I live than anywhere else in the country.... I think colored people have pride of race. It does not mean that they look down on the white people; it means that they prefer to be among themselves as general rule. They like to associate among themselves.[81]

Such arguments, even when we see through their claims of African Americans' satisfaction with the existing state of affairs, reveal the speaker's basic belief that public order was actually *more* compatible with the prevailing arrangements of racial domination—that is, that the southern status quo, as it had been developed since Reconstruction, could be maintained. He may have been correct about the rural South—it is not clear that its subnational authoritarian regime would have ever given much ground on civil or political rights without outside intervention. But in the urban spaces of the North, with their continual upheaval and large, dense populations, this was not an argument to be taken seriously. There, deep discontent was understood as tantamount to a time bomb, and when riots did occur, they were far more costly than would have been the case in a less intensely developed area. Accordingly, regulation of intergroup conflict and public endorsement of nondiscrimination were seen as necessary for *keeping* social peace, not for upending it. Representatives from cities' own local FEP boards (which had been implemented on a permanent basis by several cities and states, including Chicago and New York state, by 1949) advocated on behalf of a national law, adding to the previous arguments the idea that FEP was an important measure to keep the "powder keg" of race from exploding in their cities. James Sheldon, chair of the New York Metropolitan Council on Fair Employment Practice, argued that

> if people were permitted to discriminate against others because of their skin color or religion in a city like New York, the whole structure of life would soon break down.... In an urban area like that for which I speak here, it is more than desirable, it is basically necessary that government should provide safeguards so that all Americans may enjoy equal opportunities regardless of their race or their religious beliefs.[82]

Clarence Anderson, the executive secretary of the Metropolitan Detroit FEP Council, was even more direct:

> We [in Detroit] get the jitters. We feel that we are sitting on a powder keg. Our race riot of last summer is still fresh in our memories.... Whatever measure of racial harmony we enjoy today in our industrial racial relationships in Detroit is largely attributable to the work of the present FEPC... [which has been] more important than mere civil society and union cooperation.[83]

These two may have overstated the importance of their own organizations, but their perspective was clear, and clearly urban: state regulations against discrimination, and institutions to oversee their enforcement, help resolve intergroup conflicts. And the previously noted statements by elected representatives of these cities arguing for the desirability of such legislation fits with this perspective. Conflict resolution is much more important in urban areas, where violence is more costly, can involve more people, and cannot be quelled in the same way a rural uprising can be. Coming up with ways to avert such violence and actively manage group relations in the context of an inexorably changing status quo, rather than trying to reinforce a more static one, was the urban approach to race.

Finally, one very important "non-observation" should be noted. During this time, urban racial conservatism was absent from the national legislature. The record of hearings on civil rights during this era reveals no city representative from outside the South opposing the liberal position on the issue in question. This is notable because of the division and racial conservatism that was present in these cities' streets all along and later became quite central to their politics. For although they lacked the elaborate legal architecture of white supremacy constructed in the southern states, and despite their sometimes self-righteous pride at not being *as racist* as southerners, many urban residents in the North and their political leaders fiercely resisted residential, social, and school integration (and still do, though less blatantly), and many more harbored serious doubts about the prospect of close proximity to African Americans (and still do). But this division or ambivalence over the important changes afoot in national race relations is not reflected in the record of *how these places represented themselves in the nation*. These representatives, and their local allies, articulated a position that sought to manage racial conflict by likening African Americans, at least rhetorically, to other newcomer groups and to establish and sustain institutions that could manage potentially explosive social conflict. They also redefined racial issues in ways that were directly relevant to urban life, focusing on the plurality of groups, on the usefulness of new rules for changing social norms, and on the grave danger of not finding ways to manage inevitable change (as opposed to trying to resist social change or relying strictly on privately or individually evolving attitudes to deal with changes as they arose). This liberalism became the core of the city position on racial issues during this era and would be reflected in city representatives' voting on controversial issues, as well as in the later "blue" alignment that would be dominated by city representatives.

5.3 Urbanicity and Roll Call Voting

For the rest of the chapter, I will demonstrate that these ideas and patterns are also observable in the behavioral record of congressional voting. If city representatives were urbanizing the liberal position on race, we would expect them to be cohesive on these issues, despite the obvious conflicts they experienced at home. We found that to be true in the discursive forum of the congressional hearing. Turning to blunter forms of behavior, analysis of roll call voting shows that urban division was similarly absent and city representatives were cohesively liberal on these issues during this period. Beginning in the broadest terms, we can see that city representatives tended to be more liberal than their non-urban counterparts on racial or sectional issues during this era. One common measure of congressional ideology is the DW-NOMINATE scores developed by Poole and Rosenthal (1997). These scores incorporate information from all congressional roll calls and estimate legislators' overall ideology. For much of American history, congressional ideology and conflict seem to have revolved around a single partisan "dimension," which Poole and Rosenthal describe as having to do with "the role of government in the economy," or statism.[84] At some times, however, the NOMINATE score reveals a second dimension of conflict on which legislators seem to organize some of their voting behavior. This dimension, they argue, has to do with race and region, and it operates most frequently when race is a salient issue in national politics. The Long New Deal was just such a moment: the recurrent split within the Democratic Party between southerners and the rest of the party fed a second dimension in congressional conflict. Looking closely at the relationship between these NOMINATE scores and urbanicity, however, reveals that this second dimension is not "just" a matter of race and region: urban representatives were on average much more liberal on this dimension than non-urban representatives.

Figure 5.3 illustrates this reality by plotting the DW-NOMINATE second dimension scores for different groups over time. The scores range from –1 ("Liberal") to 1 ("Conservative"), so the higher the line on the graph, the more conservative the group. We can see immediately that urban representatives are more liberal on this second dimension, even when we exclude the southerners whose regional preferences do so much to drive it (see Figure 5.3b). Especially early in the period, when the second dimension was most powerful (the late 1930s to late 1970s), urban representatives were on average far more liberal than their non-urban counterparts. Later in the period, it seems that the dimension captures more purely regional differences, but nonsouthern urbanites were also more liberal on this dimension than the other groups from 1930 to 1960. Again, Democrats always constituted a substantial majority of this group after 1931.

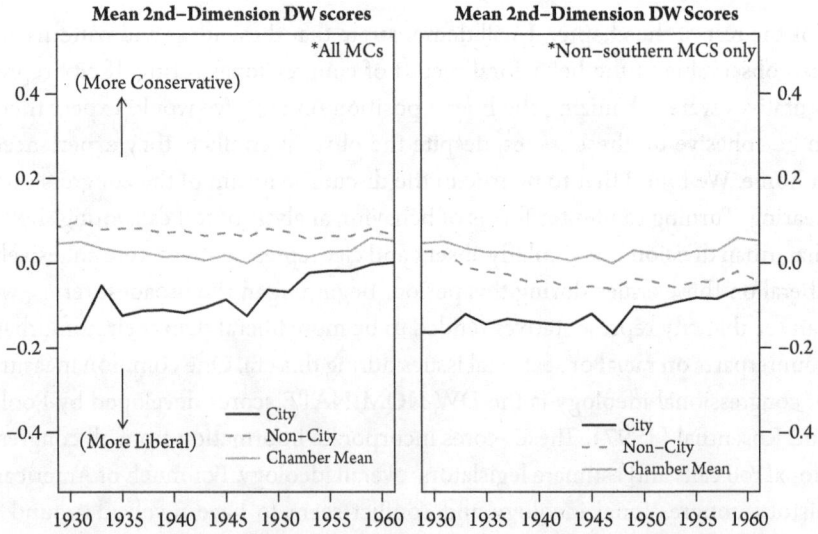

Figure 5.3 **Group Means on DW-NOMINATE Second-Dimension Scores, 1930–1960.** At left, means for city- vs. noncity representatives. At right, all nonsouthern. This dimension is typically interpreted as racial or regional conflict in voting. Higher values mean more racially conservative/southern, lower values more racially liberal/nonsouthern.

Table 5.2 **Linear Regression of DW-NOMINATE Second Dimension Scores, 1930–1970**

Variable (#categories)	Coefficient	(Robust Standard Error)
Urbanicity (7)	−0.053*	(0.029)
Democrat (2)	.353*	(0.018)
South (2)	.524*	(0.021)
Intercept	−.166*	(0.013)

Note: Cell entries are estimates from regression of DW-Nominate second dimension scores on covariates at left. City representatives were on average more "liberal" than suburban or rural representatives on issues of race and region. *$p < .01$; N = 6,313; $R^2 = .70$.

Sources: CSR data; AIP; Voteview.

This gap persists, or even grows, when we account for partisan affiliation and other factors. Table 5.2 shows results of a linear regression of NOMINATE second dimension scores (on measures of district urbanicity, congressional party, and region) over the Long New Deal. While being a southerner or a Democrat is associated with an increase in the measure (i.e., a tendency to align with the conservative side of this dimension), representing an urban constituency makes one far more likely to support the liberal position. On average, urban representatives are about .15 to the left of a suburban representative from the same section and party (about a third of a standard deviation) and .25 to the left of rural representatives on this measure. Urbanicity is thus associated with broad-brush racial liberalism on the second dimension, even when we account for party and section.

Because these NOMINATE scores incorporate information from votes on all topics and procedural matters, however, they are noisy, and substantive judgments about the content of the ideological dimensions they describe are inductive and *a posteriori*. To focus more precisely on the relationship between urbanicity and support for civil rights liberalism in roll call voting, we can examine particular roll call votes from this era that were substantively about civil rights and analyze representatives' behavior on these votes.[85]

Using the substantive issue codes from the American Institutions Project, we can identify roll call votes about civil rights in the House of Representatives over time. From 1899 to 1961, there were fifty-eight votes about African American civil rights in the House (see Table 5.3). Most of these votes related to proposed legislation about lynching, fair employment, and general civil rights. Using data from these votes, we can investigate how different groups of legislators voted and what factors were associated with support for racial liberalism and add these elements to the evolving picture of how race came to rise on the agenda during this era.

Table 5.3 **House Roll Calls About Civil Rights for African Americans by Congress, 1899–1963**

Year*	No. of Votes	Subject(s)
1899	3	Frederick Douglass Statue
1921	22	Antilynching
1937	4	Antilynching
1939	2	Antilynching
1945	3	School Integration
1949	11	Fair Employment
1957	6	Civil Rights Commission
1959	7	Civil Rights Commission
1961	1	Civil Rights Commission
Total	58	

Note: *Year Congress began.

Source: AIP data.

One straightforward way to determine the "liberal" position on these civil rights bills is to estimate the position of the African American community, which was the driving force behind them and was understood to be their chief beneficiary.[86] To this end, we can identify what position was taken by the majority of African American members of Congress on the votes themselves as a shorthand for the "black" or "pro–civil rights" position on the particular roll call. For the Long New Deal the black position on civil rights is quite easily identified, because there were so few black members of Congress.[87] Throughout the era under investigation, whenever there was more than one black member voting on the same roll call, they agreed, indicating that there was at least a modicum of consensus on the black position. From 1899 to 1927, there were no black members of Congress. There were also few moments when civil rights reached the formal agenda during this time, but for votes that predate Oscar De Priest's appointment in 1927, I identify the position taken by a majority of Southern Democrats on these civil rights issues (specifically, opposition to a memorial for Frederick Douglass and opposition to federal intervention in lynching cases) and assume that the *opposite* of this southern position is the African American position. Having identified the position taken by black members as the "liberal" position, we can evaluate the tendencies of other groups of representatives to agree with that position.

Figure 5.4 describes the average support for racial liberalism by different blocs of legislators, and from these two graphs we can see changes over time. In each figure, the proportion of a group of legislators agreeing with the black members' position is plotted over time. Each point represents the proportion of that group taking the liberal position on a given roll call (with any African American members dropped from the analysis because their votes were used to determine the dependent variable). The lines represent the smoothed average for the bloc. First, we can see that by the mid-1940s, nonsouthern Democrats were indeed more likely than Republicans to support racial liberalism, though each of these groups was far more likely to vote liberally than Southern Democrats. The sets of votes from before 1937 are included in this analysis to show where the parties were coming from: in 1899 and 1920, Republicans were nearly unanimous in their support for the black position on civil rights votes (these particular votes were to approve a memorial for Frederick Douglass in 1899 and a series of votes on the Dyer antilynching bill in 1921). As late as the 1930s, they still tended to support this liberal position on average, but the average Republican support for civil rights declined slowly beginning in the 1940s and then rapidly beginning in the late 1950s. There were some instances in which Republicans were quite divided on these issues, and some in which they were even more united against the black position than southerners were; the latter include a series of roll calls on amendments to the complex omnibus civil rights bills of the late 1950s, which included strong measures to enforce employment nondiscrimination, among other steps.

For their part, Southern Democrats were consistent in their opposition to racial liberalism, though their solidity ebbed over time. By the 1960s almost one in five Southern Democrats was taking the liberal position on civil rights (though it is difficult to say exactly why from these data alone), though most remained vehement opponents of racial equality, seeming to prioritize that position over potential compromises with their northern allies. The tripartite account does reveal a large change among nonsouthern Democrats, however. Inconsistent but fairly evenly split in their voting on the 1921 Dyer bill, this group had become solidly in favor of the black position on civil rights votes by the time antilynching legislation returned to the agenda in 1937, and its members were more consistent than Republicans—basically unanimous—in their support for racial liberalism from the 1940s on. Even more telling, however, is who was leading this group and seemingly powering the progressive racial agenda of the time. In the right-hand graph of Figure 5.4, the top line shows that nonsouthern urban Democrats were essentially unanimous in their support of racial liberalism throughout the Long New Deal. While nonsouthern non-urban Democrats were almost as supportive as their urban copartisans by the end of the period, even though they were certainly split on the issue early on, their support was always more tenuous and at

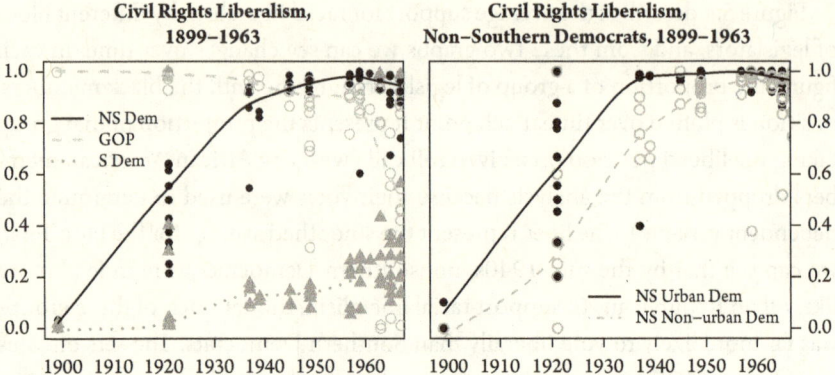

Figure 5.4 **Proportions of Legislators Supporting Liberal Position on House Civil Rights Votes, 1899–1963.** Left: While Republicans and Democrats were opposed on civil rights votes in earlier years, nonsouthern Democrats had changed their position by the late 1930s and were more likely than Republicans to support civil rights by the mid-1940s. Right: Among nonsouthern Democrats, city representatives were more likely to support civil rights earlier and were more supportive of them later. Source: Voteview; AIP, CSR.

certain moments subject to deep division, as we can see from the two outlier points after 1960. Throughout the 1940s and 1950s, however, it certainly appears that compared to all other groups, urban Democrats were the most consistently in agreement with the African American position on these racial issues. This is consistent with a previous finding that support for racial liberalism in Congress was associated with urbanicity, though the disaggregation of the nonsouthern Democrats is clearer here.[88]

This relatively strong support for racial liberalism among nonsouthern Democrats stems not only from urban representatives, but more specifically from urban representatives who came from places with strong institutions of horizontal integration, especially those local organizations that most fully incorporated African Americans. Chicago and New York (and later, Philadelphia, Detroit, and Los Angeles) were the homes of local Democratic parties that included their growing African American voting blocs fully enough to send black representatives to Congress. Even before the New Deal, local politicians in these cities had courted black voters, who were often quite cohesive as a group and at times may have been pivotal in city- and statewide elections (Keiser 1997). In Chicago especially, courting and working through black political leaders were key parts of electoral strategy for both Republicans and Democrats through the mid-1940s.[89] Participation in local governing coalitions meant that African Americans had a seat at the table, albeit typically not an equal position. Nonetheless, because African Americans were in their coalition, even representatives from all-white constituencies had black local partners and were indirectly reliant on black votes for the maintenance of their organization's power, which in turn had effects on their own access to resources and position.

Nevertheless, several questions remain. Was urbanicity generally associated with racial liberalism? Were representatives from strong local parties more supportive of racial liberalism, as city delegation theory would predict (given a city interest in social peace)? Were representatives with city delegation partners who were black more likely to support racial liberalism? In Table 5.4, I use a multivariate regression framework to approach answers about the effects of cities and city delegations while simultaneously accounting for the common alternative explanations—that support for racial liberalism is explained by section, party, and constituency composition. If local institutions and organizations nudge representatives to support racial liberalism, then these factors—in this case, traditional party organizations and black partners in a city delegation—should be positively correlated with taking the liberal position on racial issues, even beyond the other explanatory factors. The analysis includes the following data and variables (with results listed in Table 5.4; alternative specifications of this model, including alternative measures of district class and racial composition, do not substantively affect the significance or direction of the key coefficients of interest).

The unit of analysis is a vote by a representative on a civil rights roll call. The dependent variable is the same as that used in Figure 5.4: a binary indicator of agreement with the "African American" position on civil rights votes. Again, the African American congresspersons whose votes were used to construct the dependent variable are excluded from the analysis, so this analysis estimates the relationships between *white* representatives' support for racially liberal positions and several key explanatory variables.

We are particularly interested in the variables measuring political factors associated with the representative's home jurisdiction. First, the ordinal CSR score is included. We would expect high urbanicity scores to be associated with racial liberalism in representation, in keeping with the evidence shown previously in this chapter and the implications of urbanicity for elite preferences outlined in Chapter 2. In addition to this district-level measure of urbanicity, two measures of city delegation characteristics are included. The first is an indicator for whether a white representative is part of a city delegation with a black local copartisan. For instance, a white Democrat from Chicago would have a 1 on this measure after the election of Arthur Mitchell in 1935, while a Republican from Chicago would have a 1 from 1928 to 1935, when Oscar De Priest represented the First District. Representatives not from cities, from cities without a black delegation member, or from locally partisan cities with a black member in the *other* party but not their own receive scores of 0 on this measure. If having a black member fosters racially liberal voting in the rest of a city delegation, the coefficient on this measure should be positive.

The city delegation measure of organizational IHIs included is a measure of local party strength, a key institutional variable associated with cohesion in city delegations. As in Chapter 4, this measure of organizational IHI strength is adapted from David Mayhew's (1986) "traditional party organization" scores, which measure the strength of local party organizations in controlling nominations at midcentury.[90] Because Democrats had coalition partners (African Americans and racially liberal unions such as the CIO) pushing for civil rights and were themselves much more closely associated with traditional party organizations by this time in almost all parts of the country, I also hypothesize that the relationship between traditional party organizations will be stronger among Democrats than Republicans, so I include a multiplicative interaction of partisanship and local party organization (TPO*Dem).[91] The relationship between local organization and racial liberalism should be stronger for Democrats than for Republicans if this hypothesis is correct.

In addition to these variables associated with urbanicity and local political organization, I include alternative explanations that we know to be importantly associated with positions ultimately taken on race during this era. Section is a key variable, so I include an indicator for whether a representative is from outside the South.[92] The emerging literature indicates that nonsouthern Democrats were taking the lead on these issues, so I include an indicator for nonsouthern Democrat as well.

Finally, support for civil rights may be prompted by large African American populations in a member's district—the electoral connection hypothesis. Though the population patterns described earlier meant that there were relatively few districts in which African Americans comprised a large share of the voting population (and some of those districts are excluded from this analysis because they had black representatives), this is still an important potential explanation for racial liberalism, so I include an estimate of the share of the voting-eligible population that was black. Available data from Adler (2012) provide good measures of the proportion of the population identified as black at the congressional district level for all districts that encompass at least one entire county going back to the 78th Congress.[93] For city districts that are subdivisions of a county, however, a finer-grained measure is necessary because of residential segregation, so I develop measures for these districts using the GIS technique outlined earlier in this chapter and in Appendix B. Data for this variable at low levels of aggregation are limited to decennial census years in cities with census tracts (which existed only in select counties in these years—although fortunately these counties include most cities with more than one congressional district), so I estimate each of these districts' black population based on the data from the closest decennial census.[94] For districts in the South, where the vast majority of African Americans could not vote during this time, the percent of the electorate that was black is zeroed out; voting records and the exclusionary all-white primary instituted in many of these states during this time make it clear that southern representatives were not responsive to this group, even the few who could vote. I expect the coefficient on percent black to be positive if pressure from black constituents prompts responsiveness and racial liberalism. Conversely, a negative coefficient may indicate some evidence of racial threat, as in Key (1949).

All of the votes on civil rights during the Long New Deal (1933–1963) are pooled in this analysis. Separately, analyses excluding antilynching legislation votes, which did not really have important implications in northern cities, yield substantively similar results to those presented in the following, revealing that the patterns of voting were common to all subsets of the civil rights agenda in Congress. The model presented here is estimated using fixed effects for each roll call to account for general fluctuations in support for the liberal position on particular votes, and robust standard errors are grouped by legislator because some individuals voted on many of these roll calls, making for some particularly nonindependent observations.

Table 5.4 **Logit Regression of Factors Associated with Agreement with African American Position on Civil Rights**

Variable	Coefficient	(Std. Err.)	Marginal Effects
CSR (7)	0.116**	(0.031)	.012
Black Partner (2)	1.368	(0.875)	–
TPO (4)	0.128	(0.101)	–
Dem (1)	–1.554**	(0.402)	–.15
TPO*Dem	0.466**	(0.144)	(See Figure 5.5)
Non-South Dem. (2)	2.149**	(0.370)	.19
Non-South (2)	1.692**	(0.356)	.25
%Margin of Victory	–1.694**	(0.268)	–.17
&Far Left	–0.365	(3.582)	–
%BlackVEP	4.210	(2.572)	–
%Blue collar	2.959	(2.385)	–

Note: Marginal effects estimated as expected change in likelihood of agreement given one-category shift in the dependent variable, with other variables held constant at appropriate values (*p < .05, **p < .01; N = 7,620; Psuedo-R^2 = .49; estimated with an intercept, vote-level fixed effects, and robust standard errors clustered by legislator). ***City representatives and those with a black partner in their city delegation were more likely to support civil rights. Local black partnership was a perfect predictor of support; those observations are dropped from this model. Exclusion of the variable does not reduce the magnitude or significance of the other predictors of interest. *p < .05 **p < .01, N = 10, 313, R^2 = .47.

Sources: CSR; AIP; Voteview.

These results support the key hypotheses about urbanicity and city delegations. First, urbanicity was positively and significantly associated with racial liberalism during the Long New Deal (1933–1963). A representative from a city district was on average about 4 percent more likely to support the racially liberal position than an otherwise similar representative from a suburban district, and 10 percent more likely than a representative from a rural district to do so. Representatives with a local black partner were almost uniformly in support of the racially liberal position; having a black partner is not quite statistically significant in the model, but this may be because there is so little variation in this measure—over the course of the long New Deal, only three votes were cast by city congressmen with a local black partner against civil rights—two in 1937 and one in 1963. In between, this connection appears to reach the level of sufficiency for support of civil rights liberalism. Again, for much of the urban interlude this indicator would only apply to Democrats from Chicago and New York, two central players in the Democratic urban order. But these two pillars of the Democratic Party, riven by race at home, were *completely cohesive* on civil rights in the House between 1937 and 1963.

The relationship between local party organization and racial liberalism is more complicated to interpret, but the expectations outlined earlier are supported by the data. Figure 5.5 illustrates how likely Democrats and Republicans from different local partisan contexts were to differ in their support for racially liberal positions on these roll calls. Moving across the horizontal axis, local party strength increases from left to right. The lines on the graph represent the predicted probability of support for the racially liberal position for members of each party.[95] Among Republicans, the relationship between local party organization and racial liberalism is weak and statistically insignificant. Among Democrats, however, the relationship is quite strong: a Democrat from a strong local party (i.e., TPO = 4 on this scale) was approximately 26 percent more likely to support the racially liberal position than a Democrat from a place without local parties (i.e., TPO = 0), even when we account for other factors.[96] This result supports the theory that the relationship between local party organization and racial liberalism was stronger among Democrats, both because of the party's more enduring relationship with that organizational form and because their African American coalitional partners were the principal proponents for racial liberalism during this era.[97] These racial issues were the heart of the intraparty conflict, and they define the second dimension of political conflict in the House.[98] But cities themselves, despite the potential for division at home posed by the rapid influx of African Americans into metropolitan areas, were very likely to support the racially liberal position

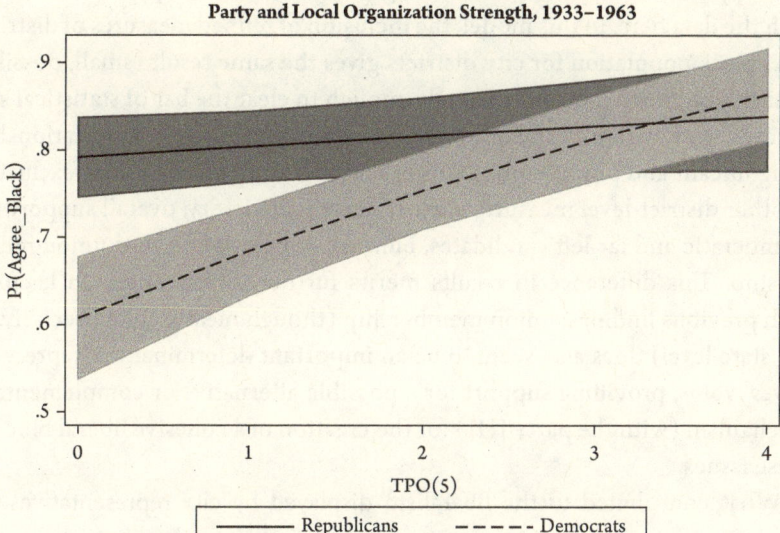

Figure 5.5 **Predicted Probability of Support for Pro-Civil Rights Position by Party and Local Party Strength (Interaction Interpretation), 1933–1963.** Each line and 95 percent confidence interval represents the estimated probability of supporting civil rights liberalism for members of each national party at different levels of traditional party organization strength. Estimated in Stata holding other variables constant at appropriate values.

on these issues, even as they threatened to destroy the basis of their national alliance with the South. This was especially true of those Democrats coming from cities with strong partisan institutions. These cities' politicians, even if they did not represent African Americans themselves, were politically linked at home and in the nation to those who did, and as the products of strong parties they may have been more sensitive to the demands of their broader subnational party organization—those who needed black votes at a citywide or state level.

Other findings of this regression analysis may be worth noting here. First, in keeping with what we would expect, there are large sectional effects that support the model of a tripartite system on these issues—a nonsoutherner was about 25 percent, and a nonsouthern *Democrat* an additional 19 percent, more likely to support civil rights liberalism. Second, the data are consistent with findings by Schickler, Pearson, and Feinstein (2010) and Schickler (2016) of little direct electoral connection between local black population and support for racial liberalism during this time, and this appears consistent with the data here. In this model, the inclusion of refined measures of district-level black population for city districts gives the same result (small, possibly positive, but not estimated precisely enough to clear the bar of statistical significance), though in some other models not presented here the relationship is significant and positive; its status is sensitive to the inclusion or exclusion of other district-level measures such as margin of victory, overall support for Democratic and far-left candidates, blue-collar population, and union membership. This difference in results merits further investigation. In keeping with previous findings, union membership (though measured imprecisely, at the state level) does also seem to be an important determinant of representatives' votes, providing support for a possible alternative or complementary mechanism (with the party IHI) for the creation of a cohesive liberal bloc on these issues.

What contributed to the liberalism displayed by city representatives on the divisive issue of race? A companion analysis of city delegations shows the relationship between party structure and cohesion on civil rights issues in Congress, as city representatives tended to agree with their local colleagues. As in Figure 4.4 showed for all roll call votes, Figure 5.6 shows the cohesion on civil rights votes for the four largest city delegations from the 1930s to the 1960s. The cities with strong IHIs were more cohesive on civil rights. Los Angeles, with its weak local partisan institutions, was the first to show signs of fracture as race claimed the national spotlight in the early 1960s, and when all cities showed division later on, Los Angeles was the most deeply divided of the four on civil rights.[99]

As in Chapter 4 this delegation cohesion is a function not merely of national party affiliation, but also of local party form. When we analyze the probability of a pair of legislators agreeing on a civil rights roll call, based on their affinity on a range of likely factors, local party organizational forms are independently associated with agreement. Table 5.5, which presents the results of such an analysis, demonstrates this reality. Breaking delegation cohesion into its basic parts, these analyses take legislative dyads (i.e., two members casting votes on a particular piece of legislation) as the unit of analysis, as in the analyses in the last part of Chapter 4. The dependent variable in each probit analysis is agreement (or not) by the two representatives on a given civil rights vote. Agreement (in support or opposition) means that these representatives are "cohesive" on the vote in question. The independent variables at the left of the table are measures of similarity between the congresspersons who make up the dyad: similarity in national party affiliation (SameParty), urbanicity (CSRsim), district percent African American (Blacksim), and district percent blue-collar (Classsim).[100] Each of these variables is expected to be positively associated

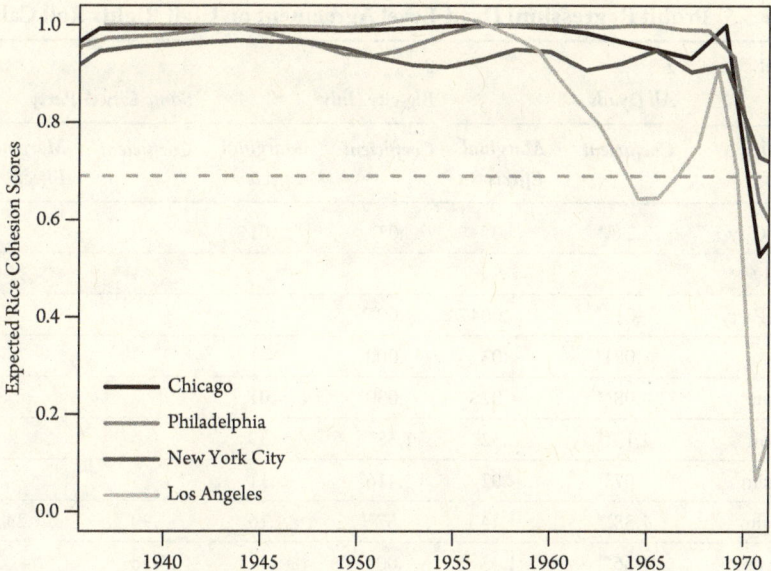

Figure 5.6 **Average City Delegation Cohesion on Civil Rights Votes.** Similar to Figure 4.4, these lines represent the average annual cohesion score for each delegation on civil rights roll call votes, smoothed over time for better visibility. Dotted line indicates congressional party average on all roll calls.

with agreement on roll calls (if significant), because similarity on a given dimension should ostensibly contribute to similarity in representation. The three models examine the observable implications of city delegation theory (as in Chapter 4) for different sets of vote-dyads. Model 1 includes all votes on civil rights roll calls during the Long New Deal (78th through 87th Congresses). Model 2 includes only big-city dyads, that is, only those dyads whose members are both from cities, restricting the sample and providing a tougher test for the jurisdictional and organizational hypotheses. Model 3 cuts the sample down again, this time to dyads from the same city and same party, to help compare strong-party cities to weak-party cities. The key explanatory variables of interest are all highlighted in gray in Table 5.5: SameCity for Models 1 and 2, and hiTPO for Model 3.[101]

In Table 5.5 we see that the same basic patterns that were present in vote agreement generally in Chapter 4's analysis of dyadic voting are repeated in this subset of votes. In Models 1 and 2, the coefficient for SameCity is statistically significant in the hypothesized direction. Even when accounting for other important factors, representatives from the same city were more (about 7 percent more, in the model that includes all representatives) likely to agree on civil rights votes. Among same-city, same-party dyads, organizational form mattered, too: being from a strong-party city meant that such a pair was about 11 percent

Table 5.5 **Probit Regression: Dyad-Level Agreement on Civil Rights Roll Calls**

Model	1 All Dyads		2 Big-city Only		3 Same City & Party	
Variable	Coefficient	Marginal Effects	Coefficient	Marginal Effects	Coefficient	Marginal Effects
SameCity	.21**	.07	.03*	.015		
hiTPO					.44**	.11
SameParty	.015*	.0047	.09**	.02		
State	.081**	.03	.000	–		
Region	–.08**	–.025	–.039**	–.01		
Section	1.13**	.32	1.38**	.39		
CSRsim	.07**	.02	.416*	.11		
Racesim	1.38**	.44	.57**	.16	.99**	.24
Classsim	4.56**	1.45	.004	–	5.36	–
%FarLeftsim	–.24*	–.07	.16	.05	–.15	–
Psuedo-R^2	.19		.24		.16	
N	2,288,558		177,655		6,430	

Note: Cell entries are regression estimates similar to analysis in Tables 4.5 and 4.6, but restricted to civil rights roll calls. Key explanatory variables of interest highlighted in gray. Marginal effects for statistically significant coefficients estimated as expected change in likelihood of dyad agreement given one-category shift in the dependent variable, with other variables held constant at appropriate values (*$p < .10$, **$p < .05$). Significance estimated with nonparametric shuffling procedure described in Rader, Pinto, and Erikson (2014); significance at $p < .10$ means that observed test statistic (Z-score) lies outside 5–95 percentile range of test statistics for that coefficient in simulated models. Estimates with an intercept, Congress-, and vote-level fixed effects not listed here.

more likely to agree.[102] Dyads from strong cities, bound together by membership in strong local party organizations in a way that members from weak-party cities were not, were more likely to agree on this crucial area of policy than even same-party dyads from weak-party cities, where politics were not as integrated across the face of the city and different territorially based constituencies within the city were more independent of each other. As we know from the previous analysis of civil rights liberalism, these urbanites (again, particularly those from strong-party cities) were very likely to take the liberal position on these issues. Urban cohesion on this issue of civil rights, in the face of solid opposition from the South, laid the groundwork for the issue evolution of the 1960s and the subsequent racial realignment.

5.4 After the Landmark Legislation

All of the foregoing data in this chapter have been from the Long New Deal period, when national Democratic leaders successfully held their fragile and fractious coalition of liberals and reactionaries together and Republican leaders were gradually becoming less attached to their party's ancient commitments as the Party of Lincoln. They show that the tripartite division on race was apparent long before the 1960s, and that urbanites were particularly staunch supporters of civil rights measures (even though they were rarely successful). In 1964 and 1965, dramatic events accelerated this process. In 1964, Lyndon Johnson signed the Civil Rights Act, which was passed by a bipartisan (though urban Democrat–*led*) coalition over a bipartisan (though Southern Democrat–*led*) filibuster. Republicans then nominated a participant in that filibuster—Barry Goldwater—for president. Goldwater blended the Republican business establishment's ostensibly principled opposition to statism with the states' rights rhetoric common to southern opposition to national civil rights. He won several southern states for the GOP for the first time since Reconstruction but lost the rest of the nation in a landslide that also delivered historic majorities to the Democrats in Congress. In 1965, the Voting Rights Act was passed, outlawing the regime of racial political exclusion that had defined southern politics since the nineteenth century. Other civil rights acts followed in other spheres.

As shown by Schickler (2016) and others, these events were not the sharp disjuncture posited by Carmines and Stimson (1989); rather, they were consistent with the positions taken with increasing frequency by the elements of America's tripartite politics since the 1930s. The key difference of the 1960s was how salient the issues were and the clarity with which the parties' leaderships now staked out their stances on them. Because of the actual changes these landmark laws entailed, the realities of civil rights laws were also more apparent to many nonsouthern white Democrats who were not particularly attached to civil rights. Latent conservatism (perhaps prompted and informed by Goldwater's rhetoric, but consistent with pre-1964 polling as well) was unleashed. This conservatism was signaled in many ways over time, including white flight from the cities, voting for Republicans, opposition to school and housing integration, and increasing levels of racial resentment based on stereotypes or perceived group competition.

Chicago was immediately sensitive to this change in white valence on civil rights. When Mike Royko made the pithy observation about the lack of difference between southern whites and Chicago whites reproduced in this chapter's epigraph, it was an exaggeration—there were lots of differences between

Chicagoans and southerners. Most urban northerners had no particular affection for southerners, and there were almost certainly more white racial liberals in northern cities like Chicago than there were in southern cities. But racial liberalism was never the only attitude of Chicagoans, and there was a kind of tidal shift in how racial attitudes were expressed over the short time between 1964 and 1966.

For an illustration of this shift, and of how city representatives might have perceived it, we can examine the correspondence of Rep. Barratt O'Hara (D-Chicago), who represented a largely white district on the South Side of Chicago situated at the front lines of neighborhood-level racial conflict in the 1960s. O'Hara himself was a throwback of sorts. A veteran of the Spanish-American War who had served as Illinois lieutenant governor before rejoining the army in World War I, he was elected to Congress in the late 1940s and stayed there through the tumult of the 1960s. He was staunchly liberal on race—he never voted against the racially liberal position on a civil rights roll call, and his archival correspondence shows that he spent a lot of time responding to letters from constituents on civil rights issues. The bulk of them (at least those that have survived and were catalogued in his papers) were written during the 1960s, in response to contemporary events. Reading his constituents' views sheds light on big-city white Democrats' views and the reasoning behind them, revealing that they were divided on race—some urged him to support civil rights, but most argued against racial liberalism, especially after 1965.

The contrast between local and distant issues is evident in the valence of constituent letters he received in the 1960s. For instance, in 1962, as Congress considered bills to eliminate Jim Crow–era poll taxes and literacy tests meant to disfranchise black voters, O'Hara's constituents wrote to him in strong support of these measures. Few organizations wrote in opposition to the bills, and many in favor of them. Individuals were more mixed, but early in the decade the preponderance supported civil rights. Their justifications for this support somewhat reflected the urbanizing language of their representatives but especially drew on moral claims. One constituent wrote that southern white supremacy made him "aware of the weakness of our case in attempting to set ourselves up as a moral example to the world."[103] Another urged the same support, hoping that "we all be judged by our actions, not our skin colors."[104] Another likened southern repression to Nazi-era German authoritarianism: "I feel strongly that we as a people are demoralized by allowing this condition to go unchecked—I used to think the Germans were 'rotten' for allowing Nazi brutality to flourish by not doing anything about it—Are we rotting?"[105]

These concerns were probably not a high priority, however, even for liberal white Chicagoans. For one thing, the archives do not include many letters from individuals in favor of civil rights, especially not before the 1960s. One of

O'Hara's constituents wrote a brief letter requesting information on "cooking and food preparation" and then included a postscript urging him to "support all bills to further integration and end discrimination... so that we will truly have an integrated society with equality for all."[106] Even Chicagoans in support of civil rights legislation made nonmoral arguments in its favor, mirroring the "danger of disorder" position. In keeping with this theme, one woman wrote to O'Hara reminding him that he might convince Rep. Everett Dirksen to cooperate on civil rights by reminding him that "the Negroes are well-organized now and there's no telling what's going to happen if the [bill] doesn't go through."[107] Another made the complicated argument that "in this shrinking world (and exploding populations!) where most of the humans are 'colored' we cannot afford to slight or 'condescend' to certain 'colored' peoples."[108] Others saw the same social phenomena but drew the opposite conclusions, opposing "the civil marches which breed hatred and violence" and arguing that "civil rights bill[s] cause more violence, riots, and hardship on people than good."[109]

Many Chicagoans became personally fearful of being caught up in racial tensions. In 1963, one resident who had been part of "the only white family on [the] block" for years said that "life was peaceful until the Alabama situation," but that harassment by neighborhood teens had made her very frightened of late.[110] Another wrote to O'Hara with a long list of grievances, including Mayor Daley's leadership of the NAACP parade, cited several street crimes carried out by African Americans, and quoted J. Edgar Hoover's claim that the "rights of society in many jurisdictions today are being trampled [by] habitual criminals"; this letter writer also included a pamphlet alleging that Martin Luther King had attended "communist training school."[111] The fiercest opposition expressed by constituents was to the very local and personal subject of residential integration. During debate over the Civil Rights Act of 1966, which included a housing nondiscrimination policy, hundreds of Chicagoans wrote to O'Hara to oppose fair housing legislation, often under the mistaken impression that they would either be evicted from their homes or be forced to sell their homes to African Americans. As was common in other cities, an expanded view of homeowners' rights found its way into this protestation.[112] One Chicagoan flatly stated that "I consider my home 'My Castle'—therefore I am completely opposed to the 'Open Occupancy,' which violates my constitutional rights as a property owner."[113] Another argued that the nondiscrimination policy was a "direct violation of Article 3 and 4 of our Bill of Rights."[114] Still another wanted to "keep on enjoying the privilege of choosing my own tenants and buyers," also mistakenly citing the Third Amendment as a likely legal basis for such an appeal.[115] The jealous protection of potential real estate prerogatives was framed as a dear right; prohibitions of nondiscrimination were seen as existential threats. "Do you recall that our precious country was founded *because* of *oppression*?" one letter argued.

"Is this housing bill not very similar? It takes away one of the freedoms that our ancestors strove and fought for.... It is most unfair to force a law-abiding citizen into a position where he has no 'freedom of choice.'"[116] Wrote another: "*Freedom from force* and *freedom of choice* are two important freedoms which should not be sacrificed for the sake of the minority. 'The greatest good for the greatest number' is a better basis for progress in non-discrimination in the long-run." More nakedly racist views infused with race panic also frequently run through these letters. One of O'Hara's constituents argued that "as long as Washington advises negro parents that they may send their children to school for the express purpose of getting 'their civil rights,'... we will have nothing but jungles in every large [city] across the nation."[117] Another complained that "South Shore used to be a very wonderful part of Chicago. It is now a jungle. We are not safe on the street day or night. 85 percent of the crimes are committed by negroes."[118] Another wrote that civil rights legislation had led to "end results [of] people burning and looting.... Murder and crime is accepted as a freedom and a way of life. Our leadership has brewed a society of crack-pots and sex-maniacs."[119] One constituent from Alphabet City on Chicago's East Side declared, "It is high time that someone call a spade, a spade. These marchers are disrupting the peace and tranquility of a neighborhood.... THE PENDULUM IS SWINGING TOO FAR."[120]

Perhaps the most common conception of the relationship between rights and community among Chicagoans opposing the bill was a sort of separatist multicultural vision, leading to the appeal that the city should not be a melting pot, but rather a place to preserve the apparently distinct cultures of different ethnic and racial groups, nearby but separate. They frequently argued that fair housing would be a major setback for race relations. This local vision of street-level multicultural separatism was revealed in sentiments such as "as my representative it is your duty to preserve the churches, schools, and community that I hoped my children would grow and live in."[121] One South Sider concluded a long letter: "All people have the right to 'integrate' but they must find others who are willing to 'integrate' before they can exercise the right. All persons have equal rights. The ability to exercise those rights should not be handed to any group on a silver platter at the expense of others."[122] Another endorsed Malcolm X in a roundabout way to take this idea to its extreme:

> There must be a number of prominent negroes who could take the lead in a "Back to Africa" movement. Because of your experience in African affairs, you could undoubtedly find ways in which this idea could be coordinated with the aspirations and needs of the new African nations.... [A] number of prominent anthropologists do not believe that people of different racial backgrounds naturally tend to

integrate.... [That] is why there is so much opposition among whites and negroes alike to peaceful integration.[123]

Finally, many letter writers stated plainly that they would be watching this issue closely and would base their support for (or opposition to) O'Hara in the next election on this issue alone. As one put it, "The passage of [the open occupancy bill] will have disastrous results. I'll be anxious to see how you will cast your vote. When you needed us to get re-elected we were behind you. Now it's your turn to back us."[124] This is the kind of clear signal that would catch the eye of most congressmen and be tallied directly in the constituent pressure column as they made calculations on roll call votes.

Nonetheless, despite all this rancor and division, Chicago's Democrats (like most urban Democrats throughout the country) remained steadfast in their support of civil rights legislation, even through the tumultuous 1960s. Overall, it appears that in this district at least, those with intense feelings on race were averse to neighborhood integration while supportive of other, more remote civil rights. The letter writers typically (though not always) argued in polite terms, without invective or obvious racism. Their conceptions of whose rights should be strictly protected were racially informed but were not couched explicitly in terms of biological or immutable social hierarchy. Rather, they employed the language of citizen rights to argue for a (racial) cultural separatism based on what they saw as divergent values held by different communities. They had also begun to employ (though probably had not mastered persuasively, from a legal standpoint) the language of property rights for both homeowners and communities in favor of preservation of the status quo. What even those in favor of civil rights did not argue much was that either they or African Americans were individuals in the classic sense—detached from their affinity groups or capable of being understood in the absence of community ties. This lacuna may be related to the policy substance that prompted their letters: housing, which is place-based and the foundation of community (as opposed to voting or the workplace). Just as urban representatives had earlier spoken in favor of civil rights using the group-based language of the city, now everyday Chicagoans were using the same framework to argue against integration.

The positions of South Side Chicagoans are not necessarily representative of all white urbanites' views, of course. On the East Coast, far fewer complaints were made about civil rights to a similarly senior and outspoken congressman in a roughly analogous (in terms of working-class composition and demographic transition away from overwhelmingly white) New York district, John Rooney (D-Brooklyn).[125] Many organizations wrote to O'Hara and Rooney to voice support for antidiscrimination measures, especially the liberal activist trio of labor unions, churches, and civil rights groups. And a key finding in Schickler

(2016)'s exhaustive treatment of the transformation of liberalism during this era is that urbanites tended to be *more* liberal on civil rights (and other dimensions of liberalism) than other nonsoutherners. But even the self-professed liberal white urbanites may not have supported *all* civil rights measures, and it is also naïve to believe they were strongly in support of racial equality at any time during this era—there is very little evidence of that, and plenty to the contrary. Instead, white urban opinion should be considered as deeply divided on race, with differences across issues, time, and space.

Despite all this rancor and division, most urban Democrats remained steadfast in their support of civil rights legislation, even through the tumultuous 1960s. The key insight of these examinations is the unity of city representatives on race during the Long New Deal, despite the division of their constituents. How did the role of local institutions play out in roll call voting as civil rights issues rose in controversy after 1964? To answer this question, we can turn to votes in the period immediately *after* national party leaders clarified the parties' positions on civil rights: 1967–1971. When we analyze these votes in the same way that we analyzed the votes during the Long New Deal in Table 5.4, all of the key relationships

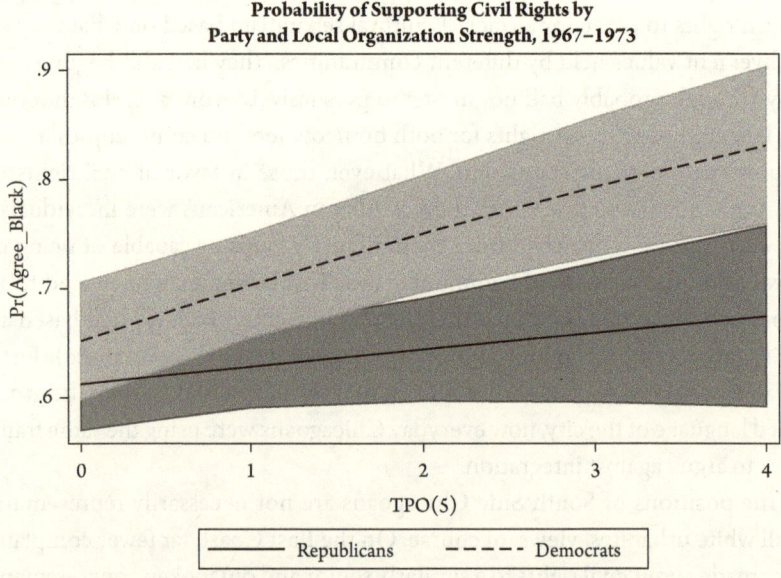

Figure 5.7 **Predicted Probability of Support for Racially Liberal Position by Party and Local Party Strength (Interaction Interpretation), 1967–1971.** As in Figure 5.5, the lines and 95 percent confidence intervals depict the probability of support for the racially liberal position on civil rights votes based on a multivariate logit regression analysis with the same covariates as in Table 5.4. Estimated in Stata holding other covariates constant at appropriate values.

remain substantially the same: urbanicity and region are still important predictors of support for the liberal position. Significantly, the role of local institutions remains intact as well. Figure 5.7 shows the relationship between local party strength and support for civil rights liberalism in this time period, similar to Figure 5.5

Compared to the early period, there is one key difference: while there is still little relationship between local party strength and Republican behavior, the *overall predicted probability* of GOP support has dropped from 80 percent to 60 percent. Among Democrats, the relationship between local party strength and support for civil rights measures is slightly weaker than it was before (and less precisely estimated because there were fewer votes in this window) but barely changed—the strong-party Democrats were still over 80 percent likely to support the civil rights agenda, even in the face of significant constituent backlash. After the backlash, white Democrats from strong local parties were still about 10 percent more likely to support civil rights than their counterparts from weak-party cities. The local party glue may have been even more important when civil rights was controversial than when it was a distant sectional issue for the rank and file. This analysis is consistent with Figure 5.6, which illustrates that all city delegations were split by the 1960s, but the split was much deeper in the cities with weaker parties. The bridges built by these local institutions were not washed away by the urban crisis, but rushing waters of racial backlash did have large effects on American politics more broadly.

5.5 Discussion

The results of the roll call analyses in this chapter are consistent with the growing consensus that nonsouthern Democrats were the strongest advocates for racial liberalism throughout the urban interlude, but it adds an important twist by focusing on urbanicity and local institutions. This group assumed this position despite the obvious threat that it posed to their national alliance with southerners; the delicate balancing act they had to pull off between local factors and national coalition made this liberalism somewhat harder to see. Local factors, however, were also important even when we account for section and party, as demonstrated in the previous multivariate regression analysis. First, having a local black copartisan made representatives almost completely reliable on race; such representatives, like Barratt O'Hara, supported the liberal position consistently, even though their constituents (who were likely all white) held much more conflicted views on such matters.

By the same token, Democrats from places with strong local party organizations were more likely to support racial liberalism, ostensibly responding to pressures from within their party—whether from across town or from up the chain of command. Democrats whose districts were more atomistic, or less connected to other constituencies through organizational IHIs, were less likely to support the racially liberal position. These findings provide support for the central theoretical claim of city delegation theory, that local institutional factors color national representation, fostering political cohesion despite social fracture. In the case of race, city representatives were cohesively liberal, beyond what might be predicted based on district characteristics or simple national partisan affiliation. The historical and normative implications of this insight are more complicated than the city representatives' behavior, however. They can help us understand the relationship between urbanicity and the "dimensions" of liberalism, as well as our understanding of how race operates in and shapes the American political system.

Previous accounts of the dissolving Democratic Party have spotted a break between southern and nonsouthern Democrats on race that expanded over the course of the Long New Deal. Those analyses show that the range of issues upon which the two wings split grew over time, as southerners interpreted a growing swath of substantive policy areas as potentially threatening to their racial agenda and repeatedly sided with Republicans to form a conservative coalition on a number of priorities for nonsouthern Democrats.[126] At the same time, nonsouthern Democrats began to provide stronger support for civil rights policies relative to their local Republican rivals. At the state level, Democrats outside the South began to position themselves as more supportive of civil rights than their intrastate Republican rivals.[127] In Congress, nonsouthern Democrats, especially those from cities, became the most likely and consistent advocates of civil rights by the mid-1940s, while Republicans adopted an ambiguous posture or worked to weaken civil rights provisions when they did arise on the agenda.[128]

These observations, which help explain the positions taken by the two major parties on race in the mid-1960s, force an important reevaluation of what is driving politics and partisan change. Carmines and Stimson (1989) argue that national party elites have a great deal of discretion in adopting new positions when engaged in forging coalitions and recasting new conflicts in national politics in the search for political success. But the new revision, stated most persuasively in Schickler (2016), focuses not on the highest level of political leadership—presidential nominees, congressional leadership, and the narrowest cohort of their advisors who formulate a party message that is broadcast out to the electorate—but rather on the mezzo-level of state and locally rooted politicians and their civil society allies that come to create a conversation within a party that filters up and out. For instance, Schickler, Pearson, and Feinstein (2010), looking more closely at nonsouthern Democrats, argue for a causal role for coalitional partners that structured or constrained the choices available to elites by the 1960s—they credit progressive labor unions and African Americans in this respect, but many other groups within the New Deal coalition outside the South were no doubt important as well. The real action in this account is not among national elites associated with presidential campaigns but at the party's middle level: activists and civil society groups closely associated with the party who articulated a program and mobilized the mass base. This is similar to the perspective adopted by Schlozman (2015) and others, who argue that deep down, parties are congeries of ideologically motivated movements or interest groups; antiracist activists and leftist labor unions fit this narrative quite well and were important mezzo-level players in the development of New Deal liberalism. From this perspective, the "ultimate break-up of the New Deal coalition was built into the structure of the alignment that emerged during Roosevelt's administration" and was not contingent on reactions to events in the early 1960s.[129]

This important claim—that the key building blocks of the Democratic Party outside the South were strong proponents of (national) racial egalitarian policies during this critical era, and that this commitment ultimately undermined the broader Democratic coalition—fits a broader narrative in which southern pathology is marginalized over time and nonsouthern racial egalitarianism is somehow naturally ascendant. Schickler, Pearson, and Feinstein (2010) argue that, having achieved a majority within the Democratic Party, programmatic liberals could fight southern racism and embrace racial as well as economic liberalism. This view is also linked with the Manichaean understanding of race in American political history, pitting recalcitrant white supremacists against idealistic "transformative egalitarians."[130]

When we look closely at those nonsouthern elements of the Democratic coalition—many of whom were not naturally predisposed to civil rights liberalism and were often clearly racist in other contexts—we should pause and see that the story is more complicated. Were the political forces associated with the rise of twentieth-century racial liberalism all ideologically committed to transformative egalitarian racial policies? At the local level, the bedfellows were just as strange as they were in the national alliance, with racial domination a frequent and apt descriptor of political organizations' function at the city level. But *representatives* of these cities, especially those from cities with strong traditional party organizations (and in these Congresses, such representatives were generally the products of those local organizations), were consistently liberal on race in national politics, even though they themselves had essentially no black constituents, and even though the constituents and organizations with which they did have relationships had mixed records on race at best. The same institutional players seem to have been simultaneously on different "sides" on race at different levels of politics, if the idea of two "sides" maintains coherence.

This cohesive racial liberalism from representatives of constituencies and organizations that were not dedicated to racial egalitarianism—who were, in fact, often in direct, violent conflict with the black newcomers in their cities—muddies the waters in our understanding of racial orders in American politics and makes the "Tocquevillian" picture of a naturally ascendant, *ideological* antiracism less clear. There is no doubt that idealistic activist groups played a crucial role in keeping elite attention on these issues, but organizational dynamics contributed to the end result as well, keeping representatives from cities with strong IHIs (which linked the representatives of apathetic, ambivalent, or hostile whites with black cross-town members of the same organization or political community) more closely attuned to a citywide position of racial liberalism. This makes the midcentury proponents of racial liberalism seem less like a coherent "institutional order" than an "uneasy alliance," which deployed new arguments about city life to justify civil rights policy not because they were all selflessly committed to helping defend minority rights or obliterate whiteness as a governing principle, but because African Americans were closer allies than the South.[131] This is encouraging for those who would promote the rights of vulnerable minorities, for such institutional links may help provide support for such changes without reliance on saints or altruists. The programmatic antiracists played a key role in this shift and set the liberal agenda in many instances, but their power was wielded through institutions that were not themselves programmatically antiracist, merely politically pragmatic and united as city blocs.

Normatively, this support for civil rights (and the later passage of landmark legislation) embodied a paradox of representation, because the racial division in cities was not reflected in the national conversation. Usually, a disconnect between constituents and a representative is seen as a democratic failure (denial of civil and political equality is also a democratic failure, of course). In the case of civil rights, the evidence, from before, during, and after the mid-1960s, is fairly clear: a substantial plurality of white Americans, including those in the large cities of the northeast quadrant of the country, have not been particularly supportive of racial equality, and many continue to hold racist views. Even though naked "old-fashioned" racism usually draws rebuke (or defensiveness, if one is accused of it) from across the political spectrum today, opposition to policies that support group equality is not a fringe position in American politics. It is typically expressed through a variety of more sophisticated coded appeals to group identity or by paeans to a "color-blind" official philosophy.[132] These are the long-held positions of the chief justice of the Supreme Court and a major platform plank of the Republican Party today. But it's not only Republicans who take such positions. When direct democracy institutions provide citizens unmediated access to lawmaking, even relatively liberal white majorities tend to vote against racially progressive measures.[133] Time and again, all manner of democratic American institutions at many levels have demonstrated a marked taste for oppression, marginalization, and unfair treatment of minorities and vulnerable groups; this is one reason why civil rights activists have so often pursued justice through the courts, where the tyranny of majorities is filtered through the procedures of jurisprudence and a clearer recognition of the rights of individuals.[134]

There is a longstanding "dilemma" at the heart of American democracy, a psychological and communal disconnect between our supposed liberal ideals and our racially repressive reality.[135] We should never trivialize the successes of the civil rights liberals, which saw major protections for a minority group ratified by a Congress representing constituencies that were predominantly—whether latently or actively—opposed to racial equality. But how to escape that dilemma and build actual policies that live up to those ideals? The city delegations of the Long New Deal provide a clue. There, we see durable support for minority rights by white politicians. These politicians, rooted in local politics, bound to local copartisans, and motivated by the urgency of urban governance, did not let group difference undermine other imperatives and sustained alliances ("uneasy" though they may have been) by representing only the liberal side of their communities' race politics.[136]

The cohesive city position represented in national politics was developed not at the mass level, but at the mezzo-elite level, among activists, local officials, and congressional representatives. The scale of the local polity in cities means that politics there are necessarily *mediated*, and individuals take part in politics through social groups and power brokers more than they must in smaller places. As Louis Wirth put it, city-dwellers are "associated with a greater number of organized groups."[137] This observation recognizes a key fact of city life: we usually interact with and are known to each other—socially and economically, but also politically—not as whole persons but as identity-based aspects of persons, as dimensions or attributes that give cues (which are often only partially accurate) to others and shape our interests, behaviors, and preferences. When there are so many others about, and there is so much to do, we are not isolated Jeffersonian yeomen, but members of groups. The recognition of the group basis of politics was a key insight of pluralists, and it became a key tenet for progressive liberals.[138] But what does it mean to be members of groups as well as citizens of the nation?

City representatives were working this question out when they spoke about race in a new way during the urban interlude, referencing pluralist experiences more common to urbanites. In his history of modern American ideas, Menand (2001) outlines four different conceptions of the emerging idea of cultural pluralism articulated in the early twentieth century as cities grappled with diversity in close proximity, as huddled masses arrived in American cities. These visions of American society were alternatives to both melting pot assimilation and exclusionary-authoritarian Anglo-Saxonism in that they sought to "acknowledge ethnic difference as a fact of twentieth-century American life, and to recognize it as a virtue."[139] But the role of groups and their relative positions within these visions varied significantly, ranging from a justification of permanent hierarchies to the conviction that such categories were inevitably on the wane as the nation approached an evermore cosmopolitan future.[140] Each of these pluralisms had its proponents and described different aspects of social life in American cities. However urbanites conceived it, however, pluralism was necessary for understanding and managing city life and provided a commonsense language through which urbanites could acknowledge group claims and argue reasonable positions on the issue of African American civil rights.

Though the dynamic global population flows made pluralism an inescapable fact of city life, that does not mean that the practitioners of pluralist politics saw cosmopolitan transcendence of group identities as the end goal, or that they believed that all groups would contribute equally to the new Americanism. The hierarchical organizations described repeatedly by scholars of urban politics were not managed by philosophers like John Dewey; rather, they were the creations of the same kinds of men who would riot, race-bait, and show group favoritism in their governance. In Congress, they supported positions that were somewhere between seeing culture as a resource for shared communal advance and seeing it as an asset for strengthening American society as a whole. In the cities, their positions were more conservative, recognizing the legitimacy of democratic participation by marginal groups (itself a major advance for the time!) but simultaneously working from a seat of power to sustain group stratification. But in both places, they were pluralists, not liberals in the most basic sense of attending primarily to the individual as the fundamental unit of politics.

These ideas about the plurality of our society and the importance of *groups* in defining American culture and politics were a departure from important earlier ideas in American politics. Mediated, group-based politics is different than Jeffersonian yeoman liberalism because it demands less of the individual for participation in the polity. It also leaves more leeway for leadership and power brokering through representation. This leeway was critical during the formative period of support for civil rights in American politics because it allowed a space for elites to articulate support for ideas that were not exactly in line with most of their constituents' views on race and to create a formidable (and ultimately successful, though only after *decades*) political alliance to overcome conservative recalcitrance and obstruction. The recurring, stable partnership of the traditional party organization—an IHI that privileged loyalty above most other values—provided a forum in which such deals could be reliably made and monitored over repeated interactions. If, as the political philosopher Ian Shapiro contends, a primary normative promise of democracy (along with empowering majorities) is to minimize the possibility of domination, then we must think hard about the institutional arrangements that promote that end. In a pluralist society, formal, longstanding organizations of mutual political interest (but not necessarily of ideological affinity) that build bridges between groups are among such institutions.[141]

Similarly, the cohesive racial liberalism supported by these IHIs points us toward another insight about democracy in diverse societies. There is a recurrent stream of "pessimistic" scholarship finding that diversity inhibits support for statism.[142] Translated to American politics terms, conflict on the second dimension undermines liberalism on the first dimension. Though they focus on the provision of public goods and frame the challenge as one of coordinating collective action under suboptimal conditions rather than of false consciousness, these findings are in some ways the descendants of Marxian analyses that identified the nefarious ways that working-class ethnic divisions undermined (supposedly) objective class interests.[143] But in the dual liberalism of the urban political order, we find the strongest support for civil rights liberalism coming from the *most* heterogeneous communities in the nation. The two dimensions seem to reinforce each other. Here is where the mediation and coordination efforts of IHIs enter the picture: Democrats who prioritized economic interventions built and sustained cross-racial alliances to defend that first dimension. Some analysts of local politics today have identified other instances in which the challenges of diversity to effective and active governance can be mitigated with institutions like political parties and logrolls.[144] To make such arrangements and support such a government, it is not necessary to embrace the most altruistic versions of antiracism, or to deny the importance of ethnoracial group identities in public and political life. It is only necessary to be able to work across group lines, something made easier by institutions that support the formation of coalitions of common interest rather than separation and retreat from a common public life. Just as institutions can produce "racism without racists," in Eduardo Bonilla-Silva's (2003) famous formulation, so too might they foster racial justice without relying on (or waiting for) a wave of wokeness.

The most visible and dramatic events of the racial realignment took place in the mid-1960s and beyond: Goldwater's embrace of racial conservatism, the GOP's "Southern Strategy," the backlash to central-city riots, and the transition by white southerners to the GOP that was more or less complete by the 1990s. The groundwork for this change, however, was laid much earlier, when racially liberal representatives from cities articulated a new, distinctively urban position on the racial issues of the day. When Hatton Sumners tried to defend lynching as a kind of tool of traditional frontier democracy (as quoted at the beginning of this chapter), he was making an argument that would not have been accepted in a city. In cities, such spontaneous, popular violence sometimes did erupt, often in defense of the established racial order. But under conditions of urbanicity, such acts were seen from above as a significant *threat* to the community's well-being, not a defense of it. John Rooney, then a young congressman but eventually a mainstay of the Brooklyn Democratic organization, said seemingly in reply (though fifteen years later) that few would bewail the passing of the frontier days. In an America seemingly obsessed with the mythologies of the rugged frontiersman, such a statement entails at least a little controversy. In that instance, he was arguing on behalf of fair employment legislation, which (like city Democrats' efforts to pass antilynching measures) would fail before southern obstruction in Congress. Rooney argued that the interdependence of modern urban life made the institutions and practices of the frontier obsolete, and that it was time to embrace the city perspective, including the pluralism and rules it entailed. In this respect, he voiced a city position, on a city issue, in support of members of his city delegation.

Rooney and his colleagues from similar local traditional organizations that were the heart of the urban political order, and of the New Deal Democratic Party, brought a new style and idea of community to national politics. Their continued cohesion in the face of potentially divisive issues like race (which are thought to undermine support for economic liberalism) fostered the development of double liberalism. By bringing many groups into their fold, the new stock politicians of the cities' Democratic organizations built a cultural tradition and political brand of group accommodation and bargaining that was expansive enough to include African Americans as well—and their socialization to prioritize local ties and organization made their commitment to group pluralism strong enough to withstand the racist pushback within their national party (and within their cities). It was from this traditional party impulse toward identity-based appeals, logrolling, and concern for local outcomes that the urban political order now known as blue America was born.

6

The Cities on the Hill

Urban Power in Congress

> Reece: It happens that I come from a small city. Now, we do not look upon our sanitation problem there as a federal problem.
>
> Moses: If you lived here [in New York City], and you had New Jersey just across an arbitrary line, you would feel differently about it.
>
> —Exchange between Rep. Brazilla Reece (of Johnson City, Tennessee) and Robert Moses, hearing of Subcommittee on Public Works and Construction, July 28, 1944

The foregoing chapters have illustrated the microdynamics of the urban political order: conditions of city life make certain governance commitments important; city leaders began to pursue national urban policies consistent with these commitments in the 1930s; and the urban political order was held together in part by local institutions, which foster unity in representation. These developments have created an extremely heterogeneous but nonetheless growing and united bloc-of-blocs that is now the core of support for city-friendly policies in American politics. In this chapter, the macrodynamics of the urban political order in congressional representation are analyzed using original data from the CSR dataset. Over time, since the initial move by city leaders toward becoming a bloc-of-blocs in the Democratic Party in the 1930s, the urban–rural partisan divide has grown in stages to its current state. Today, it is as large and stable as it has ever been. Given that about 80 percent of Americans live in urbanized places, one might think this could be an advantage for pro-urban politics. As we shall see, however, this is not necessarily the case. As the relationship between partisanship and place character has grown, city representatives' legislative power has become more fragile, rather than stronger.

This chapter's analyses provide pieces of a descriptive "macro"-level picture of important twentieth-century political changes, describing how national politics developed after city leaders built a cross-city coalition and defined and defended dual liberalism, even at the peril of national partisan dominance.

6.1 The Urban Bloc(s) in Congress

The urban–rural partisan cleavage is now at its historical peak and is not solely a function of the increasing ethnic and racial diversity of urban areas over that time period.[1] This gap is not the most powerful predictor of vote choice—partisan gaps on ideology and race are even bigger—but place character is so important because representation is based on residence: legislators formally represent geographic constituencies, not sectors of the economy or age cohorts or other possible cross-sections of society.[2]

A representative is tied to a particular built environment and the persons who dwell within it—and to the extent that urbanites, suburbanites, and ruralites are affiliated and represented differently, this connection may intensify political conflict along a place character dimension. While individual voters' preferences and behavior are important, however, they do not contribute decisively to policymaking. Ultimately, the system of representation distills the preferences of individuals in communities into seats in legislatures; thus, this urban–rural divide may be not only represented but magnified within national political institutions. A relatively close victory (say, 55 to 45 percent of votes) is quickly exaggerated to 1–0 as votes are translated into seats in winner-take-all constituencies, so even seemingly small place-character effects can be magnified in the process of representation. The increasing identification of one place type with a particular political alliance or ideology, moreover, may feed back into the system, prompting further geographic sorting, heightening polarization, and deepening division.[3]

At the broadest level, this book focuses on the relationships between place character, local political institutions, and national representation. As the exchange between Reece and Moses that begins this chapter illustrates, many modern city problems are insoluble without action at higher levels.[4] Pollution, guns, and other governance challenges do not suddenly stop at the New Jersey state line. As an alternative or complement to at-home policies, city political forces organize at higher levels to shape the broader contexts in which their communities govern themselves. Even someone as locally powerful as Robert Moses, that master (re)builder of the modern metropolis, could see the benefit in that. As shown in Chapter 3, such attempts to create national urban policy were important from the earliest days of the New Deal.[5] Redistribution, labor law, regulatory policy, public works projects, and a host of other market interventions are perhaps better planned and paid for at the national scale, where interjurisdictional competition—between large cities and between cities and their own suburbs—is less of an undermining force. Urbanicity predisposed city elites toward what we call a liberal position on each of these interventions, and that position, when advanced, has typically been given voice in national politics by the Democratic Party since at least the New Deal.

But not everyone has agreed with the city position that Moses espoused or has seen the problems of the city as the problems of the nation. All along the way, the urban political order has faced serious challenges from representatives of other kinds of places, who resent the attention cities get, prefer less interventionist state action, and are less apt to forge coalitions for all kinds of policies.[6] Brazilla Reece's position in that hearing has been the more common one for most Americans for most of the nation's history. Still, because cities are so vital to all facets of American economic life and cultural reproduction, they have punched above their weight since getting together in the 1930s. And to sustain forward progress on many fronts in an ever-changing world, policies that help us manage our fastest-changing and most productive communities will always be important.

The focus of this chapter is to show how the growing urban–rural political cleavage has manifested itself in congressional power and how city positions have fared over the *longue durée*. While previous studies have described urban power in the House over several decades, there has been no analysis of the power of city interests over the century and a half since the consolidation of the national two-party system.[7] Although it is something of a truism that today's Democratic Party is the urban party, the parties have not always been organized along this continuum. Sectional conflicts, or long periods of fairly one-sided national politics, used to be more typical, with no nationalized place-character divide.[8] Theoretically and in practice, even if some political conflict is urban–rural, its partisan split need not be national; in some places we might have the "typical" contemporary configuration, while in others Republican cities might be surrounded by Democratic outlying areas.

During the New Deal era, however, a new place-character basis for politics emerged. The shift was driven by big-city leaders' campaign to seek aid from the national level to fund local emergency relief efforts and circumvent the constraints felt so harshly during times of fiscal duress—efforts by "local and national political entrepreneurs [who] used federal programs to introduce and solidify a new system of alignments in American politics," and the Democrats' more robust response to that entreaty.[9] The urbanicity cleavage has nationalized since then, so now cities in all parts of the country and of all ages tend to be more Democratic than their outlying areas, both in the electorate and in Congress. Given our present demographics (with ever-increasing proportions of Americans living in metropolitan areas and the suburban fringes), an elite partisan politics with opponents arranged according to constituency place character is likely to be contentious and closely fought, as we have seen in recent electoral cycles.

Examinations of city representation in Congress and national politics have been too rare.[10] Previous studies focusing explicitly on city representation in Congress have examined the influence of city constituencies on legislators or the power of a city bloc to pursue an urban agenda. In what may be the first scholarly indication of the congressional geographical sorting to come, Mayhew (1966) finds that midcentury city Republicans were cross-pressured by constituency and party. On housing roll calls from the 1950s, city Republicans voted against their party. Conversely, city Democrats found their support for those same bills to be compatible with both their urban constituencies *and* their national party—probably because they had formulated the party position on such issues themselves. However, there *were* high levels of defection by noncity Democrats, especially those from the South, on these city-friendly policies. Similar conflict was evident in the housing debates of the 1930s, with noncity Democrats hesitant to increase spending and institute a program of state-run housing.[11] Though the urban–rural partisan divide had not yet matured in Congress at this point, its seeds were clearly there. Picking up a similar theme but looking at later data, Wolman and Marckini (2005) systematically explore the developing character and strategic position of the urban bloc over the three decades in which suburban preeminence solidified, finding that city influence in Congress did not wane as much as might be popularly believed, but that the growth of suburban constituencies (at the expense of nonmetropolitan areas) has left Congress "thoroughly dominated by suburban representatives."[12] This chapter updates and expands each of these endeavors, focusing on three strategic tools available to the putative urban political order: cohesion, majority status, and chamber leadership. Urban cohesion has been increased by the cities' continuing shift to the Democratic Party, and chamber leadership among city representatives has been made more *potentially* strong, but certainly more brittle, by the outflow from the Democratic Party of noncity constituencies.

6.1.1 Measuring District Urbanicity

Throughout this book, I have used a new dataset (the CSR dataset) that I assembled to identify city legislators and delegations for use in quantitative analyses of roll call patterns. In this chapter, I dive a bit more directly into this dataset, first with a description of how and why I collected this information. To study city representation in Congress, we need some standard of what constitutes a city district. Unlike states and persons, however, cities are accorded no formal representation in the national legislature. Congressional district boundaries often blithely cross municipal boundaries, so identifying an "urban" or "city" district may not be straightforward. Worthy approaches typically rely on the availability of census data listing the districts' proportion of rural, suburban, and urban residents. Mayhew (1966) used this approach, combined with an accounting of percentage in the district who rented their homes. Wolman and Marckini (1998) identified a district's character with its largest population group, categorized as central city, suburban in-metro, out of metro, or a mixture. These studies represent the best examples of attempts to identify and track urban representatives in the House using census data.

These techniques are straightforward, but they share two shortcomings. First, comparing factors across long time spans is not easy, as readily available census data for congressional districts only go back a few censuses, so getting a long-term picture of city power or the urban–rural divide may be impossible using this approach. To study much of the Long New Deal, a period of particular interest for this study, another tack must be taken entirely. Second, the central city of a Census Bureau–defined metropolitan area may not conform to our idea of what a city is in national terms. Sioux City, Iowa, is the center of a metropolitan area, but it does not really conform to our intuitive understanding of a city because it is still very small—we would not think of it when listing urban places, so should we consider a congressional district anchored by such a place urban? Mayhew (1966) attempts to fix this problem by applying a threshold of percentage of residents in the district who rent their homes. This approach appeals to a certain dimension of what urban residential patterns are like, but it is too exclusive: it jettisons some districts within large cities if they have too few renters, even if those residents are part of the large political communities we call cities.

The alternative approach employed here is to identify *a priori* the set of large cities at a given time and then identify the districts that these places comprise. This approach circumvents practical challenges with census definitions but also uses an explicitly political definition of the city that is fairly resilient to the changes in urban forms we've seen in American history. Lieberman (2009) defines a standard of "city" that allows for consistent, intuitively satisfactory comparisons over time. By this definition, a place is considered a big city if its population constituted 0.1 percent of the total national population in the most recent census. This is a nice round number, and the actual list of cities it produces fits well with what one would intuitively expect. It is also theoretically compelling: each modern congressional district (if such districts were exactly equal in size) makes up 1/435 of the nation, or 0.22 percent. Thus the 0.1 percent threshold is just shy of a majority of a district. For a city to have its "own" district in Congress, it should at least be close to a majority of a congressional district.[13] In this approach, *size* is the key definitional element of urbanicity in defining cities over time: without a large population, a city cannot make a strong claim for representation in the legislature, especially in the context of partisan conflict along an urbanicity cleavage, in which city is pitted against hinterland.

Following in this vein, I created a new dataset useful in studying city representation in Congress. For each census up to 2000, Lieberman (2009) has identified the cities that constituted at least 0.1 percent of the national population. Using this list (updated for the 2010 census) and congressional district atlases, I coded each district in U.S. history as a city, suburban, or rural district (hence "CSR data"; see Appendix A for more details).[14] The result is a dataset spanning American history that allows us to analyze place-type representation in the national legislature and to see the partisan distribution of these different kinds of districts over a wider swath of history than was possible before.[15] In the analyses in this chapter, I use a three-category CSR score (city, suburban, and rural) for the sake of visual clarity; in regression analyses in previous chapters, a more refined seven-category (which allows for more gradations in districts between city and suburb, and between suburb and countryside) variable is used unless otherwise noted. For a clearer picture of which cities the CSR counts as large at different times, Figure 6.1 shows which cities made the list in a few selected censuses as the American population spread from the East and North to greater regional parity.[16] We can see that over time, cities became less clustered regionally. This fact in itself may have fostered a more *national* urban order as the pockets of places with big cities (and their attendant challenges) spread from the Rust Belt to every part of the nation. The remainder of this chapter is devoted to some descriptive analyses of city congressional history.

6.1.2 City Representation over Time: The House of Representatives

The place character of representation in Congress has shifted over time. First, from Figure 6.2a, we can see how the number of urban districts rose in the early twentieth century and leveled off just as the New Deal solidified. City representation in Congress has not declined much in terms of overall numbers.[17] Since the 1930s, the real change has been the growth in suburban districts, from about 10 percent of seats to about half of all seats, while the share of rural districts has diminished.[18]

Figure 6.2b displays the partisan distribution of the different kinds of districts: dark (imagine it's blue) Democrats on the bottom of each category, with light (imagine it's red) GOP seats above. From this figure, we can see the historical development of the urbanicity cleavage in Congress: from 1865 to

1929, city and rural districts were alike in how they split between the parties (there were very few suburban districts during this time, but they were all Republican), and both city and rural districts were fairly responsive to national shifts: when one rose or fell a lot, so would the other, as in the rapid sequence of partisan rotations in the 1890s.

After 1931, however, a new pattern began to take hold. First, there was a large jump in the Democratic share of city districts as the New Deal assembled its city-based coalition of labor, newly mobilized ethnic whites, and eventually African Americans. Republicans regained some of these urban seats intermittently in the 1940s and 1950s, but as Mayhew (1966) notes, these urban Republicans had to "do violence to party principles" when choosing to support many city-friendly policies.[19] On the substance of urban policy, Democrats were better positioned to reconcile party programs and constituency pressure. Thus, except for the dip in the 1940s, Democrats have held a large majority of urban districts since the 1930s; since the 1960s, that urban advantage has been remarkably consistent and has grown slightly, even as the overall strength of the parties nationwide has fluctuated. At the same time, the share of rural districts held by Democrats fell, fairly gradually, until a big drop with the 1994 takeover of the chamber by Republicans, in which many rural southern districts converted to the GOP column. Until the 1960s, the suburban middle zone of the graph was exclusively GOP territory, but the Democrats have made some gains in this area since. As time has gone by there have been fewer total rural districts, as suburban rings have grown and large cities have become more evenly spaced across the country.

The key observation from these graphs is that the development of the urbanicity cleavage in the national legislature over the twentieth century has left us with red country and blue cities in Congress: before the New Deal the two parties each featured sizable city and rural factions, but since then they have each acquired a distinctive place-character identity. The bottom half of the graph has gotten "bluer," and the top half has gotten "redder": this has been a core development in American politics over the past eighty years (not just in recent cycles) and the institutional corollary of the growth of the urban–rural divide in the electorate.

Within the set of city districts, two further observations are notable. First, the partisan differential along the urbanicity dimension even *within* the set of city districts has grown. Among "core" districts (those which are contained within a city rather than straddling different place types), only two were Republican as of 2016, and Democrats have long held more than 90 percent of these districts. The other kinds of city districts, which may also span other parts of the metropolitan or adjacent rural areas, are more evenly distributed between the two parties, though in each category Democrats tend to hold a majority.

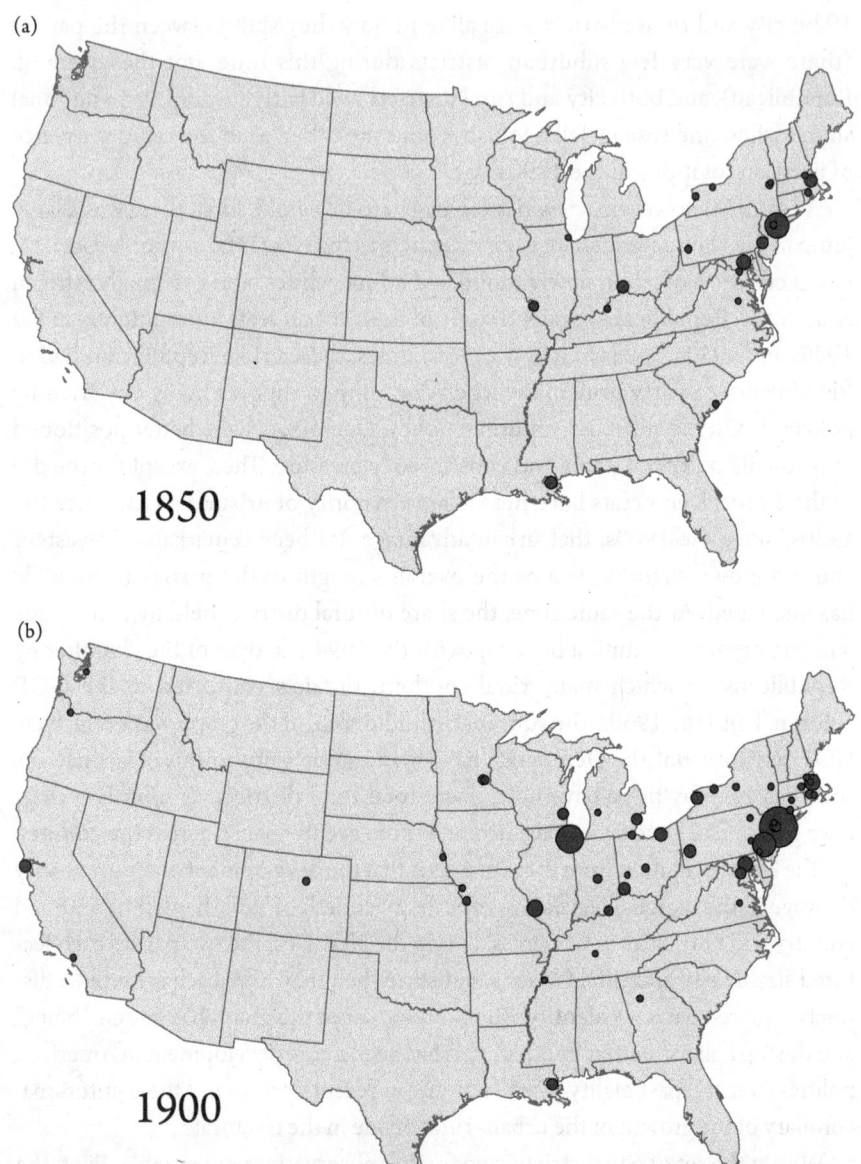

Figure 6.1 **Cities with More than 0.1 Percent of National Population, at Fifty-Year intervals.** Circle sizes are relative to city's share of national population for that year.
Source: Lieberman (2009).

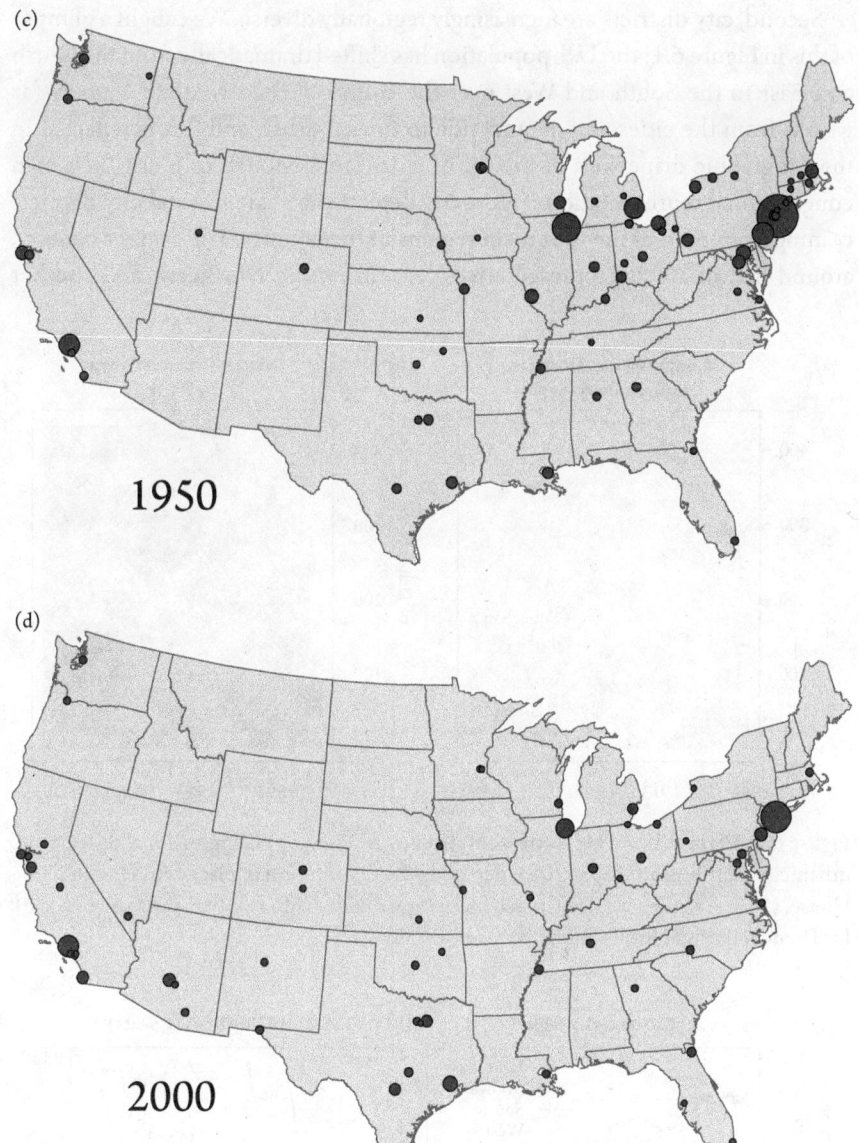

Figure 6.1 Continued.

Second, city districts are increasingly regionally diverse. We caught a glimpse of this in Figure 6.1; the U.S. population has shifted dramatically from the North and East to the South and West over the course of the twentieth century (as well as from the cities and countryside to the suburbs), and this is reflected in the geographic dispersion of the set of cities large enough to merit their own congressional representation. Figure 6.3 depicts the share of total city districts coming from each of the four main regions of the country. For nearly a century, around half of all city representatives came from the Northeast, and another

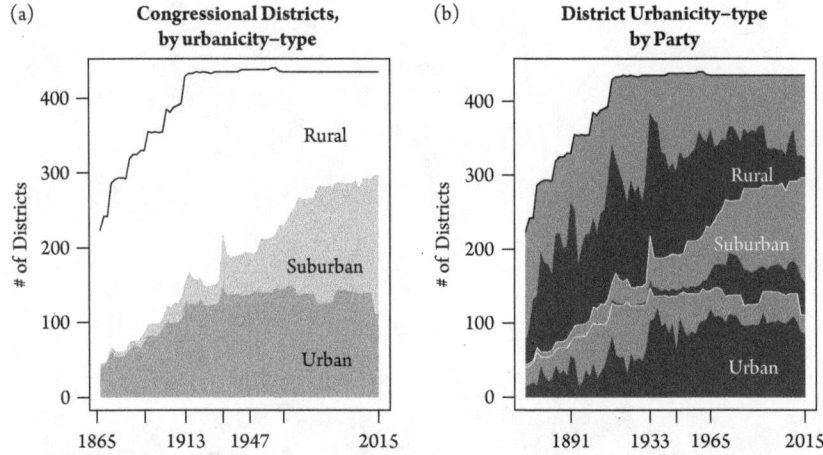

Figure 6.2 **Place-Character Representation over Time.** (a) Congressional district urbanicity distribution, 1865–2015, depicting the distribution of place types in the House. (b) The same graph, with each place-type divided into two partisan tranches: dark for Democrats, light for Republicans. Source: CSR data.

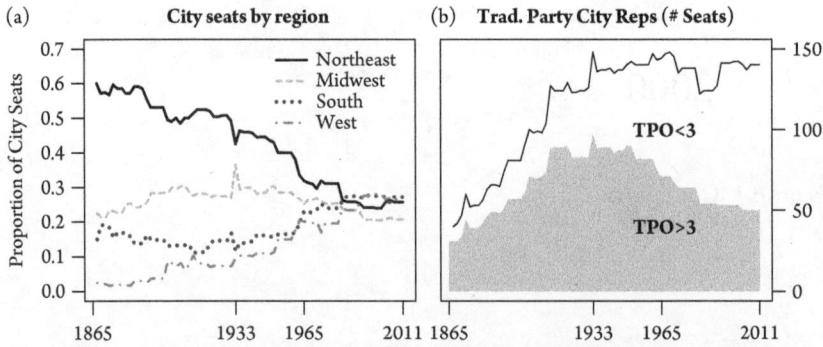

Figure 6.3 **Proportion of All City Districts by Region and Organization type.**
(a) Each line depicts the share of city districts from each of the four main census regions over time. (b) The number of total city representatives from cities with a history of strong traditional party organizations. Sources: CSR data; Mayhew 1986.

quarter from the Midwest. Very few came from the West, and those from the South typically represented districts that were grossly malapportioned, so even larger southern cities did not have core districts.[20] By the late twentieth century, however, city representation in Congress had reached a point of virtual regional parity: a city representative was as likely to come from the West or South as from the Northeast or Midwest. This regional shift has surely colored the content of any urban agenda, but what is most notable about this change is that despite increasing geographic diversity, the urban bloc has become *more* cohesive, in partisan terms, as we can see from Figure 6.2, and in terms of finer-grained measures of congressional behavior such as roll call votes. The urban political order is more national now than ever before.

As a byproduct of the dispersion of city districts to the South and the West, there has been an institutional change as well. One of the key institutions of horizontal integration, which fosters greater city delegation unity, is the traditional party, as analyzed in Chapters 4 and 5. These organizations are found mainly in cities, and mainly in the Northeast and Midwest.[21] Figure 6.3b shows that the number of city representatives coming from places with traditional party organizations (defined for this figure as a TPO greater than 3 on Mayhew's measure) has been in decline since midcentury. Though the intracity power of most of these local parties has been diminished significantly since the early twentieth century in any case, important elements of their style of politics and integrative potential remain in the cities where they continue to exist. Because of this qualitative and numerical decline in TPO power, these organizations' role in bridging the heterogeneous constituencies of the urban order has no doubt diminished since the Long New Deal, when strong traditional party districts were at their peak, holding about 100 seats. Future research on bridge-building institutions may help us understand the new dynamics that bind constituencies together.

The growing identification of the Democratic Party with its city constituency can also be seen by looking directly at Democrats as a share of city representatives—and, vice versa, city representatives as a share of Democrats in Congress. Figure 6.4a and 6.4b tell the story: most city representatives are Democrats, and an increasing share of Democrats are from cities, making up nearly a majority of the party since the final departure of the South in the 1990s. After the 2010 congressional losses, city representatives actually constituted a narrow majority of the Democratic caucus. At no time in U.S. history has there been a more urban party—a party more identified with cities, their citizens, and all that this entails—than the contemporary Democratic Party. This trend affects the strength of city power in the chamber: as city representatives become a larger share of a major party, they become potentially more powerful when that party is in the majority, but more power*less* when it is not.

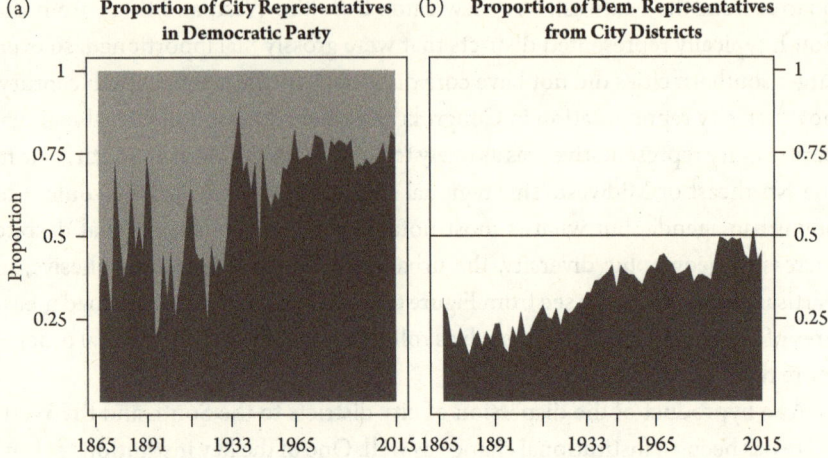

Figure 6.4 **Partisanship and Place Type over Time.** (a) The partisan balance of city districts, with Democrats on the bottom and Republicans on top of the graph. (b) The proportion of Democratic members of the House of Representatives that have been from city districts. Source: CSR data.

These analyses of the CSR data show clearly that we are living in a nation of blue cities and red countryside—or at least that Congress represents such a nation. They also reveal the *sequence* of the growth of the urbanicity divide. First, urban constituencies became distinctive and advanced their policy goals in a manner shaped by the conditions of urbanicity and institutions of horizontal integration. Only later did more conservative, rural areas react and pull away from them. We can see this sequence and measure the cleavage more clearly than in Figure 6.2 by tracking group seats fractionalization (GSF), a summary measure that identifies how different groups (here, city, suburban, and rural representatives) are from each other on some measure (here, partisan affiliation).[22] The intuition of the measure is the association between district place character and party, or how likely you would be to guess the place character of a representative's constituency if all you knew about him or her was party membership. Figure 6.5 illustrates that the urban–rural cleavage has grown in the House. In Figure 6.5a, we see that overall disproportionality of the urbanicity cleavage was generally at very low levels in the early twentieth century and has risen quickly and fairly steadily since the New Deal. In our contemporary Congress, it is as high as it has ever been. In Figure 6.5b, the unweighted constitutive elements of GSF for each place type are plotted over time. This measure, seats disproportionality (SD), reflects how different each place-type is from the rest of the chamber. Urban districts first became distinctive in the 1930s; over time, the suburbs have become much less distinctive in their partisan representation as they have grown in number and become less homogeneously Republican.

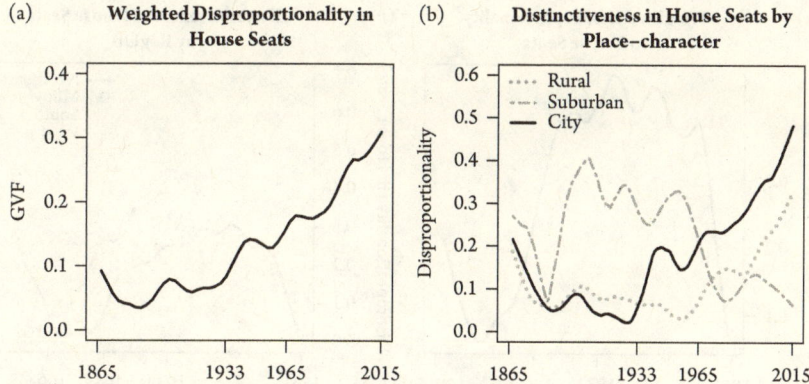

Figure 6.5 **Place Character-Based Partisan Cleavages in Congress.** (a) The summary measure of weighted disproportionality. Higher values mean city, suburban, and rural districts are increasingly different from each other in partisan terms. (b) Each line plots changes in the component parts of the aggregate weighted disproportionality measure at left. Higher values mean a given bloc is more different from the other blocs. Lines in both subplots lowess-smoothed for better visibility. Source: CSR data.

Rural districts, however, have become increasingly distinctive—in favor of the GOP—only since the 1960s.

The absolute magnitudes of GSF measures are not easily interpreted, but we can see that urbanicity is important by contrasting that cleavage with the other variable commonly seen at the heart of the red–blue divide. The typical narrative about political polarization usually involves the "red" and "blue" states, grouped on a roughly regional basis. But regional differences are smaller than they once were and less important than the urbanicity cleavage. In Congress, at least, regional division has fallen since a peak around midcentury, though it has seen a resurgence over the last decade. We can see this in Figure 6.6: 6.6a shows changes in GSF (analogous to Figure 6.5) since 1865, while 6.6b shows changes in SD since then.[23] Though regional distinctiveness in partisanship has increased since the 1990s, it has been driven mainly by the Northeast and South, regions that themselves have strong urban and rural identities, respectively. The overall level of regional distinctiveness is still lower than it used to be, and lower than urbanicity differences.

The foregoing description of city members in the House of Representatives over time leaves us with two important new observations, which we can interpret visually in Figure 6.5: first, the urbanicity cleavage has matured in two main steps since 1933. Initially, city districts became disproportionately Democratic in 1933, forging a national urban political order and initiating a trend that continues to the present. Then, beginning in the mid-1960s, noncity districts changed. Suburban districts became *less* distinctively

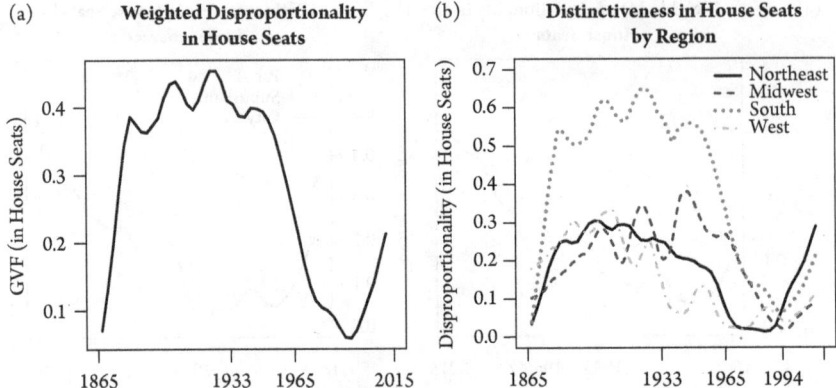

Figure 6.6 **Region-Based Partisan Cleavages in Congress.** (a) Overall regional disproportionality. Higher values mean higher differences across regions. (b) Distinctiveness disaggregated by region. Higher values mean a given bloc is more different from the other three blocs. Lines in both plots lowess-smoothed for better visibility. Source: CSR data.

Republican (while continuing to become more numerous), and rural districts became more distinctively Republican (and less numerous). Before the New Deal, place character was not an important dimension of partisanship at the national legislative level; since then, the cleavage has grown in importance and become more monotonic—the more "city-like" a district is, the more likely it is to be Democratic.

The second observation is related to the first and will be more fully elaborated in the next section, which concerns actual legislative behavior by these city representatives. City legislators have become more Democratic even as they have become more diverse geographically. At the beginning of the New Deal, 80 percent of city representatives came from what would become the Rust Belt of the Northeast and the Midwest (see Figure 6.3). With its fairly similar patterns of settlement, industrial relations, and Civil War legacies, such a bloc might seem easier to hold together than a bloc representing city constituencies evenly spread across the four major regions of the country. Yet we see *greater* partisan similarity among cities even as the list of cities becomes more regionally heterogeneous (and more different from each other in terms of their developmental histories and trajectories). City representatives today are more stably Democratic than they were at midcentury, and they are more cohesive as a voting bloc. The maintenance and development of this geographically diverse coalition are rooted in the common city experiences that are shared across cities from diverse regions. These include the city-killing forces of deindustrialization and suburbanization, as well as the basic characteristics of urbanicity, which fostered common responses to such challenges, and common national goals, even among cities that shared little politically before the construction of the urban political order.

6.2 Urban Power in the House

Cities across the country have become more identified with the Democratic Party over the past eighty years. The governance demands associated with urbanicity in the waning of the Fordist industrial era, and the intensifying constraints cities face, have prompted the growth of a substantive city agenda in national politics since the New Deal. This growing urban agenda marks a departure from the past in large part because many of its policies deal directly with the uncertainties and challenges of modern urban life; the work by city representatives to articulate and advance such measures since the New Deal era have been described in detail elsewhere.[24]

However, even though a national urban agenda has become more important for cities, city districts have not become more numerous. Given that city districts make up at most a third of the House (and usually less), pursuing an urban agenda requires strategy and institutional leverage; some of these were described in previous chapters. In this section, I explore key elements that might foster legislative success for cities given the obstacles presented by a growing urban–rural partisan divide. Three strategic imperatives are common to the pursuit of any such nonmajority bloc's goals: attain leadership positions to influence the agenda; be cohesive, especially when bloc members (in this case, cities and other kinds of places) do not automatically agree; and gain reliable allies with either common interests or a propensity to logroll or compromise in order to provide extra votes for the bloc. The remainder of this chapter analyzes different aspects of these strategic imperatives.

6.2.1 Chamber Power Positions

Within Congress, the increasing identification of the parties with different kinds of places has led to the institutional exaggeration of the smaller urbanicity cleavage in the electorate. This place-character divide may be further exaggerated if the *leaderships* of the two parties are also sorted by place character. Especially in the House of Representatives, the majority party has significant control over the legislative agenda. Leadership controls what kinds of policies are considered: its members will likely only allow a bill to be seriously considered when a majority of its own party prefers the bill to the status quo; anything else may not see the light of day.[25] Though this agenda power is mostly *negative* power, membership in the leadership group of the House majority is quite valuable, especially for a subpartisan group like the city bloc that may struggle to achieve chamber majorities on its own but also needs to advance positive legislation to further an urban agenda—on city issues, the status quo is always changing, so urban policy must adjust accordingly.[26] In this model of legislative control, the majority median, committee chairs, majority-party members of important committees, and party floor leadership have outsize influence on the shaping of substantive agendas and the precise content of legislation. For all these reasons, it is useful to explore how successful city representatives historically were in securing leadership positions, becoming members of the cartel that could control action in the House.

For over fifty years beginning with the New Deal, the diverse Democratic Party alliance held almost uninterrupted majority status in the House of Representatives. Many of the key legislative battles that took place during this time were as much between different factions of the Democratic Party as between Democrats and Republicans.[27] The most famous struggle was between (mostly rural) southerners, who had been the party's core since Reconstruction, and (mostly urban) northerners, many but not all of whom were relative newcomers to the Democratic caucus. Thus, while the city wing often enjoyed greater numbers and closer links to Democratic presidents, the moderate/conservative southern wing had advantages in ideological centrality and seniority.

City power within the House cartel has *not* tracked broad city representation in the chamber. The overall number of city representatives in the House grew for roughly the first third of the century and then plateaued between 135 and 145 seats, a level it has not exceeded to the present day, accounting for about one-third of House members, as illustrated in Figure 6.2. Within the leadership, however, the pattern has been more uneven but also potentially more promising for the city institutional order.[28] Figure 6.7a estimates the agenda-setting power of representatives from different place types over time, plotting the proportion of members of the legislative cartel—members of the majority-party leadership and committee chairs—who represent city constituencies. As in Figure 6.2, the dark gray shaded area at the foot of the figure is for city representatives, the light gray is for suburban representatives, and the white area on top is for representatives from outside major cities' metropolitan areas. The endpoint of the urban series in the 112th Congress is indicated with a small circle for visibility. The labels on the x-axis indicate Congresses when the chamber's leadership changed hands (there was mostly Republican control before 1931, for one Congress in the 1940s, and from 1995 to 2007), a horizontal line at 0.5, and a black line showing the proportion of overall seats in the House held by city representatives (as in Figure 6.2).

Figure 6.7a tells a dramatic tale. While city representation in the chamber overall has been fairly steady, as indicated by the black line hovering around 0.3, city inclusion in the leadership has been volatile: the dark gray shaded area careens up and down. By the late 1930s, city representatives made up nearly half of all leadership positions, peaking in the 77th Congress, when John McCormack (Boston) served as majority leader, Adolph Sabath (Chicago) as chairman of the Rules Committee, and Mary Norton (Jersey City) as chair of the Labor Committee. New York City alone had six committee chairmen in its delegation in the 77th Congress, though none had particularly important portfolios. The city's place within the Democratic chamber leadership dropped precipitously during the postwar era, despite mostly Democratic chamber control. This was an era in which some northern city districts were closely contested, and a wave of quick reversals—seats shifting Democrat–Republican–Democrat over a very few Congresses—erased city seniority among Democrats in some cases; there were also some notable retirements among old-guard city Democrats during this time. Beginning in the 1950s, however, city power in the Democratic leadership grew until these representatives achieved a numerical majority during the 1980s. In the 101st Congress, half of the chamber's key roles were again filled by city representatives, including Speaker; majority leader; majority whip, and the chairs of the Rule,[29]; Ways and Means; Banking, Finance, and Urban Affairs; Education and Labor; and Public Works and Transportation committees. After a half-century of contending with the powerful conservative southern wing of the party, city representatives had established control over important areas of city legislation. While the urban interlude is often seen as the peak of city power, a strong case can be made for the 1980s as well, at least in this important representative institution. Of course, power in the House leadership is one thing, policy success another. The 1980s and 1990s are generally seen as a period of retrenchment on urban policy in particular as a result of divided government and President Reagan's drive for domestic policy austerity (Caraley 1992).

This moment of city chamber power was short-lived. The loss of the House by the Democrats in 1994 did not evenly impact different kinds of places: there were few city Republicans at this time, and the city presence in the House leadership dropped significantly, replaced by a largely suburban, but increasingly rural, Republican leadership. By 2005, only two of the twenty-seven House cartel members were from cities, the lowest level of city power on this measure since the 83rd Congress.[30] This was also a half-century high tide point for *rural* membership in the cartel—over the prior decades, rural power in the chamber had waned, but with the maturation of the urbanicity cleavage, Republican leadership has to a great degree meant rural or exurban leadership. With the frequent changes in House leadership that have occurred in recent years, levels of city representation in the leadership cartel have become even more extreme. After the Democratic gains of 2006 and 2008, city representatives made up a greater share of the cartel than ever before, including the Speakership and the chairs of the Ways and Means, Commerce, Foreign Affairs, Veterans Affairs, and Judiciary committees; after 2010, however, they lapsed back to near-historic lows.

City representatives' strengthening ties to the Democrats and the waning security of noncity Democrats has meant that city representatives are overrepresented in the leadership when Democrats control the House but underrepresented when Republicans control the chamber. Wolman and Marckini (2005) attribute much of this tie between a Democratic majority and city power to the increasing seniority of many city Democrats.[31] Their findings, which end in 1995–1996, have been amplified in the ensuing decades. As the city–country divide has grown in the chamber as a whole, the institutional implications for cities in the nation have become something of a feast or famine: when Democrats control the House, city representatives make up more of the leadership than ever; when the GOP controls the agenda, city representatives are not included in the leadership.

Figures 6.7b and 6.7c reinforce this narrative of chamber power for city representatives. In each figure, the partisan place-character divide is illustrated within sets of representatives with particular power over city issues. Figure 6.7b depicts the proportion of representatives from each kind of place on the "prestige" committees: Rules, Appropriations, Ways and Means, and Budget.[32] These committees have broad jurisdictions that impact virtually all significant policy, so members of these committees may be particularly powerful. City and suburban representation on these committees has grown, and rural representation diminished, roughly parallel with the proportions of such members in the chamber as a whole. Even more than in Figure 6.2, however, the partisan place-character divide is amplified on these powerful committees. Figure 6.7c shows membership by place character and party on the most important House committee for city issues, Financial Services.[33] On this committee, cities have always been overrepresented, especially around the middle of the twentieth century, when city representatives made up over half of the committee (vs. a third of the chamber), because of the committee's important role in oversight of large housing and urban development programs. Suburban Republicans have since become more numerous, while rural representation on this committee has greatly diminished. On issues controlled by this committee, which include urban and regional development and many of the specific programs established to help cities manage the paradox of urban governance, the dividing lines between city Democrats and noncity Republicans are particularly clear.[34]

Taken together, these analyses the role of place character in leadership and important committees reinforce two observations. The clearest long-run historical trend here is the diminution of rural power on committees and in leadership. Rural interests were once dominant in the most important institutions within the House, but metropolitan representatives, and ostensibly their perspectives, now predominate. This makes sense, as the vast majority of Americans today live in urbanized places, if not in central cities. The exception to this trend is that when Republicans are in control, rural representatives do have an outsize share of power positions, though still less than they once did.

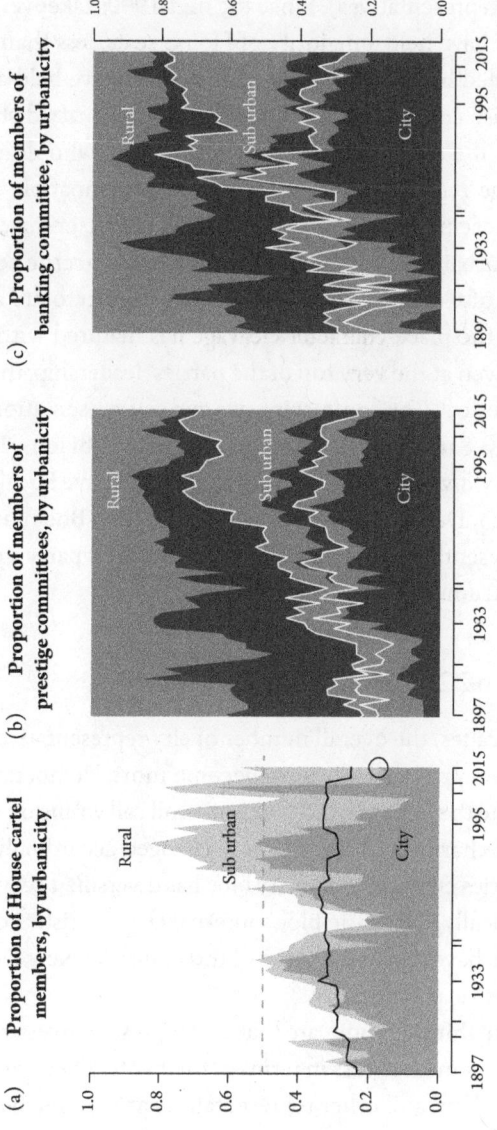

Figure 6.7 **City Representation in House Leadership, 1901–2015.** (a) Members of House leadership cartel, by urbanicity. (b) Membership in House prestige committees by urbanicity and party. (c) Membership on House Finance (Banking/Urban Affairs) Committee by urbanicity and party. Ticks on time axis indicate change in House majority control. Sources: CSR data; Charles Stewart Committee Roster Data.

The other important observation is the volatility of city power that has resulted from the place-character partisan divide. Before the GOP takeover of the 1990s, just under half of House committee chairs were from urban districts, and the proportion of committee chairs from different kinds of places had held fairly steady for two decades (though there was a gradual increase in the share that went to suburban representatives). Since the mid-1990s takeover, however, whenever Republicans have held a majority of House seats, less than five committees have been headed by urbanites; when Democrats have held a majority, more than half of House committee chairs have come from city districts. This pattern may be due to the aging-out or defeat of partisans who do not fit the place-character cleavage representatives more naturally compatible with their districts (i.e., those whose party affiliation and district character match the partisan character of the urbanicity cleavage) can more easily accrue seniority as the place-type sorting of Congress continues.[35] As in the electorate and in the legislature as a whole, the place-character cleavage has matured within legislative party leadership. Even at the very top of the parties' leadership, the divide is clearly present, if not perfect. The contrast in style and self-presentation between Barack Obama and, say, Sarah Palin or George W. Bush is obvious. But within Congress the urbanicity divide is manifest as well. The past five Speakers of the House—Newt Gingrich, Dennis Hastert, Nancy Pelosi, John Boehner, and now Paul Ryan—each represent constituencies in sync with their party's placement on the urbanicity spectrum.

6.2.2 City Voting in the House

Over the past eight decades, the overall number of city representatives has held fairly steady and these representatives have become more Democratic. In this section, I will investigate the pattern of city power in roll call voting on the House floor. Has the political character of the city bloc changed accordingly? Has the frequency of city victories changed as the city bloc has diversified geographically but consolidated politically? Have the bloc's internal characteristics changed as different kinds of cities have displaced some of the industrial New Deal core as representatives of cities?

The most immediate things to note are that city representatives are typically the most liberal members in Congress in terms of their voting behavior, and that a gap opened between them and other representatives around the beginning of the New Deal, timing we might expect from Figure 6.2. City representatives were the most assertive forces behind various important policies of the New Deal, including relief employment programs, public works construction projects, housing subsidies, and new labor regulations. Support for this suite of market interventions came to define liberalism, and to a great extent what it meant to be a "Democrat," in national politics. We can see this trend in an analysis of a common measure of congressional behavior/ideology, DW-NOMINATE scores (1st Dimension; lower scores interpreted as more liberal). Figure 6.8 illustrates that urbanicity is indeed associated with liberal voting on the primary dimension of conflict: city representatives have long been more liberal than rural or suburban representatives on the first dimension, and Figure 6.8a shows that this is true within each party as well.

Figure 6.8b illustrates that there was little place-character divide before the 1920s: the lines for each kind of district track each other, and the chamber mean, fairly closely. After 1933, however, the city average is consistently well below (i.e., more liberal than) that of the other kinds of places and the chamber mean.[36] Rural districts are generally slightly above average, and above the other groups, on this dimension, while suburban districts are in between, closely tracking the chamber mean. This is what we would expect, given the theorized relationship between urbanicity and preferences about statism, as well as the party–place-character divide illustrated in Figure 6.2. Central city districts are to the left on this dimension (i.e., have lower scores on average), while rural districts lie the furthest to the right. Of course, the first dimension DW-NOMINATE scores also capture party affiliation, so this explains much of the gap in place types on this dimension. Figure 6.8b shows that when we account for party (and region, among Democrats), the gap between representatives of different kinds of places is still clear. The top pair of (dashed) lines are the mean first dimension scores among urban and non-urban nonsouthern Republicans. The gray line in the middle is the chamber mean. The Morse-dashed line that arcs up and down across the graph is the mean for all southern Democrats.[37] The solid lines running slightly downward across the bottom are the means for nonsouthern, non-urban Democrats and nonsouthern, urban Democrats, respectively. In each party, city representatives are, on average, more liberal on this measure than their non-urban sectional copartisans. For Republicans, this difference was largest during the urban interlude, when a sizable gap opened up between urban and non-urban members of that party, but it has diminished and even become slightly inverted over the last two decades (though there are now very few city Republicans in any case, and the vast majority of them represent mixed urban–suburban constituencies). Still, during the urban interlude, there seem to have been important defections among city Republicans on statism.[38]

Among Democrats outside the South, urbanites have been consistently more liberal on this dimension than those from outside cities. Though both groups have moved slightly to the left over the past decades, the *gap* between them has remained fairly constant. One important observation from this figure is the switch that occurs between Southern Democrats and urban nonsouthern Democrats in the early 1920s, well before the surge in nonsouthern Democrats during the New

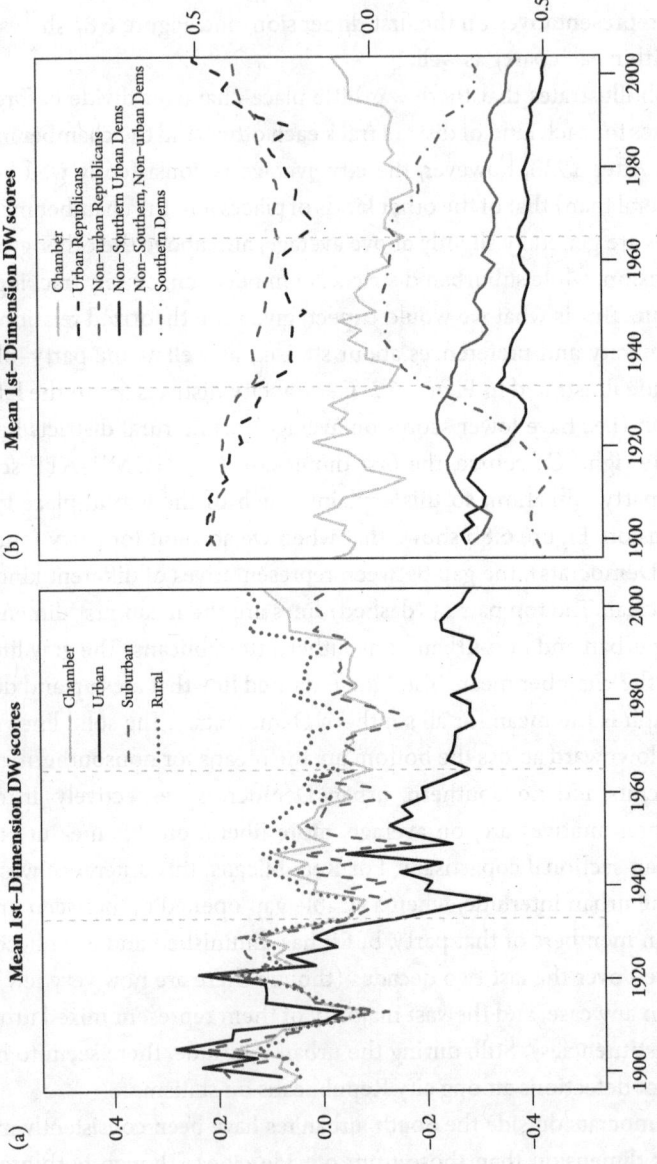

Figure 6.8 **Mean DW-NOMINATE First-Dimension Scores.** (a) Mean scores by party and urbanicity/Democratic (b) Mean scores by urbanicity group over time. Lower scores mean more liberal/Democratic votes. Sources: CSR data; Voteview roll call data.

Deal. This dimension measures partisan conflict, typically over the economy, and it indicates that something changed in the 1920s, wherein the urban Democrats became the furthest "left" on this dimension, and the most likely to disagree with Republicans, while Southern Democrats became more centrist. Southerners remained slightly to the left of center on this dimension for the entire period of the Long New Deal, before eventually moving back toward the rest of their party.[39]

That switch in the 1920s was a major intraparty change; city Democrats became the most consistent opponents of congressional Republicans, and southerners became relatively less staunch in their opposition to the GOP. This shift marks the beginning of the conservative coalition and of the partisan place-character divide, as the collection of progressive liberals, especially those Democrats Buenker (1973) identifies as "new-stock" immigrants, began to take the reins of the national Democratic Party. While city representatives did not constitute a majority of the party's national delegation in Congress until the 1930s, they did seem to be asserting their muscle in intraparty politics during this period, most notably in the contentious nomination of Al Smith for president in 1928 (and the failed attempt at his renomination in 1932). Smith lost to Hoover, but between him, Roosevelt, and Truman, Democratic nominees were closely linked to large cities for the next quarter century, reflecting and reinforcing the preeminence of urban forces within the party.[40]

City representatives thus came to be the most partisan Democrats during this era, redefining what that partisan identity really meant. Given their marginality on statism (i.e., their typical distance from the median voter), trends in other strategic considerations are also very important to consider. The potential influence of a voting bloc is related to its size, cohesion, and factors exogenous to the bloc itself, such as the ideological distribution of other voters.[41] To the extent that a bloc is large and cohesive, and the rest of the voters are not united against that bloc, the bloc can be said to have influence. The most common example of a powerful bloc in Congress is the congressional party, which aims to be large and cohesive enough that it does not matter much what the other voters do.[42] The city bloc has never constituted a chamber majority in the House, nor has it been entirely drawn from one political party, so it has always needed to court allies.

Figure 6.9 illustrates trends in city bloc voting over twentieth-century congressional history.[43] On each measure, the city position is defined as the position taken by a majority of city representatives casting a vote on a given issue, unless specifically clarified otherwise. Figure 6.9a shows the proportion of roll call votes on which the city bloc won, with "winning" meaning the majority of city legislators agreed with the chamber majority. The solid line is the share of *all* roll call votes on which the city position was also the winning position. Because many votes are one-sided, this proportion is typically quite high, above 80 percent of all votes until the 1990s. The gray dashed line in Figure 6.9a shows the percentage of *contested* votes on

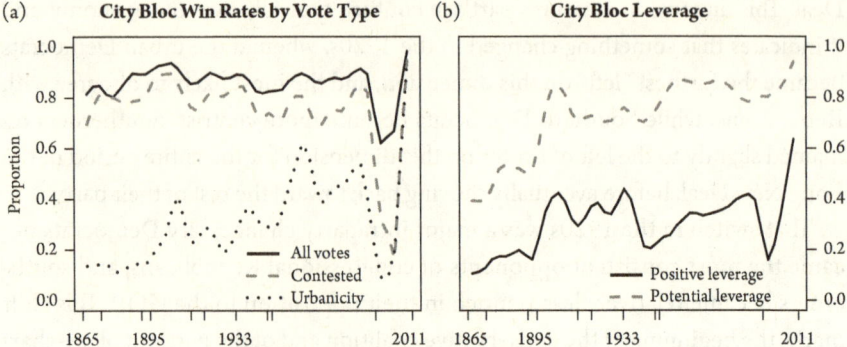

Figure 6.9 **City Bloc Roll Call Voting, 1865–2011.** (a) Proportion of votes in each category in which the city position won. (b) Proportion of contested votes on which the city bloc had potential and positive leverage, respectively. X-axis ticks indicate change in House majority control. Sources: CSR data; AIP data; Voteview roll call data.

which the city bloc won. Contested votes are those with the support of less than three-quarters of the chamber. The dotted line shows the proportion of urbanicity cleavage votes on which the city side won. These are votes on which the majority of city representatives disagreed with the majority of noncity representatives. Again, the thin vertical lines mark important changes in chamber control. As in Figure 6.7, city power in the legislature has become much more volatile and contingent on chamber control. This is especially true on urbanicity votes, on which the city bloc generally fared better until the mid-1990s, when Republican control of the chamber dramatically decreased city success. This was not the case during the long period of mostly Democratic control from 1933 to 1995. Especially early in that era, despite Democratic control and the Democrats' urban tilt, when city and noncity representatives disagreed (which happened on about a fifth of all votes, as opposed to about half of all votes since 1994), the city position generally *lost*, or only won about half the time in the 1960s and 1970s. The percentage of urbanity-cleavage votes on which the city position won from one Congress to the next was fairly steady and generally increasing, however. Once again, the new, more volatile party alignment has led to more feast-or-famine prospects for city success.

Figure 6.9b illustrates measures of congressional leverage for the city bloc, following Wolman and Marckini (2005). The gray dashed line is the proportion of contested votes on which city representatives had potential leverage. These are votes on which the total number of city representatives was greater than the difference in voting between non-urban voters, so that if the city bloc was perfectly cohesive, it was in a position to decide the vote one way or the other. This has been true of a large and slowly increasing proportion of votes for over a century. Given that the size of the city bloc has not grown for decades, this is an indication that noncity representatives have become more evenly divided, leaving more potential opportunities for a cohesive city bloc to cast decisive votes. City representatives are usually not *perfectly* cohesive, however, so a more realistic and useful measure is the black line, which traces the percentage of contested votes by Congress for which the city bloc had positive leverage. Wolman and Marckini (2005) define positive leverage votes as votes on which "the majority of city representatives cast the decisive winning votes."[44] This means that the votes of noncity representatives would not have been sufficient to carry the vote without city allies, and that most city representatives voted to pass the ultimately successful measure. As with overall win rates and leadership positions, the leverage of the city bloc has become increasingly sensitive to partisan control. The prior trough, in the 1930s, is a reflection of large Democratic majorities and a sometimes-divided city bloc: on many votes, city votes were not necessary for passage, even though a majority of city representatives supported most of these measures, and on others the closer partisan split among city representatives themselves made them less cohesive. The trough beginning in the 1990s, however, reflects the fact that the city position was defeated on a large proportion of votes, while the peak in the 110th and 111th Congresses reflects the fact that city votes were, more often than not, necessary for passage and enough to put a proposal over the top.[45]

6.3 Discussion: City Representation in the House

In this chapter, I have illustrated the development of an urban–rural cleavage in the House of Representatives over the past eighty years. The existence of that cleavage in contemporary partisan politics is now well known, and the sociological differences between city and country have been observed for a century. The precise development, in terms of sequencing and causal relationships, of the partisan divide, however, has been less clearly delineated because of researchers' narrow time horizons and a focus on individual voters rather than institutional representation. Authors focusing on spatial polarization have often focused on voter behavior and the city–suburb divide, with special attention paid to the 1950s or 1970s as key moments in the development of this cleavage.[46] This city-suburban partisan divide is real and has been important since even before the New Deal, but among voters and in the halls of Congress, cities and suburbs are becoming more *alike*, not diverging, as partisan differentiation matures along the full urbanicity continuum.

Looking further back in time raises new causal possibilities. In Congress, at least, the city bloc formed before voters began moving to the suburbs in droves (and well before suburbs made up a large portion of the House). The urban–rural partisan divide began with New Deal Democrats' urban gains and accelerated in rural shifts away from the Democrats about thirty and sixty years later. Republicans were reduced to a suburban and exurban redoubt in the 1930s and made gains in the South first in presidential politics and after decades of party building that succeeded in gathering that less city-fied region into their stronghold.⁴⁷ In the North, the disappearance of urban Republicans starting in the 1930s led to the development of cohesive Democratic urban blocs in many industrial cities. Though some urban liberal Republicans lingered, they were on borrowed time well before Rockefeller's 1964 defeat by Goldwater conservatives in the GOP primary.⁴⁸ Most scholarly focus on this elite partisan realignment has been on the conversion of the South, its drift away from the New Deal coalition, and the resilient force of racial conservatism in regional and national politics.⁴⁹ This was a very important development, but such accounts partly overlook the main change during this time, which was the growth and consolidation of the urban political order within the Democratic Party, which substantively changed what it meant to be a "Democrat" and brought a host of city-centric interventions to the agenda fairly abruptly.

The most disruptive of these agenda changes, as we saw in Chapter 5, was the re-emergence of civil rights for African Americans, though the congressional politics of labor and other issues took on similar coalitional dynamics.⁵⁰ Southerners, from their place as the long-established core of the party, did not change much on size-of-government preferences or on white supremacy. They only changed parties, and it took them decades to do it. Needing an active state to alleviate their governance challenges at home, city representatives pursued a program of mutual exchange with their copartisans but were rebuffed on a range of issues and eventually began to pursue other strategies, and other alliances, incompatible with the South's chief priorities.⁵¹ Over time, as the urbanicity cleavage has matured, city representatives have created a metropolitan party that they can control—but also a situation in which they are more vulnerable to being left powerless in the minority, as has been the case for several congresses. This perilous dynamic is strengthened by the inefficient spacing of Democratic big-city voters, their dense population (which makes them likely to be "packed" into lopsided districts under any districting scheme), and the shrinking cities of the Rust Belt, as we saw in the elections of 2016.

Cities, more than other kinds of places, have a particular incentive to forge an active, united bloc in the national legislature. They often face common challenges of urban life that can be addressed with similar policies. Among these policies are major market interventions that cities are ill-situated to implement themselves locally. In this context, cities have actively turned to state and national levels to ameliorate some of their governance challenges.

Before the New Deal, there was nothing distinctive about city representatives in partisan terms; as a group, they mirrored the national partisan split. The New Deal changed that and made urbanicity an important cleavage in national politics. But as we saw in Chapter 3, this shift wasn't just something the New Deal did *to* cities; it was also something city leaders did to set the course of the New Deal.

Even before FDR took office, city representatives, practicing a style of politics distinctive to the traditional party organizations that were their local forebears, recognized the increasing peril cities faced under conditions of industrial capitalism and sought to use national resources and national political alliances to alleviate their governance problems. Since the New Deal, not only has national unity among cities grown, through the vehicle of the Democratic Party, but rural constituencies have become more associated with the Republicans, strengthening the place-character divide at the highest levels of national representation. This change was not initiated by migration to the suburbs (the first shift predates most of that migration), though it was surely accelerated by it. It was also not merely a function of white flight and race: all but two urban congressional districts had overwhelmingly white electorates in the early 1930s, when the urbanicity rift opened up.[52] The progressive liberalism of the New Deal brought city issues to the fore in national politics, and city representatives pursued these policies from their position as an important, if not pivotal, bloc.

Casually, we often think of the middle of the twentieth century as a sort of golden age for American cities. More Americans lived in the large central cities of the industrial era at that moment than at any other time in our history, and it embodied a kind of "metonymic moment" for cities in the nation.[53] As illustrated here and in Chapter 3, it also marked a time when important city issues were central to the national agenda. The relative social decline and recurrent problems faced by many cities after the 1960s reinforce this view of the Long New Deal as a golden age. That impression is fairly nostalgic, because city efforts at policymaking during that era were so frequently stymied or distorted by resistance from the conservative coalition or southern copartisans. As cities become more closely identified with the Democratic Party, the median congressional Democrat and the Democratic leadership are more likely than ever before to represent city constituencies—a new situation for an American political party. These leaders, in committee and chamber alike, may be particularly attentive to and protective of big-city perspectives and interests on many issues.

However, given that a large majority of representatives are *not* from cities, and that when Republicans hold majority status cities go virtually unrepresented in the leadership group and are very unsuccessful in roll call voting, city power in Congress today is also more brittle and vulnerable than it was during the Long New Deal, when Democratic majorities were less urban but more safely entrenched. City power on the Hill thus faces a deep, fundamental uncertainty in terms of chamber power and intraparty power.

In the Conclusion, I will explore this uncertainty through a look at how the urban–rural divide is manifest in the mass public and where the strongest possibilities for a resurgent urban political order lie: in the expanded metropolitan political order.

7

Conclusion

Notes for a Metropolitan Political Order

> New York City... where more than seven million people live in peace, and enjoy the benefits of democracy.
> —WNYC Radio 1930s-era station identification

> Let me say... that I know very little about New York, and if I never know any more I will be just as happy.
> —Rep. Graham Barden (D-NC), chairman of House Committee on Education and Labor[1]

There are certain places that are unexpectedly connected in American cultural and political life; Chicago and Mississippi are such an unlikely pair. From the North Side of Chicago, home of the millionaires' Gold Coast, the neighborhoods of the bungalow belt, the Magnificent Mile, and a famously vertiginous skyline, it's a quick right onto Lake Shore Drive. Within minutes, you're on the Dan Ryan Expressway heading south, weaving fast through a ten-lane canyon carved through the South Side, where the Gold Coast can seem a million miles away, and which reminds us of the faults and folly of some twentieth-century projects that have led to twenty-first-century inequality. Cut southwest onto I-57 South, and nine hours later, you'll arrive in the broad plains of the Mississippi Delta, mostly empty and stretching pancake-flat from horizon to horizon, home to many of the richest and poorest Americans in the middle of the nineteenth century. Generations of Americans traveled this route in the twentieth century's Great Migrations, but mostly in the opposite direction: from south to north, from agricultural semifeudalism to industrial urban inequality, from flat fields to tall towers.

This path through the middle of the country is also an axis upon which America's racial politics have turned. Five of the first six African Americans to serve in the U.S. Senate came from either Mississippi or Chicago, though a century of political exclusion interrupted their seatings. In 1963, as racial tumult beset the South and just a year before Johnson's signing of the Civil

Rights Act, these very different places actually had more in common politically than we might think. Mississippi was represented by five white Democrats in the House of Representatives (no one *other* than white Democrats had been elected in Mississippi in the twentieth century). Chicago's North Side, part of a strong local machine organization for a generation, also sent five delegates to the House, also all white Democrats. Each delegation was a consistent, archetypal element of the New Deal Democratic coalition—the urban machine and the Solid South—and both places had profited from a close relationship with the national government, bringing home pork and having outsize influence on many policies from positions of seniority.

In both places, too, a clear racial hierarchy was in place. In Mississippi, white supremacy was sustained by law and private violence. The story of the strongest bastion of Jim Crow white supremacy is well known, from the infamous restrictions on black public and political life that would be tested and fought so dramatically in the coming years to the murders of civil rights leaders Medgar Evers and Chicagoan Emmett Till. In Chicago, America's most racially segregated large city, the hierarchy was less obviously violent but still real. The hegemonic local Democratic organization practiced a politics "with a sharp racial edge," marginalizing black political forces or coopting their leaders as lieutenants of the dominant citywide machine.[2] Everyday white Chicagoans were not focused on building a postracial utopia either. Over the decades of the Long New Deal, some fought for racial justice and integration, but others bombed black would-be homeowners or threw rocks at Martin Luther King. Most were silent, worried, or indifferent. Entrenched patterns of racial segregation were strengthened first by neighborhood vigilantes, then by law and regulation (such as redlining and restrictive covenants), and later by discrimination and strong cultural norms.[3]

However, the early 1960s marked the last time that Chicago and Mississippi were both, for all intents and purposes, stable white polities within the Democratic fold. The way that racial politics played out in these two kinds of places is perhaps the most important political development of the twentieth-century United States. In both Chicago and Mississippi, an essentially all-white electorate was transformed from the outside into one in which there were many African Americans. In Mississippi, court cases and voting rights legislation reintroduced African Americans into that state's formal political processes as Jim Crow institutions were dismantled, so the electorate became about 35 percent black quite quickly (up from basically zero). The reaction by white Mississippians—almost all of whom (at least those who had participated in the political process) had been Democrats—was partisan exit. What had been a one-party Democratic state became a Republican stronghold. Over the next five decades, Mississippi would become a comfortably red state, with over 80 percent of white Mississippians supporting Republican presidential candidates in recent elections.

In Chicago, even more than in other northern cities, the Great Migrations of the first half of the twentieth century brought hundreds of thousands of black immigrants to the city from the South. From 1910 to 1940 to 1970, Chicago went from 0 percent African American, to 8 percent, to about 33 percent. By the 1970s, there were about four times as many black Chicagoans as there were *total residents* in all of Mississippi's cities combined.[4] Just as Mississippi saw a backlash to the Freedom Summers, Chicago would also see decades of backlash, especially in response to pushes for open housing and political incorporation, with recurrent conflict between groups of citizens and deep contention among elites. But *unlike* Mississippi, the city continued to represent itself as staunchly Democratic, and liberal, in national politics. In 2016, Hillary Clinton won nearly seven votes for every one cast for Donald Trump, winning a majority in every ward of the city. Clinton did *particularly* well there, but Chicago has had routinely massive Democratic victories for decades.[5] While race turned Mississippi's congressional delegation from Solid South Democrat to red Republican, Chicago's North Side has maintained an uninterrupted shade of blue since the 1940s.[6] This continued support for national Democrats, despite the divisive potential of race, is partly attributable to the fact that Chicago's representatives were from a city, but also partly attributable to the fact that Chicago's representatives were from the *same* city; the local institutions of the common political community and strong local party organization made Chicago's representatives more likely to agree on all issues, especially those most relevant to the city. For Chicago's (and other cities') delegation in national politics, race was important but not overwhelming, and members stayed united on it just as they did on other issues. And the institutions that kept diverse coalitions together during the New Deal have weathered the storm, at least in national politics, through to today.

7.1 Seeing Red and Blue More Clearly

In the aftermath of the 2016 elections, many analysts turned to the urban–rural divide to explain what happened. Indeed, the ultimate results showed not so much an across-the-board valence shift to the Republicans, but an elaboration of this urbanicity cleavage. Rural areas got redder, and large metros got bluer. We now know that it's not red states, blue states, but red countryside, blue cities, with purple suburbs in between. Some argue that this is a recent development, while others say the urban–rural divide has always been there. The reality is more complicated: just as in Congress, mass partisanship has not always been associated with urbanicity everywhere, even though there has always been a cultural tension between city mice and country mice. A developmental account, examining elections over time and among counties, can help us understand the relationship between urbanicity and voting more clearly.

The simplest place to see the urbanicity divide emerge in the electorate is in analysis of voting returns at low levels of aggregation. Analyses of red and blue America often stop at the state level, because of the logic of the Electoral College, because 50 places are clearer to see than 3,000, and because it's easy for pundits to wax poetic about state or regional cultures. But it is important to look closer to see what's really happening in our elections. The first thing to know is that on a grand scale, there is an increasingly strong relationship between population density and support for Democratic presidential candidates, which has not always been present.[7] For instance, Figure 7.1 shows county-level results from four elections: 1932, 1960, 2008, and 2016. In each of these subfigures, the points represent the margin of victory in the two-party vote for the Democratic candidate (y-axis) in relation to the (log of) population density (x-axis) of a given county. Because there are so many counties, a local fit line is also drawn to show the underlying relationship.

In each of these elections, city areas are generally credited with being key to the Democratic candidate's successes.[8] And to some extent this is true: in each election, the Democratic candidate won most big-city counties comfortably. But in the earlier elections, there is no *relationship* between density and Democratic support: both Roosevelt and Kennedy did about as well in sparsely populated areas than they did in densely populated places. The cloud of middle-density but extremely pro-Roosevelt counties are mostly found in the South, where there was basically no Republican Party in the early 1930s, but FDR did well in the West too.[9] And Hoover and Nixon (the opponents of Roosevelt and Kennedy, respectively) didn't do poorly in *all* metropolitan counties, as you can see from the many dots below the horizontal lines near the righthand side of the graphs. Fast-forward fifty years and things have changed quite a bit. While there is still a cloud of points, and the relationship isn't perfect, it is clearly much stronger. In 2016, Clinton won about 80 percent of the votes in the densest counties of the nation but less than 20 percent in the least dense. Even since 2008, the relationship has become noticeably steeper and more monotonic, especially at the rural end, where Clinton's performance relative to Obama's in 2008 turned out to be particularly important in the Electoral College.[10]

We can peer into the dense clouds of Figure 7.1 by disaggregating by state. For various historical reasons, county density is very uneven across states—northeastern counties are particularly small, and western counties are particularly big, with unevenly spaced populations. This makes comparing them all

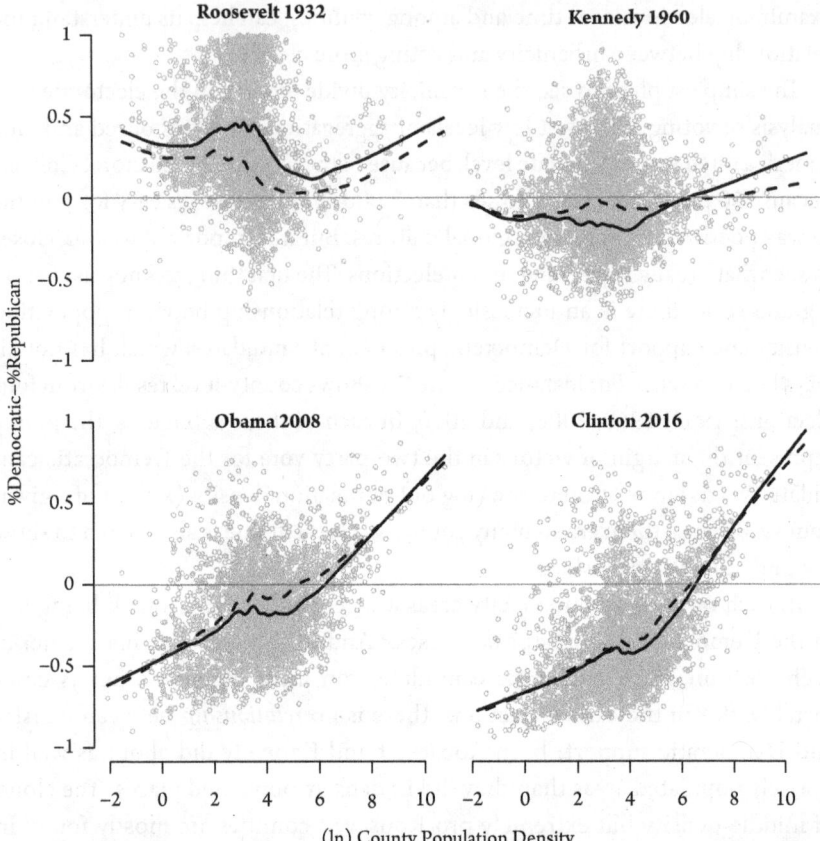

Figure 7.1 **County Support for Roosevelt (1932), Kennedy (1960), Obama (2008), and Clinton (2016) by Population Density.** Y-axis is the proportion of votes cast for the Democratic candidate minus the proportion for the Republican candidate. X-axis is the log of population density (persons per square mile). Solid lines are local-fit curves for all counties; dashed lines are local fit lines for all non-southern counties. Sources: Clubb, Flanigan, and Zingale (2006); Townhall.com (2016 results) Data.gov (2008 results); National Historic GIS (County size).

at once on a density measure potentially misleading. Fortunately, we can break them up and see a striking pattern across states that also helps explain the development and spread of the urbanicity cleavage. For the same elections examined in Figure 7.1, Figure 7.2 shows the density–vote relationship in twenty-five selected states over time.[11] The developmental story here is subtle but very important, because it relates specifically to the big-city-driven narrative of political transformation described in previous chapters. For the 1932 election, there is no cross-state pattern of positive association (just is there a relationship between density and Democratic support when all counties are put together in the same pool). A few states show a fairly strong relationship, but in most the relationship is either flat or nonmonotonic. More basically, in many states, especially in the South, there is almost no variation in county population density: almost all counties were fairly sparsely populated.[12] Both mathematically and theoretically, it is difficult for a relationship to exist when there is so little variation in one variable. Also, in many cases there is a large spread along the vertical axis, indicating large intrastate differences, albeit not differences associated with density. In a few states, however, there is a clear, monotonic relationship between density and vote choice. This was the case in New York, home of FDR, La Guardia, and the nation's most urban city. Even as the city was famously divided at home (casting votes for FDR and electing a largely Democratic congressional delegation, but not a Democratic mayor, for instance), the difference between its policy needs and those of upstate constituencies produced a partisan rivalry that proved quite lasting—and that would eventually be replicated in nearly every other state with a large metropolitan area. Among the other states shown, only Massachusetts shows a similar pattern in 1932.

By the more closely contested election of 1960, the "New York" pattern of a stronger relationship between population density and support for Democratic candidates had at least partially spread to several other states with large cities such as Ohio, Illinois, Michigan, Missouri, and Pennsylvania. Like New York, these were key swing states that held the balance of national power and also had some history of state-level rivalry between urban and rural political forces. By 1960, the modern pattern had begun to appear in at least a handful of states, with populous city counties becoming relatively Democratic, although rural areas remained relatively unaffected. This pattern of urban areas becoming distinctively Democratic sooner and rural areas shifting toward the GOP later was also true of congressional representation, as we saw Chapter 6. As states developed their own large metropolitan areas as the American population spread across the continent from the Northeast and saw the emergence of their own urban–rural divides, the pattern was replicated elsewhere. Fifty years on, the New York pattern has spread to nearly every state with a sizable metropolitan area.[13] Even Nebraska, a state where Republicans often win every county in national elections (at least through 2016), has an urban–rural divide of about the same magnitude as New York—only with a different intercept. The only notable exceptions are southern states in the Black Belt with large rural populations and no big cities (like Alabama and Mississippi) and Texas, where heavily Latino border counties support the Democrats. Even there, the average relationship in nonborder counties is basically the same. The urbanicity divide appears to have been fully nationalized—not all at once, but in stages, replicating the path upon which New York embarked in the 1930s.[14]

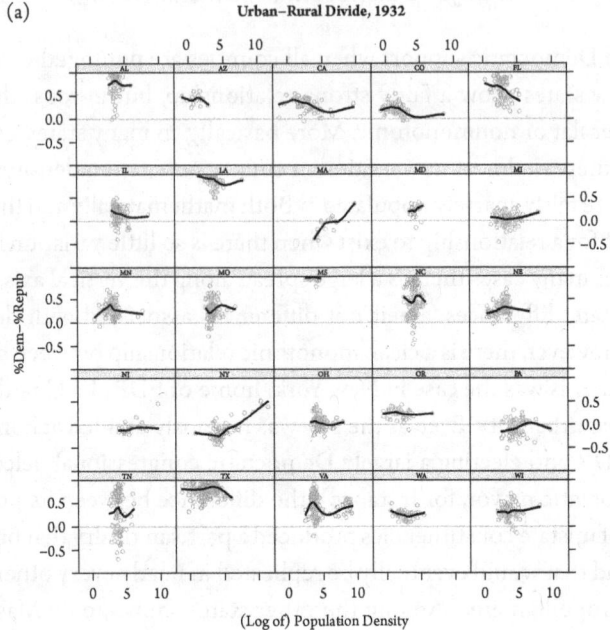

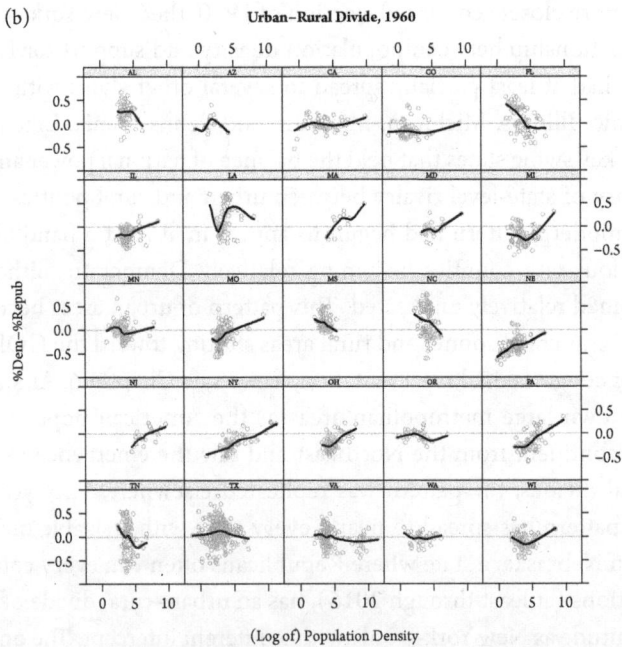

Figure 7.2 **County-Level Support for Democratic Candidates in 1932, 1960, 2008, and 2016, by Population Density in 25 States.** Y-axis is the proportion of votes cast for the Democratic candidate minus the proportion for the Republican candidate. X-axis is the log of population density (persons per square mile). Lines are local-fit curves for visual clarity. Support for F.D. Roosevelt (1932), J. F. Kennedy, Obama (2008), H.R. Clinton. Sources: Clubb, Flanigan, and Zingale (2006); Townhall.com (2016 results) Data.gov (2008 results); IPUMS NHGIS (County size).

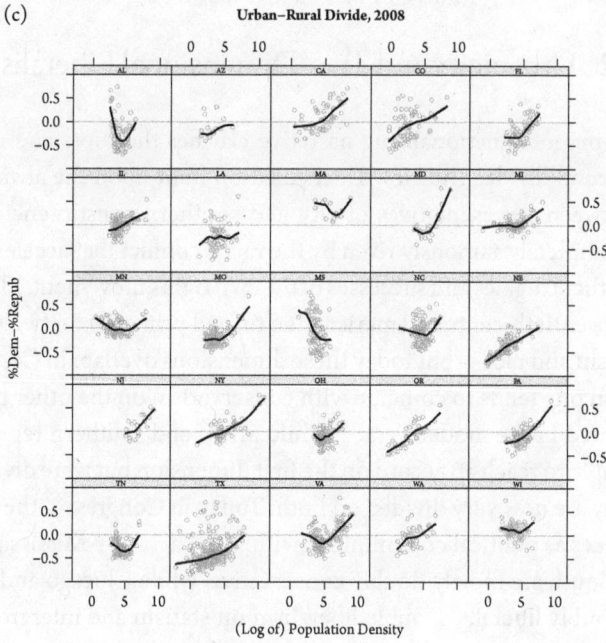

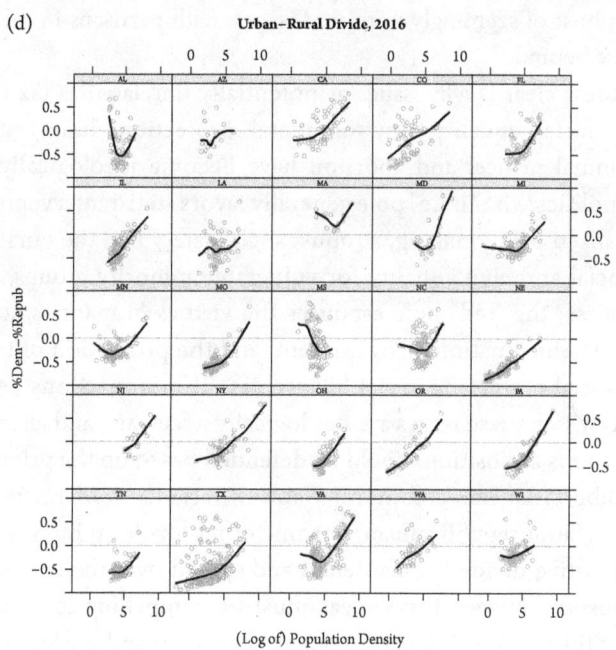

Figure 7.2 Continued

7.2 Urbanicity and Two-Dimensional Liberalism

This developmental, nationalizing narrative clarifies the roots and meaning of the urban–rural divide. The New Deal coalition built upon the always tenuous alliance between representatives of city and southern constituencies has now vanished completely, famously riven by the racial conflict that accelerated in the 1960s with the struggles and successes of the civil rights movement. Elite political conflict in twentieth-century America then turned primarily on two substantive axes—statism and race—but today these dimensions overlap: in Congress, conservatism on one tends to coincide with conservatism on the other to an extent unprecedented in the modern era.[15] While urban and southern representatives were once able to reach an accord on the first dimension but were divided on the second, they are now very divided on both. Today in Congress—the distillation of these places as political communities within the nation—Mississippi and the rest of the South are mostly doubly conservative, while Chicago and most large cities are doubly liberal.[16] Double liberalism on statism and intergroup politics has come to sweep up other issues, such that elite positions have also become sorted on a host of seemingly unrelated issues, with partisans in the electorate sorting close behind.[17]

What is less clear is *why* issues as potentially unrelated as tax rates, labor regulation, racial equality, environmental protection, immigration, drug policy, criminal justice, and abortion have become ideologically linked in American politics. The "blue" pole generally favors statist intervention in markets, centralized policymaking, a robust social safety net, the pursuit and defense of social and civil equality for vulnerable minority groups, and social permissiveness; the "red" pole espouses the virtues of markets, lower taxes, generally restrained national government, and the promotion of traditional/Christian social mores and social hierarchies. The connections between the party positions on these issues are not logically necessary, and alternative sets or combinations of positions could be defended based on the principles elaborated by libertarianism, communitarianism, variants of Marxism, dogmatic Catholicism, labor republicanism, or some other ideology. But the extant liberal–conservative divide has hardened and spread over the past decades, so the relationship between these ideas must be compelling to *someone*. If we think about the relationship between place character and the kinds of politics required to effectively manage different spaces, however, the role of urbanicity in helping to shape political conflict is compelling: liberal commitments are *urban* commitments.

The epigraphs at the beginning of this chapter reveal American attitudes about New York City and are representative of an important conversation about the place of cities in the American experience. In these pages, I have argued that place character and the distinctive governance challenges of urban communities are at the heart of contemporary modern political polarization because place character is related to governance—related to the character of the state and the ways that groups are treated in politics. The doubly liberal set of positions taken up by representatives of "blue" America resonates more in urban settings, an idea alluded to in the popular discourse on the red–blue divide but usually attributed to state or regional cultures, or to the attitudes of individuals who dwell in different places. Surely it is true that the ideas, particular histories, climate, and contingencies of states and regions matter in the formation and maintenance of citizens' political preferences. However, material conditions and lived experience on a human scale—the kinds of built environments we navigate, the varieties of persons we interact with, and the manner in which these things change, or not—are also important shapers of worldview and political outlook.

Statism and group pluralism, the hallmarks of double liberalism, are more important features for sustaining order in urban political communities than they are in other contexts. The values and perspectives articulated by Thomas Jefferson and his allies in the republic's early days were firmly rooted in the soil of an agrarian civilization and predicated upon the continual expansion into and American domination of fertile "open" territory. The many interrelated transformations of the industrial revolution, which Jefferson could not have foreseen but which would have dismayed him, and the associated development and growth of urban forms gave rise to a host of new governance demands and institutions developed to deal with them. This is not to say that all core progressive liberal policy commitments are somehow inappropriate or unpopular in rural spaces, or that urbanites won't support any conservative values. For instance, wealth redistribution and some traditional moral norms enjoy broad support in all kinds of places, and ideological and opinion divide are much smaller than red and blue maps of political identities and choices would have us believe. The key claim here is that liberal positions seem much more useful for governance and regulation of large, densely populated, heterogeneous communities. They are commitments made by city leaders attentive to their city's interest: to managing rapid economic change, to averting massive and costly social unrest, as a response to cultural changes. They embody compromises that help sustain the local body politic.

These solutions for urban life were transferred into national politics with the ascendancy of the Democratic Party's progressive liberal wing in the New Deal. Thus, the main commitments of the Long New Deal—statist intervention in the economy through regulation, redistribution, and public goods provision; the recognition, tolerance, and accommodation of group difference; and state institutional adjustment to new social conditions generally—are *urban* commitments, made national by the Democratic Party's new urban bloc-of-blocs in the 1930s, even as its local polities were episodically riven by deep racial, class, and social conflicts. This is the spirit conveyed by the WNYC station announcement, which is still aired to describe a certain kind of community to which the urban bloc aspires. These commitments made a marriage of convenience with the South—which often preferred not to "know any more" about such communities—less and less convenient as time wore on. Local development patterns and local political institutions and arrangements, not simply demography, constituent ideology, or southern pathology, played key roles in the divergent outcomes of Chicago and Mississippi.

The roots of today's red–blue moment were present within the Democratic Party of the New Deal, in an urban wing that "moved first" by developing distinctive policy goals and norms that would eventually overwhelm the national alliance with a southern wing that never fully supported either statism or group pluralism. Seeing this helps unlock a historical puzzle at the heart of the New Deal's dissolution, positing that by fostering cohesive representation in support of positions that would enhance a city's organic "health," cities and local political institutions played an unexpected role in bringing a new approach to urban policy and issues of racial equity to the national legislative agenda. This move was the basis for the mutually reinforcing dimensions of conflict we see today.

These many complex subjects—the political dynamics of the New Deal, the development of liberalism, the conversion of the white South from solidly Democratic to red Republican, the increasing polarization of contemporary American politics—are obviously important, and they have received an appropriately large amount of scholarly attention. The links between these processes become clearer when we explicitly attend to urbanicity and the manner in which cities represent themselves in the broader polity. Cities and their leaders reshaped the content of American politics to meet their special, urgent governance demands, which is easier when national policy is city-friendly. These demands, which include significant interventions in economic behavior and adjustment to changing social conditions, including the inclusion of new groups, fostered the development of progressive liberalism, a set of ideas and an approach to politics developed at the local level and later adapted to national politics. Despite the potentially divisive challenges of diversity, cities have represented themselves as unified in national politics.

7.3 A Metropolitan Political Order

Over the course of the Long New Deal, faith in the capacity of progressive liberal policies to address the challenges of modernity was high, and the mood in cities was a general optimism for the future. Of course, the intervening decades eroded that optimism and tempered the persuasive force of city-friendly ideas in national politics. Structural changes in the economy (especially the decline of Fordist manufacturing, compounded by automation and competition from low-wage competitors in the United States and elsewhere) and population shifts to the suburbs and Sunbelt left many urban centers hollowed out. Some Rust Belt cities today are half as large as they once were, and the communities that remain sometimes struggle to provide even the most basic forms of order; contemporary Detroit and Flint, Michigan, are the most shocking examples of this phenomenon. The most successful cities may have now regained their midcentury populations in absolute terms, but relative to their metropolitan areas and the nation as a whole they are much smaller than they once were. New York City once sent twenty-six representatives to Congress; today, that number is down to eleven, even though the city itself is still home to "more than seven million people," as WNYC bragged in the 1930s.[18] The (central) city can no longer claim to be the part that stands in for the whole of American society. At the same time, fewer city representatives come from places with strong local party traditions (and these parties have mostly become weaker where they do persist). The result of both of these trends limits the potential impact of locally-rooted bridge-building institutions.[19]

The political prospects for the urban political order have shifted. The maturation of the urbanicity divide, the Republican consolidation of the (white) South, and continued net population flows to suburban areas mean that the pivotal political force in American politics is clearly suburban.[20] The political consequences of this trend, which Gainsborough (2001) identifies as the "suburbanization" of American politics, are still being negotiated; the general trend is toward further privatization of both government and personal life, a shrinking retreat from the private sphere, and a reflexive aversion by many, at least rhetorically, to the kinds of regulations that smooth the operations of city life but seem more like headaches in other contexts. The city–South Democratic alliance fell apart because southern partners would not compromise on the kinds of social regulation—that is, on issues of labor and race—helpful in keeping cities peaceful and productive. In the wake of that change, at a political moment when cities' institutional power in national government is on the ebb, it is tempting to seek disconnection from national politics. At least one thoughtful observer has proposed a kind of deep confederalism: if national politics is hopelessly polarized, let cities have broad sway over their internal affairs in order to help solve the world's pressing problems.[21] Carving out a sphere of autonomous action for city-friendly policies is appealing, especially if we grant that certain elements of polarization are based on reasonable differences in the kind of government best suited to manage different kinds of spaces.

Efforts to shore up local democracy and reinvigorate civic engagement are certainly desirable, but the lessons of the urban order teach us that local action is not enough. Such a retreat, beyond being practically and constitutionally difficult, would not be desirable. First, many progressives' commitments expand beyond their own communities to others. Confederal arrangements, with their inherent decentralization, would leave vulnerable persons even more exposed to material hardship and civil discrimination. More basically, however, cities are more connected with each other and the rest of the nation and world than before, meaning that externalities will inevitably continue to cross boundaries. The logic of interjurisdictional competition remains as well; this means we should expect cities to continue their pursuit of city-friendly policies for the same reason they did back in the 1930s.

To pursue those goals, cities have new potential coalitional partners. As the urbanicity cleavage has matured, the "next most urban" places—suburban areas and smaller cities—have become the most likely allies.[22] However, while demographic patterns are shifting in a way that makes political partnerships between cities and their suburbs more plausible, the local jurisdictional-political organization of these places is not. In some sense the *point* of suburbs is their high level of political fragmentation, so as more Americans live in such small places, this fragmentation may continue to undermine the possibilities for effective policy solutions. Local politics in such small, relatively homogeneous democracies have dynamics that may especially undermine programs of public investment or redistribution.[23] When the divides between small and homogeneous communities are wide, the potential for mass- or elite-level bridge building is more limited. Fragmented metropolitan areas, smaller political communities, and the increased rarity of fora in which groups are forced together means that many issues can be ruled out of local politics.[24] Without the IHIs of common polity, or common political identity fostered by comembership, the prospects that local democracy can help do the "big things" required to maintain American preeminence or alleviate all manner of mounting inequality seem dim.

This lack of bridges is a major problem that new forms of local IHIs might help mitigate. From a policy or political perspective, two possibilities for reducing political fragmentation and reinvigorating the power of local IHIs seem apparent—though neither seems particularly likely to occur in the short term. The first is to redraw the meaningful lines of political division and identity by strengthening regional approaches to local governance. Because the metropolitan area is the real functional unit of contemporary social and economic life, there is a flourishing ecosystem of ideas about how to build regional governments in pursuit of more rational or equitable policy implementation.[25] Such an agenda aims to strengthen institutions' planning and resource allocation decision making at a regional level, incorporating both central city and suburbs and effectively create a new, meaningful, and more inclusive jurisdictional IHI. Some areas have made impressive achievements in moving toward such regional governance: Portland (Oregon) and Minneapolis are perhaps the most notable American examples of these efforts, and other variants of metropolitan governance are even more common than powerful regional authorities. City–county consolidation is fairly common, especially in the South.[26] And in newer cities where outlying areas have not been incorporated and fenced off from the common weal, assertive annexation rules for newly developed areas is also a promising tack for building metropolitan unity by simply expanding the central city.[27] In most areas, though, metropolitan governance remains weak, devoted to only some specialized areas of policy, and often fairly divorced from the most salient politics of the day. Better integration of transportation, community development planning, schools, policing, and other vital service provisions would make these regional metropolitan connections clearer for both leaders and citizens by making plain the reality of metropolitan interdependence (as opposed to illusory suburban independence), and pave the way for more robust institutional connections down the road.

The same obstacles that have impeded efforts at regional governance have no doubt hindered regional representational cohesion as well. We observed the outcome of this situation in Chapter 4: 20th-century metropolitan-area delegations were less cohesive than city delegations in almost all cases. Some notable suburban areas such as Orange County, California, and Long Island have longstanding political cultures and organizations that seem purposively founded in opposition to the priorities of the city they touch. In those cases, and in other suburban contexts, change may be afoot. Long Island's Nassau County was once the home of perhaps the last (or only) real suburban Republican machine; since the 1990s, it has routinely gone for Democratic presidential candidates (and its congressional delegation is currently split between two Democrats and one Republican.) In Chicagoland, my work-home of Evanston was the home of the antimachine, anti-immigrant sentiments embodied in the temperance and municipal reform movements. Now it is just as Democratic as its big-city neighbor. Farther west in that metro area, an archetypically suburban congressional seat held by Republicans for three decades (first by Donald Rumsfeld, then by Phil Crane) turned over in the Democratic wave of 2005 and has now gone to the Democrats in four of the last five election cycles. Out west, Orange County, California, the paragon of historian Rick Perlstein's "Nixonland," has not quite joined the rest of the state's coastal counties in consistently supporting the Democrats, but its rapidly changing demography (the county's largest city, Santa Ana, is now about 75 percent Latino) has pushed it to the tipping point;[28] in the last election, Clinton actually won fairly comfortably in a county that Jimmy Carter lost by 45 percentage points in 1980. These suburban political shifts indicate that the suburbs and city are now closer than ever before on national issues. Such changes may make coordination across municipal boundaries more likely and may eventually persuade municipalities to cede some elements of their "sovereignty" (which under the actual workings of federalism is a thin fiction in any case) to a broader authority and build a more inclusive, effective political community. Thus might the pursuit of regional solutions to metropolitan governance problems coincide with new political dynamics far away in Washington.

A second possibility for reducing political fragmentation and reinvigorating local IHIs is to shift not the meaningful borderlines, but the people. The sprawling population patterns that have accelerated over the past century as American life has been reorganized at automobile scale have pushed us far beyond the boundaries of central cities, past the lines that once collected many, many Americans in the same local polity.[29] This sprawl has been encouraged by some technologies and preferences, but also by government policies. Municipal fragmentation has been both a side effect and an accelerant of the phenomenon.[30] Among sprawl-financing policies include publicly funded and nationally subsidized road-based transportation networks, low energy prices (especially gasoline, relative to comparable countries) with considerable externalities, subsidies for homeownership, and a system of primarily local financing for public schools. Eliminating or reversing these policies can have the simultaneous effects of reducing sprawl as a developmental form and including more persons in shared local jurisdictions.[31]

Similarly to eliminating subsidies for sprawl, reducing the costs of city life can help bring populations back into central cities. Technology has a role to play here. Some of the advances of the Internet age are fairly spatially dependent: densely populated areas can provide effective, free wireless Internet more easily, and technology can improve service delivery in cash-strapped cities. Integrated, multimodal, and environmentally friendly transit networks (including subways, buses, light rail, bicycle shares, and private ride sharing) work better in densely populated areas. Reduced crime rates have made some cities, especially those most connected to the global economy and certain flourishing economic sectors, very attractive as revitalized communities. As redevelopment efforts continue, local governments should use policies (especially for affordable housing) that make this development, which is generally good for the city's organic interest, sustainable in the long run. It is also possible that today's younger cohorts have a taste for urban life that their parents did not, though the jury is still out on that count.[32]

In planning and policymaking circles, sprawl is increasingly seen as a cause of all ills, so fighting it is often seen as a sort of panacea. Changes to the calculations involved in how people make their residency decisions are possible insofar as those calculations are driven or shaped by policies. If people lived closer together, there are reasons to believe many personal and social ills would be diminished, from greenhouse gas pollution to income inequality to obesity. Of course, other problems might fill the void—everyone who has lived in a densely populated space knows such communities have their serious aggravations. But if membership in the same political community fosters common interest, at least among elites, then reducing sprawl may actually foster something like liberalism by strengthening institutions that help to overcome the "diversity problems" that complicate sharing and statism. By building bridges between central cities and their suburbs, leaders can simultaneously address many of their problems at home and help build a new *metropolitan* political order.

Other features of the American system mean that a metropolitan political order will remain vulnerable to exclusion from power. Though she won a substantial plurality of the votes cast in the 2016 election, Hillary Clinton did not win the presidency and the city-based Democrats are in the minority of both chambers of Congress. This outcome is due to inefficient distribution of these representatives' supporters as much as anything else. Democratic margins were massive in large metropolitan areas but didn't help much in states where cities are shrinking fast. And new research on the kinds of places where Clinton's support was weakest relative to Obama's indicates that rural voters may not rejoin a coalition of mutual exchange, because anti-urban resentment is central to their conception of politics.[33] A more likely course for success, not only in politics but in policy, is to build shorter bridges to suburban jurisdictions that are now experiencing what we used to think of as city challenges—infrastructure decay, market inefficiencies, aging and increasingly diverse populations—that can best be solved through cooperation with regional partners instead of by building walls to separate themselves from the central city. Building a metropolitan political order is not only compatible with urban policy goals—it is also going where the votes are, as an ever-increasing share of Americans—well over 80 percent at last count—live the interdependent lives of metropolitan urbanites, even if their self-conception as suburbanites blurs this reality. This metropolitan strategy must be pursued in tandem with an effort to maintain support for the urban agenda in the smaller cities scattered throughout the nation that face problems shared by all cities and can benefit from the doubly liberal policies that help solve them. Essentially, the metropolitan order should be the same one Richard J. Daley called for in that hearing on reapportionment in 1964.

7.4 Cities on the Hill

The biblical image of a shining "city on a hill" has often been employed to describe or justify America's status as an exceptional nation. The phrase was a favorite of Ronald Reagan, who employed it frequently over decades. In his televised farewell address, Reagan devoted several paragraphs to describing his vision of the city upon a hill as

> a tall, proud city built on rocks stronger than oceans, windswept, God-blessed, and teeming with people of all kinds living in harmony and peace; a city with free ports that hummed with commerce and creativity. And if there had to be city walls, the walls had doors and the doors were open to anyone with the will and the heart to get here. That's how I saw it, and see it still.[34]

This imaginary, model capitalist-Christian alternative to Communism has been adopted as a touchstone of Reagan's legacy, and the idea of the United States as a model community is closely linked with the concept of American exceptionalism, a concept that has itself come to approximate extreme patriotism in its common usage and is most commonly associated with conservative causes. As a sort of metaphorical inversion, this book examines a time when cities were particularly active on the Hill—Capitol Hill—and self-consciously promoted an example of politics and society markedly different from that of today's Party of Reagan. Digging into the relationship between these phrases may transform our interpretation of both American exceptionalism and the city on a hill.

The idea of American exceptionalism is rooted in the paradox that prompted Werner Sombart to ask why there was "no socialism in the United States" in 1906.[35] This alleged absence demanded explanation from a Marxian perspective because of America's advanced capitalist development. From a further remove, we can see other important exceptional features of the United States that can help us answer Sombart's question. As Lieberman (2009) notes, as far back as Jefferson, the United States has always seemed to have a deep unease with cities and the kind of citizens and society they engender. This has certainly been manifest in our national mythology, but also in our political institutions, which have always privileged place over people.[36] The result has been a general weakness of cities in national politics that is unusual by international standards. In other modern democracies, a larger share of the population lives in large cities, and there is often a single metropolis that dominates the cultural, economic, and political life of the nation.[37] Not so in the United States. However, there have been moments when cities have had their say in national affairs. The Long New Deal was as close as we have come to an exceptional (for America) "moment of urban triumph" in which a cross-city political alliance moved the needle of American politics significantly to the left.[38] This alliance—supported by a urban mass hodgepodge coalition that included large numbers of the ethnic white working class, unions, African Americans, and others—promoted and passed the major social welfare legislation that would prove to be as close to socialism or workers-party leadership that the United States has seen to date.

But this urban triumph and the political forces that gave it muscle present a theoretical puzzle for Sombart and his interlocutors. Many plausible explanations for the absence of socialism (or its variants) in the United States have been proffered in the century since Sombart asked his question, and among the most frequently recurring have been variations on the theme of division within the working class, as "the complex web of backgrounds from which the American proletariat emerged is often seen as rendering unity along class lines all but impossible."[39] Such a perspective argues that diversity—particularly diversity in salient identities that cannot be easily changed—undermines the potential for what we think of as liberal politics, or socialism, in the parlance of Sombart's time.[40] Diversities of background and interest are particularly salient in cities, where all sorts of differences are both magnified and compressed within physical space, where principles of toleration and democracy are tested most seriously, and where common interests or preferences are elusive.[41] Such conditions are not conducive, contemporary social scientists argue, to statism, social provision, and intergroup comity.[42] As we might expect, city politics have never been easy or consensual, especially at the local level. But the broader truth is that significant national moves to the left for several generations now have been powered by these hodgepodge alliances from such heterogeneous places. Today, a liberalism that is supposed to be undermined by diversity seems in some ways to be driven by it (even as it is also opposed and limited by a conservative reaction). The party of the diverse cities supports social welfare provision to individuals (and because it supports national programs, it makes provision even those individuals who don't typically support such provision), more substantial public goods provision, the imposition of rules to govern large institutions, and generally inclusive and adaptive norms for managing the unavoidable pluralism of our rapidly changing contemporary society. Even if they do not win all the time, if such a politics is most ardently supported by the most diverse places, this prompts a reexamination of how diversity affects the politics of statism and group relations, perhaps with special attention to how social and political experiences (and the political cultures they generate, or that help people make meaning of them) that differ by place character have real, important effects far from the sites where they are developed.

The assignment of the label of "city on a hill" to the American experiment is thought to originate in a sermon by John Winthrop, a Puritan minister who was, in Reagan's words, "an early freedom man."[43] But freedom as Reagan typically meant it—an individual's lack of encumbrance by the state—was not a theme in Winthrop's text. The Puritans, after all, were not noted for their commitment to individual freedom.

In his now-famous "Defense of Christian Charity" of 1630, Winthrop likened the new Puritan colony in Boston to a city on a hill, as the American experiment's success or failure would be closely followed by those back in England and ostensibly attributed to the righteousness and faithfulness with which the Puritans followed their holy path. Winthrop was himself alluding to the Sermon on the Mount, in which Jesus exhorts his followers to lead exemplary lives of good works as a model for others.[44] In Winthrop's view, the exemplary conduct of those in Jesus's hilltop "city" would be marked by Christian love and reciprocal obligation under the guiding advice of the Golden Rule and a selflessness worthy of sainthood. For Winthrop, the path to be followed by the Puritans was not one of openness or individual liberty; rather, he conceived of their mission as one that could only be pursued in a closely knit community in which some individual desires were subordinated to the common good. Winthrop emphasizes these ties of mutual obligation:

> We must be knit together, in this work, as one man. We must entertain each other in brotherly affection. We must be willing to abridge ourselves of our superfluities, for the supply of other's necessities. . . . For we must consider that we shall be as a city upon a hill. The eyes of all people are upon us.[45]

Winthrop preached unity in pursuit of the common cause presented by external threats and urged exemplary conduct in the name of Christian love and charity, but also in the name of their community's survival. He couched this approach in the context of apparent concern about why, within the band of colonists, "some must be rich, some poor, some high and eminent in power and dignity; others mean and in submission." Theorizing how a diverse community (his emphasis, after all, is on differences of wealth and status among the group of settlers) can remain unified (especially against outsiders), Winthrop argues that "diversity" of wealth is a good to all, because under such conditions "every man might have need of others, and from hence they might be all knit more nearly together in the Bonds of brotherly affection." He was worried that the success of the colony was far from assured, given the many perils of the New World.[46] He was hopeful that divisions could be overcome in the name of common cause, in the interest of the city itself.

We do not need to venture into Ronald Reagan's imagination to see American communities self-consciously seeking to lead the world and exemplify a new, distinctive vision of political community. We can see this in the character and substance of city representation in national politics—how the cities represent themselves on Capitol Hill. Actual cities have lived up to Winthrop's aspiration better than those pessimistic about the challenges of diversity might predict: in the face of all manner of internal crisis and conflict, they have frequently united to speak with one voice on the challenges of the day and have established and developed an urban political order that has come to define American liberalism as a force in our politics, first in conflicts within the Democratic Party and then in conflicts between the national parties.

Just as Winthrop's Pilgrims were faced with an external threat that was to bind them together despite their differences, so too did the urban political order create a cohesive bloc out of disparate parts when faced with the extreme crises of modern capitalism during the Depression and the subsequent era of suburbanization and capital flight.

The member cities of the urban political order in the twentieth century faced more and deeper divisions—in terms of class, region, race, religion, national origin, and general worldview—than Winthrop would have been able to imagine. These polyglot communities fostered an approach to politics that grappled with difference and recognized it (even if only symbolically at times) while seeking to bring these new members into an existing political framework and preserve the health of their cities. Internal struggles did not go away, but in national politics they were subordinated to the common interest in the fight against the structural threats to cities presented by the twentieth century. Within- and cross-city unity was forged even though the cities themselves had long faced (and continued to face) the deep threat of internal disorder as economic and cultural heterogeneity made consensus more difficult and raised the stakes of politics. The result was an ongoing, imperfect, but inclusive negotiated compromise, which was not made on equal terms for all groups but which nonetheless allowed for progress to be made even as local conflicts remained deep and dire, simmering or exploding according to local conditions; sometimes, these supralocal successes helped to provide solutions (of varying partiality and durability) to the conflicts and problems of city governance within a federal polity.

This is how city leaders saw themselves during this era. When WNYC announced that its listening audience comprised members of a community where "more than seven million people live in peace and enjoy the benefits of democracy," and when Chicago's Anton Cermak described his ascendant Democratic machine as "a house for all peoples," they were attempting both description and inspiration. The progressive liberalism developed in these cities and supported by their representatives in national politics reshaped America's self-presentation in the world. These cities sought to spread their brand of politics—doubly liberal, pluralist in cultural and political approach, and with faith in limited statist intervention as a way to soften capitalism's rough edges and strengthen the bonds of membership in the national community—to the nation, and eventually, in the aftermath of World War II, to the world. They met with mixed success, but their political project shifted national domestic politics, nudging the doubly conservative South away and strengthening the power of the urbanicity cleavage over time.

These city leaders, speaking at the moment of metropolitan metonymy, sought to apply a politics developed in cities to a nation that had seldom been comfortable with urban life and would soon face the dramatic urban crises of the 1960s. They were speaking in the center of the national political conversation, on Capitol Hill, referring not only to the grand ongoing experiment of city democracy but also to a world beset by different visions of how to deal with the flux of modernity. Illiberal models were ascendant in many places, but leaders in American cities advanced a set of policies and political commitments that sought to deal with the significant, urgent challenges of the modern world while still taking democracy as a fundamental premise. In a world of constant threats and increasingly global economic insecurity, the city on a hill—the American political solution to economic modernity and cultural diversity that Reagan saw as a beacon of hope for the world—was built by the cities, on the Hill.

The current political divide between city and country, intensified and reinforced by ideological and identitarian cleavages, presents a seemingly intractable puzzle. Will we as a nation be able to meet our urgent governance challenges, from climate change to increasing inequality, to persistent terrorism, to accelerating economic structural change? Will our leaders seek solutions through negotiation with whom they do not share a great deal in common, or will they seek refuge in communities of social affinity and ideological purity? The answers to these questions remain obscure when a disagreement about the very notion of governance—whether to do it, whether to try to solve problems pragmatically together—lies at the heart of our red and blue differences.

Appendix A

HOUSE CSR SCORES

As described briefly in Chapter 6, the quantitative analyses in this study are based in part on an original dataset of measures indicating the place character of congressional districts, or CSR scores (for "City–Suburban–Rural"). These CSR scores differ from the urbanicity scores used by Mayhew (1966) and Wolman and Marckini (2005) because they are available across a wider stretch of time (since they do not rely upon the availability of district-level census data, which has been the standard approach in previous studies) and because they begin with the premise that urbanites are members of large political communities. For each of these reasons, the CSR codes are more theoretically useful for study of the urban–rural divide over time. This appendix describes how CSR scores are developed and compares them to previous efforts to measure congressional urbanicity.

A.1 Previous Approaches: Census-Driven

Previous analyses of city representatives' power or behavior in the House have begun with district-level census data to identify districts. Mayhew, in his pioneering study of cross-cutting pressures on legislators from different kinds of places, uses a census-based approach combined with an accounting of the percentage of residents in the district who rented their homes. He relies on data from *Congressional Quarterly* from 1962 and then applies the measures for those Congresses forward and backward over his time period. He is thus restricted to a relatively few postwar Congresses based on data availability.

Wolman and Marckini (2005) (hereafter "W-M") adopt a similar approach, but because they wrote in 1998 they are able to include more Congresses over time. They begin with census data for the Congresses just after the decennial census and reallocation of seats (1963, 1973, 1983, and 1993). These data allow them to determine the proportion of a district's residents living in central cities, the proportion living outside of central cities but in metropolitan-area counties, and those living in counties outside metropolitan areas. Based on whether a majority of the district's residents fall into one of these categories, they code the district urban, suburban, or nonmetropolitan, respectively. Districts that do not have a majority from one place type are coded as "mixed."[1]

Each of these census-based analyses identifies districts by place character, but their approaches have several shortcomings. The most obvious is the time constraint: because these approaches rely on available census data, they are restricted to a few Congresses. This limits the scope of questions they can ask. For a study concerned with the changing place of cities in American political development, using only a few recent Congresses, even when spread over three decades (after the urban–rural divide has grown), limits the things we might see. Another approach, less dependent on the availability of census data (which was relatively limited in availability before 1960), would be an improvement.

Beyond this main time limitation, each selection process includes potentially limiting choices in categorizing city districts. Mayhew is not concerned with the full range of urbanicity: his analysis is primarily concerned with city representatives, so he labels representatives on a binary measure, as either city or noncity. City representatives are those with very few nonmetropolitan residents and lots of renters. This purposefully excludes representatives from areas of cities with relatively high rates of homeownership, prioritizing land tenure over political membership in the conceptualization of what counts as urban. In practice, this approach means including districts from smaller, perhaps more working-class, places where there are lots of renters and excluding more affluent areas of some cities, which are often nearer to the edge of the city/suburban border. This decision is perhaps appealing sociologically, but not politically. Because size is a key characteristic of urbanicity, membership in the large political community of the center city (and thus inclusion in its institutions of horizontal integration) is relevant, so over the long run the opposite choice seems more appropriate for identifying city districts. Relying on political boundaries, rather than proportion of rentals, may be more appropriate over time as well if the rental rate varies significantly over time or across cities.

W-M's selection and coding does rely primarily on municipal boundaries in determining whether a district is mostly city, suburban, or nonmetropolitan. Their approach is limited in two ways, however. First, they do not attempt to characterize "mixed" districts, which are those without a majority from one of the three place types. It is likely that for most of these districts some judgment can be made about the balance—for instance, a predominantly urban–suburban mix or a predominantly rural–suburban mix. Their approach is unnecessarily modest and leaves out potentially useful information from this "in-between" category. More than fifty seats in each of their Congresses go essentially uncategorized.

Second, and probably less importantly in practice, W-M's approach does not distinguish between large and small cities, even though central cities can in practice be quite small and not fit our intuitions of what a "city" is. For most districts, this is not a problem, because a small city's population will not make up a majority of a congressional district, but if a district contains several small cities and is drawn in an idiosyncratic way, it might; again, membership in a common political community is theoretically important in this study, so distinguishing districts in which most members live in the same city from those in which they come from different local political communities is helpful.

A.2 CSR Codes: Size-Driven

For this study, I develop measures of district place character that are consistent and applicable over time, that are sensitive to the full spectrum of place character (i.e., not just binary), and that result in scores that fit well with our intuitions of what a city is. Because urban forms have changed so much over time, focusing on rental rates or other lifestyle characteristics may not be flexible enough. Instead, I adopt the approach taken in Lieberman (2009), which gives priority to place size relative to the nation in determining what a city is and measures the urbanicity of a congressional district based on its spatial relationship with such cities. This approach has the advantages of being consistent over historical time and not distinguishing between one kind of city over another (in terms of development or home tenure patterns), apart from the large versus small.

The CSR measures are developed as follows. I begin with Lieberman (2009)'s list of cities with more than 0.1 percent of the national population in a given decennial census (hereafter referred to as "large cities"). This standard is identified by Lieberman as a useful definition for cross-time comparisons. It enjoys face validity insofar as the list of cities fits an intuition of which kinds of places should be included in a set of cities, and the character of the places is allowed to vary over time. More rigorously, 0.1 percent is just shy of one-half of one congressional district under conditions of equal apportionment, so such places would theoretically be able to exert significant control over at least one congressional district.[2] There were sixty places that met this standard in 2010, totalling about fifty million city-zens. The set of cities in this list has become more varied geographically over time. From a concentration in the North and East, the set of cities has spread to the South and West, and the number of cities in the set has increased over time. The list of cities, with lines representing the years they are included in the dataset, is presented graphically by region in Figure A.1.

A.3 CSR Codes: Scoring Procedures

With Lieberman's list in hand, each congressional district is assigned a series of scores based on its position in time and space relative to that list. The first score (CSRnum) is an indicator of whether a district has significant spatial overlap with a city on the list for that decade. If a district overlaps with a current city, it is given a score of "city." If it overlaps with a large city that was on the list but has dropped off the list within two decades, it is labeled as a "former city." This is because such communities will no doubt retain some of their political importance, even if their relative (or absolute) size has declined, and to distinguish such formerly city districts from those that have never been part of a big city. If the community overlaps with a city that joins the list in the next decade, it is labeled "future city" to mark cities that are growing and may have actually reached the threshold but have not been remeasured by the census yet. In the analyses of the book, I use only the contemporary measures, not the former- and future-city indicators, though the major insights are robust to using those more capacious measures. Districts that do not overlap with a city, former city, or future city are given a "noncity" label.

Each district is also given a more qualitative measure describing its character. These scores are developed by carefully examining each district's geographic extent and evaluating its mix of place characters. Thanks to the tireless efforts of Lewis et al. (2013), which was released as I was refining these measures, GIS maps of the districts can be overlaid on a large city's boundaries to determine to what extent the district is enclosed within the large city. For older Congresses, I also used maps available in the congressional atlas series, and Congresses before 1983 are scored using maps and district descriptions from Martis et al. (1982), an invaluable source. Districts that are entirely within a city from Lieberman's list are coded as "C," wholly suburban districts are coded as "S," and those that do not overlap with a large city (or its suburbs) are coded "R." Coding mixed districts is less straightforward. While W-M lump many of these districts into a single category and effectively discard them, CSR codes attempt to give a more informative qualitative description of where a district falls on the place-character continuum, which allows for a more fine-grained scale of urbanicity to be used in some of the book's analyses. A district that is primarily within a large city but also includes significant suburban areas is coded "C/S," a district that is predominantly suburban but also includes some significant portion of a large city is coded "S/C," and so on. Once these qualitative CSR codes are

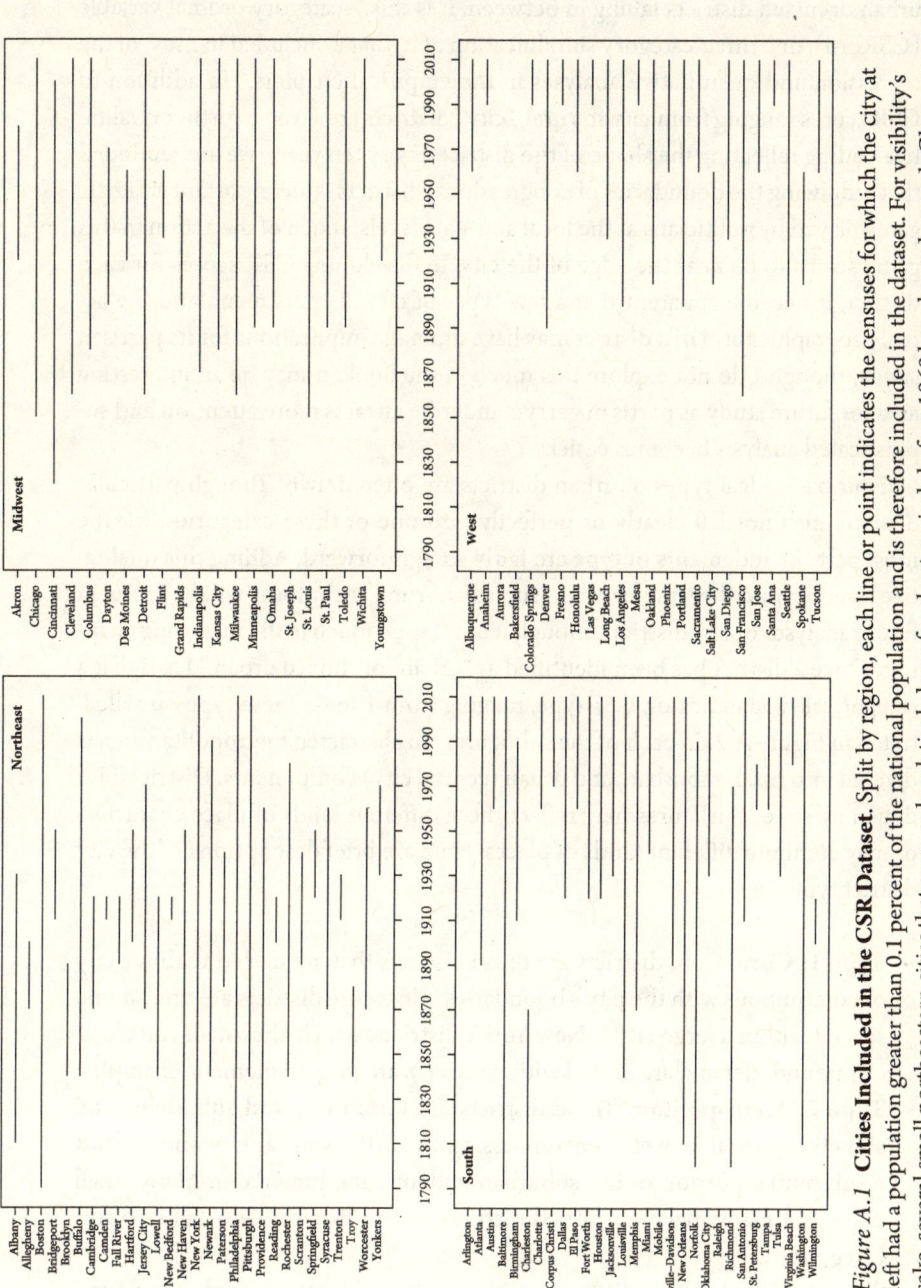

Figure A.1 **Cities Included in the CSR Dataset.** Split by region, each line or point indicates the censuses for which the city at left had a population greater than 0.1 percent of the national population and is therefore included in the dataset. For visibility's sake, several small northeastern cities that were only relatively large for short periods before 1860 have been dropped: Gloucester, Marblehead, Middlebrough, Nantucket, Newburyport, Newport, and Salem (MA); Portsmouth (NH); Moyamensing, Northern Liberties, Kensington, Southwark, and Spring Garden (PA); and Williamsburgh (NY). Sources: Lieberman (2009); U.S. Census.

given, districts are also given a quantitative measure on an ordinal CSR scale ranging from 1 (noncity/rural) to 7 (entirely city), with predominantly suburban or mixed districts falling in between. It is this 7-category ordinal variable (CSRord), or a three-category simplification of it, that is included in most of the regression and quantitative analyses in the empirical chapters.[3] In addition to CSR scores ranging from city to rural, "city" districts are given a further qualitative coding reflecting the shape of the district. Every ten years, we are reminded that redrawing the boundaries of congressional districts is an important strategic game played by politicians at the local and state levels; much of the action in this game seems to lie near the edge of the city. In developing CSR scores for each district, it became apparent that a few types of city districts recur, and the actual geographic form of a district may have dramatic implications for its partisan status; though I do not explore this much in the book, it may be an interesting area for future study as partisan gerrymandering attracts more attention and sophisticated analysis becomes easier.

Four basic ideal types of urban districts are often drawn. Though particular districts may not fall clearly or perfectly into one of these categories, for the most part the judgments of type are fairly straightforward. Adding this qualitative layer beyond the simple urban–suburban–rural trichotomy will be useful in future analyses of city districts, though it is not used much in the foregoing chapters. Once a district has been identified as "urban" or "mixed urban," I assign it a categorical type indicator, CSRtype, ranging from 1 to 4. These types are illustrated in Figure A.2. In each of the subfigures, an abstracted metropolitan area is divided into rural, suburban, and urban (central city) components. District lines drawn by state legislatures may reflect these different kinds of place characters or may combine different kinds of places. Here are brief descriptions of the city district types:

- **Type 1: Core.** Core districts are those districts that are nested within a city or coterminous with the city's boundaries. Most core districts are one among several within a large city—New York's districts, which almost all run along city boundaries and are nested within the city, are the paradigmatic examples.
- **Type 2: Metropolitan.** These districts are mixed city and suburban (and sometimes rural as well), encompassing all of the central city and at least a substantial portion of the suburban and/or rural hinterland. Many small cities and many malapportioned districts before *Baker v. Carr* fall into this category.
- **Type 3: Sliced.** These districts combine city residents with suburban and/or rural residents, typically in a way that makes the city look like a pie that has been sliced up. If a city is large enough to merit more than one district, this type of district is often an attractive alternative to creating districts that

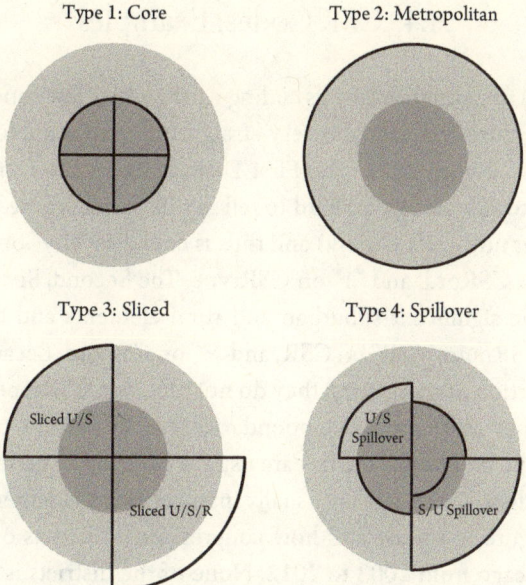

Figure A.2 **Illustrations of Ideal Urban District Types.** Each figure represents a metropolitan area with a central city (shaded dark grey) and a suburban area (shaded light grey) surrounded by nonmetropolitan white space. Dark grey lines represent some common types of congressional-district boundary patterns. The balance of geography within a district determines the CSR score assigned to it.

are more internally homogeneous with respect to urbanicity. Many districts that resulted from the forced redistricting following *Baker* look like this, as do many of the districts that have resulted from court enforcement of the Voting Rights Act.

- **Type 4: Spillover.** These "remainder" districts combine urbanites with residents outside the central city, most often because there is some area of the city left over, or geographically anomalous, that cannot be fit into a more city-based district. There are not many spillover districts, and for a district to qualify as this type, it must be from a city that has at least one core district, to illustrate that the spillover is not just one of many pie slices.

Finally, during the coding process, the large city with which the district is associated (as a city or suburban district) is noted, and in the case of very large cities, the part of the city represented is also noted (e.g., the South Side of Chicago, the San Fernando Valley in Los Angeles, or the neighborhood of Manhattan in New York City). Recording the city allows for city delegation–level analyses as well as analyses of metropolitan-area and suburban delegations, as in Chapter 3, and acts as a handy referent when identifying the constituencies of representatives in other contexts.

A.4 CSR Codes: Examples

It may be useful to examine how this coding works with a few concrete examples. For instance, Figure A.3 uses the very straightforward example of districts in Colorado from 2003 to 2012. The First District traces the Denver city limits (marked by shading, though it's hard to tell in this map because the boundaries track each other unusually closely) and thus is coded as "city" on CSRnum, "C" on CSR, "7" on CSRord, and "1" on CSRtype. The Second, Sixth, and Seventh districts include significant suburban and rural elements and are each coded "noncity" on CSRnum, "S/R" on CSR, and "3" on CSRord. Because they do not include any portion of a large city, they do not receive a CSRtype score.

Because congressional district boundaries usually do not track municipal boundaries at all, and because cities are usually not almost perfectly sized for a congressional district, the scoring usually involves more judgments than it does for Denver. Figure A.4 illustrates how congressional districts overlapped with the city of Chicago from 2003 to 2012. None of the districts is entirely within the city boundaries (again indicated by the shaded area), though the territory of the gerrymandered Fourth District is effectively inside Chicago. All of the other districts that overlap Chicago have significant suburban components, and some are primarily suburban. Thus, while the First, Second, Third, Fifth, Seventh, and Ninth districts are all coded "city" on CSRnum, they vary between "U/S" and "S/U" on CSR, with CSRord scores from 5 to 7, depending on the balance of the city/suburban mix.

Such elaborate and complicated district-drawing schemes have become more common over the past decades, as cities have been accorded fewer districts and lines must often be drawn with considerations other than contiguity in mind. The phenomenon of suburban sprawl also complicates these judgments. Before the twentieth century, few cities had satellite communities that could reasonably be called suburbs: Cambridge (Massachusetts), Brooklyn, and some of the neighborhoods that are now part of Philadelphia were a few notable exceptions.[4] For most cities, suburbanization became noticeable politically around the time of the 1930 Census, when medium-sized congressional districts appeared outside the central city's boundaries. This year is when I begin coding more suburban districts for many cities. In practice many of these districts included city, suburban, and rural components—sometimes older cities like Lowell (Massachusetts) became functional suburbs, while sometimes suburbs like Brooklyn were incorporated into their central cities—and it is often very difficult to tell where the development line between "suburban" and "rural" ends for both historic and contemporary Congresses. I have done my best to code these accurately, using historical street maps where available and knowledge of the development patterns of these cities and states. For most districts, however,

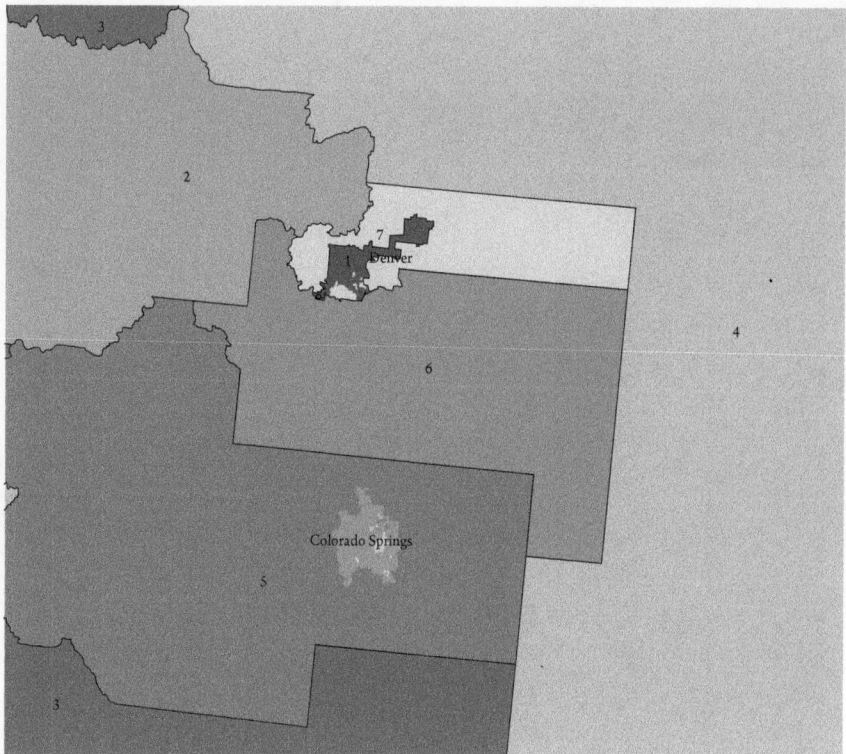

Figure A.3 **Congressional Districts: Denver and Colorado Springs Metropolitan Areas, Colorado, 2003–2013.** A real-life example of metropolitan congressional district-drawing. Districts are outlined in bold lines and numbered. Central city boundaries are shaded to contrast with surrounding areas. Note that Denver's city boundaries are roughly coterminous with the first congressional district.

geographic extent serves as a good indicator of population density, given the assumption of relatively equal district sizes mandated by law since the 1960s, and the fact that central cities are almost always more densely populated than their suburbs (if not necessarily as densely populated as *other* cities and *their* suburbs) helps in coding the suburban and mixed districts.

A.5 Comparing CSR and Census-Driven Measures

As a test of concept and measurement validity, it is worthwhile to compare the CSR scores with the previous standards where possible. In the following I compare the CSR codes to those developed using census measures of central city, suburban, and rural populations in Wolman and Marckini (2005) and Mayhew (1966).

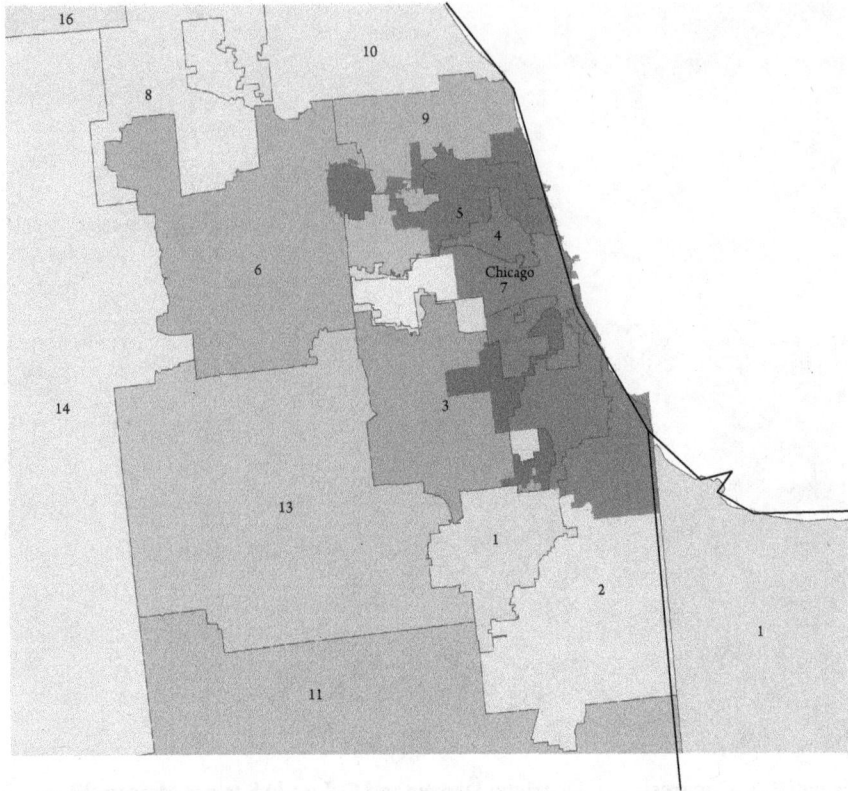

Figure A.4 **Congressional Districts: Chicago Area, 2003–2013.** Congressional districts are labeled and given different light shades. Central city footprint shaded dark. Note that city and congressional district boundaries are not related, and several city districts take the "sliced" shape in Figure A.2.

Though a chief advantage of the CSR is that it codes many more congresses, we can directly compare the different approaches for districts that they both code to see how different they are. Table A.1 summarizes a few such comparisons, and in it we can see a few things. First, the CSR total is the same as Mayhew's total for the 1950s. This is very encouraging, though we know that the two methods include slightly different sets of representatives because of the use of rental housing as a selection criterion in Mayhew's set. The aggregate figures for the CSR categories roughly track those based on the W-M (census-based) approach when we account for the fact that CSR3 forces mixed districts into one of the three categories. If forces make judgments about the sixty-six "mixed" districts from 1963 in the Wolman and Marckini table, the categories are closely matched in that year. There do seem to be sizable systematic differences, however: the CSR scores tend to have many more rural districts and fewer suburban districts than W-M, even when we assume that their mixed districts could be forced into one of the categories. But how different are the two systems of categorization, and what is driving this

Table A.1 **Comparison of CSR Scores with Past Census-Based Urbanicity Scores**

Source	Year	City	Suburban	Rural	Mixed	Notes
Mayhew	1950s	140				City v Non-city
CSR	1953	140	63	227		CSR3
Wolman Marckini	1963	94	94	181	66	
CSR	1963	143	88	205		CSR3
Wolman Marckini	1973	103	131	131	70	
CSR	1973	135	132	168		CSR3
W-M	1983	88	191	93	63	
CSR	1983	122	158	153		CSR3
Wolman Marckini	1993	84	214	83	54	
CSR	1993	141	144	148		CSR3
Wolman Marckini	2007	92	235	71	62	Estimated
CSR	2007	140	152	143		CSR3

Note: Cell entries are counts of congressional districts in each place-character group for selected congresses, for CSR data and previous efforts to code congressional district urbanicity. W-M refers to Wolman and Marckini.

Sources: CSR data; Wolman and Marckini (2005); Mayhew (1966); 2007 American Community Survey.

difference? I look closer by applying W-M's coding system to the 110th Congress and comparing it district-by-district to the seven-category ordinal CSR scores for that Congress. The cross-tabulation is presented in Table A.2.

From this table, we can see the implications of using the different systems of identifying city districts and measuring district-level place character, as well as a potential source of conflict for the CSR scores. While most of the districts on which the W-M method is decisive in the 110th lie on or near the "matched" diagonal (from top-left to lower-right, in the top three rows, indicating that the CSR score is in agreement with W-M's data for most districts), there is one major area where the scores disagree: the CSR's use of only large cities as central cities makes this approach likely to score districts as rural even if they do in fact include large suburban or "urban" populations *from small cities that do not account for 0.1 percent of the population*. There are fifty districts labeled as rural in the CSR but as suburban using the W-M method, forty-one more that W-M would find to be mixed, and three more that W-M would call urban but that CSR calls rural (or, really, "noncity"). This is troubling at first glance.

Table A.2 **Comparison of CSR Scores with the Wolman-Marckini Categories**

W-M Category	CSR Score								
	R	RS	SR	S	SC	CSR	CS	C	Total
Nonmetropolitan	56	0	10	0	0	1	0	0	67
Suburban	50	0	47	65	12	20	26	0	220
Urban	3	1	1	0	1	11	42	29	88
Mixed	41	0	8	0	0	9	2	0	60
Total	150	1	66	65	13	41	70	29	435

Cell entries are counts of congressional districts in each place-character group on 7-point CSR scale and estimated W-M categories for the 110th Congress. Highlighted cells indicate categories where the two scores differ significantly for a large number of congresses.

Sources: CSR data; U.S. Census.

Looking closer, however, these are all districts that include small cities and/or their suburbs: cities such as Pensacola (Florida), Erie (Pennsylvania), and Rockford (Illinois) are among the largest cities in these districts, while most of them are more like the South Carolina Fifth district, which runs along the border with Georgia and includes a few very small central cities in one loosely connected metropolitan area complex.

This closer look reveals that researchers should not adopt the Census Bureau's definition of central city uncritically for all analyses, because it does not have a high threshold for what is considered a metropolitan area. The Census Bureau definition of a central city is tied to that of a metropolitan area:

> The general concept of a metropolitan area (MA) is one of a large population nucleus, together with adjacent communities that have a high degree of economic and social integration with that nucleus. Some MAs are defined around two or more nuclei.... An MA must contain either a place with a minimum population of 50,000 or a U.S. Census Bureau-defined urbanized area and a total MA population of at least 100,000 (75,000 in New England).... In each metropolitan statistical area and consolidated metropolitan statistical area, the largest place and, in some cases, additional places are designated as central cities under the official standards.[5]

Our contemporary settlement patterns blur the lines between populated and unpopulated areas, and also between city and suburb. In the 2016 Census, over 262 million people (just over 85 percent of the national population) lived in the

525 metropolitan areas identified by the U.S. Census definition as such.[6] A category of "city" that broad may be useful in differentiating and categorizing zones of economic activity, but it is not appropriate for assessing the strength of cities in national politics, because not all "central cities" are really cities—the Census Bureau definition does not sufficiently consider size as a key component of urbanicity. These smaller places may be relative centers of local activity, but there are real differences in kind and degree that obviously differentiate them from places like New York and Chicago, which have been on the Lieberman list for a long time, as well as from even smaller cities that have dropped out of the large-city category such as Syracuse (New York) or Providence (Rhode Island). A list of cities that includes Anderson (South Carolina), Pascagoula (Mississippi), and Benton Harbor (Michigan) is too inclusive for a study of cities in national politics and misses the importance of size as a dimension of urbanicity while overemphasizing centrality. And while the residential character of some of these districts that include the smaller cities and their surrounding areas may include developments like those in the suburbs of the larger cities, these districts do not have the same political dynamics that characterize the ideal-type metropolitan area—one large polity (large enough to merit representation in the nation) surrounded by many smaller ones, bound by economic activity but separated by political geography.

These districts, by and large, are better understood as consisting of small towns and their fringe areas; their inclusion as suburbs and cities in W-M and the census is an artifact of a census category, the central city, that is outdated (because the threshold size for central cities was decided when the national population was much smaller) and mostly intended to track economic and social variables, not political ones. The disparity between the W-M data and the CSR ultimately hinges on one's answer to the question: Can you have suburbs without a city? Suburbs are not classically rural communities, but most Americans are no longer cowboys or farmers in any case. These communities are sparsely populated areas far from a major city. I have adopted the vocabulary of rurality, which fits most of them even using W-M's categories, but their label of "nonmetropolitan" may be just as appropriate—even if they are included in Census Bureau metropolitan areas. Once we look more closely at those districts with apparently too-low CSR scores and see that they really are not associated with major cities, the utility of the CSR scores becomes clearer, as we see that they attend to the changes in place-character representation over time.

Beyond this issue of suburban rurality, the CSR approach has other potential issues as well, of which I have been conscious throughout the coding and whose potential distorting effects I have tried to minimize. The method is more subjective at the margins than a blind reliance on outside census figures and might be potentially distorted by a coder's differential knowledge about different places or their subjective interpretations of the maps. For instance, if a coder knew more about developmental patterns in some cities than in others, he or she might be able to more precisely gauge the balance between city and suburban character in those places. These potential sources of error were mitigated to a great extent by the use of textual legal descriptions of districts and historical maps of districts and cities. The advantage afforded by not being limited to recent Congresses for which census data are available, a starting point may distort what we mean by city representation, is considerable and outweighs this pitfall.

Second, this definition of "city" remains essentially neutral beyond a population threshold. It may therefore be appropriately exclusive of some small cities and allow the kinds of communities that count as cities to evolve over time, but it also excludes some places that may be considered more "urban" by certain conventional understandings of the term than those in the set. For instance, Gary, Indiana, is never included in the set; though it seems to have a self-conception as a city, its built environment is recognizably "urban," and it has been the subject of urban politics study,[7] it was never big enough to merit inclusion as a city large enough to represent itself in national politics. Santa Ana (California) and Mesa (Arizona) are included after 2000, however, even though they are basically large suburbs of sprawling late-twentieth-century cities. Indeed, one could quite reasonably argue that Gary is a more "urban" community than even Phoenix, even though the latter includes almost twenty times as many members. That is basically Mayhew's approach. But this issue is as much a function of American social and economic development as a problem with social scientific classification, and it fixes on a perhaps nostalgic or outdated conception of what a "city" is or should be. Any list of major cities over time has to adjust for changing patterns of how people live and using size as an ultimate yardstick seems the best way to do this. This is an acknowledged conceptual hazard of the CSR method of classification, and analyses bear it in mind.

Appendix B

CITY DISTRICT DEMOGRAPHY

Legislative behavior is a function of intracameral and extracameral influences, though political scientists may not all agree on their relative importance. Intracameral influences include congressional parties, institutional incentives such as rules, committee assignments, and prestige.[1] Extracameral influences include some mix of personal preferences and ideology and constituency preferences and pressure.[2] In evaluating the role of constituency pressure in shaping legislative behavior, district-level demography is an important source of information—one that is often used as a helpful heuristic for identifying which legislators might be concerned with particular issues or may be faced with cross-cutting pressures.[3] For analyses of the Senate and contemporary House of Representatives, there are a wide range of readily available measures from the U.S. Census and the Inter-University Consortium for Political and Social Research. Because this study is particularly concerned with place character, and most variation on this dimension takes place within states, the House is the more interesting chamber. Historical House district–level demography is trickier, because it is a less used unit of analysis than state- or county-level demography. For the most recent Congresses, the Census Bureau has tabulated good measures on a number of variables at the district level, and these are available on the Census website. For older Congresses, a researcher must rely on the somewhat idiosyncratic collections made by other scholars for their own purposes. Some of these are readily available and have become invaluable public goods. For the 87th to 104th Congresses (1961–1997), census data have been gathered by Lublin (1997a).[4]

Analyses in Chapters 4 and 5 in this study focus on the Long New Deal, including the 1930s, as a time period of important political change, and these older Congresses require further data collection, because census data for these years are not available at the district level. Mayhew (1966) uses *Congressional Quarterly* data from 1962 to conduct his study of city districts, combined with information from the *Congressional District Data Book* released by the Census Bureau in 1961.[5] He then traces these districts backward across fifteen years to identify the city districts in his study of 1947 to 1961. But his study of housing issues does not take any demography apart from homeownership into account and includes no other demographics. Adler (2012) has created a very valuable dataset going back further, to 1943, using county-level measures to create congressional-district measures. This dataset includes such variables as percent African American, union households (at the state level), and percent blue-collar and is an important resource, but for a study of city districts over the Long New Deal it is insufficient in two respects. First, 1943 is not quite far enough back to study the 1930s. We could apply values from the early 1940s to the 1930s and be reasonably confident that they would be related, but the 1940s was a particularly "mobile" period for many Americans, especially black Americans leaving the South for the cities of the North during wartime mobilization, in what we know as the Second Great Migration. So especially on race, measures from the mid-1940s are likely significantly higher than those from the 1930s. This may be true on other measures as well.

Second, and more important from an analytical perspective, because Adler's data are based on county-level measures, they work very well for rural districts (for which counties can be aggregated) but not city districts (which are subdivisions of counties). Using this approach, Adler's recipe states that "urban counties that contained multiple congressional districts were divided geographically and demographically according to the respective number of districts."[6] This means that for city districts within the same county, the countywide measures are applied to each district (or divided equally, in the case of raw totals). This is the best that one can do with county-level data, but in densely populated places with high levels of spatial segregation (a characteristic of all major American cities during this period), this approach will mask cross-district heterogeneity, making it look as though populations are spread evenly across districts within a city delegation even when they are not. This is especially important in examinations of racial segregation, which was stark, because equalizing the percent African American across districts gives a potentially misleading impression. For instance, in Adler's data it would appear that every district in Chicago had about 10 percent African American voters; in such a circumstance, every congressman might have had the same incentive to respond to that black population's demands for reelection or renomination. In fact, as we saw in Chapter 5, only two or three Chicago congressmen (out of ten) had more than a handful of black constituents at this time because of residential segregation. This pattern is well-known but usually not accounted for in congressional studies.[7]

In this study, because I am particularly interested in racial dynamics and congressional representation, it is important to rule out the direct electoral connection between African American constituencies and city congressmen who do not represent them. I thus need more accurate measures of racial populations at the district level, not the county level. Fortunately, there are geographic techniques that can help us get better estimates of congressional districts below the county level for some cities in some Congresses even before the 1960s. Analyses in Chapters 4 and 5 use preliminary measures that reflect the true demographic heterogeneity of these districts during the 1930s through 1950s. I develop the measures using the following techniques.

B.1 Building District-Level Estimates in Large Cities

To create more accurate district-level demographics for city districts, we must build from lower levels of aggregation, not assume demographic evenness from the top down. To construct city districts from county data is akin to constructing all districts from state data: better than a completely naïve estimate, but blind to within-area heterogeneity.[8] Census tracts are an appropriate subcity level of aggregation for this: they are much smaller than congressional districts, and most fall within district lines. So I build my estimates of city district demography from the bottom up using tracts.

Today, the entire country is divided into census tracts, but this was not always the case. When the tract was first introduced as a unit in 1910, counties in only nine city areas were divided into tracts: New York City, Chicago, Boston, Baltimore, Cleveland, Philadelphia, Pittsburgh, Milwaukee, and St. Louis.[9] By 1930, twenty-four counties in fourteen states had been divided into tracts; by 1940, seventy-four counties in twenty-nine states; and so on. Of course, not all of these counties need to be disaggregated into tracts to get better congressional district measures. Some, like Syracuse or Omaha, were too small to be divided into more than one district. Others, like Nashville or Memphis, were probably large enough for multiple districts but because of unequal districting (a practice most egregious in, but not exclusive to, the South) did not get them and thus sat within a single congressional district. For each of these kinds of cities and their districts, Adler's method works better. Some of the districts for which Adler's measures need improvement can be identified by the fact that they have equivalent measures for variables that are very unlikely to actually be equivalent: the number of black residents or blue-collar workers, for example. These are the districts for which more sensitive measures need to be developed.

The remainder of this appendix describes how I developed the more accurate district-level measures, using the example of race in Chicago districts from the 79th Congress (1945–1947). To fix these measures, I first identify the districts that are estimated using county-level "top-down" measures. All districts from the same state and Congress that share equivalent measures of percent African American and median family income with at least one other district are

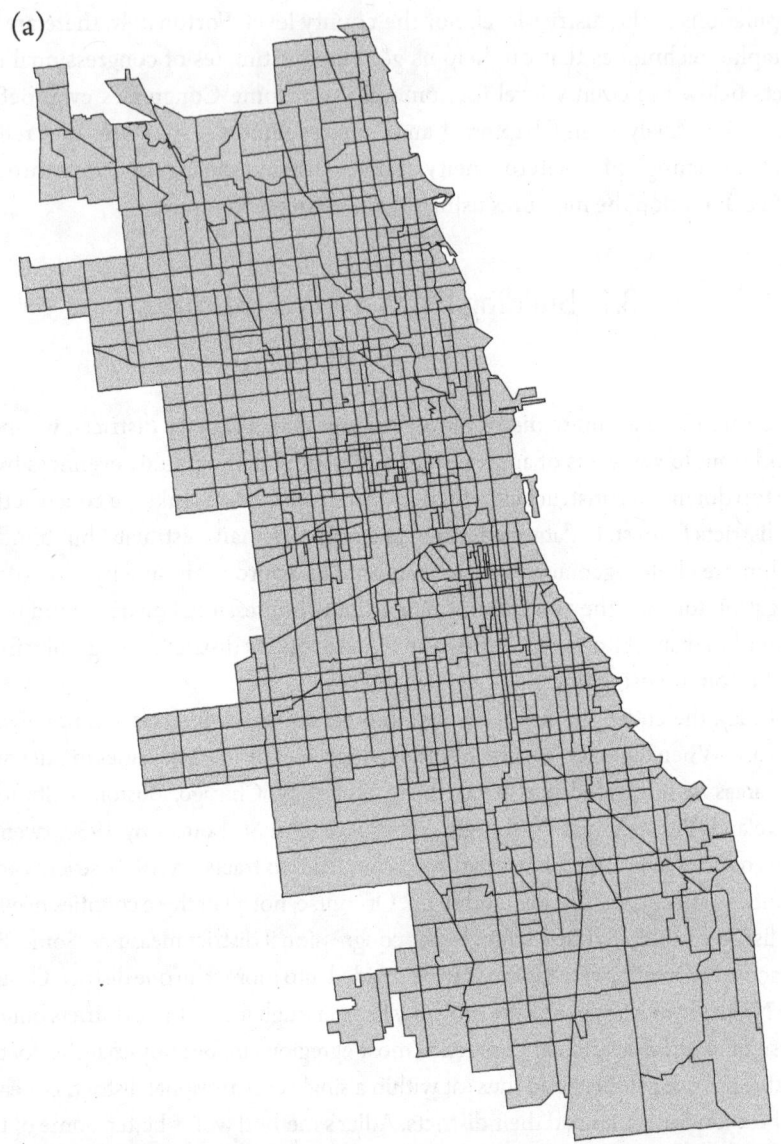

Figure B.1 **Chicago Census Tracts and Race, 1940.** (a) Chicago census tracts, 1940 Census. (b) Proportion black in census tracts. The North Side and outlying areas were almost entirely white, while tracts on the South Side and near West Side were over 75 percent black.

(b)

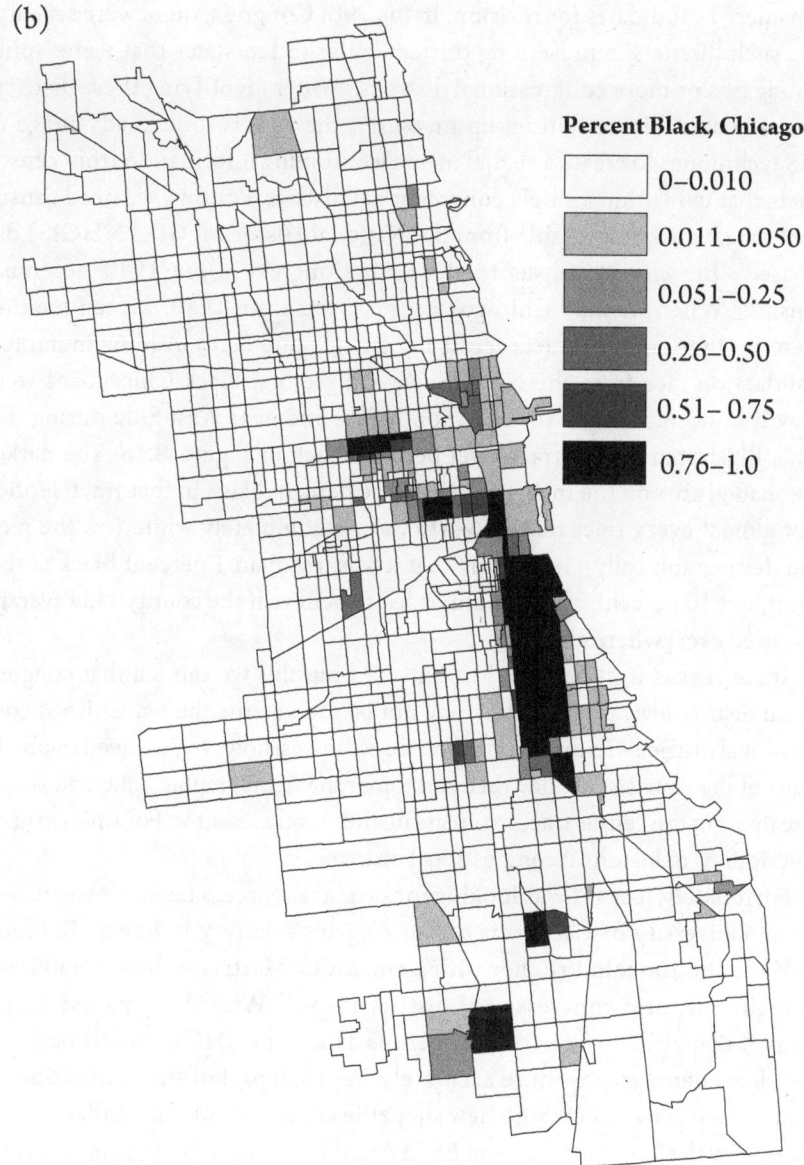

Figure B.1 Continued.

considered candidates for revision. In the 79th Congress, there were seventy-one such districts, representing thirteen cities in ten states that were "split" among two or more congressional districts.[10] After identifying these districts as candidates for the bottom-up measures, the goal is to take advantage of GIS techniques to create a spatial match, combining information from census tracts that fall within a single congressional district. For this, we need census tract data, which is available from the National Historical GIS (NHGIS) database.[11] The closest census to the 79th Congress is the 1940 decennial census.[12] When we map Chicago's census tracts from 1940, we can see that there are thousands of tracts across the city (Figure B.1a). Adding in numerical data on race from the NHGIS, we can see that black Chicagoans were heavily concentrated on the near South Side and near West Side during this time, illustrated by the tract-level percent black in Figure B.1b. The darker the shaded area on the map, the higher the percent black in that tract. Notice that almost every tract on the North Side is completely white (on the map and demographically), indicating that it was less than 1 percent black at this point, not 10 percent, as we would be led to believe if the countywide average was used everywhere.

These census tract data are helpful, and from this we can tell that congressional district-level percent black will not be even across the ten Chicago congressional districts. To make more precise estimates, however, we need to obtain maps of the districts, overlay them on top of the demographic data, and aggregate up from the census tracts to create district-level measures. For this, we need descriptions of historical congressional districts.

Fortunately, just as I was looking for such a resource, a team of researchers at the University of California at Los Angeles—Jeffrey B. Lewis, Brandon DeVine, and Lincoln Pritcher with Kenneth C. Martis—released a new set of digital historic congressional district maps.[13] With these painstakingly created shapefiles, we can overlay census data from NHGIS to estimate district-level demography more accurately. For each part of states with tracted land in each census, I create a new shapefile composed of the smallest pieces created by the "intersect" tool in ESRI ArcMap software. This operation creates small pieces that can be aggregated up to create district-level estimates. Most small census geographies lie completely within a congressional district, so they are unaffected by this change. For tracts that don't, or for portions of counties that are also split by district lines, the intersect tool creates fragments of those geographies that can be attributed to the correct district. In such cases, census count estimates (such as the number of persons or the number of blue-collar workers) are divided proportionately according to the fragment's share of the tract's (or county's) overall area. For instance, if a tract had 100 people in it but a congressional district line ran through it such that 40 percent of it was in District 1 and 60 percent in District 2, 40 of those people would be attributed to District 1. The assumption in this operation is that persons are evenly distributed within the tract; as with Adler's procedure, this may not perfectly match reality, but it is a far more realistic assumption than to assume that persons are distributed evenly across districts within an urban county, which we know to be importantly unrealistic.

Finally, having created small-unit estimates for the pieces of the congressional districts, I simply add up those counts to create district-level estimates and create percentage estimates of the district's constituency composition using standard statistical software.

The end result of the spatial join is a map that resembles Figure 5.2, with the pattern of census tract-level segregation from Figure B.1 amplified at the level of congressional districts. The pattern is starkest in Chicago because of its high levels of racial segregation and very large black population, but the general point holds across all the large cities with multiple congressional districts examined here. Figures B.2 through B.4 show the spatial patterns for New York, Philadelphia, and Los Angeles in the 79th Congress. The shading is the same across cities (but *not* quite the same between tract and congressional district— no district in the 1940s was close to the Illinois First), so we can see how residential segregation aggregates into representational unevenness. For each city, (a) depicts census tract–level percent black, with bold lines outlining city congressional districts, while (b) depicts the congressional districts, shaded according to the percent black. In each city, the Adler "top-down" data attribute the same value of percent black to each district in the city (or county, in the case of New York City, which includes all five counties); with those data, each entire city would be some shade of light gray—though there would be a little variation across cities (Los Angeles would be lower than the others shown here). In each place, black residence was uneven, and there were a number of representatives with virtually no black constituency—yet, as shown in Chapter 5, these representatives were consistently cohesive and liberal on civil rights issues in the run-up to the 1960s.

States redraw their district boundaries sporadically, most often after the decennial census. For long stretches in the early twentieth century, many district boundaries went unchanged. When they change, I draw a new map for that area and recalculate the district-level measures.[14] The new estimates for the "split" city districts are then reinserted into the dataset for analysis, better (though still imperfectly) reflecting the true district attributes, and ostensibly serving as better estimates of this aspect of constituency pressure, at least according to our theories of how pressure might work if it is related to numbers. Overall, these fixes are most relevant to the percent black in city districts, which is typically the

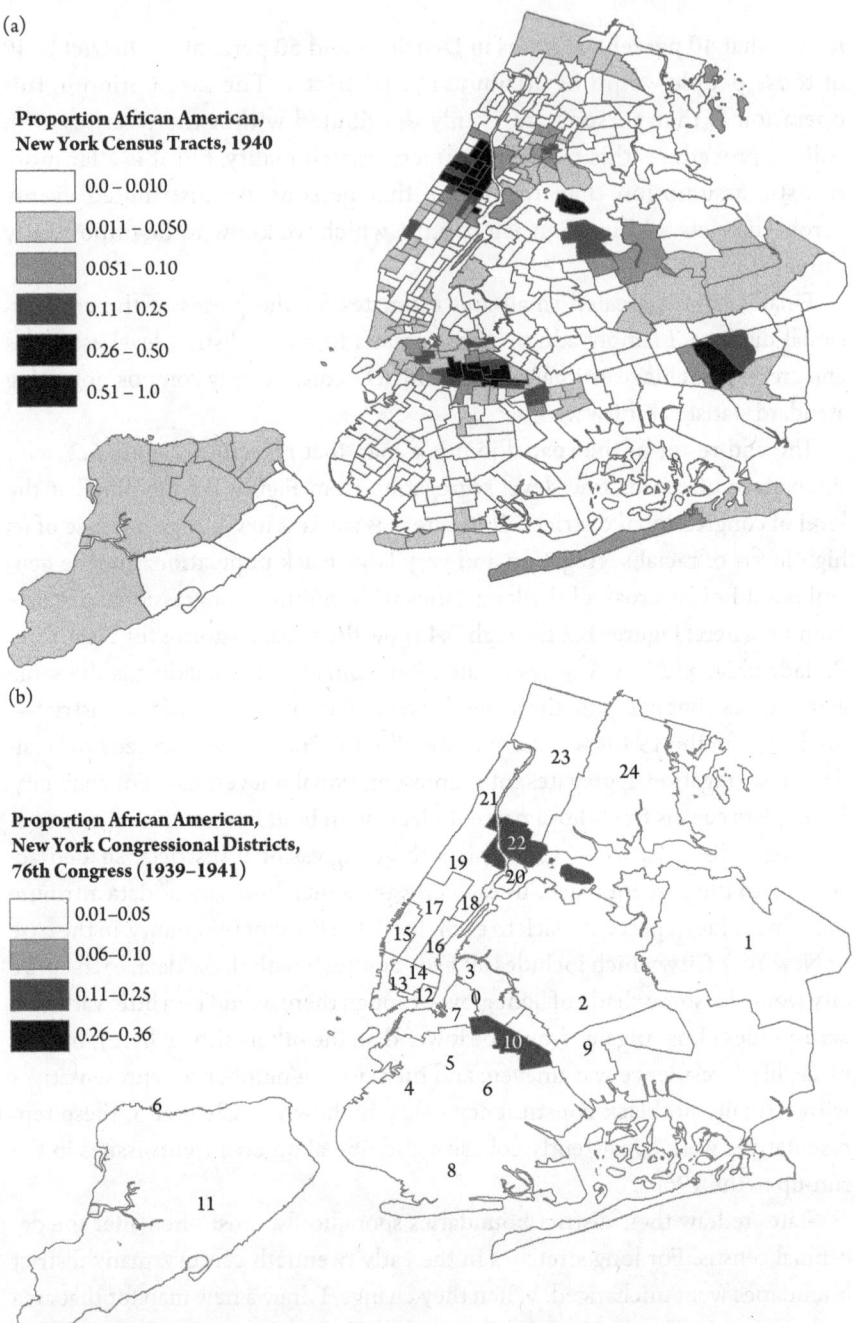

Figure B.2 **New York City (and Surrounding Urban Areas), Percent Black, 1940.** (a) Proportion black in Census Tracts, 1940 Census. (b) Proportion black in 1945 congressional districts, based on 1940 Census. Sources: IPUMS NHGIS and Lewis et al. (2013).

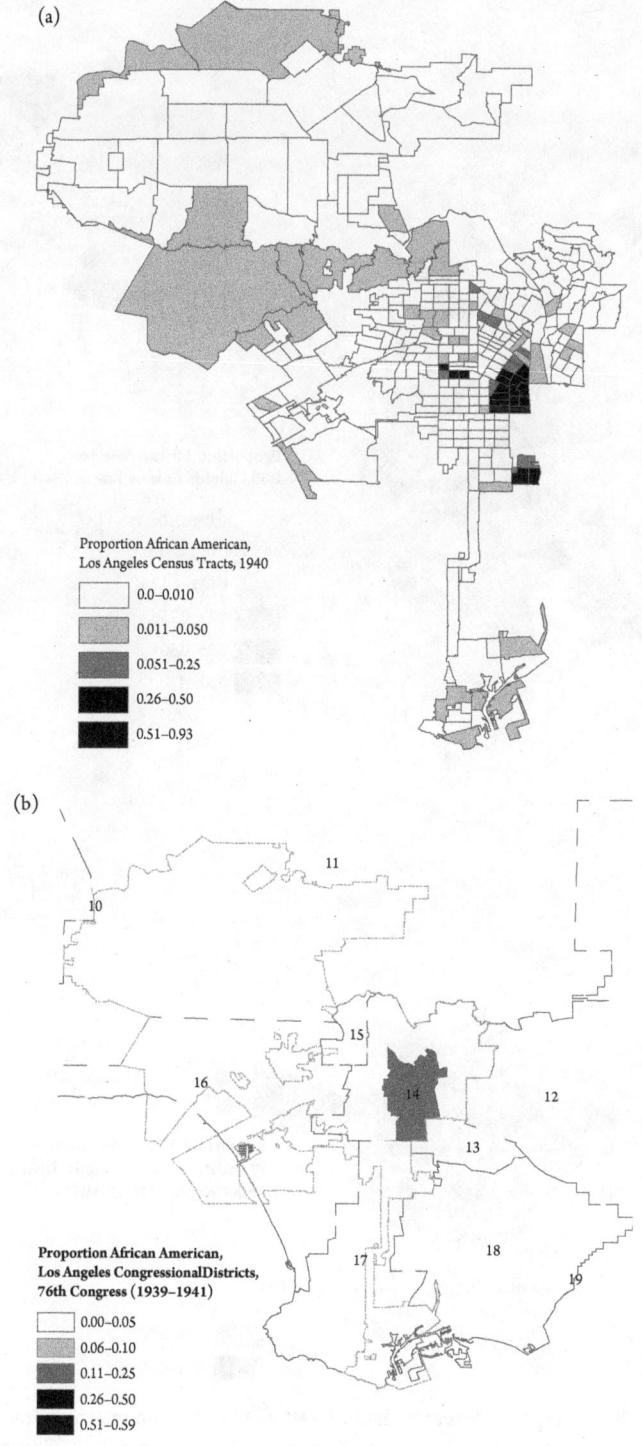

Figure B.3 **Los Angeles, Percent Black, 1940.** (a) Proportion **black** in census tracts, 1940 Census. (b) Proportion black in 1945 congressional districts, 1940 Census.
Sources: IPUMS NHGIS and Lewis et al. (2013).

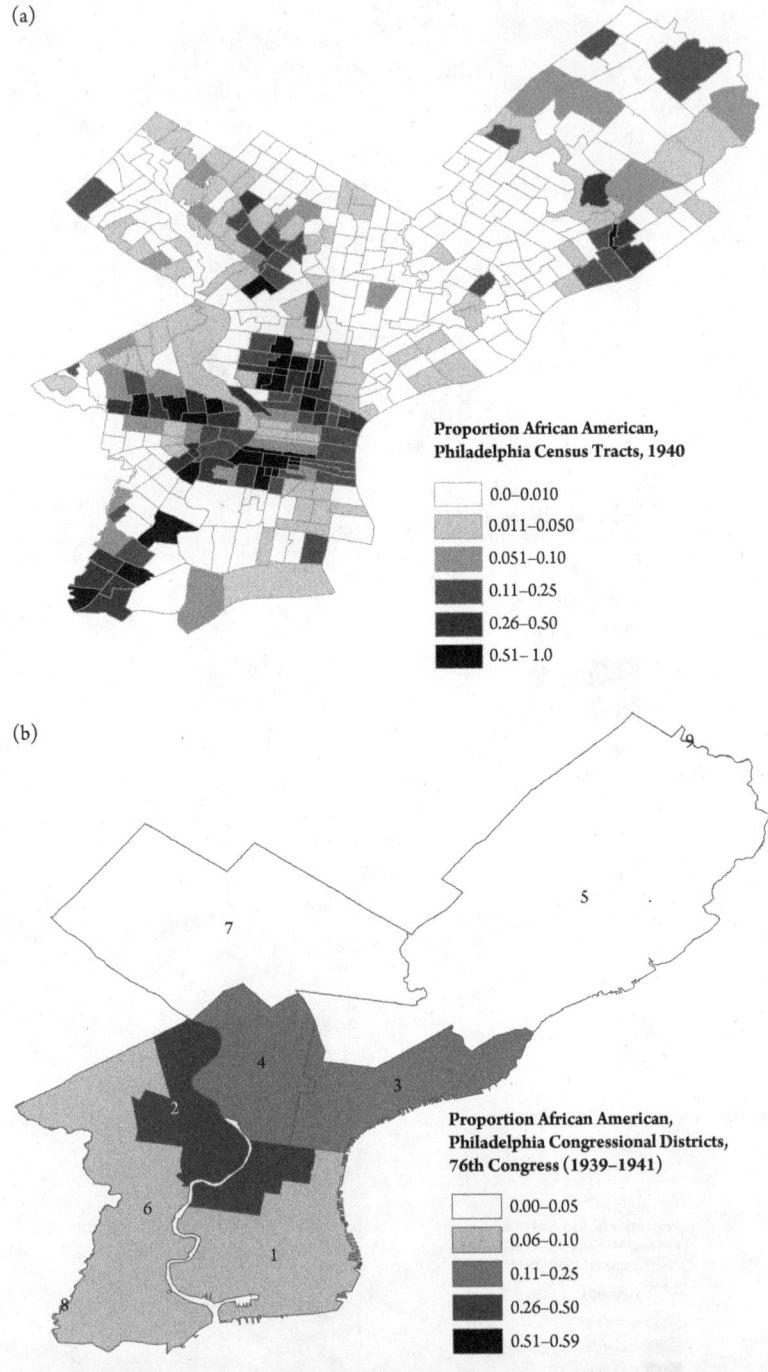

Figure B.4 **Philadelphia, Percent Black, 1940.** (a) Proportion in census tracts, 1940 Census. (b) Proportion black in 1945 congressional districts, 1940 Census.
Sources: IPUMS NHGIS and Lewis et al. (2013).

most unevenly spaced variable in these analyses (as well as the most theoretically important for the analysis in Chapter 5). The cities affected are New York City, Chicago, Los Angeles, Philadelphia, Pittsburgh, Boston, Cleveland, Baltimore, Buffalo, Detroit, Cincinnati, San Francisco, St. Louis, and Milwaukee. In the book's multivariate analyses, I apply this fix to measures for the city districts in Congresses ranging from the 75th (1937–1939) to the 86th (1959–1961), those that predated Lublin's more accurate district-based census data.

Appendix C

URBANICITY REGRESSION RESULTS

This appendix includes a pair of tables of regression analyses that show that the urbanicity divide is not simply a function of other likely explanations correlated with (but not identical to) urbanicity. First, at the county level, Chapter 7 shows several graphs depicting a relationship between population density and support for Democratic candidates over time. More densely populated counties also have distinct demography: they tend to be more diverse and wealthy, for instance. County density also varies a lot because of regional patterns in the geographical size of counties: northeastern counties are particularly small, western counties particularly expansive. Although the county level is not the best place to disentangle density from other highly correlated factors (aggregate data make the analysis noisier than individual-level data), using census data to account for county-level relationships shows that dense counties are more Democratic even when we account for race, class, and region, as in the following ordinary least squares linear regression of results from 2008 and 2016 (see Table C.1).

Second, at the individual level, Chapter 6 refers to the marginal relationship between place character and support for Obama in 2008. This estimate is based on the logit regression shown in Table C.2 using data from the 2008 National Annenberg Election Survey.

These analyses underscore the fact that an independent relationship exists between voting behavior and place character. They cannot conclusively identify the causal relationship between place and views—no observational data can, and it would be difficult to devise an experiment to do so because most Americans get to choose the place they live. This book does not argue that sorting has not occurred among individuals, but I do argue that the place-character divide, *especially at the elite level*, predates geographic mass sorting. A more conclusive closer look at the independent relationship between voting and place is a rapidly developing area of study.

Table C.1 **County-level Linear Regression of Support for Obama in 2008 and Clinton in 2016**

Variable	Obama 2008 Coefficient	(Standard Error)	Clinton 2016 Coefficient	(Standard Error)
Pop. Density (ln)	0.060*	(0.003)	0.032*	(0.001)
Northeast	0.062*	(0.019)	0.016	(0.009)
Midwest	0.020	(0.014)	−0.043*	(0.006)
South	−0.291*	(0.014)	−0.156*	(0.007)
% African Americans	0.935*	(0.031)	0.677*	(0.015)
% Hispanic	0.434*	(0.034)	0.307*	(0.015)
% Asian	1.619*	(0.215)	1.172*	(0.090)
HH Med. Inc (10k)	0.030*	(0.005)	0.000	(0.002)
Intercept	−0.270*	(0.021)	0.198*	(0.006)
N	3112		3109	
R^2	.46		.61	

Note: Cell entries are regression estimates. West is regional base category. Linear regression of county-level support for Obama in 2008 and Clinton in 2016 on the natural log of population density and regional indicators (West as base category). $R^2 = .46$; $N = 2,830$.

Sources: Townhall.com (2016 results); election data from Data.gov (2008 results); IMPUS NHGIS.

Table C.2 **Individual-level Logistic Regression of Support for Obama in 2008**

Variable (#categories)	Coefficient	(Standard Error)	Marginal Effects
Urbanicity (3)	0.17*	(0.025)	.042
Conservatism (5)	−1.159*	(0.019)	−.29
Income (3)	−0.258*	(0.024)	−.064
Educ (3)	0.108*	(0.023)	.026
Age (10yrs)	−0.002	(0.003)	−.00
Male	−0.273*	(0.034)	−.067
Hisp	1.021*	(0.075)	.22
Black	3.912*	(0.121)	.51
Asian	0.286*	(0.130)	.069
Attend Church (5)	0.173*	(0.013)	.043
Northeast	0.115*	(0.053)	.028
Midwest	0.219*	(0.050)	.054
South	−0.356*	(0.048)	−.088
Intercept	1.932*	(0.109)	NA

Note: Cell entries are regression estimates. Marginal effects estimated using Stata, holding other covariates constant at appropriate levels. Even when controlling for other potential confounding factors, there is an independent association between place character and vote choice. *Ceteris paribus*, an urbanite was about 8–9 percent more likely than a rural-dweller to choose Obama over McCain.
*Statistically significant at $p < .05$.

Source: National Annenberg Election Survey 2008.

NOTES

Chapter 1

1. Snowiss 1966, p. 630.
2. Most notably, these include *Baker v. Carr* (1962) and *Reynolds v. Sims* (1964).
3. Legislative malapportionment was particularly egregious in the South and the West, and in state legislatures, but it existed in all regions and in national congressional districts as well. See Snyder and Ansolabehere 2008, p. 30. More broadly, these authors chronicle the historical roots of malapportionment, the political and judicial prologue to the voting equality decisions of the early 1960s, and the effects of subsequent changes in representation. *Reynolds* and *Baker* ushered in a system of apportionment in which nearly all legislative bodies approached parity, though inequalities persist, particularly in the Senate, which is exempt from the ruling because of Article I of the Constitution.
4. The principle used to defend such inequities was representation by place: the idea that each county, or township, should be represented in a legislature on a roughly equal basis (the same principle that guides representation in the U.S. Senate), even though the industrial revolution had driven population to the cities and away from the countryside.
5. Emphasis added. U.S. House Committee on the Judiciary, Subcommittee No. 5, "Apportionment of State Legislatures," August 6, 1964, HRG-1964-HJH-0043, pp. 504–505. Perhaps Vorys was fortunate that Luce was not there to read the quote himself, having died in 1946. The passage is clearly taken out of context, for Luce (a Boston Republican with evident affection for cities) would probably not have wanted his work to be used in service of Vorys's cause. On the page previous to the one quoted by Vorys, Luce writes that "the most powerful motive [for the continuation of malapportionment] has been jealousy, suspicion, and fear of the cities," and later he argues that the cohesive power of the cities was overrated in the case of Massachusetts anyway. Luce 1930, pp. 364–367.
6. Katznelson 2009; Connolly 2010.
7. Daley and his lieutenants were obsessed with loyalty to the Democratic Party, which they saw it as a virtue beyond all others. See Snowiss 1966 and the taped conversation between Daley and President Johnson, November 16, 1964, recording no. 6370, Miller Center Archives, University of Virginia.
8. These marching orders were communicated via "idiot lists" of positions to be taken. See Biles 1995, p. 61.
9. U.S. House Committee on the Judiciary, "Apportionment of State Legislatures," p. 473.
10. Along with spatial centrality, these three dimensions constitute the distinctive characteristics of urbanicity. See, e.g., Wirth 1957 and the discussion in Chapter 2.
11. The dimensions of liberalism are (1) interventions in markets to ameliorate the failures of capitalism (statism), and (2) adaptation to cultural change through the recognition of new

constituencies and nondeference to traditional social mores. Being liberal on each of these dimensions is "double liberalism," an ideological configuration I identify as distinctively urban.
12. Banfield and Wilson 1963.
13. Trounstine 2008.
14. Keiser 1997; Erie 1988; Pinderhughes 1987.
15. Gelfand 1975, p. 28.
16. Buenker 1973, ch. 6.
17. Bateman and Taylor 2007; Lieberman 2001; Katznelson 2005.
18. I borrow the "Long New Deal" label for this historical period from Chen 2009, though the label may not originate with that work.
19. Lieberman 2009; Conn 2014; Nall 2010.
20. See, e.g., Dahl 1961; Wilson 1962; Banfield and Wilson 1963; Katznelson 1982.
21. Dilworth 2009a; Peterson 1981; but see Trounstine 2009 for a review of the recent resurgence of local politics studies.
22. These techniques typically explain away place and context either as part of an error term or as a set of regular attributes that can be included in a more complete but still placeless model of behavior. See, e.g., Ethington and McDaniel 2007; and King 1996.
23. For instance, how national political views are shaped by local contexts; see Hopkins 2010; or Hajnal and Abrajano 2016.
24. Brenner 2009.
25. Ibid., p. 134. Dilworth 2009b is a kind of collective manifesto for the reinvigoration of the study of urban politics with a specific eye toward American political development. This study draws on several of those essays for scholarly inspiration, hoping to contribute to an ongoing reinvigoration of research in this direction.
26. Bridges 1984, p. 15. An important analogous point is central to the study of international relations, in which states are situated within a broader system and outcomes frequently depend on the two-way interaction between that system and its constituent parts. For recent pieces on the resurgence of local studies to understand national politics, see Trounstine 2009 and Ethington and McDaniel 2007 for reviews; see Enos 2017, Hopkins 2010, Hajnal and Abrajano 2016, and Newman 2014 for substantively and methodologically innovative treatments.
27. See, e.g., Rae 2003; Caraley 1976; and Sugrue 1996.
28. These rules are sometimes imposed at the local level as well. TELs place constraints on the size of government, though it is unclear how effective they ultimately are in practice. Kousser, McCubbins, and Moule 2008.
29. Mollenkopf 1983. This is the main theme of Chapters 2 and 3.
30. Lieberman 2009.
31. Ethington and Levitus 2009, pp. 155, 165, refer to this period as the early "Metropolitan Era," and I will at times refer to it as the "urban interlude," to emphasize its exceptional status as a moment within national political history, or as the "Long New Deal," to emphasize the strains of political and policy continuities within this era of mostly Democratic control of national institutions. Several studies take stock of national–local interaction and the urban order's political advances and setbacks during this era, including Buenker 1973; Gelfand 1975; Mollenkopf 1983; and Biles 2011.
32. Buenker 1973; Lieberman 2009.
33. Especially in presidential elections. See Eldersveld 1949; and Andersen 1979.
34. Mollenkopf 1983, p. 60.
35. Hofstadter 1948 for the classic account of this position, and see Kennedy 2009 for a summary of works with a similar perspective.
36. Plotke 1996, p. 169. Kennedy 2009 argues that the New Deal's coherent contribution was a set of institutions that provided Americans security against the vagaries of markets—one manifestation of the second principle of progressive liberalism identified by Plotke. Mayhew 1986 also labels the nonsouthern Rooseveltian reform wing of the extended New Deal alliance "progressive-liberal." Buenker 1973 traces the development of "liberalism," finding it in the progressivism of local urban politics, especially among new-stock immigrant parties.
37. Buenker 1973, chs. 1, 6.
38. Plotke 1996; Skowronek 1982; Katznelson 2012.
39. Bridges 1984, p. 3; Katznelson 2009 and Connolly 2010 expand this theme.

40. Rakove 1975; Snowiss 1966; Wilson 1960; Mayhew 1986.
41. Mayhew 1966, ch. 6.
42. Connolly 2010.
43. See Chen 2009 for an excellent defense of this periodization. This choice of period is roughly the same as that selected in two parallel studies of the midcentury realignment found in Schickler 2016 and Katznelson 2012. This is an apt label for the era because the partisan labels and dynamics of the time were *relatively* stable, and began with Roosevelt's 1932 election.
44. Ethington and Levitus 2009.
45. Among these strategies were logrolls, "urbanizing" issues, and affinity partnerships; each created different political dynamics that will be described in Chapter 2.
46. Lieberman 2009; Ethington and Levitus 2009.
47. Plotke 1996 defines a political order as "a durable mode of organizing and exercising political power at the national level, with distinct institutions, policies, and discourses." I use the term similarly, but in this text I focus on a specifically *urban* political order, which includes many of Plotke's distinctive forces (such as labor unions, whose numbers came mainly from cities) but emphasizes the conditions of city life and governance that predispose leaders to the set of political commitments known (and explicitly defined by Plotke) as progressive liberalism. This urban order is not quite as powerful an assemblage of persons and political forces as Plotke's Democratic order, which is closer conceptually to what others have called a "regime" influential enough to dominate politics for a period of time. The urban political order consisted of cities, their members, their representatives, and their advocates, and it won some battles but obviously lost others along the way. In this, my use of the term "political order" is more akin to the "institutional orders" in Smith and King 2005, which exist concurrently with competing and opposed orders. See Schickler 2016, ch. 3, for the changing content of liberalism during this time.
48. Connolly 2010; Mollenkopf 1983, ch. 2; Katznelson and Mulroy 2012.
49. Carmines and Stimson 1989.
50. Schickler 2016; Katznelson and Farhang 2005.
51. And for the Republicans to create organizations in the South to receive them; this change was ironically sped up by the reapportionment revolution that finally brought representational parity to more densely populated areas. See Black and Black 2003; and Snyder and Ansolabehere 2008.
52. This label is applied by Mayhew 1986 to describe this form of organization. He applies it to political organizations that have thorough control over internal operations (especially nominations for office), but it is also strongly associated with the "machine" style of politics characterized by interparty linkages sustained through particularistic exchange.
53. Mayhew 1986; Erie 1988.
54. At many times and places, traditional party organizations were themselves very factionalized and not at all united. This was the distinction between *machine politics*, a style of political culture, and the *political machine*, which was an intermittently consolidated political project. See, e.g., Mayhew 1986; Bridges 1984; Ansell and Burris 1997.
55. Though not *absolutely* likely—recent censuses have found that a majority African Americans and immigrants live in suburban areas.
56. Bishop 2008; see also Nall 2010.
57. Schickler 2016.
58. Lapinski 2013, p. 13; Katznelson and Wawro 2010; Schickler 2001; Baumgartner and Jones 1993.
59. Previous analyses in this area, such as Mayhew 1966; Wolman and Marckini 2005; and Caraley 1976, restricted themselves to analyses of subsets of years after 1950 (see Appendix A) and so missed most of the action of the urban interlude.
60. See Lapinski 2013, ch. 2, for this theoretical point and description of the AIP data, which provide a fine-grained substantive coding of congressional roll call votes.
61. For that matter, not every issue gets a roll call vote, either—sometimes committee agendas are *more* inclusive.

Chapter 2

1. Thomas Jefferson, letter to James Madison, December 20, 1787, *Papers of Thomas Jefferson*, quoted in Gosnell 1937, p. vii.
2. Banfield and Wilson 1963, p. 101.
3. There are many translations and adaptations of this fable; here I use the version endorsed by the U.S. government: read.gov/aesop/004.html.
4. Sassen 2005.
5. Whether those others are moderates or ascribe to ideologies that don't easily map onto the main parties' conservative–liberal continuum is a matter of debate. See Fiorina, Pope, and Abrams 2004; Abramowitz and Saunders 2005; and Carmines, Ensley, and Wagner 2017 for this debate.
6. Cramer 2016; Green, Palmquist, and Schickler 2002.
7. This history is the fascinating subject of many excellent books. See, for instance, Mumford 1961 for a classic and Conn 2014 and Barber 2013 for recent updates. For clarity, here I provide a brief sketch of the relevant contours of American urban history as well as some recommended readings for students of the subject. People have always been drawn to cities. This is true in a physical sense; cities grow and grow and are now home to most of humanity. But it is also true in another sense, as thinkers have pondered the meaning, effects, and possibilities of common life for millennia. The great American urbanist Lewis Mumford observed that cities are great "theaters of social action." The Greek *polis* was an ancient site of such investigation, despite Aesop's admonitions, and tellingly, the sages of that tradition investigated the world not through monastic or hermetic introspection, but through lively Socratic dialogue, or the necessarily communal activity of tragic theater—a form in which wisdom comes as often from the crowd known as the chorus as from divinely inspired insight. Preindustrial cities were mostly small, what we might call towns today, but they still afforded a life of differentiated opportunities in an overwhelmingly agricultural age. The medieval German observation that "city air makes you free" was more than just a legal principle; it reflected a vision of spiritual emancipation fostered by an urban lived experience. Most *American* cities originated as hubs in extractive and productive networks and have been the site of many attendant ills and dangers: lawlessness, pollution, inept and corrupt political leadership, social conflict, and individual spiritual anomie. In America, miasmic city air was believed to be as likely to kill you as to make you free. City life was often balefully contrasted with the mythology of a frontier nation populated by self-protecting, independent yeomen, as in the famous quote by Thomas Jefferson that began this chapter. Jefferson's belief that the true "Empire of Liberty" would be a rural one, shared by his allies in the preeminent political faction of the early republic, was reinforced by a range of eighteenth- and nineteenth-century public policies that encouraged dispersed settlement, including expansion of national borders (through military conquest and purchase) and rural land grants (for veterans and homesteaders); see Frymer 2017. Early America was not an urban nation, especially compared to its European cousins. For most of the twentieth century, too, national policies favored sprawl over denser forms. In between those eras, however, there was an exceptional political moment when the United States *was* open to urban leadership and city-friendly policies. During the period of rapid urbanization around the turn of the twentieth century, as our cities grew and grew, national leaders approached with new urgency the analysis of city life not just from an aesthetic or moral perspective, but in terms of actually managing these communities, which were unprecedented in their scale, density, and pace of development. The challenges and experiences of urban life were a central preoccupation of early social scientists, who were more ambivalent than Jefferson but nonetheless fairly pessimistic about the prospects for the "good life" within the city. Frederick Tonnies's (1887) *gemeinschaft* and *gesellschaft* are still useful concepts for explaining the changes wrought by the urban revolution; as the population moved from the country to the city, traditional (and largely informal) hierarchies and ways of life characterized by thick ties were replaced by thinner ties and more reliance on formal rules and clearer lines of authority. Louis Wirth describes this contrast as a change from a country situation in which people can make contact as full personalities to an environment in which urbanites encounter each other fairly anonymously in "highly

segmented roles" (see Wirth 1938, fruitfully excerpted in the excellent resource LeGates and Stout 2016). The radically changed lived environment, amplified and accelerated in America, seemed to have powerful deleterious effects on human beings. Packed with new arrivals both domestic and foreign, be-smogged by round-the-clock manufactories, and riven by persistent class and ethnoracial conflict, America's cities were already drifting into disrepair by the 1920s when spatially attentive sociologists used the new tools of social science to find that density caused "an impoverished social life and psychological withdrawal." See Baldassare 1978, p. 41, for a review, though these models have been refined. Together, the distinctive circumstances of the United States and the challenges of the industrial city have imbued our culture with a persistent pastoralism and suspicion of urban life. The urban crisis of the mid-twentieth century did little to allay the concerns of the city's critics, and there was a mass exodus from central cities, many of which, especially in the postindustrial Rust Belt, have seen their populations halved since their peak. Overall, however, central-city population has actually remained fairly steady since midcentury, as immigrants replaced those who left and the geographically unbound cities of the South and West grew rapidly. This population shift was driven by several significant factors, including individuals' preferences for larger and/or less expensive homes and sparser, smaller, more homogeneous communities (especially among whites); technologies such as the automobile that allowed more diffuse settlement and production patterns; and public policies that encouraged new home construction, homeownership, and residential racial homogeneity. The results of this movement were the sprawling, politically fragmented metropolises, often centered on poorer, semi-abandoned, and ill-kempt central cities, of contemporary America. There is a vast sociological literature on the causes and effects of suburban construction and migration; see Massey and Denton 1993; Dreier, Mollenkopf, and Swanstrom 2004; and Hirsch 1983 for the best treatments. Thus, the inexorable march of the modern world has made the United States into an urban nation—though, significantly, not a *city* nation. Today, more than 85 percent of Americans live in metropolitan areas, a far cry from the self-sufficient yeomen of Jefferson's ideal. But a majority of today's *metropolitan* Americans—indeed, a majority of all Americans since the 1970s—live in the smaller local polities that lie outside of central cities. This is true even as the twenty-first century sees a cautious renaissance of city life. The urban crisis left America's central cities shattered shells of their former selves. By the late 1980s, the combined effects of fiscal crisis, white flight, and federal disinvestment meant that many cities could not govern themselves effectively. Crime, drug use, and physical decay created spaces that were less auspicious sites of the possibilities of freedom than reliquary reminders of a bygone era. Popular representations of the city reinforced this notion: the lawless streets of *The Warriors* and *Death Wish* were no place for civilized people. Of course, civilization never really left the cities, and today a number of factors point to a city renaissance. It seems like we are making progress. Fundamentally, there has been a massive drop in urban crime since the beginning of the 1990s, a necessary condition for many who have a choice of residential options. There is probably unresolvable debate about what caused this drop in crime, though changes in economic conditions, altered approaches to policing and criminal justice, and new technologies have all likely played significant roles. Concurrent with this change, cities have been "rediscovered" as the kind of settlements that can help us meet many of the challenges of our age—though it is important to observe that the notion that American cities were ever "forgotten" is imbued with a certain white, middle-class bias; even during the height of the disinvestment crisis, central cities were still magnets for new arrivals, the site of vibrant and resilient local communities, and the primary centers of cultural production. While those central cities that were most heavily reliant on Fordist manufacturing for their economic health lost population, many others grew or maintained their numbers throughout the twentieth century. Other technologies are improving responsiveness to public safety and infrastructure challenges. A rejection of midcentury High Modernist authoritarian design and planning principles has emphasized human scale in city aesthetics. And though deindustrialization has meant the disappearance of many stable working-class jobs, it has also meant the disappearance of much of the pollution that assailed our lungs and offended sensibilities for so long. This pivot in city history is crucial, because if we can solve or even alleviate some of the governance challenges that caused and characterized the urban crisis, the multiple advantages of city life may become widely apparent again. Economists emphasize the productive advantage inherent in dense places, where innovation can thrive on the easy exchange of ideas; see Glaeser 2011. Public health scholars have identified density and walkable community design as important tools in the fight against obesity (see Smith et al. 2008). City-dwellers have lower per capita carbon emissions compared to their more rural peers, perhaps making a return to dense communities a partial solution to climate change, though so far the overall good effect of dense cities has been decreased by the metropolitan sprawl that surrounds them; see Jones and Kammen 2014. The rediscovery of more closely built communities can theoretically foster all of these positive outcomes, and it augurs well for city rebirth that urbanist principles have been adopted as the current developmental paradigm. Planners often call this "New Urbanism," but much of it is a simple refurbishment of existing plans. Some, but not all, New Urbanist plans suffer from their status as urbanist veneers within broader suburban seas of automobile dependence. In short, cities are cool again, and not only for their capacity for innovative cultural production. Though cities have recovered some cultural and intellectual cachet, not everyone agrees that a city life is the best life. We all have experiences with cities of some kind, and we also know intuitively what makes them different. These differences can elicit strong, often-opposing reactions—they are crowded, exciting, expensive, dangerous. With the city's existential crisis on the wane, though, the poetic distillation of the city as a site of "opportunities for common life and a significant collective drama" (Mumford 1937, p. 59) or as a "concrete jungle where dreams are made" becomes more alluring (Carter and Keys 2009).

8. As will be clarified later, these governance imperatives are possibly, but not necessarily, related to the lived experiences of individuals within the city. This observation will entail an argument that relies on both the aggregation of individuals' experiences and preferences *and* a more ineffable sense of the interests of a city's corporate whole.

9. A note on terms: "Urban" places are settlements characterized by relative density and nonextractive economic activity. A "city" is a political community typically consisting of the largest (usually in terms of both population and geographical extent) central jurisdiction in an urban space. Sometimes a city fills an urban space, but more often in today's United States, an urban area extends beyond city boundaries. In certain contexts, this distinction between "urban" and "city" is relevant: for some purposes, the U.S. Census defines an urban space as any nonrural area (i.e., a city and its suburbs, also known as a "metropolitan area"). In many nations, the entire metropolitan area is governed by a single, growing city government, making the metropolitan area the appropriate unit for some cross-national urban analyses. In this study, I sometimes employ "urban" and "city" somewhat interchangeably to refer to the same kinds of communities and spaces at one end of an urban–suburban–rural sociological continuum. To emphasize the *political* aspects of the *city*, however, I will tend to use that term.

10. See, e.g., Wirth 1957. Local centrality is often included in this suite of characteristics as well, but some newer approaches to urban sociology (e.g., the "Los Angeles school") deemphasize the centrality of a particular area in favor of more polynodal understandings of the metropolis; the political implications of sociological centrality per se for national representation of policy preferences are unclear, though centrality (or, rather, peripherality) does seem to play a role in the resentment identified among rural voters against urbanites by Cramer (2016).

11. In thinking about a city, and what is distinctive about it, it may be helpful to think of density in terms of either population (whether residential, employment, or both) or activity (as in a high rate of economic or social activity, such as the number or volume of transactions; intensity of land use, as measured by firm or population density; or real estate values per unit of ground area). These indicators are frequently coincident and are classic hallmarks of many models of urban sociology based on the concentric zones identified by Park, Burgess, and McKenzie (1925). Alternative models, such as those that deemphasize concentricity of activity, do not diminish the importance of the three main characteristics of urbanicity. In a metropolitan area, the downtown area of the central city tends to have the highest density, and density often diminishes more or less monotonically as one moves farther from that center, though today there are often locally dense nodes of such activity outside the center as well.

12. Glaeser 2011.

13. See, e.g., Mumford 1961; Rae 2003; Sassen 2001.

14. Tonnies (1887) developed this framework of *gemeinschaft* and *gesellschaft*, roughly understood as "community" and "society," respectively, to theorize this contrast as large cities first began to grow.
15. In urban studies that focus on density and heterogeneity, the metropolitan area is often an appropriate unit of analysis, as most economic activity within the United States is not tightly constrained by municipal boundaries, and the central city along with its suburbs often constitute something close to a functional unit of economic activity. The U.S. Census at times assumes this perspective and defines "urban" areas as a metropolitan area plus its surrounding counties, and the Brookings Institution approaches urban policy issues through the lens of a "Metropolitan Policy Program." A similar perspective can be seen when comparing cities around the world: the New York metropolitan area, not just New York City, for example, is often the frame of comparison for other supercities such as London, Tokyo, or Mexico City, because of variation across countries in the forms and importance of local government.
16. In some cases, size is the necessary condition for heterogeneity as well. Where residential or economic-functional segregation is pronounced along key lines (as is often the case in American cities), only geographic inclusiveness makes these places particularly heterogeneous.
17. Katznelson 1982.
18. To be sure, inequality and the conflict it produces are still chronic problems within cities, but in recent decades these differences have become less stark than the divides between local polities within larger metropolitan areas. This observation is the central insight of the community of scholars and practitioners who, seeing that segregation and inequality are now even starker at the metropolitan level than within central cities, argue for a growth in regionalism as a way to promote equity between citizens. See, e.g., Dreier, Mollenkopf, and Swanstrom 2004.
19. Gainsborough 2001. Perhaps the more apt metaphor for the city boundary is the moat or wall (as opposed to the trench that might denote an intracity boundary), an obsolete version of the boundary, and one that more dramatically divided the city from its outlying areas, as in the Calvino epigram in Chapter 1.
20. Other characteristics can refine this understanding, and new concepts can help us poetically illustrate the "only in a city" juxtapositions, paradoxical spatial dynamics, and attitudes that increasingly have come to characterize the modern global metropolis. See Sassen 2005.
21. For instance, among recent canonical works, Browning et al. 2003; Alesina, Baqir, and Easterly 1999; Kaufmann 2004; Trounstine 2008; Hajnal 2007; and Erie 1988 all examine dynamics and outcomes at the local level, focusing in particular on intergroup relations in urban political space. Similarly, classic studies such as Dahl 1961; Banfield and Wilson 1963; and Sayre and Kaufman 1965 all looked to the local level, although sometimes to make broader external claims by analogy.
22. I use this portmanteau to indicate that I am considering not only actual citizens, legal residents, or somehow otherwise "formal" members of the city as the set of persons whose political dispositions are shaped by urbanicity. New arrivals may be shaped, too, and may be politically active and relevant to such considerations. Of course, given that electoral pressures are always prominent in most officials' minds, legal citizens and registered voters' preferences have especial institutional importance.
23. The relationship between context and attitudes is a contentious subject and has been for as long as scholars have systematically investigated individual behavior and preferences. See Oliver 2010 for a review of the relationship between context and attitudes, and Ethington and McDaniel 2007 for an examination of the idea of place/space effects in political geography. Many of these studies suffer from a fairly intractable problem. People (at least those with means and who do not face discrimination) can generally choose where to live in the United States, making it difficult to identify the direction of causation: cities may shape people's preferences, or people may have preferences that affect their choice of residence.
24. Rousseau 1762, Book II, ch. 3.
25. We might think of this city interest as a variety of long-term sociotropic calculation, in which individuals' or groups' particular interests are included in an evaluation of the sustainable, multigenerational health of the fictive corporate person of the city. Ultimately, this matter is not easily resolvable, but there may be significant overlap between the abstract "organic" interest and the concrete "city position" or "accord" fostered by city institutions of horizontal

integration and supported by a city delegation in representative politics, as described later in this chapter. This citywide accord is likely to reflect the interests of those elites who are most reliant on the overall health of the city; although in the worst case, these elites are purely corrupt rent-seekers, they also have incentives serve the city's long-term interest as well as their own. At a minimum, the order provided by IHIs can be seen as at least a partial good (when contrasted with the plausible alternative of open-ended disorder), even if the order and accord are not satisfactory to all parties. I return to this point in the discussion of IHIs later.

26. Such leaders will likely be attuned to the aggregated interests of citizens (as well as their own particular interest) as well, but the point here is that citywide concerns are more salient at the elite level than at the mass level.
27. As judged inductively by Poole and Rosenthal 1997. The significance of the second dimension waxed and waned in importance over the twentieth century but was particularly behaviorally orthogonal to the first during the urban interlude. Over time, conflicts on that dimension were folded into the first, such that the two dimensions are not as analytically separable as they were before.
28. There is persistent definitional confusion over terms in American politics—"liberal" ideas and positions are not identical with classical "liberalism," and "conservatives" seek to enact sweeping, sudden changes as often as they seek to preserve the status quo—so this discussion will highlight the importance of place character in informing and defining the main positions on many issues, ultimately suggesting something akin to "city" and "country" as replacement terms for our contemporary political ideological poles.
29. The dimensions are estimated by Poole and Rosenthal 1997 and captured in their DW-NOMINATE scores. Current iterations of this research agenda are available in McCarty, Poole, and Rosenthal 2006 and at www.voteview.com, where they refer to the substance of the first dimension as "the role of the government in the economy." As a caution, the precise content of this substantive judgment is fairly inductive and may not apply to previous eras, especially before the New Deal. See Noel 2014 and Katznelson, Clinton, and Lapinski Forthcoming for new approaches that seek to separate economic ideology from party. These new approaches are compatible with the narrative of Chapter 3, in which a city coalition brings such issues to the center of the agenda.
30. As opposed to alternative interventions such as purely voluntary regulation by associations of firms (though this is also fairly common), state ownership of firms, rationing, or centrally directed production; see Katznelson and Pietrykowski 1991.
31. Wirth 1938.
32. Wirth 1938.
33. In this case, regulation essentially serves to enhance the probability for cooperation in a "prisoner's dilemma" in which the diner and the restaurant are the participants. The state takes steps to ensure the quality of the meal and promises to punish the diner if he defects by not paying the bill. As well as benefiting diners, this system can also benefit restaurants that *would have been* conscientious in any case: an "A" in the window can serve as expert testimony that at the very least, an establishment is not dangerous or negligent. Thus, all restaurants have an incentive to be conscientious and are rewarded for it.
34. Today, technologically innovative alternatives to formal state regulation have arisen and may serve this information purpose even more effectively—for instance, user-review smartphone applications may alert potential diners of a particularly unhealthy restaurant—but it is unclear how reliable or durable such systems will prove.
35. Here, I conceive of common goods as (1) goods with broad benefits from which it is very hard to exclude nonpaying users, like clean air, public safety, or fire protection (the classic definition of a public good); (2) goods for which it would be possible but more inefficient to limit use to paying users, like parks or highways; and (3) goods that are technically exclusive but open to use by all and often constructed or subsidized by the state, such as public transportation.
36. Though for some goods likely to be valued everywhere, it may be more *important* that the good be effectively provided by the state in certain contexts. For instance, in a sparsely populated area, a murder is unlikely to cause a costly riot; even if it did, we could just wait for the next growing season to recoup the losses. In a city, such reactions have often occurred

because of the much higher accumulation of value and density of potential witnesses and property-destroyers.
37. Bateman and Taylor 2007.
38. In terms of use value, the Central Park is clearly more valuable than an equivalently sized parcel located far from a significant population. This is one instance in which exchange value reflects this difference: many people have paid millions for proximity to Central Park.
39. Individuals, even those who do live within walking distance to the park, may also value the public good of the park less because in a less dense residential environment there are often private spaces directly behind people's homes. In such a context, people may quite reasonably be even less inclined to support or pursue provision of further public parks.
40. This practice typically stopped when state authorities intervened and set up special districts to govern water distribution and use. See, for instance, Burrows and Wallace 1998 on New York; Erie 1992 on Los Angeles; and Cain 1983 on Chicago. For comparative narratives of the development of publicly owned, generally available public water, see Smith 2013.
41. Alesina, Baqir, and Easterly 1999.
42. Meltzer and Richard 1981.
43. Meltzer and Richard 1981 further extrapolate that such preferences will result in more redistributive *policy*, but the preferences driving this model need not actually lead to policy changes to be real; this is why the study of institutions matters. Additionally, other factors, especially political ideology or beliefs about an individual's responsibility for his or her own fate, surely inform preferences about redistribution, but one's place in the income distribution (as well as other indicators of socioeconomic status) is indeed a powerful predictor. See, e.g., Alesina et al. 2011.
44. Assessing preferences for redistribution across levels of government makes the story more complicated. These preferences may be formed at the local level if individuals' information about their place in the income distribution is local, but to the extent that income distributions differ across space, such assessments may produce counterintuitive results, such as a locally rich person in a very poor locality wanting less redistribution than a locally poor person in a wealthy place, even though the latter may actually have more wealth or income. We have reason to believe that citizens form at least some of their preferences about redistribution based on information about equality and deservingness they gain locally; see Newman 2014. In practice, redistributive policies may not be in the organic interest of the city if enacted locally; they may be unsustainable at the local level because of the kind of external constraints described by Peterson 1981 and Hackworth 2007, among others. In this view, redistribution is more functionally suited to higher levels even though the taste for it is developed locally. Consequently, we may not see heightened redistribution at the local level, despite local demand for it, but merely in stronger *support* for redistributive policies, albeit at higher levels.
45. Martin Luther King, Jr., famously called such uprisings "the language of the unheard."
46. Alesina et al. 2011.
47. To labor the metaphor of an organic city interest, we could think of cities as organisms that require greater inputs to maintain homeostasis.
48. This is not to imply that being urban and supporting statist interventions are equivalent; this is not the case, as there are certainly many economic conservatives in cities and many liberals outside of them. But cities foster a predisposition toward these interventions, especially among those tasked with maintaining the health of the city, so we should expect an association between urbanicity and statism.
49. Bridges 1984, p. 20.
50. Erie 1988.
51. Buenker 1973.
52. Alesina, Baqir, and Easterly 1999. At higher levels, this divide was present from the birth of the urban political order, as we shall see in Chapter 3, and it has been consistent in modern congressional representation, as shown in Figure 6.8.
53. Kousser, McCubbins, and Moule 2008.
54. Hackworth 2007.
55. Peterson 1981.
56. White 1890.
57. Rae 2003, p. xii.

58. Throughout this book, I use the term "supralocal" to refer to levels of government above the local, primarily state and national.
59. Poole and Rosenthal 1997.
60. Habyarimana et al. 2009. There is a large literature in economics and political science theorizing the reasons why diversity might undermine statism—especially public goods provision, but also redistribution, especially when groups are concentrated at different parts of the income distribution. For instance, the perception that African Americans are the primary beneficiaries of welfare spending is believed to undermine support for redistribution among white Americans. See, e.g., Gilens 2000.
61. This perspective was articulated by Allport 195), but for a review of subsequent literature, see Oliver 2010.
62. Group threat theory is often called "realistic" group threat. See Key 1949; Blalock 1967; Oliver 2010. A key methodological challenge in studies of contact and threat is the problem of residential mobility and endogeneity: environments may change persons, or persons may relocate into environments that suit their tastes. This challenge is most pertinent to those who find the racial contact hypothesis at work, as it seems less likely that persons locate themselves in order to be *closer* to groups they do not like. Observational or quasi-experimental studies that find evidence for threat, such as Oliver 2010 and Enos 2010, are less vulnerable to this fundamental inferential problem.
63. Sugrue 2008; Keiser 1997; Biles 1995; Frymer 2007; Jones-Correa 2000.
64. Sugrue 1996; Joyce 2003.
65. Notably, however, our understanding of these intergroup conflicts has become more nuanced as scholars have explored the role of broader context in the particular contact or threat. See Oliver 2010; Enos 2010; Hopkins 2010. One corollary finding related to the threat hypothesis is that diverse communities have lower levels of interpersonal trust and social capital; that is, even when people from different groups are not fighting outright, they are not getting along and cooperating very well either. See Putnam 2007.
66. Ansolabehere and Jones 2011; Mayhew 1974.
67. Key 1949; Trebbi, Aghion, and Alesina 2008; Lublin 1997b.
68. At least on racial grounds—the separation of whites into ethnic enclaves is generally exaggerated, but concentrations of black Americans in particular spaces within the city was (and still is) pronounced. Massey and Denton 1993; Katznelson 1982.
69. Oliver 2010, ch. 2.
70. Keiser 1997.
71. There are many reasons social peace is preferable to heated division: humanitarian concerns that persons not be injured or killed, desire for a feeling of mutual affection or respect with co-members of one's community, respect for private property, the promotion of commerce or other practices that are strengthened in circumstances of physical security, aesthetic affection for particular historic buildings or districts, and so on.
72. See the New York City Commission on Human Rights website at http://www1.nyc.gov/site/cchr/about/inside-cchr.page.
73. Stone 1989.
74. How *effective* these groups are at delivering substantive justice or reform for minority groups remains a question, but the existence of such institutions, with their goal of keeping social peace through reform and persuasion rather than repression, is itself an expression of the organic interest of the city.
75. Indeed, this dimensional framework is borrowed from Poole and Rosenthal 1997, who mathematically separate these dimensions in legislative roll call voting patterns.
76. In one oft-cited study, local jurisdictions provided fewer public goods when levels of diversity were high, indicating that it may be difficult for groups to overcome their ethnic or racial differences and govern at the local level. See Alesina, Baqir, and Easterly 1999; Alesina and Glaeser 2004; see also Habyarimana et al. 2009 for experimental evidence in a different context. But see Hopkins 2011; and Boustan et al. 2013 for counterpoints.
77. Buenker 1973, ch. 6.
78. The exception is when a city's population hits a sweet spot equal to the size of a legislative district at a particular historical moment (such that the district would encompass the city as

a whole, rather than a subdivision of the city or the city and its surrounding areas, which may have very different interests). This is fairly rare, but such a district would be the closest we can often get to a condition of identity between a city and a seat in a legislature.

79. As I will illustrate in Chapter 4, these constituencies are often *particularly* heterogeneous collections of districts, especially when it comes to race and class.
80. Katznelson 1982.
81. Mayhew 1966; Wolman and Marckini 2005; Caraley 1976.
82. Indeed, I implicitly adopt this framework myself in the earlier discussion of the relationship between urbanicity and liberalism and in Chapter 6's analysis of the development of the urban bloc and its ability to pursue an "urban agenda" over time.
83. Gelfand 1975, p. 28.
84. By comparison, consider the centrality of London to English/U.K. society, or Paris to French society. See Monkkonnen 1988.
85. See Erie 1992 on California rivalries, Burrows and Wallace 1998 on New York.
86. Mollenkopf 1983; Ethington and Levitus 2009.
87. Many authors highlight different aspects of this project and its importance for the New Deal, including Dorsett 1977; Mayhew 1986; Andersen 1979; Mollenkopf 1983; Buenker 1973.
88. Bridges 1984; Connolly 2010. Dahl 1961, often cited as a kind of textbook of political pluralism, draws its data entirely from observations of interest-clashes in even the small city of New Haven, CT—all major critiques of that school of thought indicate that they *underestimate* the amount of conflict actually present in city politics.
89. See Cannato 2002; but also Rae 2003, introduction.
90. DeLeon 1992.
91. By integrating local politics, these institutions are able to more effectively transmit the city interest "vertically," up the political food chain to higher levels of government.
92. Which in turn undermines the possibility for two-dimensional liberalism. Gainsborough (2001) finds that the "suburbanization" of American politics leads to a strengthening of political localism and increasing support for small-government policies, while Oliver (2001) finds that homogeneity leads to diminished political participation and civic capacity. Shrinking the political community seems to shrink the public sphere and tighten the public purse strings.
93. The Chicago metropolitan area, often called Chicagoland, has an extremely high number of local governments, making for a politically fractured metropolitan community, but most big cities are similarly surrounded by suburban rings.
94. Oliver 2001; Oliver 2012. Fewer participants in both relative and absolute terms.
95. Some of the suburbs that are very dark grey are indeed highly unequal. But at least two of these—Barrington Hills to the northwest and Lake Forest along the lakefront, which are each over 90 percent white with median incomes over $150,000—are small communities made unequal not by the cohabitation of rich and poor but by the presence of some extremely rich households, which throws off the statistics. They are not places where different kinds of people are thrown together into a diverse polity. The overall trend of the map would look similar if we mapped other major dimensions of diversity, such as race and ethnicity.
96. Advocates of metropolitan governance schemes implicitly emphasize the importance of jurisdictional IHIs in the articulation and implementation of policies reflecting a broad "organic" interest of the metropolitan community; these institutions are usually fairly weak or restricted in their substantive areas of authority in the United States.
97. For instances or conceptual outlines of strong local parties in cities, see Banfield and Wilson 1963; Bridges 1984; and Mayhew 1986. For classic accounts of machine politics, see Gosnell 1937; and Erie 1988. Bridges 1997 outlines instances and characteristics of reform regimes, and Trounstine 2008 draws an important connection between these institutional arrangements and partisan-style machines, conceptualizing each kind of political order as a subset of the broader category of "monopoly." Stone 1989 conceptualizes the elite urban regime and describes some of its characteristics in action in Atlanta.
98. This question refers to an inquiry about one's ethnicity based on a glance at a last name. Even in Chicago, the capital of Polish America, I am asked this on an almost daily basis—still an exchange common among white Chicagoans (and others).
99. Huntington 1968.

100. Again, this citywide "accord" may be undemocratic and may reflect neither the "will of all" of the city's residents nor the abstract "general will" of the city as a corporate body (though ideally it will include elements of those) while remaining an enforceable policy or position that results from the deliberation and workings of IHIs. I choose the language of "accord," as opposed to "city interest" or "consensus," to reflect this idea—that there may be winners and losers, and that it is certainly possible that an accord will not necessarily reflect consensus or the city's organic interest.
101. Mayhew 1966; Mayhew 1974; Fenno 1973. This mix of factors is in itself something fairly distinctive about American legislative politics, in which relatively decentralized party institutions make strict party-line voting something less than a given, as it is in most other Western democracies. In the ideal abstract, a legislature is something of a microcosm of broader society, with the views and preferences of its constituent parts brought to bear on political questions for deliberation and policy adjustment. In reality, along the way to final legislative decisions, unavoidable collective action and social choice problems give rise to legislative institutions that shape the way constituencies' preferences are aggregated into policy.
102. In fact, they are both important. See Aldrich 1995; Krehbiel 1998; Cox and McCubbins 2004. For a review of this literature, see Aldrich 2011, ch. 7. When cities turn to higher levels of government to pursue solutions to their local governance problems, both constituency and party should therefore be taken into account.
103. These differences may be softened by a member's party affiliation in Congress, a truism in the study of legislatures. But such studies rarely examine subdelegations, or patterns among them, which is the explicit focus of city delegation theory.
104. Districts from the same state are within the same jurisdiction and so share *that* IHI. But the greater geographic extent of states and the immediacy of local ties may make local jurisdictional institutions relatively more powerful integrators. Empirically, state delegations of any significant size are not usually very cohesive, and being from the same state tends to be, *ceteris paribus, negatively* related to cohesion, as demonstrated by analyses in Chapter 4.
105. See Dorsett 1977 for details on local organizational distribution of WPA funds.
106. Phillips and Brooks 2010; Welch and Bledsoe 1998; Pinderhughes 1987; Keiser 1997.
107. For instance, when a local municipal employees' union sought a pay rise in 1950, its members did not restrict themselves to local officials but wrote to Rooney for support in their battle with the mayor. Raymond Diana and CIO Government and Civic Employees Organizing Committee, letter to John Rooney, December 6, 1950, Box 82, Folder "CIO," John J. Rooney Papers, Brooklyn College.
108. Mayhew 1986 shows that strong parties were powerful shapers of local outcomes. Bridges 1984 calls the political machine the "characteristic form of city government" in the nineteenth century, and though these institutions were weakened by reform and other factors, their structures and legacies are still evident in the cities they once dominated and were certainly the most powerful single political forces in many cities during the urban interlude. See Erie 1988; Mayhew 1986. There are certainly other very important organizational IHIs, including reform slating groups, labor unions, and, to a lesser extent, community organizations. Any group that brings together elites and city-zens from across the face of the city to resolve governance challenges could qualify for the designation. Overall, the political party is the most effective, durable, and replicated such institution in American urban history.
109. Mayhew 1986. This is the definitive text on such organizations in the mid-twentieth-century United States.
110. Snowiss 1966; Buenker 1973.
111. Biles 1995.
112. Snowiss 1966, p. 629.
113. Mayhew 1986; Wilson 1962; Snowiss 1966; Rakove 1975.
114. Stone 1989, p. 180.
115. Burns et al. 2009; Burns, Gamm, and Allard 1998; Weir, Wolman, and Swanstrom 2005b.
116. Flanagan 1999; see also Chapter 3.
117. Mollenkopf 1983; Dorsett 1977; Eldersveld 1949.

118. Katznelson and Farhang 2005 analyzes the intentionality and frequency of the conservative coalition. Katznelson and Mulroy 2012 more closely analyze its temporal and substantive dimensions, particularly how this partnership contributed to party change in the Long New Deal. Gelfand 1975; Mollenkopf 1983; and Biles 2011 each focus on how the coalition impeded northern Democrats' pro-city policy agenda.
119. Two examples from the Long New Deal era can illustrate this idea. First, bloc unity was used quite effectively by southerners in Congress to defend their regional racial order. See Katznelson and Farhang 2005; Katznelson and Mulroy 2012. Southerners frequently and increasingly "defected" from their co-partisans on a range of issues, forming the conservative coalition with Republicans that was a recurrent feature of national politics for decades. Because they actually defected, and because the positions they took were compatible with their true issue preferences, their victories did not appear to be pyrrhic, and they gained significant leverage as the pivotal bloc in the legislature. See Katznelson and Mulroy 2012; Sitkoff 1978. Second, a similar strategy was employed concurrently in electoral politics by the fast-growing African American population in some large northern cities to advance their civil rights agenda and gain meaningful incorporation into local and national party organizations. Previously loyal to the Republican "Party of Lincoln," African American electoral support was still in flux during the 1930s and 1940s, and black power brokers sought to extract concessions (mostly civil rights policies and material inclusion in the spoils of office) from their suitors in each party. See Sitkoff 1978, pp. 88–92; Keiser 1997, pp. 7–9, 26–33. This strategy lost power over time, however, as a return to the Republican fold began to seem self-defeating to African Americans. Most national Republicans, reduced to a non-urban, nonsouthern redoubt during the 1930s and 1940s, had basically no African American constituents to appeal to, and their extreme fealty to business interests and hostility toward the New Deal meant that many significant antiracist regulatory measures were seen as opposed to their new core principles. See, e.g., Chen 2009. Each of these groups was able to leverage pivotal cohesion into meaningful results.
120. Burns et al. 2009.
121. Again, the conditions of urbanicity mean that the status quo does not usually work for very long; social and economic flux mean that policies must change to address new realities and associated governance challenges. Thus, city representatives must typically forge coalitions for positive action, not merely block policy changes that would harm their cities (though they must seek those as well).
122. I conceive of unity as a precondition for strategic action, because a fractious, divided bloc cannot properly be said to be a strategic actor. However, the unified bloc is itself the product of strategic action, because cohesive representation may not reflect the "true" positions or divisions within or between cities.
123. Cox and McCubbins 1993.
124. Cox and McCubbins 2004; Wolman and Marckini 2005. Again, southern representatives were particularly aware of these tools in advancing their own goals during the twentieth century. Lieberman 2001; Katznelson 2012.
125. Mayhew 1966.
126. Burns et al. 2009.
127. Weir, Wolman, and Swanstrom 2005.
128. Mayhew 1966; Aldrich 2011, pp. 23–24.
129. Katznelson and Mulroy 2012.
130. Fleck 2008; Bateman and Taylor 2007.
131. Mayhew 1966.
132. The "uneven" logroll that was the heart of the Democratic coalition also fits with an understanding of how urbanicity and Peterson's (1981) logic fit together as an example of collective action on statism. Cities had relatively more resources and could ostensibly have provided some of these goods/interventions on their own, but they were constrained from doing so. In turning to the national level, they were forced in effect to provide certain goods to other constituencies (for whom such interventions were less important and/or more costly, because the conditions of urbanicity did not obtain) in order to ensure that such interventions were made *in cities*. This helps explain why less densely populated areas

actually received *more* federal largesse during this time, according to Bateman and Taylor 2007, and still do, according to Cramer 2016.
133. Katznelson and Mulroy 2012.
134. Though they do not use the term "urbanize," this model is drawn from Burns et al. 2009.
135. Burns et al. 2009.
136. Jackson 1985; Nall 2010; and Gainsborough 2001 tell the story for the mid- to late twentieth century, but this divide was present from the start (though suburbs were initially a trivially small segment of the population). See, e.g., Bass Warner 1978; Cain 1983.
137. Weir, Wolman, and Swanstrom 2005.
138. Gainsborough 2001.
139. Mayhew 1986; Erie 1988.
140. Erie 1988; Keiser 1997; Biles 1995.

Chapter 3

1. C. A. Dykstra, "Relief from the Municipal Point of View," Annual Proceedings of the U.S. Conference of Mayors, 1934.
2. House Committee on Banking and Currency, "To Create a U.S. Housing Authority," August 3, 1937, p. 27, HRG-1937-BCU-0002.
3. The American Municipal Association is now the National League of Cities, which engages in more national advocacy work, similar to the U.S. Conference of Mayors, but for a more inclusive set of communities.
4. Flanagan 1999.
5. On the development of postwar urban policy and the subsequent retreat from it, see also Biles 2011; Gelfand 1975. On the Reagan revolution and slashed urban aid, see also Caraley 1992.
6. Mollenkopf 1983, p. 16.
7. Mollenkopf 1983 makes this key observation about the 1930s, though his focus is on the postwar years. Flanagan 1999 also identifies this theoretical insight about the birth of intergovernmental lobbying.
8. Burns et al. 2009; Weir, Wolman, and Swanstrom 2005.
9. Similar flows occurred in advanced European countries as well. Population numbers from U.S. decennial censuses.
10. Nearly all of the Progressive reformers' efforts and rhetoric were infused with some mix of paternalism, xenophobia, belief in Anglo-Saxon supremacy, limited faith in democracy, a vision of the common good, fiscal conservatism, bourgeois self-satisfaction, and a reliance on management expertise. Whether the bosses or the reformers were somehow better is a long debate in urban politics and political science; both groups were too diverse and the issues at stake are too complex to render a succinct verdict in the case.
11. See White 1890 for a particularly famous statement of this position. This position was itself inevitably and inherently "political" in a broader sense, but Progressives used the term in the narrow sense of having to do with partisan politics.
12. Gelfand 1975, p. 14.
13. Dilworth 2011, ch. 7.
14. Dykstra, "Relief from the Municipal Point of View."
15. Monkkonen 2004.
16. Ibid.
17. Fiorello LaGuardia, "The Federal Work Program and Cities," Annual Proceedings of U.S. Conference of Mayors, 1937.
18. Ibid.
19. Beito 1989; Parke Brown, "Kelly Bill Beaten; 58 to 66," *Chicago Tribune*, January 13, 1932, p. 1.
20. Senate Committee on Banking and Currency, "Relief to Municipalities," May 3, 1933, HRG-1933-BCS-0021, pp. 15–16.
21. See Katznelson 2012 on the contrast between U.S. and other responses to the Depression; and Lowi 1969 on the transformation of American politics during this era.

22. On the particularly controversial subject of race, this amalgam of liberal groups (or at least their leadership) would advocate consistently on behalf of civil rights throughout the Long New Deal, contributing to the national parties' evolving divergence on such issues. This transformation is the focus of Chapter 5.
23. There were many other groups, but these appear frequently in the record of urban issue hearings during the 1930s.
24. Frymer 2007.
25. E.g., Arthur Sears Henning, "Democratic Factions Fight for 1940 Rule: Left Wingers Battle to Retain Grip," *Chicago Tribune*, November 11, 1938, p. 1. See also hearings in the 1930s on recruitment rivalries and AFL resentment of CIO successes; see, for example "National Labor Relations Act," vols. 1–4. House Special Committee to Investigate National Labor Relations Board, December 1938, HRG-1939-INL-0001–HRG-1939-INL-0004. While the conception that this era was particularly and unusually auspicious for gains by organized labor, a working-class interlude in David Greenstone's famous phrase, the cohesion of the factions within the movement should not be understated nor should the liberalism of its rank and file.
26. Based on a search of congressional hearings using ProQuest Congressional.
27. The NLC was known as the National Municipal Association in its early years.
28. No witnesses appeared before Congress on behalf of the NLC until the 1930s; when the organization did voice a position in congressional testimony, it was represented by Sherwood Reeder, a member of the NLC's committee on federal policy, who appeared several times on its behalf. Reeder was also a member of the executive committee of the U.S. Conference of Mayors and often appeared on behalf of both organizations to clarify their positions on technical matters. While Reeder was no doubt a fine spokesperson and an expert in municipal government (he went on to be the city manager of Richmond and Norfolk), the NLC lacked a certain star power, perhaps as a byproduct of its inclusivity and hinterland origins (it always included many smaller cities, which were wary of the urban behemoths among them).
29. *Chicago Daily Tribune*, "Mayors Asking Liberal Loans, Aid for Jobless: Urge Five Billion Dollar Public Works Program," June 2, 1932, p. 6.
30. U.S. Conference of Mayors, *Born in Detroit* [film], https://www.usmayors.org/the-conference/about/
31. Carter Glass, in "Unemployment Relief," Hearing before Senate Committee on Banking and Currency, June 1932, HRG-1932-BC-008, p. 18.
32. C. L. Dykstra, "The Municipal Viewpoint," Annual Proceedings of U.S. Conference of Mayors, 1934.
33. Flanagan 1999, p. 434.
34. Dorsett 1977.
35. Mollenkopf 1983.
36. Eldersveld 1949.
37. Bridges 1984; Shefter 1976; Burrows and Wallace 1998.
38. Although government functions in New York City were generally merged in the consolidation of 1898, some county administration persists, and the city's political organizations remain a collection of county- and borough-based groups.
39. Tammany had been dominant in New York politics in the decades before the five counties merged, and the opportunities rivals saw to weaken the Tiger's grip on City Hall contributed to the dynamics of city consolidation. See Burrows and Wallace 1998, ch. 69.
40. Dorsett 1977, ch. 4.
41. Flanagan 1999, p. 435.
42. Dorsett 1977.
43. Ibid.
44. Ibid., ch. 4; Flanagan 1999.
45. Even more impressively, the Democrats have won 99 percent of Chicago seats since 1963; see the CSR Database.
46. Albeit with a major internal struggle during the 1980s, when African Americans demanded more substantial inclusion in political and policy good distribution.
47. Dorsett 1977, p. 88; Gosnell 1937.

48. See Dorsett 1977 for some details on Kelly's relationship with FDR and in national Democratic Party politics, particularly his gathering of support for FDR's third term at the 1940 Democratic National Convention in Chicago. Daley's actions on the national stage, particularly at the Chicago convention in 1968 and in his mobilization efforts to provide Kennedy a narrow victory in Illinois in 1960, were much more notorious, but he was also a frequent correspondent with Johnson throughout his presidency and organizer of the 1964 convention, helping to advise the president on party leadership, election strategy, and how to resolve the Mississippi Freedom Party controversy. See conversations between Daley and Johnson in 1964 and 1965, recordings 5254, 5231, and 6369, Miller Center Presidential Recordings Archive, University of Virginia, millercenter.org/scripps/archive/presidentialrecordings/johnson/.
49. Mayhew 1986.
50. These western cities often had fairly conservative local leadership and heated class and racial conflict, in part because there were no organizations to effectively build and sustain alliances among elites and their constituencies. See Bridges 1997; Sonenshein 1994; DeLeon 1992.
51. Flanagan 1999, p. 435.
52. U.S. House Subcommittee on H.R. 3082 and Other Bills to Provide Loans Through Reconstruction Finance Corporation, "To Provide Loans Through Reconstruction Finance Corporation," Feb. 13, 1934, HRG-1934-BCU-0003, p. 181.
53. Lieberman 2001; Katznelson 2005.
54. Much of the story of the rise of urban issues to the national agenda has been told well elsewhere; see, e.g., Gelfand 1975. Here, I add observations specifically germane to the urbanicity paradox (high demand, constrained resources for governance) and to the strategies city representatives pursued to overcome their situation of marginal urgency.
55. Caraley 1976.
56. Dreier, Mollenkopf, and Swanstrom 2004, ch. 4.
57. This list was assembled from a search of the LexisNexis Congressional Hearings database using the search terms "federal aid to local governments" and "federal aid to municipalities," two standard subjects for hearings, and restricting results to between 1900 and 1940 to create the table. Extending the search back in time produces only a few more hearings; extending it forward toward the present produces hundreds more. The period 1930–1933 is clearly an inflection point when the substance and frequency of these hearings changed dramatically.
58. This was determined by the substance of the hearings and the witnesses who appeared before the committee: on topics that were possibly urban, witness lists that were primarily persons from or representing cities were taken as signs that this was a city issue. Topics that were obviously not urban, such as "Forestry," were coded as such.
59. John McCormack, testimony before House Committee on Rivers and Harbors, March 10, 1932, HRG-1932-RRH-0010, p. 4.
60. Ibid.
61. Ibid.
62. Gelfand 1975, pp. 17–24.
63. Senate Committee on Education and Labor, "To Create a U.S. Housing Authority," April 14, 1937, HRG-1937-EDS-0013, p. 100.
64. Unemployment in large industrial cities was higher than the national average, and the potential for unrest there made increased or extended relief particularly valuable. Though massive road-building projects were already contributing to city-killing suburbanization by the 1920s, city officials supported them from the start because of the massive local stimulus they provided. Biles 2011, p. 3.
65. Senate Committee on Banking and Currency Hearing, "Unemployment Relief," June 2–13, 1932, HRG-1932-BCS-0008.
66. Ibid., pp. 14–15.
67. Ibid., p. 17.
68. Ibid., p. 17.
69. At this point, Wagner, Roosevelt, and other leading Progressives such as Republicans Robert La Follette and La Guardia were avowedly opposed to deficit spending on principle (see

Leuchtenburg 1963, p. 37), but the inclusion of bond issuance in these loan programs presages the later adoption of Keynesian countercyclical budgeting.
70. HRG-1932-BCS-0008, p. 17.
71. Ibid., p. 18.
72. Ibid., p. 29.
73. Ibid., p. 41.
74. Ibid., p. 166.
75. Ibid., p. 178.
76. Ibid., p. 189.
77. Senate Committee on Banking and Currency, "Relief to Municipalities," May 3, 1933, HRG-1933-BCS-0021, p. 5.
78. Ibid., emphasis added.
79. Ibid.
80. Mayhew 1966; Fleck 2008.
81. House Committee on Ways and Means, "National Industrial Recovery," May 18–20, 1933, HRG-1933-WAM-0006, p. 299.
82. Testimony of Nathan Straus, Administrator of U.S. Housing Authority, before Senate Committee on Education and Labor, April 7, 1939, "To Amend the U.S. Housing Act of 1937," HRG-1939-EDS-0007, p. 29.
83. House Committee on Banking and Currency, "Amendments to U.S. Housing Act of 1937," April 28, 1938, HRG-1938-BCU-0004, p. 16.
84. And Meeks's *district* did not get any of the fat pie, either.
85. Author's analysis of first-generation USHA grant figures given by USHA Administrator Nathan Straus before Senate Subcommittee on S. 591, Committee on Education and Labor, HRG-1939-EDS-0007, pp. 27–28.
86. Gelfand 1975 and Biles 2011 chronicle the growth of the conservative coalition and resistance by noncity Democrats to a cabinet-level "urban" department beginning in the 1930s. Mayhew 1966 quantifies the relatively frequent defection by noncity Democrats from the party's alliances built on inclusive exchange over the 1940s.
87. House Committee on Banking and Currency, "To Create a U.S. Housing Authority," August 3, 1937, HRG-1937-BCU-0002, p. 101.
88. To identify urban roll calls for this time series, I used data from the American Institutions Project (AIP) dataset, which assigns substantive issue codes to all roll calls in congressional history up to the 100th Congress. See Katznelson and Lapinski 2007 for a detailed description of the dataset. AIP data are also used in later chapters to identify certain kinds of votes.
89. Gelfand 1975.
90. Dykstra, "Relief from the Municipal Point of View."
91. Ibid. Harry Hopkins, "The Cities and Relief," Annual Proceedings of the U.S. Conference of Mayors, 1933.
92. Harold H. Burton, "An Industrial City Looks at Relief," Annual Proceedings of the U.S. Conference of Mayors, 1937.
93. Unidentified speaker at 1932 annual gathering of the U.S. Conference of Mayors, cited by Dykstra, "Relief from the Municipal Point of View."
94. Dykstra, "Relief from the Municipal Point of View"; Hopkins, "The Cities and Relief."
95. Harold Ickes, "Cities and the Public Works Programs," Annual Proceedings of the U.S. Conference of Mayors, 1933.
96. Figures drawn from "Final Report on the WPA Program, 1935–43," compiled by Brent McKee at wpatoday.org.
97. Lawrence Veiller, quoted in Biles 2011, p. 9.
98. As Senator Robert Wagner put it in 1934: "I think 60 years ago they were talking about housing conditions in New York City, and the very same houses are in existence today and being used by people." See Senate Committee on Banking and Security, "National Housing Act," May 16–19, 1934, HRG-1934-BCS-0024, p. 26.
99. Biles 2011.
100. Quotes in this paragraph from National Housing Act of 1934.
101. Massey and Denton 1993; Rae 2003.

102. Senate Committee on Banking and Security, "National Housing Act," May 16–19, 1934, HRG-1934-BCS-0024, p. 143. See also Biles 2011, introduction.
103. Testimony of Nathan Straus, Administrator of U.S. Housing Authority, before Committee on Education and Labor, April 7, 1939, HRG-1939-EDS-0007, p. 34.
104. Flanagan 1999, p. 427.
105. Ibid., p. 430.
106. Ibid., p. 12.
107. Submitted testimony by John Smith, Acting Mayor of Detroit, "To Create a U.S. Housing Authority," Hearing of House Committee on Banking and Currency, August 3–6, 1937, HRG-1937-BCU-0002, p. 4.
108. "To Create a U.S. Housing Authority," Hearing of House Committee on Banking and Currency, August 3–6, 1937, HRG-1937-BCU-0002, p. 27.
109. Flanagan 1999, p. 428.
110. Fiorello LaGuardia, "The Federal Work Program and Cities," Annual Proceedings of U.S. Conference of Mayors, 1937.
111. Dykstra, "The Municipal Viewpoint."
112. Caraley 1992.
113. Flanagan 1999.
114. See usmayors.org/issues.
115. Eldersveld 1949; Andersen 1979.

Chapter 4

1. Banfield and Wilson 1963, p. 101.
2. Snowiss 1966, p. 630.
3. Rae 2003; Sugrue 1996.
4. Katznelson 1982; Massey and Denton 1993.
5. DeLeon 1992; Cannato 2002.
6. Though each of these smaller cities had their own particular histories. See Mayhew 1986 for state-by-state narratives of party strength and development. See Dorsett 1977 for closer case studies of several machines' relations with the national Democratic leadership under FDR.
7. That Democrat was an incumbent governor, who defeated a Chicago-backed insurgent. See Wilson 1962, p. 67.
8. Mayhew 1986, p. 45.
9. Paper trails were frowned upon, and these men were not typically writers of memos by disposition in any case. Lomasney's Law governs political communication within the party organization: "Never write it down if you can speak, never speak if you can nod, never nod if you can wink." See Buenker 1973, p. 208.
10. New York's Democratic organization was perhaps the first organizational IHI developed to build cohesive political authority over the face of an American city, a process that occurred when Tammany Hall consolidated under Fernando Wood and then became dominant under Richard Croker in the nineteenth century; see Bridges 1984. Spread over five counties after the formation of Greater New York, New York's Democrats were often less unified than Tammany in its heyday, but they still organized around party operations that exerted citywide influence.
11. Prosterman 2013.
12. Though DeSapio was unsuccessful in his effort to replace Adam Clayton Powell with someone more loyal to the organization in 1958. See Wilson 1962, p. 47. On early Tammany, see Bridges 1984. On the relationship between Tammany, business, and labor, see Shefter 1976. On the long trajectory of Tammany and the traditional organizations, see Bridges 1984. On Roosevelt, La Guardia, and the party bosses, see Dorsett 1977. On the internal strength of New York organizations, see Mayhew 1986; and Banfield and Wilson 1963.
13. Besides those he had partnered with during his own time as an activist liberal congressman, especially Emanuel Celler and Sen. Robert F. Wagner.
14. La Guardia and Marcantonio shared both ideological and ethnic bonds and corresponded at times in Italian, although the two sparred quite seriously later, as La Guardia allied with moderate democratic labor organizations and Marcantonio with the Communist left.

15. La Guardia was accused of using this resource, among others, to help Marcantonio unseat James Lanzetta in La Guardia's old East Harlem district. See Dorsett (1977); James Lanzetta, telegram to Fiorello La Guardia, August 24, 1934, Fiorello La Guardia Subject Files, Vito Marcantonio correspondence, Film 127, Slide 1588, New York Municipal Archives.
16. Fiorello La Guardia, telegram to Emanuel Celler, February 4, 1936, La Guardia Collection Subject Files: Congressional Correspondence Roll 24, Slide 0064, New York Municipal Archives.
17. Emanuel Celler, telegram to Fiorello La Guardia, January 29, 1935, La Guardia Collection Subject Files: Congressional Correspondence Roll 23, Slide 2431, New York Municipal Archives.
18. Fiorello La Guardia, telegram to Henry Steagall, January 29, 1935, La Guardia Collection Subject Files: Congressional Correspondence Roll 23, Slide 2430, New York Municipal Archives.
19. Emanuel Celler, telegram to Fiorello La Guardia, January 30, 1935, La Guardia Collection Subject Files: Congressional Correspondence Roll 23, Slide 2427, New York Municipal Archives.
20. Paul Betters, telegram to Fiorello La Guardia, January 31, 1935, La Guardia Collection Subject Files: Congressional Correspondence Roll 23, Slide 2428, New York Municipal Archives.
21. Fiorello La Guardia, telegram to Jesse Jones, January 31, 1935, La Guardia Collection Subject Files: Congressional Correspondence Roll 23, Slide 2426, New York Municipal Archives.
22. William Sirovich, letter to Fiorello La Guardia, March 16, 1934, La Guardia Collection Subject Files: Congressional Correspondence Roll 23, Slide 2323, New York Municipal Archives.
23. Though as the son of a senator, Wagner, who was mayor from 1954 to 1965, enjoyed significant advantages in initial political placement over the typical New York politician, as did his son Bobby. Ultimately, Mayor Wagner broke with Tammany Hall and defeated its preferred challenger for the Democratic mayoral nomination in his third successful run in 1961. The other three-term mayors were La Guardia, Koch, and Michael Bloomberg.
24. Esther Berman and Robert Zucker, letters to Robert F. Wagner, Jr., May 1954, New York Municipal Archives.
25. Unsigned letter to Robert F. Wagner, Jr., undated, 1954, New York Municipal Archives.
26. James V. Valvo, letter to Robert F. Wagner, Jr., undated, 1954, New York Municipal Archives.
27. Ellsworth H. Sommer, letter to Robert F. Wagner, Jr., May 4, 1954, New York Municipal Archives.
28. Anna Spano, letter to Robert F. Wagner, Jr., May 6, 1954, New York Municipal Archives.
29. Rhoda A. Salon, letter to Rober F. Wagner, Jr., May 5, 1954, Robert F. Wagner, Jr. Papers, New York Municipal Archives.
30. Robert F. Wagner, Jr., form letter to New York Congressional Delegation, May 15, 1954, New York Municipal Archives.
31. "New York Democratic Delegation Denounce Undersecretary of the Army Slezak and Deputy Under Secretary Higgins for Their High-Handed tactics," press release, May 20, 1954, New York Municipal Archives.
32. Louis B. Heller, "The Quartermaster Purchasing Agency Should Remain in New York City," *Congressional Record*, May 20, 1954, pp. A3745–3746.
33. Remarks by Herbert Lehman to Congress, *Congressional Record*, June 17, 1954, p. 8426.
34. Remarks to Congress by Edward Martin and James Duff, *Congressional Record*, June 17, 1954, pp. 8429–8431. Also remarks by same Senators on June 14, 1954, p. 8154.
35. Emanuel Celler, "New York Democratic Delegation Denounce Under Secretary of the Army Slezak and Deputy Under Secretary Higgins for Their High-Handed Tactics," *Congressional Record*, May 13, 1954, pp. A3751–3752. Coudert did acknowledge the mayor's letter of May 15.
36. Emphasis added. James Donovan, letter to Robert F. Wagner, Jr., May 24, 1954, New York Municipal Archives.
37. "Removal of New York Quartermaster Purchasing Agency to Philadelphia," *Congressional Record*, May 19, 1954, p. A3697.
38. The office was merged with another agency at the Philadelphia Quartermaster Depot, and then, to throw salt in the wound, Congress held investigative hearings about corruption at the NYQMPA

that had apparently been fostered by New York's superior restaurant scene. See Senate Permanent Subcommittee on Investigations, Committee on Government Operations, "Textile Procurement in the Military Services [Part 1]," January–July 1955, HRG-1955-OPS-0013, p. 212.
39. The bill, H.R. 3881, which was originally proposed in 1963 but not adopted until 1964, was a national mass transportation bill to establish a program supporting expanded, comprehensive metropolitan-area mass transit systems. The bill's material dimensions were strongly beneficial for cities, providing grants and financing incentives to encourage local and state governments to develop larger systems that would serve more people and transcend local boundaries. See House Committee on Banking and Currency, "Urban Mass Transportation Act of 1963," February–March 1963, HRG-1963-BCU-0004. This is the kind of public goods infrastructure provision that is particularly valuable in densely populated areas.
40. Stuart Rothman, letter to Joseph E. O'Grady, May 22, 1964, Robert F. Wagner, Jr., Papers, New York Municipal Archives.
41. The bill created the forerunner to the Federal Transit Administration and laid the groundwork for the more comprehensive U.S. Department of Transportation, which was also created during the Johnson administration. Locally, New York established the forerunner to the Metropolitan Transit Authority (MTA) just after passage of the bill. Today, the MTA manages the largest and busiest mass transit network in the nation.
42. Bernard Ruggieri, memorandum to Mayor Robert F. Wagner, Jr., June 4, 1964, Robert F. Wagner Papers, Slide 361, New York Municipal Archives.
43. Robert F. Wagner, Jr., telegram to New York Democrats in House of Representatives, June 12, 1964, Robert F. Wagner Papers, New York Municipal Archives.
44. Robert F. Wagner, Jr., telegram to New York Democrats in House of Representatives, June 23, 1964, Robert F. Wagner Papers, New York Municipal Archives.
45. Roll call data from CSR, Voteview. Nine Republican "yeas" came from the New York metropolitan area, where Republican governor Nelson Rockefeller would soon use the bill's programs to the city's great advantage.
46. Since 1933, barriers to international trade had been gradually reduced through bilateral agreements with foreign governments negotiated by executive branch personnel. Relative to the previous trade regime, in which high tariffs were more common, this executive approach was generally seen as conducive to international trade because it provided a framework for negotiated, bilateral, simultaneous action between two countries, rather than relying on unilateral action (e.g., by Congress), which tended to produce protectionism and higher barriers to trade. See, e.g., Weingast, Goldstein, and Bailey 1997 for a summary of the history and political economy of these acts. Note that this set of agreements is legally distinct from, but politically parallel to, its more famous multilateral cousin the General Agreement on Tariffs and Trade, which was also controversial in the United States in the 1950s.
47. House Committee on Ways and Means, "Renewal of Trade Agreements Act," March 1958, HRG-1958-WAM-0008, p. 2185.
48. Ibid., p. 2529.
49. Ibid., p. 2213.
50. Ibid., p. 2135.
51. Ibid., p. 2146.
52. House Committee on Ways and Means, "Trade Agreements Extension: Part 2," January 31–February 4, 7, 1955, HRG-1955-WAM-0003, p. 1781.
53. Ibid., pp. 2467, 2790.
54. 1950 U.S. Census. Bureau of Labor statistics (see http://www.bls.gov/mlr/1993/02/art4full.pdf) show that this number fell by about 13 percent between 1950 and 1960, so when these debates were happening in 1958, this sector should have been among the loudest voices of protest.
55. 1940 U.S. Census.
56. Weingast, Goldstein, and Bailey 1997.
57. Emanuel Celler, letter to Robert F. Wagner, Jr., April 15, 1958, Robert F. Wagner Papers, New York Municipal Archives.
58. George Buchheister, letter to Robert F. Wagner, Jr., on behalf of Rep. John Rooney, April 3, 1958, Robert F. Wagner Papers, New York Municipal Archives.

59. Rep. Eugene Keogh, letter to Robert F. Wagner, Jr., April 3, 1958, Robert F. Wagner Papers, New York Municipal Archives; Keogh is described as a Tammany lynchpin by authors such as Hersh (2008).
60. Emphasis added. Albert Bosch, letter to Robert F. Wagner, April 10, 1958, Robert F. Wagner Papers, New York Municipal Archives.
61. The fourth logically possible combination of positions, opposition to both recommittal/amendment and passage, was not taken by any representatives.
62. Author's analysis of roll call data from 80th and 89th Congresses using AIP definitions of trade and tariffs votes and CSR definitions of New York delegation. Divided votes are those on which at least one in four New York members took the position that was a minority within the delegation (i.e., the delegation was split at least 75–25 percent in one direction or the other).
63. Schlozman 2015, Greenstone 1959, Plotke 1996.
64. Paul Fino, letters to Robert F. Wagner, Jr., January 14, February 1, May 13, and October 13, 1965, Robert F. Wagner Papers, New York Municipal Archives.
65. Robert F. Wagner, Jr., letter to Paul Fino, May 25, 1965, Robert F. Wagner Papers, Reel 40572, New York Municipal Archives.
66. Letters between Robert F. Wagner, Jr., and John Lindsay, 1965, Robert F. Wagner Papers, Reel 40572, New York Municipal Archives.
67. Emanuel Celler, letter to Robert F. Wagner, Jr., November 17, 1965, Robert F. Wagner Papers, Reel 40572, New York Municipal Archives.
68. Robert F. Wagner, Jr., letter to Emanuel Celler, November 17, 1965, Robert F. Wagner Papers, Reel 40572, New York Municipal Archives.
69. One can observe this graphically in Figure 4.4.
70. Wilson 1962; Erie 1988.
71. Letters between Richard Daley and Roman Pucinski, March 1965, Richard J. Daley Collection, Series 2, Subseries 1, Box 74, Folder 5, University of Illinois–Chicago.
72. Roman Pucinski, letter to Richard Daley, April 5, 1966, Richard J. Daley Collection, Series 2, Subseries 1, Box 74, Folder 5, University of Illinois–Chicago.
73. William L. Dawson, letter to Richard J. Daley, January 14, 1964, Richard J. Daley Collection, Politics 1964, Series 2 Subseries 1 Box 68 Folder 12, University of Illinois–Chicago.
74. Letters between Raymond Krier and Richard J. Daley, Richard J. Daley Collection, "Correspondence U," Series 1 Subseries 1 Box 60 Folder 1, University of Illinois–Chicago.
75. See Snowiss 1966; and Rakove 1975.
76. In 1943, Mayor Kelly established an even smaller advisory committee designed to "steer slate making discussions and other party activities," giving him a still firmer grip on party operations. George Tagge, "Kelly Assumes Firmer Grip on Party Machine," *Chicago Daily Tribune*, November 12, 1943, p. 14.
77. See Biles 1995 for an account of this meeting.
78. Snowiss 1966, p. 630.
79. Conversation between Richard J. Daley and Lyndon Johnson, November 16, 1964, tape no. 6369, Miller Center Archives, University of Virginia.
80. Descriptions of these norms and practices are found in several discussions of Chicago legislators in action, including Biles 1995; Wilson 1960; and Snowiss 1966.
81. Interview with Raymond Simon, June 30, 2010, oral history of Chicago, Richard J. Daley Collection, University of Illinois–Chicago. Rostenkowski's father was an alderman, and Daley was between the two in age.
82. Raymond F. Simon, "Legislation" memo to Richard J. Daley, March 20, 1963, Richard J. Daley Collection, Series 2, Subseries 1, Box 61, Folder 1, University of Illinois–Chicago.
83. Cohen 2000, ch. 1; Merriner 1999, chs. 1, 3.
84. Retiring before it was an age-based imperative, Libonati claimed that it was too difficult to maintain two households, and that his wife had acute bronchitis. Rumors of pressure to retire because of links to organized crime were not substantiated (only intimated) by the *Chicago Tribune*. Several party loyalists from his territory were shuffled or replaced during the 1964 election cycle. See *Chicago Tribune*, "Daley Doubts Mob "Retired Rep. Libonati," January 16, 1964, p. N13.

85. Voteview Party Loyalty Data, voteview.com.
86. Interview with Dan Rostenkowski, June 3, 2004, Richard J. Daley Oral History Collection, Special Collections and University Archives Department, University of Illinois at Chicago.
87. Rakove 1975.
88. Wilson 1962, ch. 4.
89. While such cohesion could theoretically be marshaled for any ends, in practice these blocs have supported the "doubly liberal" program of the urban political order.
90. And described in fuller detail in Chapter 6 and Appendix A.
91. Or a "metropolitan, non-central city," in U.S. Census terms.
92. As in many other models of legislative behavior, the underlying theory is that representatives will tend to vote alike to the extent that they share characteristics and/or interests in common. Most of the time, this will mean they are members of the same congressional party, their districts have similar characteristics (e.g., a large number of farmers or African Americans), or they share some common personal experience (like being veterans). Here, the characteristic that the districts share is membership in a common local polity and/or political organization, and I am testing this model at the group level now and later at the dyad level.
93. Later, using smaller units of analysis, I will control for more factors that might foster cohesion.
94. All members of both delegations (city and suburb) from each metro area are from the same region, and most are from the same state. High cohesion in a city delegation may be attributable to the fact that members' districts abut one another. The same is true of suburban districts, however. All members within each delegation have similar scores on an urbanicity measure described in Appendix A. Of course, city delegations and suburban delegations differ in their urbanicity. The point here is that within-delegation variation on this measure is minimal and similar across delegations.
95. For instance, the Herfindahl or Simpson indexes.
96. It is also now true in the suburbs, but this phenomenon is more recent and in most cases not as pronounced.
97. These demographic measures were constructed as follows. Using the CSR data, I identified key city and suburban delegations of interest for calculations. I then gathered historical congressional district data using Lublin 1997a. To weight each of these dimensions equally, I calculated standardized income and diversity measures by congress using all districts. Then for each city delegation I calculated a delegation mean on each dimension. Then for each district I calculated the absolute difference between the standardized measure and its delegation mean on that dimension. I then sum the differences across each dimension for the delegation, and divide by the number of districts in the delegation to adjust for delegations of different sizes. I then add the scores for the two dimensions together to create the additive two-dimensional index presented in Figure 4.2. As in subsequent analyses, a given delegation must include at least three representatives in Congress to be included. This is why some of the lines in Figure 4.3 do not begin until 1930.
98. Representatives have compelling reasons to be responsive to the median voter on many economic issues, so median family income seems an apt measure of a district's class identity. Median income is highly correlated with per capita income and average educational attainment for the cross-sections used here. Other income-related measures, such as those of income dispersion like the Gini coefficient or other measures of inequality, would help us measure within-district diversity but not cross-district heterogeneity.
99. This measure is imperfect, but changes in the way race and ethnicity have been measured over time make it difficult to find a better one. In any case, because of high levels of ethnoracial segregation, this measure is highly correlated with the available natural alternatives, such as ethnoracial fractionalization or percent black plus percent Hispanic after 1970. The data for each of these measures used in *this* diversity analysis are drawn from Lublin (1997a) and therefore cover the 86th to 105th Congresses. Elsewhere, where the analyses include earlier congresses, I include similar measures using my own data developed as described in Appendix B, as well as data from Adler (2012).

100. Indeed, Vorys himself could have tried this analysis, because Rice cohesion scores are one of the oldest and most intuitive measures in all of political science. Drawn from Rice 1928, higher cohesion scores indicate greater frequency of agreement between voters. Because Rice's measures were designed for large numbers of voters and are not appropriate for comparing among small blocs of different sizes, I use the adjustment recommended in Desposato 2005 to make robust cohesion comparisons across small groups of voters. Desposato calls these scores "expected cohesion." The interpretation of these scores is quite intuitive: if a bloc has a cohesion score of .93, there is a 93 percent chance that any two randomly chosen members of that bloc agree.
101. Republicans have generally been a little more cohesive than Democrats. The parties' average cohesion scores are .73 and .81, respectively.
102. Banfield and Wilson 1963, p. 104. Many other authors on the subject agree.
103. Mayhew 1986, pp. 58–59.
104. Banfield and Wilson 1963; Wilson 1962.
105. Mayhew 1986; Banfield and Wilson 1963. Wilson 1962 reports on many of these dynamics in Chicago, New York, and Los Angeles at midcentury. Mayhew 1986 provides summaries of party strength over time in these cities.
106. The AIP dataset assigns substantive codes to all roll calls from the 45th to 104th Congresses. I use the project's substantive codes to identify the roll calls in each category here. City votes are those in the AIP categories of Public Works and Infrastructure, Public Works Employment, Urban and Regional Development, and Housing. For details, see Katznelson and Lapinski 2007; or Lapinski 2013.
107. The size of a delegation is also more relevant here, as smaller delegations seem more likely to be unanimous, but not in the previous analysis, which made a mathematical adjustment for delegation size.
108. Keiser 1997.
109. Though the mayoralty was slower to change and slower still to be openly associated with the regular party organization. Mayhew 1986.
110. Wilson 1962; Mayhew 1986.
111. These traditional models of congressional behavior—sometimes competing, sometimes integrated—suggest that the preferences of electoral constituencies and congressional parties influence representatives' behavior in Congress. See Krehbiel 1998; Cox and McCubbins 1993; Aldrich 2011. This debate is largely over the relative importance of congressional parties (as opposed to constituency pressures) in shaping legislative outcomes.
112. The raw cohesion scores for Chicago and Philadelphia are very close to what we would expect if representatives voted along party lines. For instance, if we compare expected cohesion scores based solely on partisan identification (i.e., what the cohesion score would be if members of a city delegation voted according to their partisan affiliation) to the actual scores, there is no difference over 70 percent of the time. Observed cohesion is less than expected on 20 percent of votes (and almost always when expected cohesion is 1 in Chicago or Philadelphia) and higher than expected for about 10 percent of roll calls. New York, with its notably liberal Manhattan Republicans and greater role for the jurisdictional IHI, is exceptional on this point, being more cohesive than partisan affiliation would predict more often than the other cities. Suburban delegations, and those from the other cities, are more split. This observation goes only halfway toward explaining two things. First, geographic proximity is surely a dimension of affinity, so it seems somewhat natural that city delegations would be made up of members of the same party. But given the heterogeneous demographic building blocks and political conflict in cities, this shared partisanship should not be taken for granted and does not guarantee agreement on every issue even when there is shared partisanship.
113. And if we break city delegations down into city *partisan* delegations (e.g., New York Democrats and New York Republicans), they are unanimous almost all of the time. Congressional parties are much more rarely unanimous, despite the fact that coordinating legislative behavior is their main purpose. Nevertheless, party certainly matters quite a bit.

114. Though the observation that delegation heterogeneity is generally much higher in city delegations than elsewhere indicates that something else is going on.
115. The basic model to test the jurisdictional IHI hypothesis at the dyad level is

$$\Pr(\text{Party}) = \text{City} + \text{Region} + \text{Section} + \text{State} + \text{Race} + \text{Class} + \text{Urbanicity} + E \quad (4.3)$$

where each term is a measure of similarity between the members of the dyad on the variable indicated. The underlying logic is that precameral similarities are likely to be associated with membership in the same national party. On all variables, high values indicate similarity, so a positive coefficient would mean that similarity on that measure is associated with membership in the same congressional party. For instance, "City" equals 1 if members belong to the same city delegation and equals 0 otherwise; if (as city delegation theory predicts) membership in the same city is associated with agreement on roll calls, we would expect the coefficient on this term to be positive. This would provide support for the jurisdictional hypothesis.
116. The dyad-level analysis has two other characteristics that make its logic different from most substantive measures of legislative choice, which often follow in the tradition of Mayhew (1966). First, the analysis is agnostic with respect to "direction" of behavior on a particular vote. This means that it is a thin model of representation that could be thickened if we narrowed the focus of the analysis to a particular substance on which we could realistically assess the actual content of a vote. Second, the dyadic structure of the data means that the observations do not satisfy many of the independence assumptions typical in parametric regressions; for that reason, standard errors are estimated using the insights on dyadic data analysis from Rader, Pinto, and Erikson 2014.
117. See Appendix A for further details on CSR variables.
118. Depending on the precise character of the districts in question. This measure of difference on the CSR continuum also ranges from 0 to 6, the same as the variable from which it is constructed.
119. Each estimated using the spatial techniques described in Appendix B. Adler's estimates for the foreign-born population and African Americans in some districts suffer from the issues described in regard to percent black in Appendix B and Chapter 5. The "new immigrants" of this era were not as rigorously separated from the native-born population as blacks were from whites, mitigating the problem significantly.
120. As robustness checks, I also estimated models including alternative measures of ethnoracial composition (percent black for all Congresses and different measures of percent white for later Congresses for which more ethnoracial categories were available from census data), class composition (median household income, per capita income), and urbanicity (a softer three-category variable) in alternative specifications of the model. Overall, the key relationships for the predictors of interest were stable and in the expected direction and reached conventional levels of statistical significance.
121. Estimating significance for dyadic models is controversial. Most of the results in Table 4.3 are estimated using robust standard errors, clustered by congressional district dyads (to account for continuities among districts and/or members), following the approach to dyadic analysis proposed by Green, Kim, and Yoon 2001. The inferential results for key variables of interest presented in Table 4.3 and later in Table 4.5 (those shaded in gray and used to test IHI-related hypotheses) are robust to alternative specifications, including nonparametric randomization as described in Rader, Pinto, and Erikson (2014).
122. As in other empirical analyses in this study, TPO scores (which Mayhew assigns at the state level) here are adjusted to account for Mayhew's 1986 observation that such organizations tend to be most common and strongest in cities. I adjust the scores based on the accounts available in his text. For ease of interpretation, in this analysis I then recode Mayhew's TPO scores (adjusted to account for within-state variation as described in his text) into dichotomous "strong party" and "weak party" categories; the variable used in the interaction and accompanying term is an indicator scored 1 if both members of the dyad are from places with traditional party organizations and 0 otherwise. TPO scores of 4 and 5 are counted as strong, 3 and less counted as weak. Louisiana is the only state that receives the middling 3 in Mayhew's scores; alternative treatments of this state, such as exclusion, coding as either

strong or weak, or introducing a third category, do not affect the key substantive results of the analysis.
123. Running the same tests on only those Congresses from the urban interlude actually increases the magnitude of the coefficients of interest, indicating that the relationship between IHIs and partisan affinity was particularly strong during that time, though the coefficients are positive and significant in all eras between 1943 and 1997.
124. A dyad is considered complete if both members voted on that particular roll call. Missing votes were dropped from the pool from which dyads were constructed. Representatives taking a clear position in absentia with a paired vote as recorded in the *Congressional Record* are included in complete dyads.
125. The restricted range of Congresses (vs. the earlier analysis, which included the 78th through 105th Congresses) is due to computational intensity (the voting datasets are much larger, straining my capacity), and because the Long New Deal is the crux of the book's broader theoretical narrative, which is about liberalism and party change during this era.
126. The AIP Top-Tier category of "Domestic Affairs."
127. Contested votes are those on which neither side won more than 75 percent of the vote, except in the 73rd, 74th, 75th, and 86th Congresses, for which a contested vote is one on which the majority had less than 85 percent of the total votes cast (several of these Congresses were very one-sided in favor of the Democrats, so even party-line votes were likely to have 75 percent on one side).
128. Alternative trials and samples, which included different votes, yielded results that were substantively the same as those presented here.
129. TPO is here coded 1 if the dyad comes from a high-TPO city, and 0 if it comes from a low-TPO city, as in the party affinity analysis in the previous section.
130. Though note that because uncontested votes were dropped, the votes in the analysis received between 50 and 80 percent support from the winning side in any case, so there is not a huge amount of variation here. Model 3, which includes only pairs from the same city and party, includes city-level fixed effects as well to account for unobserved features of particular cities that may make agreement more likely. Each of these models was also run without each set of fixed effects and without any fixed effects at all as a robustness check in case the high number of indicators was biasing results (or, especially, prompting false positives). In all cases, the key substantive interpretations of the coefficients of interest (i.e., the sign of coefficient and precision of estimation) were not affected by the inclusion of these indicators. In models without the indicators, the magnitudes of the key relationships were actually larger, so the results presented here are relatively conservative when compared to models that exclude the indicators for Congress, vote, and city.
131. The geographic variables are all binary indicators of similarity, so marginal effects were estimated by holding these constant at zero, which was both mode and median in each case and therefore "typical." The demographic measures of similarity (on urbanicity, race, and class variables) were held at their median. This is the same procedure used to create the estimates in Table 4.4.
132. The magnitude, though not the direction or significance of this relationship, is sensitive to one particular model specification—the inclusion of the district-level voting similarities for Democrats and far left parties. When those measures are excluded, the relationship between party strength and agreement rises to about 20 percent. The 5 percent association presented here is therefore a conservative estimate of the relationship, which may lie in between.
133. Those results not presented here for clarity's sake; city vote categories are those identified by the AIP classification system, with each being a subset of the broader Domestic Affairs category used in the models in Table 4.5.
134. Key votes are votes of particular importance to cities as identified in *Congressional Quarterly* weekly reports. See Caraley 1976.
135. Mayhew 1986, p. 157.
136. Additionally, the "reform" cities of the West and Southwest usually had smaller city delegations because of the timing of their development in national history. This does not mean their politics could not possibly be horizontally integrated, but it makes it more difficult to appreciate such institutions empirically.

Chapter 5

1. Senate Committee on the Judiciary, Subcommittee on S. 1978, "Punishment for the Crime of Lynching," March 16, 1934. HRG-1934-SJS-0003, p. 237.
2. House Special Subcommittee on Fair Employment Standards Act, "Federal Fair Employment Practice Act," May 10, 1949. HRG-1949-EDL-0005, p. 8.
3. Royko 1971, p. 139.
4. Poole and Rosenthal 1997.
5. Mayhew 1966, ch. 3.
6. See, e.g., Katznelson and Mulroy 2012 on the change in Congress, and Black and Black 2003; and Valentino and Sears 2005 on the mass realignment of racially conservative southern whites.
7. The strongest versions of realignment theory identify critical elections as moments of rapid, generational change in political alliances. See Key 1955; Burnam 1970; Mayhew 2002. In such a model, we would expect to see a clear moment in the 1960s in which some significant bloc split from a partisan coalition over an issue that had been simmering for awhile. The South and the issue of race seem to fit the bill here, but the key trouble for identifying the "moment" of realignment has to do with the uncoupling of southern votes in presidential and congressional elections during this era: the region continued to elect Democrats in great numbers through the 1980s but mostly supported non-Democratic presidential candidates beginning in 1964; not only did the region become less "Solid" during this time, but the Deep South and border states became less cohesive. If we allow for a more fragmented or syncopated process of national political change, rather than one in which an outdated system fractures sharply and re-forms durably and coherently, a softer version of realignment theory can help us understand the more gradual shift that was initiated by the New Deal alignment and did not fully mature until seventy years later. This shift was the growth of the urban–rural divide as a powerful organizing principal in national politics and political ideology.
8. Carmines and Stimson 1989.
9. The tale of this successful wooing includes a lot of organizing and outreach to conservative Christians as well. See, e.g., Edsall and Edsall 1991; Black and Black 2003.
10. And most of those who remain come from majority-minority districts, reflecting the region's continuing extreme racial polarization.
11. Eric Schickler and Ira Katznelson, working separately with several coauthors, have been central in detailing the contours of this account. See, e.g., Schickler 2016; Feinstein and Schickler 2008; Schickler, Pearson, and Feinstein 2010; Katznelson, Geiger, and Kryder 1993; Katznelson and Farhang 2005; Katznelson and Mulroy 2012.
12. The conservative coalition between southerners and Republicans was no secret at the time and has been used to explain other policy outcomes as well (see Sitkoff 1978; Mollenkopf 1983; and Lieberman 2001), but placement of this constellation of congressional alliances at the heart of the *realignment* story is a relatively recent analytical connection.
13. Key 1955 identifies 1928 as a critical election, and Andersen 1979 also includes it in her key period of urban party transformation. In addition to (or perhaps as a corollary of) being Catholic, Smith was also a proponent of Prohibition repeal, long an issue that not only offended many abstemious southerners but divided rural and urban constituencies as well. See Buenker 1973 on Smith and the *kulturkampf* over immigration and Prohibition.
14. Sitkoff 1978; Katznelson 2012.
15. As detailed in earlier chapters and in Biles 2011; Mollenkopf 1983; Katznelson and Farhang 2005.
16. Katznelson and Mulroy 2012.
17. Feinstein and Schickler 2008.
18. Katznelson 2005; Lieberman 2001.
19. Katznelson 2012; Smith and King 2005; Woodward 1955. Beyond the often-noted black–white racial divide, specifically *Anglo-Saxon* white supremacy was a prominent theme in discussions of immigration and domestic policy, as well as a core theme in the age's scientific understanding of humanity and society. See, e.g., Ngai 1999; Menand 2001.
20. Dorsett 1977; Buenker 1973; Mayhew 1986.

21. See, e.g., Sitkoff 1978; and Sugrue 2008; this perspective is also adopted by Schickler, Pearson, and Feinstein 2010.
22. Quotes from Schickler, Pearson, and Feinstein 2010, p. 688.
23. Wilson 1962 describes the relationship between ideological activists and professionals within major big-city Democratic organizations. The memoirs of Sen. Paul Douglas, a famous Hyde Park liberal Democratic reformer with a fraught relationship with the Kelly–Nash and Daley organizations, depict this tension eloquently. See Douglas 1972.
24. Frymer 2007; Nelson 2001; Boyle 1998.
25. Andersen 1979.
26. Roediger 2005; Cohen 2008.
27. Sugrue 1996; Biles 1995.
28. See Figure 6.3 in Chapter 6.
29. Mayhew 1986; Keiser 1997.
30. Buenker 1973; Erie 1988.
31. Erie 1988; Snowiss 1966; Keiser 1997.
32. Sugrue 1996.
33. Pinderhughes 1987.
34. Trounstine 2008.
35. Indeed, this period provides some of the best evidence and examples upon which this theory is based. Sugrue 1996; Roediger 2005.
36. Mayhew 1974. This is a key element of Tip O'Neill's "all politics is local" aphorism.
37. Massey and Denton 1993 is a definitive chronicle of these demographic patterns across many American cities. See also Rae 2003 for a fluent institutional account.
38. And in local politics, this spatial patterning contributed to or reinforced racial rivalries, identities, and the marginalization of African Americans within local politics for decades to come; see, e.g., Massey and Denton 1993.
39. He was also Daley's vice chair in the Cook County Democratic Party (Biles 1995) and chaired the House Committee on Expenditures in Executive Departments.
40. Massey and Denton 1993.
41. Illinois's congressional district boundaries went unchanged from 1903 to 1949. Schickler, Pearson, and Feinstein 2010 use data from Adler 2012 to estimate congressional district–level demography. However, Adler's otherwise very valuable demographic measures are based on county-level data and therefore do not account for spatial variation across districts within the same county. Thus, in that data, the percent of the population identified as black for all ten Chicago districts is the Cook County average, about 11 percent. This is problematic, especially during the urban interlude, when population was highly concentrated within central cities—producing many congressional districts within the same county—but unevenly distributed along racial and class dimensions within those cities. Using census tract–level data from the National Historic Geographic Information Systems website, www.nhgis.org, we can get better estimates of the demography of these city districts. Details on this process are found in Appendix B.
42. See Appendix B for details on how these estimates were calculated and for maps of other large cities during this era.
43. Note that the displayed map's outline actually displays the boundaries of Chicago in 1980, which were substantially the same as in 1940, with the exception of O'Hare Airport on the Northwest Side. No one lives there, so it does not affect the inference.
44. The Fifth District also had a significant Hispanic population at this time, for which reliable census measures are not available for 1940.
45. Biles 1995, pp. 21–22; Royko 1971.
46. Biles 1995, p. 10.
47. Jones-Correa 2000.
48. Biles 1995; Keiser 1997; Royko 1971.
49. Sugrue 1996 chronicles this racial combat over Detroit's color line in the immediate postwar era, and Jones-Correa 2000 demonstrates the prevalence of contemporary legal mechanisms for preventing African American "encroachment" in white neighborhoods immediately proximate to black neighborhoods. These practices were generally institutionally reinforced by federal and private housing policies.

50. The most reliable opinion data from this era come from the recuperation of polls conducted in a massive and invaluable project led by Eric Schickler and Adam Berinsky.
51. Schickler 2012.
52. Author's tabulation of responses to the 1952 American National Elections Survey variable V520047. The 32 percent is split between 18 percent wanting no action; 4 percent preferring government "taking an interest" but declining to endorse the FEP laws (state or federal) suggested by the questioner; and 10 percent preferring that government "do other things only." White nonsouthern Democratic identifying (i.e., the bottom two categories on a 7-point scale of GOP identification) members of union households were 98 respondents in a sample of 1,899.
53. See Schickler 2009, p. 50. The closer analysis in the previous sentence refers to the author's calculation of the predicted probability of support for Federal FEP legislation based on the 1952 ANES sample. The predicted probabilities are based on a probit regression analysis of responses to the survey's question V520047 on explanans for civil rights liberalism among whites based on previous scholarship, especially Schicker 2016. The tested model includes only white respondents. The dependent variable is a recoded binary indicating support for a national FEP law, and covariates include urbanicity (positively associated with support for federal FEP), subjective working class identity (no significant association), union household membership (no association), education (no association), age (no association), party identification (Democratic identification positively associated), and region indicators. Predicted probabilities generated in STATA based on that regression analysis.
54. Biles 1995, chs. 3–5.
55. Wilson 1962. At least this was true in New York. New York is probably the place we would be most likely to find dedicated grassroots ideological anti-racism, because it was a place where such ideological racial liberals (ADA, Jews, Communists, and CIO organizers) were relatively strong.
56. Schickler, Pearson, and Feinstein 2010.
57. Dahl 1961.
58. Buenker 1973; but see Dahl 1961 for a notable counterexample of Republican incorporation of Italian Americans as a competitive response to Irish control of the local Democratic Party.
59. As opposed to the hearings for omnibus civil rights legislation in the late 1950s, when dozens of members participated.
60. This table tallies appearances by House members as witnesses in hearings for either chamber of Congress, though later excerpts may quote members of the committees as well. The basic pattern revealed in this table continued past these early hearings, though more non-urban Republicans were appearing in support of civil rights legislation by the late 1950s.
61. At this point, the Illinois Republican Party had probably incorporated black voters more fully than any other organization in the country, especially in Chicago, where Mayor William Thompson's coalition relied heavily on the black bloc. The first black MC in the post-Reconstruction era was a Republican from Chicago.
62. Senate Committee on the Judiciary, Subcommittee on S. 121, "To Prevent and Punish the Crime of Lynching," February 16, 1926, HRG-1926-SJS-0003, p. 4.
63. House Committee on Rules, "Ku-Klux Klan," October 11, 1921, HRG-1921-RUH-0001, pp. 3–6.
64. Burns et al. 2009.
65. House Committee on Rules, "Ku Klux Klan," HRG-1921-RUH-0001.
66. House Committee on Education and Labor, Special Subcommittee on Fair Employment Standards Act, "Federal Fair Employment Practice Act," May 10–12, 1949, HRG-1949-EDL-0005, p. 88.
67. House Committee on Labor, "To Prohibit Discrimination in Employment," June 1, 1944, HRG-1944-LAH-0002, p. 13.
68. Ibid., p. 25.
69. House Committee on the Judiciary, Subcommittee No. 2, "Civil Rights," July 14–24, 1955, HRG-1955-HJH-0007, p. 206.
70. House Committee on Education and Labor, Special Subcommittee on Labor, "Equal Employment Opportunity," Oct 23–24, 1961, HRG-1961-EDL-0029, p. 3.
71. Ibid., p. 19.

72. House Committee on the Judiciary, "Segregation and Antilynching," January 15, 1920, HRG-1920-HJH-0004, p. 17.
73. Though in hindsight, federal regulation of the consumption of intoxicating liquors was not a great success.
74. Senate Committee on the Judiciary, Subcommittee on S. 24, "Punishment for the Crime of Lynching," February 14, 1935, HRG-1935-SJS-0001, p. 15.
75. House Committee on Education and Labor, Special Subcommittee on Fair Employment Standards Act, "Federal Fair Employment Practice Act," May 10–12, 1949, HRG-1949-EDL-0005, p. 88.
76. House Committee on the Judiciary, "Civil Rights," HRG-1955-HJH-0007, p. 204.
77. Ibid., p. 206.
78. House Committee on Education and Labor, "Federal Fair Employment Practice Act," HRG-1949-EDL-0005, pp. 12–18.
79. Theoretically, this very practical political debate echoed an earlier question posed in Allport (1954)'s landmark study of the psychology of prejudice. Asking, "Ought there to be a law?"(ch. 29), Allport answers that while prejudice should be undermined at its root where possible (through education and contact with different individuals under certain favorable conditions), passing laws to forbid outward manifestations of prejudice will both reduce some of the material harms that derive from prejudice and represent a communal condemnation of such practices and the stereotypes that drive them to send an important cue to change hearts indirectly as well.
80. Not a wild hypothesis, given Chicago's own history.
81. House Committee on Education and Labor, "Federal Fair Employment Practice Act," HRG-1949-EDL-0005, p. 44.
82. Senate Committee on Education and Labor, "Fair Employment Practices Act," August 30, 1944, HRG-1944-EDS-0004, p. 122.
83. Ibid., p. 87.
84. See Chapter 2 for a discussion of Poole and Rosenthal's (1997) twentieth-century dimensions as they relate to liberalism and urbanicity. NOMINATE scores are invaluable, statistically derived tools for estimating incredibly large amounts of information about complex behaviors. Derived from roll call votes, they are imperfect measures of ideology per se (see Noel 2014), but they are definitely good measures of patterns in MCs' propensity to ally or form coalitions with some members about whose ideology we are pretty confident. Later analyses in this chapter dig more closely into issue-specific choices, getting closer to informed judgment about votes on race.
85. Two different teams have approached the substantive coding of roll call votes: the American Institutions Project (described in Katznelson and Lapinski 2007) and the Policy Agendas Project (Baumgartner and Jones 1993; also see http://www.policyagendas.org). Though the Policy Agendas Project only provides codes for the postwar era, the two coding schemes generally agree on which roll calls can be identified as having to do with civil rights for Congresses they both code. Because the AIP dataset covers the entire Long New Deal era, votes it identifies as about "African American Civil Rights" are used for the subsequent analyses; because they identify largely the same votes for the relevant category, data from the Policy Agendas Project yield very similar analytic results for the era covered.
86. "African Americans" were not a political monolith during this era (nor have they ever been), and several important groups often disagreed on the broad philosophy of whether and how the black community should integrate with the dominant white polity. On the issues that reached the national agenda, however, and in congressional testimony on these issues, it is reasonable to identify a fairly broad consensus among African Americans in national politics.
87. The Illinois First District was for nearly two decades the only constituency in the country with a black majority and a black representative in Congress. The first such representative was Oscar De Priest, a Republican; later, he was followed by Arthur Mitchell and William L. Dawson, both Democrats. In the 1940s, Adam Clayton Powell (D-NY) joined Dawson in Congress to create a black caucus of two for the next decade. These two men had very different profiles on racial issues and different styles of engagement with their copartisans but did not disagree on any of the roll call votes examined here; both also tended to agree with major advocacy groups on national racial policy, strengthening the argument that their

position on these votes reflected the generic "black" position, rather than an idiosyncratic district-level preference. See Wilson 1960.
88. Schickler, Pearson, and Feinstein 2010.
89. Gosnell 1937; Keiser 1997.
90. TPO scores are shifted here to range from 0 to 4, instead of Mayhew's 1 to 5. Mayhew's scores are assigned at the state level, but he includes information about localities within the states

to justify his judgments. In most states, his score is based on information about city organizations, so in states for which no reference is made to traditional organizations existing outside of cities, I infer that Mayhew's score should be applied mainly to the cities he describes, and I reduce the TPO score by half for districts representing portions of that state that do not include a city mentioned by Mayhew as having a strong organization. The magnitude of this reduction is somewhat arbitrary but is meant to reflect Mayhew's observation that traditional parties are strongest in the cities, but parties outside of cities in these states typically bear "family resemblance" to each other; Mayhew 1986, p. 23.
91. Buenker 1973 also notes that traditional organizations, especially those Irish-led parties that incorporated the new-stock immigrants, were predominantly in the Democratic fold (p. 11), so Republicans from TPO states may not have actually had ties to such organizations.
92. Following Katznelson and Mulroy 2012, this analysis employs a seventeen-state definition of the South that uses Jim Crow–style legal segregation rather than secession as the indicator of "southernness." The results are robust to other definitions of section.
93. For the few votes in this analysis before the 78th Congress, I simply apply Adler's value for the 78th backward.
94. Again, while still imperfect, these estimates are an important improvement on available data.
95. The corresponding figure for Republicans is perhaps 4 percent, and not statistically significant. In estimating marginal effects, the other variables in the model are held at appropriate values to represent an otherwise statistically typical MC.
96. The 95 percent confidence intervals (not pictured) do not overlap, indicating that we can be confident that this relationship does indeed exist among Democrats. Predicted values are generated using Stata's praccum procedure, following Long and Freese 2006, sec. 9.4.
97. Schickler, Pearson, and Feinstein 2010.
98. Poole and Rosenthal 1997.
99. On civil rights votes today, all of these cities are again cohesive and liberal, but this seems unsurprising given how much demographics have changed—after decades of white flight and in-migration by African Americans and new arrivals from abroad, none of these cities is majority white any longer. Today, "urban" is a euphemism for "not white" in some contexts. But in 1970, all four of these cities were still majority white, and (more to the point) over half of their districts were still *overwhelmingly* white.
100. As in the previous dyadic analysis, precision and statistical significance are measured first using standard errors clustered at the dyad-level following Green, Kim, and Yoon 2001 and then retested using the nonparametric technique from Rader, Pinto, and Erikson 2014. All models are estimated with constant and vote- and Congress-level fixed effects (not presented here for brevity's sake).
101. For this variable, unlike in the liberalism analysis earlier in this chapter, TPO is coded 1 for dyads from strong-party cities (TPO scores greater than 3 out of 4) and coded 0 for dyads from weak-party cities (TPO scores of 3 or less; most of these have scores of 0). Because all these dyads are constituted of representatives from the same city, this is an indicator not of similarity between the dyad's districts on that measure, but of the kind of *city* from which they came. Again, all other measures are of similarity.
102. Recall from Table 4.6 that same-city, same-party dyads from strong-party cities were about 5 percent more likely than otherwise similar dyads from weak-party cities to agree on *all* roll calls; we are ill-advised to compare coefficients across models, but this may be a weak indication that the cohesive power of the traditional organization was weaker on civil rights than on other kinds of issues.

103. Philip S. Brail, letter to Barratt O'Hara, May 7, 1962, Barratt O'Hara Collection, Box 4, File 46, "Civil Rights Legislation," University of Illinois at Chicago (UIC) Library Archives.
104. Mrs. Harold Boverman, letter to Barratt O'Hara, July 4, 1963, Barratt O'Hara Collection, Box 4, File 46, "Civil Rights Legislation," UIC Library Archives.
105. Edyth E. Barry, letter to Barratt O'Hara, July 1963, Barratt O'Hara Collection, Box 4, File 46, "Civil Rights Legislation," UIC Library Archives.
106. Mrs. Earl M. Hersid, letter to Barratt O'Hara, date obscured, Barratt O'Hara Collection, Box 4, File 46, "Civil Rights Legislation," UIC Library Archives.
107. Ann Rogers, letter to Barratt O'Hara, July 15, 1963, Barratt O'Hara Collection, Box 4, File 46, "Civil Rights Legislation," UIC Library Archives.
108. A. Paige, letter to Barratt O'Hara, July 22, 1963, Barratt O'Hara Collection, Box 4, File 46, "Civil Rights Legislation," UIC Library Archives.
109. Mr. and Mrs. E. Kersten, letter to Barratt O'Hara, September 2, 1966, Barratt O'Hara Collection, Box 4, File 49, "Civil Rights," UIC Library Archives; second quote in letter from G. Fuller, same folder.
110. Helen Hamaker, letter to Barratt O'Hara, July 3, 1963, Barratt O'Hara Collection, Box 4, File 46, "Civil Rights Legislation," UIC Library Archives.
111. Mrs. F. E. Schiele, letter to Barratt O'Hara, July 9, 1963, Barratt O'Hara Collection, Box 4, File 46, "Civil Rights Legislation," UIC Library Archives.
112. See Sugrue 1996 for a detailed telling of the rise of the politics of discriminatory homeowners' rights.
113. Mr. and Mrs. J. Ryan, letter to Barratt O'Hara, 1967, Barratt O'Hara Collection, Box 4, File 49, "Civil Rights," UIC Library Archives.
114. Mr. and Mrs. E. Kersten, letter to Barratt O'Hara, September 2, 1966. This constitutional argument is inaccurate.
115. Mr. and Mrs. J. Jasieniecki, letter to Barratt O'Hara, August 27, 1966, Barratt O'Hara Collection, Box 4, File 49, "Civil Rights," UIC Library Archives.
116. Elizabeth B. Yule, letter to Barratt O'Hara, August 7, 1966, Barratt O'Hara Collection, Box 4, File 49, "Civil Rights," UIC Library Archives. Emphasis in original.
117. Mrs. E. Davis, letter to Barratt O'Hara, October 2, 1966, Barratt O'Hara Collection, Box 4, File 49, "Civil Rights," UIC Library Archives.
118. Unclear author, letter to Barratt O'Hara, August 8, 1966, Barratt O'Hara Collection, Box 4, File 49, "Civil Rights," UIC Library Archives.
119. A. Kaprelian, letter to Barratt O'Hara, July 27, 1967, Barratt O'Hara Collection, Box 4, File 49, "Civil Rights," UIC Library Archives. However, upon receiving a lengthy reply from O'Hara rooted in constitutional theory, this letter writer admitted that he had never been "so honorably spanked" on an issue in his life.
120. R. Dolemba, letter to Barratt O'Hara, August 25, 1966, Barratt O'Hara Collection, Box 4, File 49, "Civil Rights," UIC Library Archives. Emphasis in original.
121. A. Kaprelian, letter to Barratt O'Hara, July 27, 1967.
122. Charles Beck, letter to Barratt O'Hara, July 20, 1966, Barratt O'Hara Collection, Box 4, File 49, "Civil Rights," UIC Library Archives.
123. Ivan Whitkov, letter to Barratt O'Hara, July 15, 1966, Barratt O'Hara Collection, Box 4, File 49, "Civil Rights," UIC Library Archives.
124. Mrs. Chase, letter to Barratt O'Hara, August 25, 1966, Barratt O'Hara Collection, Box 4, File 49, "Civil Rights," UIC Library Archives.
125. In Rooney's papers, the overwhelming sentiment from individual constituents is in favor of civil rights, though there are far fewer letters and many are apparently from African Americans, based on surname and address.
126. Katznelson and Mulroy 2012; Biles 2011.
127. Feinstein and Schickler 2008.
128. Schickler, Pearson, and Feinstein 2010.
129. Ibid.
130. Smith and King 2005.
131. Smith and King 2005 pose the institutional orders perspective, while Frymer 1999 proposes the counterpoint with which the institutionalist perspective here aligns.

132. Gilens 2000; Mendelberg 2001; Smith and King 2005.
133. Hajnal, Gerber, and Louch 2002.
134. Though such procedures are not themselves immune from the same majoritarian pressures or group-based biases common in more democratic institutions. See, e.g., Rosenberg 1991.
135. Myrdal 1944.
136. Tellingly, the other key period of advancement for racial equality—the Civil War and Reconstruction—was characterized by a similar kind of coalition: antiracist activists like Frederick Douglass and some radical white abolitionists in the tradition of John Brown allied with many Republicans who were themselves deeply racist, or who at least preferred white supremacy in America, in pursuit of a governance plan that could tolerate or benefit from black political inclusion in the polity. See Frymer 1999.
137. Wirth 1938, p. 12.
138. Plotke 1996; but see Lowi 1969 for a pessimistic view of this development.
139. Menand 2001, p. 392.
140. See ibid., ch. 14, for discussion of four distinct strands of pluralism. The first, conceptualized by Horace Kallen, rested upon the fundamental assumptions of scientific racism and envisioned a stratified ethnic hierarchy as an appropriate and enduring condition. The second, that of Alain LeRoy Locke, argued that pride in group difference was a key resource for morale and class advancement in the modern world, but that the *preservation* of distinct cultures was folly amid the rapid changes of modern society. John Dewey's vision, third in this list, probably most closely approximates the modal position of today's liberals, stating that each group and tradition had something important and distinctive to contribute to society, and that together the various strains of tradition were "transmuted into authentic Americanism." For the fourth conception of pluralism, Dewey's "renegade disciple" Randolph Bourne went a step further to push through Americanism to "transnationalism," a soft cosmopolitanism according to which America might lead by example. Rather than weave together diverse old traditions into a rich American tapestry, as Dewey would have it, Bourne presaged Saskia Sassen's 2005 concept of "cityness," with its possibility for productive, recombinatory transformation of myriad elements into something wholly new and forward-looking.
141. Shapiro 2006.
142. Alesina, Baqir, and Easterly 1999 find a correlation between diversity and reduced public goods provision at the local level; Alesina and Glaeser 2004 find a similar relationship between diversity and welfare state redistribution at a cross-national level; Putnam 2007 finds that diversity is negatively related to trust and social capital; and Habyarimana et al. 2009 explore the coordination and preference alignment problems associated with diversity and public goods. But see Boustan et al. 2013 and Hopkins 2011 for a more thorough reexamination of, and null finding for, Alesina, Baqir, and Easterly 1999.
143. See the discussion in Foner 1984; and modern classic Katznelson 1982 for an analysis of the political-institutional roots of class-undermining ethnic conflict in New York City.
144. Trounstine and Rugh 2011.

Chapter 6

1. In 2008, the average big-city voter was about 9 percent more likely than a nonmetropolitan voter to support Obama, even when we account for other important factors known to be related to vote choice (and place character), such as ideology, race, income, religiosity, education, age, and sex. See Table C.2 in Appendix C.
2. Under the Voting Rights Act, some racial and ethnic minorities are identified as communities of interest that are not strictly spatial, though the solution to their historic political marginalization has still been rooted in territory. The controversy over the odd shapes of some of these districts reflects the dominant view of spatial proximity as the most "natural" basis for representation in the United States.
3. It is very difficult to convincingly identify the contemporary causal relationship between residential location and geographic political polarization. Gainsborough 2001 speculates that the processes are mutually reinforcing, at least in the suburbs—that suburbs

attract conservatives, who then become more conservative among likeminded neighbors. Bishop 2008 makes a similar argument about the role of political homophily in residential sorting, though this claim is not uncontroversial. It is probably not only conservatives who are moving to suburbs, as these areas have become *less* Republican, in aggregate, since the 1970s. It is unclear whether analogous processes are at play in other kinds of places—for instance, whether mostly liberals move to cities or conservatives are the most likely residents to remain in rural areas. See Abrams and Fiorina 2012; and Chinni and Gimpel 2011.

4. The logic of federalism and the disciplining power of financial institutions do not determine the character of every local outcome, but they do constrain cities seeking to promote progressive politics locally—particularly on questions of statism and public goods provision. Peterson 1981; Hackworth 2007.
5. Dorsett 1977; Biles 2011; Mayhew 1986.
6. See Cramer Walsh (2012) for a contemporary discussion of this sentiment among voters, which the author brands "rural consciousness."
7. Mayhew 1966; Caraley 1976; Caraley 1992; and Wolman and Marckini 2005 examine different facets of city representation over some parts of the postwar period. Lieberman 2009 takes a first step toward quantifying city representation over the longer scope of U.S. history but does not account for within-state variation in place character. There are no such studies of the Senate, perhaps because it is so difficult to tell whether a senator is urban. I take a first step toward such description in Appendix C.
8. Mayhew 1966 and Caraley 1976 each identify the Democrats as the party of the cities over different periods from 1940 to 1970 in analyses of the partisan breakdown on issues identified as especially important to cities.
9. Mollenkopf 1983, p. 17.
10. Lieberman 2009.
11. There were few Republican defections from their party's opposition to such programs, however, as there were fewer urban Republicans in the 1930s than in the 1940s.
12. Wolman and Marckini 2005, p. 310.
13. Employing a more rigorous "big-city" standard of 0.11 percent yields an identical list of cities for the twentieth century, though the two lists do differ slightly for the nineteenth century.
14. That is, "City–Suburban–Rural." Details are provided in Appendix A. Fuller description of the Lieberman city list can be found in Lieberman 2009. To code districts, I used maps from various sources. For recent Congresses, very useful maps are available online through the Census Bureau's TIGER GIS collection. For recent pre-Internet Congresses, the *Congressional District Atlas of the United States* (Bureau of the Census, series begins 1960) is useful; for older Congresses, Martis 1982 is an invaluable resource. Each congressional district is given several qualitative scores for this study, as detailed previously and in the CSR scoring outlined in Appendix A. Districts completely within a city are given a qualitative code of "C" and a numeric score of 7 on a CSR scale ranging from 1 to 7. A mixed district split between central city and suburban areas would get a code of "C/S" or "S/C" and a score of 5 or 6 depending on the apparent balance between place characters. As cities join or drop out of the Lieberman city set as a result of population changes, their districts' CSR scores change accordingly. I assume that cities that used to be large enough for inclusion retain some urban character, so such districts are not immediately recoded as rural when their central cities are downsized. For instance, Albany, New York, was once large enough to be a central city, but it is not any longer, so its district's code has changed from C/S to S/R/C over the years. Conversely, Fresno, California, joined the dataset after the 1990 Census, and the district's geographic extent shrank to reflect major population growth in the region, so its code has changed from R to C/S/R (actually, two C/S/R districts and two S/R districts make up the Fresno metropolitan area). Districts in states that have never had cities large enough to join the dataset, such as South Dakota or Wyoming, all receive codes of R, even though they do include some small metropolitan areas.
15. There is a high degree of overlap in the sets of districts identified as city districts under subtly different approaches. For instance, using demographics, Mayhew 1966 identified 140 city districts for his time period of study, 1947–1962. Using maps and the 0.1 percent population threshold, CSR data classify an average of 143 districts as city districts for Congresses during that time. The different selection rules employed in this classification mean that Mayhew has

more renter-heavy districts from small cities, while the CSR has more districts with many homeowners in large cities. Wolman and Marckini's 2005 technique codes as "mixed" districts those that include small central cities, while these would most often be coded as rural in the CSR data, because those cities do not reach the 0.1 percent threshold. Some of these places are captured in subsequent analyses with the CSR data that attend to cities formerly, but no longer, large enough to meet the threshold. The differences are at the margins, so broader claims about the size of the "city" bloc in Congress are robust to different selection methods. The chief advantages of the CSR data are its consistency over time where more precise quantitative demographic data are unavailable or inconsistent, as well as its higher theoretical threshold for what counts as a "city."

16. Appendix A includes a list of which cities are included for which censuses.
17. Though a closer look later in this chapter reveals that these city representatives are more diverse in their geographical origins than they used to be, and that the redistricting after the 2010 Census took a bite out of the city bloc.
18. Judgment about the number of suburban districts is the biggest difference between CSR data and Wolman and Marckini's 2005 study; they put the figure at over 50 percent. See Appendix A for a discussion.
19. Mayhew 1966, p. 78.
20. For figures and trends related to unequal district representation before the one-person, one-vote court cases of the early 1960s, see Snyder and Ansolabehere 2008.
21. Mayhew 1986; Bridges 1997.
22. GSF is computationally equivalent to group voting fractionalization (GVF), a weighted adaptation of Gallagher disproportionality, clarified to refer to seats instead of votes. GVF is a method of comparing the voting behavior of different groups by measuring the extent to which group identity is associated with vote choice. It is a quick, intuitive way of studying cleavages in an electorate. GVF is developed in Huber 2010 as an approach to studying ethnic voting. The formula for GVF is

$$GVF = \frac{1}{\sqrt{\frac{G-1}{2G}}} \sum_{g=1}^{G} \left(GVF_{g} * s_g \right) \quad \text{where} \quad GVF_g = \sqrt{\frac{1}{2} \sum_{p=1}^{P} \left(V_{g,p} - V_p \right)^2}$$

where V is the share of votes from each of G groups g for each of P parties/candidates p, weighted by s, the proportion of each group g in the electorate. Essentially, it is the sum of divergence of each group from the overall electorate, weighted by the group's proportion in the electorate. As groups become more different in their voting choices, the measure rises. The minimum possible value is 0 and the maximum possible is 1. The original Gallagher index is from Gallagher 1991. Here the groups are based on place character (urban, suburban, rural), instead of ethnicity.
23. In this plot, I employ the U.S. Census "region" definition, which splits the nation into four regions. Using the "division" definition, which divides the country into ten groups of states that are closer to pieces of the "red–blue" map (and which are themselves nested in the regions), yields very similar aggregate results and also reveals that the increasing distinctiveness of the Northeast is attributable mostly to changes in New England. The simpler regional results are shown here for clarity's sake.
24. Gelfand 1975; Biles 2011.
25. Cox and McCubbins 2004. This is the cartel model of legislative organization.
26. Wolman and Marckini 2005; Mayhew 1966; Mollenkopf 1983.
27. Lieberman 2001; Katznelson 2012.
28. Another way in which the trajectory of city power has not tracked the overall plateaued representation of cities is a result of the continued partisan sorting by place character. In addition to the leadership, another important player in the cartel model is the majority-party median voter, to whom the leadership is responsive. Over time, as the share of Democrats representing cities has grown (see Figure 6.4), the median *Democrat* has become more likely to be a city representative, though the median *voter* surely has not.

29. Claude Pepper's Florida district included Miami.
30. Before that, we need to go back to before the Civil War to find comparably weak representation of cities in the leadership.
31. The analyses in this chapter build on Wolman and Marckini 2005, filling in gaps, including more votes, extending the series forward and back, and refining the set of majority-party leaders based on Cox and McCubbins 2004.
32. This list of prestige committees is from Wolman and Marckini 2005, who adapted it from Smith and Deering 1990.
33. This committee was formerly known as Banking, Finance, and Urban Affairs, but the "urban affairs" label was dropped in 1995 when Republicans assumed the majority, a title change that in itself reflects the parties' attitudes toward city issues. The correspondent committee in the Senate remains Banking, Housing, and Urban Affairs.
34. Caraley 1976.
35. Wolman and Marckini 2005.
36. There was a brief exceptional period during the postwar Congresses when Republicans briefly held a number of city districts.
37. Disaggregating Southern Democrats by place character reveals a slight gap (in the expected direction) between urban and non-urban representatives but makes the figure less legible. Population-based maldistricting was particularly bad in the South, so even many "city" districts in this region contained very large rural areas, as noted by Snyder and Ansolabehere 2008 and Martis et al. (1982), and all southern districts were deeply undemocratic in any case. The gap within the Southern Democrats is smaller than that within the GOP and nonsouthern Democrats and disappears after the 1980s, when most conservative Southern Democrats faded away.
38. This is what Mayhew 1966 finds in his analysis of housing votes among postwar city Republicans, who supported housing legislation despite their party's opposition.
39. Though they are still more moderate on average. The recent leftward drift of the Southern Democrats' average is most likely the result of the creation of relatively safe, liberal majority-minority districts and the conversion of many southern districts to the GOP during this era, lowering the overall average for the remaining Democrats. Some of the intersectional swap among pre–New Deal Democrats may be due to over-time smoothing in the calculation of these measures; that is, we should be modest in our judgments about the precise timing of these shifts.
40. Before Smith, Grover Cleveland, the former mayor of Buffalo, had been the last Democratic nominee with significant political ties to or background in a major city. See Lieberman 2009.
41. For instance, a small bloc situated in the middle of the distribution may at times be much more influential than an enormous but relatively extreme bloc. Wolman and Marckini 2005 engage in an analysis of roll call voting by urban representatives similar to the one that follows, though their study is limited to voting on a small set of votes in a small number of Congresses. The present analysis includes all roll calls from all post–Civil War Congresses through 2013, refines the measures of leverage, and looks more closely at votes on which city representatives were distinctive.
42. Though American legislative parties have often notably *not* been cohesive by comparative standards.
43. These roll call analyses combine CSR place-character data with roll call data from Voteview.
44. Wolman and Marckini 2005, p. 304.
45. Of course, "leverage" should be understood with an important caveat. The broader argument of this book is that there is a partisan-ideological continuum that has been developing for eighty years, with city representatives at its liberal pole. With city representatives more likely to be doing the proposing from a position of chamber leadership, and to theoretically have relatively extreme (as opposed to pivotal) preferences on these issues, it is not clear how perfectly the concept of "leverage" applies to these votes: some more centrist group likely has more leverage. But following Wolman and Marckini 2005, I present these trends forward and backward to more fully describe how the position of the city bloc in the legislature has evolved.
46. Gainsborough 2001; Nall 2010.
47. Black and Black 2003.

48. Mayhew 1966.
49. Carmines and Stimson 1989; Katznelson, Geiger, and Kryder 1993; Katznelson and Farhang 2005; Katznelson and Mulroy 2012; and Schickler, Pearson, and Feinstein 2010.
50. Katznelson and Mulroy 2012.
51. Mollenkopf 1983; Sitkoff 1978.
52. Though Americans' understanding of who counted as fully "white" probably played some role in this cleavage as well.
53. Ethington and Levitus 2009.

Chapter 7

1. *Congressional Record*, April 24, 1952, p. 4382. Quoted in Mayhew 1966.
2. Sugrue 1996; Keiser 1997, pp. 44–64; Jones-Correa 2000; Biles 1995, ch. 4.
3. Sugrue 1996; Keiser 1997; Pinderhughes 1987; Erie 1988; Massey and Denton 1993.
4. U.S. Census figures from National Historic Geographical Information System.
5. See the 2012 presidential election figures from NBC News results and exit polling, http://elections.nbcnews.com/ns/politics/2012/all/president/. Obama also won Cook County's suburbs comfortably. Ward results from Chicago Board of Election Commissioners, http://www.chicagoelections.com/.
6. In Mississippi, only Bennie Thompson's district consistently elects a Democrat, a product of its Voting Rights Act–mandated black-majority electorate. Every Chicago district, despite continued high levels of segregation, routinely elects a Democrat.
7. Population density is only one element of urbanicity—though it is probably the most important one in the political theory of urbanicity. County-level measures in many cases cannot dig into the difference between city and suburban voters. The second part of this analysis will address that concern.
8. Such as they were; Clinton won the popular vote comfortably but not the Electoral College; Kennedy won the popular vote narrowly but the Electoral College comfortably; Roosevelt and Obama won both comfortably on the heels of major economic collapses overseen by their opponent's party.
9. Even when we exclude southern counties from the analysis (not pictured), the overall relationships remain basically the same: the Roosevelt linear relationship becomes more negative, though his strength in cities bends the local curve up; Kennedy's changes very little.
10. We know that densely populated, big-city counties also tend to have more of the other important dimensions of urbanicity, like ethnoracial heterogeneity, that are potential confounders in today's politics. Even when we account for region and ethnoracial and class demography, there is a strong independent association between population density and support for Obama and Clinton. The expected difference in support between a big-city county (where the average population density is over 3,000 persons per square mile) and a rural county (where it is less than 10 persons per square mile) is between 40 and 60 percent, about as extreme a contrast in political support one could find. These findings are drawn from my ordinary least squares regression analysis of electoral and census data.
11. States were chosen based on the presence of variation in county density, sufficient population and counties, and to provide geographical variation.
12. Except in Virginia, where cities of all sizes are politically independent of counties.
13. As in Figure 7.1, patterns were substantially the same, though a bit more moderate, in 2008 and 2012.
14. The relationship also appears to be fractal: analysis of 2016 results indicate that the pattern between density and vote choice is present not only nationally, at the state level, and across counties, but also *within* counties, albeit again at different levels. See Jonathan Rodden, "Red America Is an Illusion," *Washington Post*, February 14, 2017. The nationalization of voting—that is, the decline of regional or sectional effects on opinion, partisanship, and election decisions by individuals—appears to be a recent phenomenon. For current account of this trend, see Hopkins (2017).
15. Poole and Rosenthal 1997; McCarty, Poole, and Rosenthal 2006.

16. Mississippi is more consistently Republican in presidential politics than in congressional seats, but the transition among other southern states as well has made the South into a Republican stronghold.
17. Shapiro and Bafumi 2009. See also Fiorina 2004 for a broad discussion of polarization.
18. The city's population is actually at its all-time peak, with more than 8 million residents.
19. The more "elastic" cities of the South and West make up the bulk of central city growth in recent decades, but these places typically lack traditions of strong integrative organizations. See Rusk 2003.
20. During the Long New Deal, the pivotal political force was typically the Southern Democratic bloc, and its policy preferences often prevailed in important legislation. See Katznelson and Mulroy 2012.
21. Barber 2013.
22. As well as rural areas with large minority populations. This is much the coalition Mayor Daley described in his testimony in Chapter 1.
23. Gainsborough 2001.
24. Oliver 2010 finds that smaller, less diverse communities foster less participation and more biased outcomes; Dreier, Mollenkopf, and Swanstrom 2004 identify empirical trends, including heightened inequality, related to metropolitan-area fragmentation.
25. Such central thinkers as Charles Merriam were outspoken proponents of the metropolitan vision as far back as the 1930s; this agenda has never gone away but has been recently reinvigorated by scholars and practitioners such as Orfield 1997 and Dreier, Mollenkopf, and Swanstrom 2004.
26. Though city–county mergers were also used to build New York and Philadelphia, and close coordination by the Chicago and Cook County governments through the Democratic Party apparatus has helped foster political cohesion there as well.
27. Rusk 2003. There are also many approaches to metropolitan governance being advanced in other countries, so surmounting our national parochialism may yield fruitful insights as well.
28. Perlstein (2009).
29. Many Americans still live in these central cities, but relatively more increasingly live outside of these lines than was the case in the urban interlude.
30. A side effect because people's decisions to move, even if they are choosing to move out of the central city, may not be about municipal fragmentation per se. Because suburbs usually have density-prohibiting zoning laws, the shift to these areas has accelerated sprawl, because land "fills up" faster, in a legal sense, when it cannot be developed as intensely.
31. Dreier, Mollenkopf, and Swanstrom 2004, pp. 111–125; Rae 2003; Frank 2007.
32. Ehrenhalt 2013.
33. Cramer 2016.
34. Ronald Wilson Reagan, Farewell Address, January 11, 1989, Miller Center Archives, University of Virginia, https://millercenter.org/the-presidency/presidential-speeches/january-11-1989-farewell-address.
35. Sombart 1976. See Foner 1984 for a critical review of many answers to Sombart's prompt.
36. Changes to the rules of representation of the 1960s notwithstanding, the Senate (and to a proportional extent the Electoral College) continues to ignore the political principle of population-based equality in representation, because it is exempted from it by the Constitution.
37. Lieberman 2009, p. 27. See also Conn 2014 for an engaging, comprehensive treatment of anti-urbanism in American intellectual life.
38. Even if they did not move it as far as Sombart might have expected or hoped. Lieberman 2009, p. 19; Ethington and Levitus 2009.
39. Foner 1984, pp. 66–70.
40. See, e.g., Katznelson 1982 for a compelling example and discussion of this argument. A permutation of this argument in modern political economy refers to the difficulty of coordinating across ethnic-group lines for the maintenance of collective action and the provision of public goods, as in Alesina, Baqir, and Easterly 1999; and Habyarimana et al. 2009.
41. Katznelson 2009.
42. Alesina, Baqir, and Easterly 1999; Alesina and Glaeser 2004; Putnam 2007; Oliver 2010.

43. See Reagan, "Farewell Address," though the path from Winthrop to Reagan passed through some nineteenth- and twentieth-century interpretive shifts of emphasis, and twentieth-century readers seem to have found vastly more importance in Winthrop's text than any seventeenth-century Puritans did. In fact, there is no evidence that anyone ever heard or read the sermon in Winthrop's day. Reagan added the "shine" to the city. See Peterson Forthcoming.
44. Matthew 5:14–16 (KJV): "Ye are the light of the world. A city that is set on an hill cannot be hid. Neither do men light a candle, and put it under a bushel, but on a candlestick; and it giveth light unto all that are in the house. Let your light so shine before men, that they may see your good works, and glorify your Father which is in heaven."
45. John Winthrop, *A Model of Christian Charity* (1630), Collections of the Massachusetts Historical Society (Boston: 1838, 3rd Series, 7:31–48), Hanover Historical Texts Project, http://history.hanover.edu/texts/winthmod.html. Archaic spellings modernized by author.
46. Peterson Forthcoming.

Appendix A

1. Caraley 1976 apparently adopts the same approach for Congresses in 1968 and 1973.
2. In a 435-member Congress, under conditions of equal representation, each district should have about 0.22 percent of the national population (though in fact there is some variation between districts, even after the enshrinement of one-person, one-vote as a principle for representation). Thus, a more rigorous standard for a population threshold would be 0.11. In practice, this distinction does not matter much: the cities that were included by the 0.10 threshold are almost completely the same as those included using the 0.11 threshold.
3. In the empirical Chapters 3 through 5, CSRord is included as an explanatory variable in regression analyses. For graphical clarity, figures with a tripartite urban/suburban/rural distinction ("CSR3") are developed using a recoding of CSRord in which scores greater than 5 are coded "city," scores lower than 3 "rural," and scores in between "suburban."
4. Though before merging with New York, Brooklyn itself was a large enough city to be included in the dataset.
5. U.S. Census Bureau, Census Geographic Definitions, https://www.census.gov/programs-surveys/metro-micro.html.
6. An additional 27 million people live in the 152 additional "micropolitan" areas; it is unclear how these would be treated by W-M.
7. Crenson 1971.

Appendix B

1. Mayhew 1966; Aldrich 2011.
2. Mayhew 1966; Mayhew 1974; Krehbiel 1998.
3. Mayhew 1966.
4. On their own, Wolman and Marckini 2005 generated district-level measures of place character using census data going back to 1963.
5. Mayhew 1966, p. 60.
6. Adler 2012.
7. For example, Schickler, Pearson, and Feinstein 2010 seem to use Adler's (2012) data, including the race variable, without adjusting for this, though they do not make any strong claims based on this analysis. Schickler 2016 corrects this issue with an updated analysis using data from the present study.
8. Except in states with only one district, where it would work fine.
9. Here I say "city areas" because the metropolitan area was not yet in use as a unit of aggregation. The U.S. Census divided certain counties that included or were included in these cities into tracts for these early decennial periods. Not until 1970 was the preponderance of the

nation's territory assigned census tracts. See the NHGIS chart at https://assets.nhgis.org/Tract-availability.pdf for availability of tract-level data.
10. The "split" cities were New York City, Buffalo, Baltimore, Chicago, Cleveland, Cincinnati, Philadelphia, Pittsburgh, Milwaukee, Detroit, St. Louis, Los Angeles, and San Francisco. A closer look includes Boston in this list, bringing the total to seventy-three districts; its two predominantly Bostonian congressional districts also include other counties. These were the cities with at least two congressional districts within their county borders.
11. See the NHGIS website at https://www.nhgis.org/.
12. Information from the closest decennial census is used for the measures and analyses in the book. These decennial-based estimates are still far preferable to the existing data.
13. Lewis et al. 2013.
14. This estimation process is still in progress for Congresses before the Long New Deal; estimates based on the closest approximation in time and space are used for districts that have not been completed at this writing.

BIBLIOGRAPHY

Abramowitz, Alan, and Kyle L. Saunders. 2005. "Why Can't We All Just Get Along?: The Reality of a Polarized America." *Forum: A Journal of Applied Research in Contemporary Politics* 3 (2).

Abrams, Samuel J., and Morris P. Fiorina. 2012. "The Big Sort that Wasn't: A Skeptical Reexamination." *PS: Political Science and Politics* 45 (2): 203–210.

Adler, E. Scott. 2012. *Congressional District Data File [78th–105th Congresses]*. Accessed at https://sites.google.com/a/colorado.edu/adler-scott/data/congressional-district-data.

Aldrich, John H. 1995. *Why Parties?: The Origin and Transformation of Political Parties in America*. Chicago: University of Chicago Press.

Aldrich, John H. 2011. *Why Parties?: A Second Look*. Chicago: University of Chicago Press.

Alesina, Alberto, Reza Baqir, and William Easterly. 1999. "Public Goods and Ethnic Divisions." *Quarterly Journal of Economics* 114 (4): 1234–1284.

Alesina, Alberto, Paola Giuliano, A. Bisin, and J. Benhabib. 2011. "Preferences for Redistribution." In *Handbook of Social Economics*, ed. Jess Benhabib, Alberto Bisin, and Matthew O. Jackson. North Holland: Elsevier, 93–132.

Alesina, Alberto, and Edward Glaeser. 2004. *Fighting Poverty in the U.S. and Europe: A World of Difference*. New York: Oxford University Press.

Allport, G. 1954. *The Nature of Prejudice*. Reading, MA: Addison-Wesley.

Andersen, Kristi. 1979. *The Creation of a Democratic Majority, 1928–1936*. Chicago: University of Chicago Press.

Ansell, Christopher, and Arthur Burris. 1997. "Bosses of the City Unite! Labor Politics and Political Machine Consolidation, 1870–1910." *Studies in American Political Development* 11: 1–43.

Ansolabehere, Stephen, and Philip Edward Jones. 2011. "Dyadic Representation." In *Oxford Handbook of the American Congress*, ed. George C. Edwards, Frances Lee, and Eric Schickler. New York: Oxford, 293–314.

Baldassare, Mark. 1978. "Human Spatial Behavior." *Annual Review of Sociology* 4: 29–56.

Banfield, Edward C., and James Q. Wilson. 1963. *City Politics*. New York: Vintage.

Barber, Benjamin. 2013. *If Mayors Ruled the World: Dysfunctional Nations, Rising Cities*. New Haven, CT: Yale University Press.

Bass Warner, Sam. 1978. *Streetcar Suburbs: The Process of Growth in Boston, 1870–1900*. Cambridge, MA: Harvard University Press.

Bateman, Fred, and Jason Taylor. 2007. "Does the Distribution of New Deal Spending Reflect an Optimal Provision of Public Goods?" *Economics Bulletin* 8 (3): 1–5.

Baumgartner, Frank R., and Bryan D. Jones. 1993. *Agendas and Instability in American Politics*. Chicago: University of Chicago Press.

Beito, David. 1989. *Taxpayers in Revolt: Tax Resistance During the Great Depression*. Chapel Hill: University of North Carolina.

Berry, Christopher. 2009. *Imperfect Union: Representation and Taxation in Multilevel Governments*. New York: Cambridge University Press.

Biles, Roger. 1995. *Richard J. Daley: Politics, Race, and the Governing of Chicago*. DeKalb: Northern Illinois University Press.

Biles, Roger. 2011. *The Fate of the Cities: Urban America and the Federal Government, 1945–2000*. Lawrence: University Press of Kansas.

Bishop, Bill. 2008. *The Big Sort*. New York: Mariner.

Black, Earl, and Merle Black. 2003. *The Rise of Southern Republicans*. Cambridge, MA: Harvard Belknap Press.

Blalock, H. 1967. *Toward a Theory of Minority-Group Relations*. New York: Wiley.

Bonilla-Silva, Eduardo. 2003. *Racism Without Racists: Color-Blind Racism and the Persistence of Racial Inequality in the United States*. Lanham, MD: Rowman & Littlefield Publishers.

Boustan, Leah, Fernando Ferreira, Hernan Winkler, and Eric M. Zolt. 2013. "The Effect of Rising Income Inequality on Taxation and Public Expenditures: Evidence from U.S. Municipalities and School Districts, 1970–2000." *Review of Economics and Statistics* 95 (4): 1291–1302.

Boyle, Kevin. 1998. *The UAW and the Heyday of American Liberalism, 1945–1968*. Ithaca, NY: Cornell University Press.

Brenner, Neil. 2009. "Is There a Politics of 'Urban' Development?: Reflections on the U.S. Case." In *The City in American Political Development*, ed. Richardson Dilworth. New York: Routledge, 121–140.

Bridges, Amy. 1984. *A City in the Republic: Antebellum New York and the Origins of Machine Politics*. New York: Cambridge University Press.

Bridges, Amy. 1997. *Morning Glories: Municipal Reform in the Southwest*. Princeton, NJ: Princeton University Press.

Browning, R. P., D. R. Marshall, and David H. Tabb. 2003. *Racial Politics in American Cities*. New York: Longman Press.

Buenker, John D. 1973. *Urban Liberalism and Progressive Reform*. New York: Norton.

Burnam, Walter D. 1970. *Critical Elections and the Mainsprings of American Politics*. New York: Norton.

Burns, Nancy, Laura Evans, Gerald Gamm, and Corrine McConnaughy. 2009. "Urban Politics in the State Arena." *Studies in American Political Development* 23: 1–22.

Burns, Nancy, Gerald Gamm, and Scott Allard. 1998. "Representing Urban Interests: The Local Politics of State Legislatures." *Studies in American Political Development* 12: 267–302.

Burrows, Edwin, and Mike Wallace. 1998. *Gotham: A History of New York City to 1898*. New York: Oxford University Press.

Cain, Louis P. 1983. "To Annex or Not?: A Tale of Two Towns: Evanston and Hyde Park." *Explorations in Economic History* 20: 58–72.

Cannato, Vincent. 2002. *The Ungovernable City: John Lindsay and His Struggle to Save New York*. New York: Basic Books.

Caraley, Demetrios. 1976. "Congressional Politics and Urban Aid." *Political Science Quarterly* 91 (1): 19–45.

Caraley, Demetrios. 1992. "Washington Abandons the Cities." *Political Science Quarterly* 107 (1): 20.

Carmines, Edward G., Michael J. Ensley, and Michael W. Wagner. 2017. "Ideological Heterogeneity and the Rise of Donald Drumpf." *Forum* 14 (4): 385–397.

Carmines, Edward G., and James A. Stimson. 1989. *Issue Evolution: Race and the Transformation of American Politics*. Princeton, NJ: Princeton University Press.

Carmines, Edward G., Michael J. Ensley and Michael W. Wagner. 2017. "Ideological Heterogeneity and the Rise of Donald Drumpf." *The Forum* 14 (4): 385397.

Carter, Shawn and Alicia Keys. 2009. "Empire State of Mind."

Chen, Anthony. 2009. *The Fifth Freedom: Jobs, Politics, and Civil Rights in the United States, 1941–1972*. Princeton, NJ: Princeton University Press.

Chen, Jowei, and Jonathan Rodden. 2013. "Unintentional Gerrymandering: Political Geography and Electoral Bias in Legislatures." *Quarterly Journal of Political Science* 8: 239–269.

Chinni, Dante, and James Gimpel. 2011. *Our Patchwork Nation: The Surprising Truth About the "Real" America*. New York: Gotham.

Clubb, Jerome M., William H. Flanigan, and Nancy H. Zingale. 2006. *Electoral Data for Counties in the United States Presidential and Congressional Races, 1840–1972*. Ann Arbor, MI: Inter-University Consortium for Political and Social Research.

Cohen, Lisabeth. 2008. *Making a New Deal: Industrial Workers in Chicago, 1919–1939*. Cambridge: Cambridge University Press.

Cohen, Richard. 2000. *Rostenkowski: The Pursuit of Power and the End of the Old Politics*. Chicago, Illinois: Ivan R. Dee.

Conn, Steven. 2014. *Americans Against the City: Anti-Urbanism in the Twentieth Century*. New York: Oxford University Press.

Connolly, James J. 2010. *An Elusive Unity: Urban Democracy and Machine Politics in Industrializing America*. Ithaca, NY: Cornell University Press.

Cox, Gary W., and Mathew D. McCubbins. 1993. *Legislative Leviathan: Party Government in the House*. Berkeley: University of California Press.

Cox, Gary, and Mathew D. McCubbins. 2004. *Setting the Agenda: Responsible Party Government in the U.S. House of Representatives*. Cambridge: Cambridge University Press.

Cramer, Katherine. 2016. *The Politics of Resentment: Rural Consciousness in Wisconsin and the Rise of Scott Walker*. Chicago: University of Chicago Press.

Cramer Walsh, Katherine. 2012. "Putting Inequality in Its Place: Rural Consciousness and the Power of Perspective." *American Political Science Review* 106 (3): 517–532.

Crenson, Matthew A. 1971. *The Un-Politics of Air Pollution: A Study of Non-Decisionmaking in the Cities*. Baltimore: Johns Hopkins University Press.

Dahl, Robert A. 1961. *Who Governs?: Democracy and Power in an American City*. New Haven, CT: Yale University Press.

Data.gov. 2008. "2008 Presidential General Election, County Results – Direct Download." Accessed at https://catalog.data.gov/dataset/2008-presidential-general-election-county-results-direct-download.

DeLeon, Richard. 1992. *Left Coast City: Progressive Politics in San Francisco, 1975–1991*. Lawrence: University Press of Kansas.

Desposato, Scott W. 2005. "Correcting for Small Group Inflation of Roll-Call Cohesion Scores." *British Journal of Political Science* 35: 731–744.

Dilworth, Richardson. 2009a. "Bringing the City Back In." In *The City in American Political Development*, ed. Richardson Dilworth. New York: Routledge, 1–13.

Dilworth, Richardson. 2009b. *The City in American Political Development*. New York: Routledge.

Dilworth, Richardson, ed. 2011. *Cities in American Political History*. Washington, DC: CQ Press.

Dorsett, Lyle W. 1977. *Franklin D. Roosevelt and the City Bosses*. Port Washington, NY: Kennikat Press.

Douglas, Paul. 1972. *In the Fullness of Time: The Memoirs of Paul H. Douglas*. New York: Harcourt Brace Jovanovich.

Dreier, Peter, John Mollenkopf, and Todd Swanstrom. 2004. *Place Matters: Metropolitics for the Twenty-First Century*. Lawrence: Kansas University Press.

Edsall, Thomas Byrne, and Mary D. Edsall. 1991. *Chain Reaction: The Impact of Race, Rights, and Taxes on American Politics*. New York: Norton.

Ehrenhalt, Alan. 2013. *The Great Inversion and the Future of the American City*. New York: Vintage.

Eldersveld, Samuel. 1949. "The Influence of Metropolitan Party Pluralities in Presidential Elections Since 1920: A Study of Twelve Key Cities." *American Political Science Review* 43 (6): 1189–1206.

Enos, Ryan. 2010. "What Tearing Down Public Housing Projects Teaches Us About the Effect of Racial Threat on Political Participation." Paper Presented at the Center for Urban Research and Policy Workshop, Columbia University, New York.

Enos, Ryan. 2017. *The Space Between Us: Social Geography and Politics*. Chicago: University of Chicago Press.

Erie, Steven P. 1988. *Rainbow's End: Irish-Americans and the Dilemmas of Urban Machine Politics, 1840–1985*. Berkeley: University of California Press.

Erie, Steven P. 1992. "How the Urban West Was Won." *Urban Affairs Review* 27 (4): 519–554.

Ethington, Philip J., and David Levitus. 2009. "Placing American Political Development: Cities, Regions, and Regimes, 1789–2008." In *The City in American Political Development*, ed. Richardson Dilworth. New York: Routledge, 154–176.

Ethington, Philip, and Jason McDaniel. 2007. "Political Places and Institutional Spaces: The Intersection of Political Science and Political Geography." *Annual Reviews of Political Science* 10: 127–142.

Feinstein, Brian, and Eric Schickler. 2008. "Platforms and Partners: The Civil Rights Realignment Reconsidered." *Studies in American Political Development* 22: 1–31.

Fenno, Richard F. 1973. *Congressmen in Committees*. Boston: Little, Brown.

Fiorina, Morris, Jeremey Pope, and Samuel Abrams. 2004. *Culture Wars?: The Myth of a Polarized America*. New York: Longman.

Flanagan, Richard. 1999. "Roosevelt, Mayors, and the New Deal Regime: The Origins of Intergovernmental Lobbying and Administration." *Polity* 31 (3): 415–450.

Fleck, Robert K. 2008. "Voter Influence and Big Policy Change: The Positive Political Economy of the New Deal." *Journal of Political Economy* 116 (1): 1–37.

Foner, Eric. 1984. "Why Is There No Socialism in the United States?" *History Workshop Journal* 17 (1): 57–80.

Frank, Robert. 2007. *Falling Behind: How Rising Inequality Harms the Middle Class*. Berkeley: University of California Press.

Frymer, Paul. 1999. *Uneasy Alliances: Race and Party Competition in America*. Princeton, NJ: Princeton University Press.

Frymer, Paul. 2007. *Black and Blue: African Americans, the Labor Movement, and the Decline of the Democratic Party*. Princeton, NJ: Princeton University Press.

Frymer, Paul. 2017. *Building an American Empire: The Era of Territorial and Political Expansion*. Princeton, NJ: Princeton University Press.

Gainsborough, Juliet F. 2001. *Fenced Off: The Suburbanization of American Politics*. Washington, DC: Georgetown University Press.

Gallagher, M. 1991. "Proportionality, Disproportionality, and Electoral Systems." *Electoral Studies* 10 (1): 33–51.

Gelfand, Mark. 1975. *A Nation of Cities: The Federal Government and Urban America, 1933–1965*. New York: Oxford University Press.

Gilens, Martin. 2000. *Why Americans Hate Welfare*. Chicago: University of Chicago Press.

Glaeser, Edward L. 2011. *Triumph of the City: How Our Greatest Invention Makes Us Richer, Smarter, Greener, Healthier, and Happier*. New York: Penguin Press.

Gosnell, Howard. 1937. *Machine Politics: The Chicago Model*. New York: AMS Press.

Green, Donald, Soo Yeon Kim, and David H. Yoon. 2001. "Dirty Pool." *International Organization* 55 (2): 441–468.

Green, Donald, Bradley Palmquist, and Eric Schickler. 2002. *Partisan Hearts and Minds*. New Haven, CT: Yale University Press.

Habyarimana, M., M. Humphreys, D. Posner, and J. Weinstein. 2009. *Diversity and the Dilemmas of Collective Action*. New York: Russell Sage Foundation Press.

Hackworth, Jason. 2007. *The Neoliberal City: Governance, Ideology, and Development in American Urbanism*. Ithaca, NY: Cornell University Press.

Hajnal, Zoltan. 2007. *Changing White Attitudes Toward Black Political Leadership*. New York: Cambridge University Press.

Hajnal, Zoltan, and Marisa Abrajano. 2016. *White Backlash: Immigration, Race, and American Politics*. Princeton, NJ: Princeton University Press.

Hajnal, Zoltan, Elisabeth Gerber, and Hugh Louch. 2002. "Minorities and Direct Legislation: Evidence from California Ballot Proposition Elections." *Journal of Politics* 64 (1): 154–177.

Hersh, Burton. 2008. *Bobby and J. Edgar: The Historic Face-Off Between the Kennedys and J. Edgar Hoover that Transformed America*, rev. ed. New York: Basic Books.

Hirsch, Arnold. 1983. *Making the Second Ghetto: Race and Housing in Chicago, 1940–1960.* Chicago: University of Chicago Press.

Hofstadter, Richard. 1948. *The American Political Tradition and the Men Who Made It.* New York: Knopf.

Hopkins, Daniel. 2010. "Politicized Places: Explaining Where and When Immigrants Provoke Local Opposition." *American Political Science Review* 104 (1): 40–60.

Hopkins, Daniel. 2011. "The Limited Local Impacts of Ethnic and Racial Diversity." *American Politics Research* 39 (2): 344–379.

Hopkins, Daniel. 2018. *The Increasingly United States: How and Why American Political Behavior Nationalized.* Chicago: University of Chicago Press.

Huber, John. 2012. "Measuring Ethnic Voting: Do Proportional Electoral Laws Politicize Ethnicity?" *American Journal of Political Science* 56 (4): 986–1001.

Huntington, Samuel. 1968. *Political Order in Changing Societies.* Henry L. Stimson Lectures Series. New Haven, CT: Yale University Press.

IPUMS NHGIS. 2017. *U.S. Geographic Summary Data and Boundary Files.* Minneapolis: University of Minnesota. Accessed at http://www.nhgis.org.

Jackson, Kenneth. 1985. *Crabgrass Frontier: The Suburbanization of the United States.* New York: Oxford University Press.

Jones, Christopher, and Daniel Kammen. 2014. "Spatial Distribution of U.S. Household Carbon Footprints Reveals Suburbanization Undermines Greenhouse Gas Benefits of Urban Population Density." *Environmental Science and Technology* 48 (2): 895–902.

Jones-Correa, Michael. 2000. "The Origins and Diffusion of Racial Restrictive Covenants." *Political Science Quarterly* 115 (4): 541–568.

Joyce, Patrick D. 2003. *No Fire Next Time: Black–Korean Conflicts and the Future of America's Cities.* Ithaca, NY: Cornell University Press.

Katznelson, Ira I. 1982. *City Trenches: Urban Politics and the Patterning of Class in the United States.* Chicago: University of Chicago Press.

Katznelson, Ira I. 2005. *When Affirmative Action Was White: An Untold History of Racial Inequality in Twentieth-Century America.* New York: W. W. Norton.

Katznelson, Ira. 2009. "On Diversity and the Accommodation of Injustice: A Coda on Cities, Liberalism, and American Political Development." In *The City in American Political Development*, ed. Richardson Dilworth. New York: Routledge, 246–257.

Katznelson, Ira. 2012. *Fear Itself: New Deal Democracy in a Southern Cage.* New York: Norton.

Katznelson, Ira, Joshua Clinton, and John Lapinski. Forthcoming. "Where Measures Meet History: Party Polarization During the New Deal and Fair Deal." In *Governing in a Polarized Age: Elections, Parties, and Representation in America*, ed. Alan Gerber and Eric Schickler. New York: Cambridge University Press.

Katznelson, Ira, and Sean Farhang. 2005. "The Southern Imposition: Congress and Labor in the New Deal and Fair Deal." *Studies in American Political Development* 19: 1–30.

Katznelson, Ira, Kimberley Geiger, and Daniel Kryder. 1993. "Limiting Liberalism: The Southern Veto in Congress, 1933–1950." *Political Science Quarterly* 108: 283–306.

Katznelson, Ira, and John Lapinski. 2007. "The Substance of Representation: Studying Policy Content and Legislative Behavior." In *The Macropolitics of Congress*, ed. E. S. Adler and J. Lapinski. Princeton, NJ: Princeton University Press, 96–126.

Katznelson, Ira, and Quinn Mulroy. 2012. "Was the South Pivotal?: Situated Partisanship and Policy Coalitions During the New Deal and Fair Deal." *Journal of Politics* 74 (2): 604–620.

Katznelson, Ira, and Bruce Pietrykowski. 1991. "Rebuilding the American State: Evidence from the 1940s." *Studies in American Political Development* 5: 301–339.

Katznelson, I., and G. Wawro. 2010. "Political Science and History: Enhancing the Methodological Repertoire." Columbia University Working Paper, http://www.columbia.edu/~gjw10/polisci_history.8_20_10.pdf.

Kaufmann, Karen. 2004. *The Urban Voter: Group Conflict and Mayoral Voting Behavior in American Cities*. Ann Arbor: University of Michigan Press.

Keiser, Richard A. 1997. *Subordination or Empowerment?: African-American Leadership and the Struggle for Urban Political Power*. New York: Oxford University Press.

Kennedy, David M. 2009. "What the New Deal Did." *Political Science Quarterly* 124 (2): 251–268.

Key, V. O., Jr. 1949. *Southern Politics in State and Nation*. New York: A. Knopf.

Key, V. O. 1955. "A Theory of Critical Elections." *Journal of Politics* 17 (1): 3–18.

King, Gary. 1996. "Why Context Should Not Count." *Political Geography* 15: 159–164.

Kousser, Thad, Mathew McCubbins, and Ellen Moule. 2008. "For Whom the TEL Tolls: Can State Tax and Expenditure Limits Effectively Reduce Spending?" *State Politics and Policy Quarterly* 8 (4): 331–361.

Krehbiel, Keith. 1998. *Pivotal Politics: A Theory of U.S. Lawmaking*. Chicago: University of Chicago Press.

Lapinski, John. 2013. *The Substance of Representation: Congress, American Political Development, and Lawmaking*. Princeton, NJ: Princeton University Press.

LeGates, Richard, and Frederic Stout, eds. 2016. *The City Reader*, 6th ed. London and New York: Routledge.

Leuchtenburg, William E. 1963. *Franklin D. Roosevelt and the New Deal, 1932–1940*. New York: Harper Perennial.

Lewis, Jeffrey B., Brandon DeVine, Lincoln Pitcher, and Kenneth C. Martis. 2013. *Digital Boundary Definitions of United States Congressional Districts, 1789–2012*. Accessed at http://cdmaps.polisci.ucla.edu on June 6, 2015.

Lieberman, Robert C. 2001. *Shifting the Color Line: Race and the American Welfare State*. Cambridge: Harvard University Press.

Lieberman, Robert C. 2009. "The City and Exceptionalism in American Political Development." In *The City in American Political Development*, ed. Richardson Dilworth. New York: Routledge, 17–43.

Long, J. Scott, and Jeremy Freese. 2006. *Regression Models for Categorical Dependent Variables Using Stata*, 2nd ed. College Station, TX: Stata Press.

Lowi, Theodore. 1969. *The End of Liberalism: Ideology, Policy, and the Crisis of Public Authority*. New York: W. W. Norton.

Lublin, David. 1997a. "Congressional District Demographic and Political Data, 1972–1994." Accessed at http://davidlublin.com/wpcontent/uploads/2013/09/cdlublin.zip.

Lublin, David. 1997b. *The Paradox of Representation: Racial Gerrymandering and Minority Interests in Congress*. Princeton, NJ: Princeton University Press.

Lublin, David, and D. Stephen Voss. 2001. "Federal Elections Project." Washington, DC: American University; Lexington, KY: University of Kentucky.

Luce, Robert. 1930. *Legislative Principles: The History and Theory of Lawmaking by Representative Government*. Boston: Houghton Mifflin.

Manson, Steven, Jonathan Schroeder, David Van Riper, and Steven Ruggles. 2017. *IPUMS National Historical Geographic Information System: Version 12.0* [Database]. Minneapolis: University of Minnesota. 2017. Accessed at http://doi.org/10.18128/D050.V12.0.

Martis, K. C., C. L. Lord, and Ruth Anderson Rowles. 1982. *The Historical Atlas of United States Congressional Districts*. New York: Collier Macmillan.

Massey, Douglas S., and Nancy A. Denton. 1993. *American Apartheid: Segregation and the Making of the Underclass*. Cambridge, MA: Harvard University Press.

Mayhew, David. 1966. *Party Loyalty Among Congressmen: The Difference Between Democrats and Republicans, 1947–1962*. Cambridge: Harvard University Press.

Mayhew, David R. 1974. *Congress: The Electoral Connection*. New Haven, CT: Yale University Press.

Mayhew, D. R. 1986. *Placing Parties in American Politics: Organization, Electoral Settings, and Government Activity in the Twentieth Century*. Princeton, NJ: Princeton University Press.

Mayhew, David. 2002. *Electoral Realignments: A Critique of an American Genre*. New Haven, CT: Yale University Press.

McCarty, Nolan, Keith T. Poole, and Howard Rosenthal. 2006. *Polarized America: The Dance of Ideology and Unequal Riches.* Cambridge, MA: MIT Press.

Meltzer, Allan H., and Scott F. Richard. 1981. "A Rational Theory of the Size of Government." *Journal of Political Economy* 89 (5): 914–927.

Menand, Louis. 2001. *The Metaphysical Club: A Story of Ideas in America.* New York: Farrar, Straus and Giroux.

Mendelberg, Tali. 2001. *The Race Card: Campaign Strategy, Implicit Messages, and the Norm of Equality.* Princeton, NJ: Princeton University Press.

Merriner, James L. 1999. *Mr. Chairman: Power in Dan Rostenkowski's America.* Carbondale, IL: Southern Illinois University Press.

Mollenkopf, John. 1983. *The Contested City.* Princeton: Princeton University Press.

Monkonnen, Eric. 1988. *America Becomes Urban: The Development of U.S. Cities and Towns, 1780–1980.* Berkeley: University of California Press.

Monkkonen, Eric. 2004. *Police in Urban America, 1860–1920.* New York: Cambridge.

Mumford, Lewis. 1937. "What Is a City?" *Architectural Record*, pp. 58–62. Republished in LeGates and Stout, eds. 2016.

Mumford, Lewis. 1961. *The City in History: Its Origins, Its Transformations, and Its Prospects.* New York: Houghton Mifflin Harcourt.

Myrdal, Gunnar. 1944. *An American Dilemma: The Negro Problem and Modern Democracy.* New York: Harper Brothers.

Nall, C. 2010. "The Political Consequences of Spatial Policies: How Interstate Highways Caused Geographic Polarization." *Journal of Politics* 77 (2): 394–406.

Nelson, Bruce. 2001. *Divided We Stand: American Workers and the Struggle for Black Equality.* Princeton, NJ: Princeton University Press.

Newman, Benjamin J. 2014. "My Poor Friend: Financial Distress in One's Social Network, the Perceived Power of the Rich, and Support for Redistribution." *Journal of Politics* 76 (1): 126–138.

Ngai, Mae. 1999. "The Architecture of Race in American Immigration Law: A Reexamination of the Immigration Act of 1924." *Journal of American History* 86 (1): 67–92.

Noel, Hans. 2014. "Separating Ideology from Party in Roll Call Data." Paper Presented at the Conference on Congress and History, June 11 and 12, College Park, MD.

Oliver, J. Eric. 2001. *Democracy in Suburbia.* Princeton, NJ: Princeton University Press.

Oliver, J. Eric. 2010. *The Paradoxes of Integration: Race, Neighborhood, and Civic Life in Multiethnic America.* Chicago: University of Chicago Press.

Oliver, J. Eric. 2012. *Local Elections and the Politics of Small-Scale Democracy.* Princeton, NJ: Princeton University Press.

Orfield, M. 1997. *Metropolitics: A Regional Agenda for Community and Stability.* Washington, DC: Brookings Institution Press.

Park, Robert, Ernest W. Burgess, and Roderick D. McKenzie. 1925. *The City.* Chicago: University of Chicago Press.

Perlstein, Rick. 2009. *Nixonland: The Rise of a President and the Fracturing of America.* New York: Scribner.

Peterson, Mark. forthcoming. "The City-State of Boston: The Rise and Fall of an Atlantic World, 1630–1865." New Haven: Yale University Press.

Peterson, Paul E. 1981. *City Limits.* Chicago: University of Chicago Press.

Phillips, Justin H., and Leah Brooks. 2010. "The Politics of Inequality: Cities as Agents of Redistribution." Russell Sage Foundation Working Paper.

Pinderhughes, Dianne M. 1987. *Race and Ethnicity in Chicago Politics: A Reexamination of Pluralist Theory.* Urbana: University of Illinois Press.

Plotke, David. 1996. *Building a Democratic Political Order: Reshaping American Liberalism in the 1930s and 1940s.* New York: Cambridge University Press.

Poole, K. T., and H. Rosenthal. 1997. *Congress: A Political-Economic History of Roll Call Voting.* New York: Oxford University Press.

Prosterman, Eric. 2013. *Defining Democracy: Electoral Reform and the Struggle for Power in New York City*. New York: Oxford University Press.

Putnam, Robert. 2007. "E Pluribus Unum: Diversity and Community in the Twenty-First Century: The 2006 Johan Skytte Prize Lecture." *Scandinavian Political Studies* 30 (2): 137–174.

Rader, Kelly, Pablo Pinto, and Robert Erikson. 2014. "Dyadic Analysis in International Relations: A Cautionary Tale." *Political Analysis* 22: 457–463.

Rae, D. W. 2003. *City: Urbanism and Its End*. New Haven, CT: Yale University Press.

Rakove, Milton. 1975. *Don't Make No Waves, Don't Back No Losers: An Insider's Analysis of the Daley Machine*. Bloomington: Indiana University Press.

Rice, Stewart. 1928. *Quantitative Methods in Politics*. New York: Knopf.

Roediger, David R. 2005. *Working Toward Whiteness: How America's Immigrants Became White: The Strange Journey from Ellis Island to the Suburbs*. New York: Basic Books.

Rosenberg, Gerald. 1991. *The Hollow Hope: Can Courts Bring About Social Change?* Chicago: University of Chicago Press.

Rousseau, Jean-Jacques. 1762. *The Social Contract*. New York: Penguin Press, 2006 edition.

Royko, Mike. 1971. *Boss: Richard J. Daley of Chicago*. New York: Penguin.

Rusk, David. 2003. *Cities Without Suburbs: A Census 2000 Update*. Washington, DC: Woodrow Wilson Center Press.

Sassen, Saskia. 2001. *The Global City*. Princeton, NJ: Princeton University Press.

Sassen, Saskia. 2005. "Cityness in the Urban Age." Accessed at http://www.intelligentagent.com/ME/Saskia_Sassen_2005-Cityness_In_The_Urban_Age-Bulletin2.pdf.

Sayre, Wallace, and Herbert Kaufman. 1965. *Governing New York City*. New York: Norton.

Schickler, Eric. 2001. *Disjointed Pluralism*. Princeton, NJ: Princeton University Press.

Schickler, Eric. 2009. "Public Opinion, the Congressional Policy Agenda, and the Limits of New Deal Liberalism, 1935–1945." Paper Presented at the Congress and History Conference, University of Virginia, May.

Schickler, Eric. 2012. "New Deal Liberalism and Racial Liberalism in the Mass Public, 1937–1968." Paper presented at the American Political Science Annual Meeting, September 2010, Washington, DC.

Schickler, Eric. 2016. *Racial Realignment: The Transformation of American Liberalism*. Princeton, NJ: Princeton University Press.

Schickler, Eric, Kathryn Pearson, and Brian Feinstein. 2010. "Shifting Partisan Coalitions: Support for Civil Rights in Congress from 1933–1972." *Journal of Politics* 72 (3): 672–689.

Schlozman, Daniel. 2015. *When Movements Anchor Parties: Electoral Alignments in American History*. Princeton, NJ: Princeton University.

Shapiro, Ian. 2006. *The State of Democratic Theory*. Princeton, NJ: Princeton University.

Shapiro, R. Y., and J. Bafumi. 2009. "A New Partisan Voter." *Journal of Politics* 71: 1–24.

Shefter, Martin. 1976. "The Emergence of the Political Machine: An Alternative View." In *Theoretical Perspectives on Urban Politics*, ed. Willis Hawley and Michael Lipsky. New York: Prentice-Hall, 14–44.

Sitkoff, Harvard. 1978. *A New Deal for Blacks: The Emergence of Civil Rights as a National Issue: The Depression Decade*. New York: Oxford University Press.

Skowronek, Stephen. 1982. *Building a New American State: The Expansion of National Administrative Capacities, 1877–1920*. New York: Cambridge University Press.

Smith, Carl. 2013. *City Water, City Life: Water and the Infrastructure of Ideas in Urbanizing Philadelphia, Boston, and Chicago*. Chicago: University of Chicago Press.

Smith, Ken R., Barbara Brown, Ikuho Yamada, Lori Kowaleski-Jones, Cathleen Zick, and Jessie Fan. 2008. "Walkability and Body Mass Index." *American Journal of Preventive Medicine* 35 (3): 237–244.

Smith, Rogers, and Desmond King. 2005. "Racial Orders in American Political Development." *American Political Science Review* 99: 75–92.

Smith, Steven S., and Christopher J. Deering. 1990. *Committees in Congress*. Washington, DC: CQ Press.

Snowiss, Leo. 1966. "Congressional Recruitment and Representation." *American Political Science Review* 60 (3): 627–639.

Snyder, James, and Stephen Ansolabehere. 2008. *The End of Inequality: One Person, One Vote and the Transformation of American Politics*. New York: Norton.

Sombart, Werner. 1976. *Why Is There No Socialism in the United States?* Translated by Patricia M. Hocking and C. T. Husbands. New York: Sharpe.

Sonenshein, Raphael J. 1994. *Politics in Black and White: Race and Power in Los Angeles*. Princeton, NJ: Princeton University Press.

Stone, Clarence. 1989. *Regime Politics: Governing Atlanta, 1946–1988*. Lawrence: University Press of Kansas.

Sugrue, Thomas J. 1996. *The Origins of the Urban Crisis: Race and Inequality in Postwar Detroit*. Princeton, NJ: Princeton University Press.

Sugrue, Thomas J. 2008. *Sweet Land of Liberty: The Forgotten Struggle for Civil Rights in the North*. New York: Random House.

Tonnies, Ferdinand. 1887. *Gemeinschaft und Gesellschaft* [*Community and Civil Society*]. New York: Cambridge University Press, 2001 edition.

Townhall.com. 2016. "Election Results." Accessed at https://townhall.com/election/2016/president/; Compiled and formatted at https://github.com/tonmcg/County_Level_Election_Results_12-16.

Trebbi, Francesco, Philippe Aghion, and Alberto Alesina. 2008. "Electoral Rules and Minority Representation in U.S. Cities." *Quarterly Journal of Economics* 128: 325–358.

Trounstine, Jessica L. 2008. *Political Monopolies in American Cities: The Rise and Fall of Bosses and Reformers*. Chicago: University of Chicago Press.

Trounstine, Jessica. 2009. "All Politics Is Local: The Reemergence of the Study of City Politics." *Perspectives on Politics* 7 (3): 213–216.

Trounstine, Jessica, and Jacob Rugh. 2011. "The Provision of Local Public Goods in Diverse Communities: Analyzing Municipal Bond Elections." *Journal of Politics* 73 (4): 1038–1050.

Valentino, Nicholas, and David Sears. 2005. "Old Times There Are Not Forgotten: Race and Partisan Realignment in the Contemporary South." *American Journal of Political Science* 49 (3): 672–688.

Weingast, Barry R., Judith Goldstein, and Michael A. Bailey. 1997. "The Institutional Roots of American Trade Policy: Politics, Coalitions, and International Trade." *World Politics* 49 (3): 309–338.

Weir, Margaret, H. Wolman, and T. Swanstrom. 2005. "The Calculus of Coalitions: Cities, Suburbs, and the Metropolitan Agenda." *Urban Affairs Review* 40 (6): 730–760.

Welch, Susan, and Timothy Bledsoe. 1998. *Urban Reform and Its Consequences: A Study in Representation*. Chicago: University of Chicago Press.

White, Andrew. 1890. "The Government of American Cities." *Forum* 10 (December 1890): 213–216.

Wilson, James Q. 1960. "Two Negro Politicians: An Interpretation." *Midwest Journal of Political Science* 4 (4): 346–369.

Wilson, James Q. 1962. *The Amateur Democrat: Club Politics in Three Cities*. Chicago: University of Chicago Press.

Wirth, Louis. 1938. "Urbanism as a Way of Life." *American Journal of Sociology* 44 (1): 1–24.

Wirth, Louis. 1957. "Urbanism as a Way of Life." In *Cities and Society*, ed. Paul K. Hatt and Albert J. Reiss. Glencoe, IL: Free Press, 46–63.

Wolman, H., and L. Marckini. 2005. "Changes in Central-City Representation and Influence in Congress Since the 1960s." *Urban Affairs Review* 34 (291): 291–312.

Woodward, C. Vann. 1955. *The Strange Career of Jim Crow*. New York: Oxford University Press.

Yates, Douglas. 1977. *The Ungovernable City: The Problems of Urban Politics and Policy Making*. Cambridge, MA: MIT Press.

INDEX

Adler, E. Scott, 136, 182, 266, 304n119, 307n41, 318n7
Aesop, 27–29
affinity coalitions, 62–63
AFL (American Federation of Labor), 72–73, 114. *See also* unions
African Americans, 309n86; Great Migrations and, 19, 67–68, 100–101, 156–65, 184–85, 231–32, 266, 293n119, 310n99; group threat hypothesis and, 40–43, 156, 290n62; parties' relationship to, 6, 155–62, 164–75; urban politics and, 154–62, 164–75, 228
agenda control, 59–60
Agricultural Adjustment Act (AAA), 66–67
AIP (American Institutions Project), 23, 141, 177, 297n88, 303n106, 309n85
Alesina, Alberto, 312n142
Allport, 309n79
American exceptionalism, 246–50
American Labor Party, 105–7, 136
American Municipal Association, 66
American National Elections Study (1952), 161
Andersen, Kristi, 306n13
Anderson, Clarence, 174
Anfuso, Victor, 169, 172
Annunzio, Frank, 123
antilynching legislation, 152, 161–62, 165–68, 170–71, 177–79
APD (American Political Development), 5, 9–10, 20
assimilationism, 101, 163, 199–200

Bailey, Cleveland, 114
Bailey, John, 122
Baker decision, 281n3
Baltimore, 275
Banfield, Edward, 131
Baqir, Reza, 312n142

Barbour, William, 84
Bennett, Charles, 173
Berry, Christopher, 51
Biemiller, Andrew, 114–15
Big Sort, 19
Biles, Roger, 24, 297n86
bloc-of-blocs structures, 66–67, 102, 203–4, 208–16, 293n119. *See also* cities; Democratic Party
Boehner, John, 222
Bonner, Herbert, 110
Bonus Army, 93
Bosch, Albert, 116, 118
Boston, 74, 78, 83–84, 166, 275
Bourne, Randolph, 312n140
Bridges, Amy, 10, 292n108
Brookings Institution, 287n15
Brotherhood of Sleeping Car Porters, 72
Brown, John, 312n136
Bryan, William Jennings, 75
Buckley, Charles, 109, 111
Buenker, John D., 225
Buffalo, 275
Bulkley, Robert, 84–85
Burns, Nancy, 61, 164
Burton, Phil, 123
Bush, George W., 8, 222
Byrne, James, 111

capitalism, 13, 24–25
Carey, Hugh, 112
Carmines, 150–51, 153, 165–66, 189
Carter, Jimmy, 244
Catholics, 72, 152, 168, 238, 306n13
Celler, Emanuel, 16–17, 56, 62, 107, 111, 116, 119
Cermak, Anton, 77, 101, 249
charity, 93

INDEX

Chicago: Democratic machine in, 2, 7, 23, 49–51, 77, 100–101, 104, 120–24, 146–47, 192–93, 317n26; federal aid to, 90; Great Depression and, 70–71; IHIs in, 119–24, 130–35, 145–46, 303n112; population boom in, 67; racial politics in, 154–62, 170–75, 180, 189–92, 195–96, 231–32, 266–67, 275, 307n41, 308n61; suburbs of, 16, 47, 48, 243, 291n93, 291n95. *See also* Cook County; Daley, Richard J.; Democratic Party; First Congressional District (IL)
Chicago Tribune, 49, 73, 301n84
child labor laws, 170–71
Cincinnati, 275
CIO (Congress of Industrial Unions), 72–73, 114–15, 146, 182, 292n107. *See also* unions
cities: cohesiveness and, 25–26, 45–54, 61–62, 102–3, 106, 128–44; Congressional blocs and, 26, 58–63, 217–29; cross-city alliances and, 4, 6–9, 20, 58–67, 73–74, 248–49; definitions of, 286n9; Democratic Party's relationship with, 3–4, 12–15, 23, 27–29, 100–101, 175–88, 204–6, 223–27; density of, 28–30, 36, 55, 233–35, 286n11, 287n15; diversity of, 28–30, 50–51, 235–39; double liberalism and, 4, 31–33, 85, 289n48; federal power and, 3–5, 9–11, 16, 24–25, 33–38, 42–43, 57–67, 74–92, 95–101, 103, 203–4, 238–39, 245–50, 303n111; governance demands of, 2–3, 9–21, 24–25, 28–31, 33–45, 60–64, 66–71, 80–92, 99–101, 143–44, 204–6; Great Depression and, 65–80, 92–95; Great Migrations and, 19, 67–68, 100–101, 156–65, 184–85, 266, 293n119, 310n99; housing pressures in, 95–99, 191; IHIs in, 21, 137–44; immigration and, 30–31, 42–43, 156; malapportionment and, 1–3, 25–26, 281n3, 317n36; metropolitan politics and, 17, 232–38, 240–45; paradoxes of, 28–29, 32–38, 42–45, 99–101, 148–49, 198, 200–202; policymaking constraints in, 11, 28–35, 46; postindustrialization and, 242–45; racial realignment and, 149–83, 189–202, 247, 310n99; racial unrest in, 2, 7, 19, 25, 36, 41; representatives of, 21–24, 52–63, 110–11; rivalries among, 44–45, 58–59, 65–67, 69, 242; spatial analyses and, 15–21, 25, 28–29, 44–45, 47, 48, 135–36, 157–58; suburbanization and, 5, 10–11, 16–17, 20, 46–47, 62–63, 67, 125–33, 157, 189–90, 232–38, 242–45, 259–64, 291n92, 312n3, 317n30; urbanicity measures and, 136–37, 141–42, 147, 163–64, 175–88, 206–11, 232–40, 250–64, 277–79; voting districts within, 40–41, 43–45, 53–56, 58–59; white flight and, 20, 157, 189, 229, 285n7, 310n99. *See also* Chicago; group pluralism; New York; representation (political); United States
city delegation theory, 43–63, 102–5; cohesion and, 128–44, 163–74, 206, 208–16, 302n94; comparisons to suburban and metropolitan districts and, 125–28; definition of, 25, 124–25, 302n92;

explanatory value of, 137–47; heterogeneity and, 126–28; House of Representatives and, 208–27; ideology and, 5–6, 12–21, 24–33, 51, 59–63, 72, 105, 136–40, 146–56, 175–77, 197; measures of, 173–88; national politics and, 25–26; New York's representation and, 105–20; race and, 148–49, 174–75, 196–202
city districts, 19–22, 44, 54–58, 120–33, 157, 206–8, 217–27, 265–75, 290–91n78, 318n2
cityness, 312n140
city-zenship, 31–35, 38–43, 149, 213–14, 287n22
Civil Rights Act (1964), 151, 189, 230–31
Civil Rights Act (1966), 191
civil rights movement, 150–51, 295n22; cities' leadership on, 4–5, 7–9, 41, 147, 170–75; IHIs and, 26; legal strategies of, 198–99; Republican opposition to, 20; roll call voting and, 175–83; southern Democrats and, 7, 15–16, 150–51, 154–55. *See also* antilynching legislation; fair employment practices
class: IHIs and, 145–46
Cleveland, 85, 275
Cleveland, Grover, 315n40
Clinton, Hillary, 232–33, 244–45, 316n8, 316n10
cohesion (quality): city delegation theory and, 25–26, 45–54, 61–62, 102–3, 128–44, 195–202, 208–16, 302n94; definition of, 125; diversity and, 45–54, 124–28, 137–44; ideology's relation to, 5–6, 12–21, 24–33, 51, 58–63, 72, 105, 136–40, 146–56, 175–77, 197; race and, 148–49, 163–64, 184–88. *See also* IHIs (institutions of horizontal integration)
colorblindness, 198
Commission on Human Relations of Los Angeles County, 41
Commission on Organization of the Executive Branch of the Government, 110
common goods (definition), 287n34
Communism, 105, 136, 238
Community Development Block Grant program, 54
congestion, 3
Congressional Record, 111, 251, 265
Congressional Record Data Book, 266
Connery, William, 83
contact theory, 38–39
Cook County, 2, 49, 50, 50–51, 77, 121–22, 317n26. *See also* Chicago
corruption, 3, 6, 18–19, 67–68, 74–75, 77–78, 102, 105–6
Costigan, Edward, 171
Coudert, Frederic, 108, 110–11
Couzens, James, 85–86
Crane, Phil, 243
crime, 3
Croker, Richard, 298n10
CSR datasets, 22–23, 126–28, 136–44, 181–88, 203–8, 251–64, 302n97, 313nn14–15
Curley, James, 71, 74, 78, 87–88

INDEX

Dahl, Robert A., 47
Daley, Richard J., 16–17; Conference of Mayors and, 2, 16, 245, 296n48; corruption and, 6, 131; IHI cohesion and, 120–24, 133; loyalty and, 2, 14, 18, 49, 56–58, 91, 120–24, 281n7; party politics and, 18, 49–50, 77–78; strategies of, 62, 169–70, 191; street gang past of, 160. *See also* Chicago; Cook County; machines (political)
Daley, Richard M., 146–47
Dallinger, Frederick, 166
Davis, James, 84–85
Dawson, William A., 114
Dawson, William L., 50, 121, 157, 160, 169, 309n87
Death Wish (film), 285n7
"Defense of Christian Charity" (Winthrop), 248
deindustrialization, 10–11
Democratic Party: bloc-of-blocs structures of, 203–4, 208–16, 223–27, 293n119; Chicago politics and, 2, 49–51, 169–70, 189–90, 192–93; civil rights movement and, 147, 155–62, 173–202, 295n22; cohesion and, 21, 56–57, 120–25, 163–64; Cook County organization and, 121–25; double liberalism and, 12–15, 63–64, 88–89; Great Depression and, 94–95; group pluralism and, 5, 13, 19–20, 25, 32–33, 38–41, 149–83, 238–39, 248–49; House of Representatives control by, 217–22; machine politics and, 74–77, 131, 146–47; New York delegation and, 105–20, 124; rural constituencies and, 7, 60–61, 85–92, 188–95; southerners' relationship with, 5, 7, 12, 14–17, 26, 60–61, 63–64, 74–76, 86, 88–89, 97–98, 113, 148–53, 160–61, 164–76, 178–88, 206, 217–24, 230–32, 293n119, 306n7, 315n37; urban power centers of, 3–4, 12, 14, 23, 27–29, 60–61, 100–101, 128–33, 204–6, 228, 232–38. *See also* cities; double liberalism; group pluralism; IHIs (institutions of horizontal integration); machines (political); representation (political)
density (population), 28–30, 36, 233–35, 286n11, 287n15
Department of Health, Education, and Welfare, 120
Department of Housing and Urban Development, 54, 65–66, 95–96, 99
Department of Transportation, 300n41
De Priest, Oscar, 157, 178, 181, 309n87
DeSapio, Carmine, 106, 298n12
Desposato, Scott W., 303n100
Detroit, 78, 85, 98, 146, 162, 174–75, 180, 241, 275
DeVine, Brandon, 270
Dewey, John, 13, 200, 312n140
Diana, Raymond, 292n107
diversity (in cities), 29–31, 38–43, 124–28, 204–6. *See also* cities; group pluralism
Dollinger, Isidore, 109, 111
Donovan, James, 111
Dorm, William Jennings Bryan, 114
double liberalism, 101; cities as distinctive home of, 31–33, 200–202; city delegation theory and, 45–52; conflicts between aspects of, 42–43;

definitions of, 4, 32–33, 281n11, 287n27; Great Depression and, 68–71; group pluralism and, 5, 13, 19–20, 25, 32–33, 38–41, 149–64, 175–83, 238–39, 247–49; southern rejection of, 189–95; statism and, 4–5, 13, 25, 32–38, 54–55, 60–61, 80–81, 148, 222–27, 289n48, 290n60, 296n69; threats to, 291n92; urbanicity and, 238–40, 250–64. *See also* racial liberalism
Douglas, Helen, 78
Douglas, Paul, 21–22, 307n23
Douglass, Frederick, 178–79, 312n136
Dreier, Peter, 317n24
Duff, James, 110
DW-NOMINATE measure, 175–88, 223, 224, 287n28. *See also* roll call voting
dyadic models (of city representation), 133–44, 187–88, 304n116, 305n124
Dyer, Leonidas, 166, 170–71, 179
Dykstra, C. A., 69

Easterly, William, 312n142
economic management (statism), 33–38, 42–43, 54–55, 60–61, 92–95, 289n43, 296n69
electoral connection hypothesis, 182, 302n98
Ellenbogen, Henry, 91
ESRI ArcMap software, 270
Ethington, Philip J., 282n31
Evers, Medgar, 231
Experience Party, 106

fair employment practices, 161–62, 168–69, 171–74, 308n53
Fair Employment Practices Committee, 169
Fair Labor Standards Act, 73
Farhang, Sean, 293n118
Farley, James, 94–95
Farmer-Labor Party, 136
fascism, 13
Federal Emergency Relief Administration, 93–94
Federal Housing Administration, 96–97
federalism, 3–4, 11, 29, 33, 42, 63, 80, 85, 241, 244, 313n4
Federal Transit Authority, 300n41
Feinstein, Brian, 185–86, 196–97, 307n41, 318n7
Fine, Sidney, 109, 111
Fino, Paul, 112, 119
First Congressional District (IL), 159–60, 309n87
First World War, 67
Flanagan, Richard, 74–75, 99
Fletcher, Duncan, 87
Flynn, Ed, 76
Frymer, Paul, 311n131
Fuller, Claude, 88–89

Gainsborough, Juliet F., 291n92, 312n3
Gallagher, M., 314n22
Gavin, Leon, 111
Gelfand, Mark, 44, 297n86
Gingrich, Newt, 222

GIS analysis, 22–24, 182, 254, 313n14. *See also* spatial analytic methods
Glass, Carter, 86–87
Goldwater, Barry, 150–51, 189, 201, 228
Gore, Thomas, 86–88
Great Depression, 3–4, 7, 9, 15–16, 20, 25, 54, 65–71, 84, 92–99, 106–7, 156. *See also* cities; Democratic Party; federalism
Great Migrations, 19, 67–68, 100–101, 156–57, 160–61, 164–65, 184–85, 266, 293n119, 310n99
group pluralism, 214–16; cities as distinctive home to, 32–33, 38–41, 71–80, 148–64, 168–75, 238–40, 265–75; cohesion and, 124–25, 195–202; hyperpluralism and, 46, 103; IHIs and, 25–26; southern resistance to, 149–64, 195–202; spatiality and, 126–28; traditional parties and, 63–64
group seats factionalization, 214
group threat hypothesis, 40–43, 156, 290n62
Grover, James, 112

Hackworth, Jason, 11
Halpern, Seymour, 112
Hancock, Franklin, 89
Harlem, 2
Hastert, Dennis, 222
Heller, Louis, 109–10
heterogeneity, 3–5, 25–58, 73–78, 120–37, 147–48, 163–64, 201–3, 213–16, 239, 287n15
"The History and Theory of Lawmaking by Representative Government" (Luce), 1–2
Hoan, Daniel, 71, 78
Hoffman, Clare, 172–73
Hofstadter, Richard, 13
Home Owners' Loan Act, 96
Home Owners' Loan Corporation, 97
Hoover, Herbert, 93, 225, 233
Hoover, J. Edgar, 191
Hopkins, Harry, 94
Horton, Frank, 112
House Appropriations Committee, 220
House Banking Committee, 107, 218
House Budget Committee, 220
House Committee on Rivers and Harbors, 83
House Education and Labor Committee, 218
House Finance Committee, 218
House Foreign Affairs Committee, 218
House Judiciary Committee, 218
House Labor Committee, 218
House of Representative: city delegations in, 222–27
House of Representatives: leadership positions in, 217–22; Republican control of, 219, 222; rural-urban cleavage in, 223–29
House Public Works and Transportation Committee, 218
House Rules Committee, 218, 220
House Urban Affairs Committee, 218
House Veterans Affairs Committee, 218

House Ways and Means Committee, 117, 218, 220
Housing Act (1934), 96–97
Housing Act (1937), 97–98
housing crises, 95–99
HUD. *See* Department of Housing and Urban Development
Humphrey, Hubert H., 21
hyperpluralism, 46, 103

ideology, 5–6, 12–21, 24–33, 51, 59–63, 72, 105, 136–40, 146–56, 175–77, 197
idiot lists (Daley), 122, 281n8
IHIs (institutions of horizontal integration): city delegation theory and, 25, 57–63, 124–25, 140–44, 182–88; civil rights movement and, 26; cohesion of, 25–26, 45–54, 128–33, 163–64, 200–202, 241; development of, 103, 287n25; diversity and, 124–25; ideology and, 5–6, 12–21, 24–33, 51, 59–63, 72, 105, 136–40, 146–56, 175–77, 197; jurisdictional axis of, 46–47, 48, 53–54, 62–63, 103–5, 119, 125, 139–44, 291n96, 292n104, 303n112, 304n115; localism of, 21–24; national representation and, 52–57, 124–25, 145–47; organizational aspects of, 46, 49–52, 56–57, 103–5, 120–25, 139–44; race and, 148–49, 164–75, 197–202; representation and, 133–44; strategic concerns of, 58–64; suburbanization and, 242–45. *See also* cities; cohesion (quality); Democratic Party; traditional parties (as organizational IHIs)
immigration, 19–20, 100–101, 157, 163–64; assimilation discourses and, 101, 163, 199–200; cities' relation to, 30–31, 42–43, 225; racial hierarchies and, 100–101, 163–64; urbanization and, 1. *See also* Great Migrations; heterogeneity; race
Immigration Act (1924), 100–101
Impellitteri, Vincent, 106, 118
Indianapolis, 166
industrialization, 1, 239
Ives, Irving, 110

Javits, Jacob, 111
Jefferson, Thomas, 29, 239, 246, 284n7, 285n7
Jersey City, 2
Jews, 168
Jim Crow, 67, 161–62, 190, 231, 310n92
Johnson, Lyndon, 122–23, 189, 230–31, 300n41
Jones, Jesse, 107
Jones-Correa, 307n49

Kallen, Horace, 312n140
Kant, Immanuel, 13
Katznelson, Ira, 283n43, 293n118, 306n11, 310n92
Kelly, Edna, 112

INDEX

Kelly, Edward, 77, 131, 169
Kennedy, John F., 110, 233, 316n8
Kennelly, Martin, 50
Keogh, Eugene, 106
Kerry, John, 8
Key, V. O., 306n13
King, Gary, 311n131
King, Martin Luther, Jr., 191, 231
Klein, Arthur, 167–68
Koch, Ed, 56
Krier, Raymond, 121
Ku Klux Klan, 167

labor movement. *See* unions
La Follette, Robert, 296n69
La Guardia, Fiorello, 56, 70, 76, 79, 84, 89, 97–101, 105–8, 235, 296n69, 298n14
Lanzetta, James, 299n15
Lapinski, John, 24
Lehman, Herbert, 110
Levitus, David, 282n31
Lewis, Jeffery B., 254, 270
Libonati, Roland, 123, 301n84
Lieberman, Robert C., 24, 207, 246, 253–54, 313n7, 313n14
Lindsay, John, 41, 56, 112, 118–19
Locke, Alain LeRoy, 312n140
Locke, John, 13
logrolling, 14, 293n132
Lomasney's Law, 104, 298n9
Los Angeles, 44, 56, 78, 130–35, 160, 180, 271, 273, 275
loyalty (as political value), 2, 14, 18, 49, 56–58, 91, 120–24, 281n7
Lublin, David, 136
Luce, Robert, 1–2, 281n5

MacArthur, Douglas, 93
machines (political), 6–9, 49–50, 68–69, 74–77, 283n54, 291n97, 292n108. *See also* Chicago; Tammany Hall
Malcolm X, 192
Marcantonio, Vito, 107, 298–99nn14–15
Marckini, L., 206–7, 220, 226–27, 251–52, 254, 259–64, 315n31, 315n41
marginal urgency, 58–59
Marsh, Benjamin, 96
Martin, Edward, 110
Martin, Joseph, 83
Martis, Kenneth C., 254, 270
Marx, Karl, 13
Marxism, 13
Mass Transportation Bill (HR 3881), 113, 300n39
Mayhew, David, 14, 137, 182, 206–9, 213, 264–66, 282n36, 292n108, 304n122, 310n90, 315n38
mayors. *See* cities; U.S. Conference of Mayors
Mayor's Committee on Human Relations, 41
McCormack, John, 83–84, 88–89, 112–13, 217–18

McKee, Joseph, 76
McKenna, Thomas, 121
McKeough, Raymond, 91
McKinley, William V, 167
Meeks, James, 90
Meltzer, Allan H., 35, 37, 289n43
Merriam, Charles, 317n25
methodological localism, 10
metropolitan areas, 62–63, 125–28, 209–10, 232–38, 240–45, 255–57, 318n9. *See also* representation (political); spatial analytic methods; urbanicity measures
metropolitan delegation (term), 125
Metropolitan Detroit FEP Council, 174
Mills, Ogden, 85–87
Milwaukee, 78, 275
Minneapolis, 243
Mitchell, Arthur, 181, 309n87
mobility, 2–3, 11, 19, 28–29, 37. *See also* Great Migrations; immigration; white flight
Mollenkopf, John, 317n24
Moore, Arch, 114
Moores, Merrill, 166
Mortgage Bankers Association, 72
Moses, Robert, 204–5
MTA (Metropolitan Transit Authority), 300n41
Mulroy, Quinn, 293n118
Mumford, Lewis, 284n7
Murphy, Frank, 73–74
Murphy, John, 112
mutual exchange, 60–61

NAACP (National Association for the Advancement of Colored People), 72, 191
Nash, Patrick, 77, 121
National Association of Real Estate Boards, 72
National Brotherhood of Packinghouse Workers, 115
National Industrial Recovery Act, 88, 96
National Labor Relations Board, 73
National League of Cities, 73
National Municipal League, 68
New Deal, 6–7, 9, 12–15, 76
New Urbanism, 286n7
New York City, 271; city delegation from, 105–20, 130–35, 145–46, 295n38, 298n10, 303n112, 317n26; Democrats in, 36, 75, 104, 124; federal aid for, 85–87, 90; group pluralism in, 41, 126–28; jurisdictional cohesion in, 46–47, 56; local governance of, 34–35, 76–78; machine politics in, 75–77; party organizations in, 7; political infrastructures in, 23–24; population boom in, 67; racial politics in, 154–57, 160, 162, 173–74, 180, 201–2, 275; representatives of, 55–56; rivals of, 44; spatial analyses of, 271, 272; suburbanization and, 70. *See also* specific representatives

New York City Commission on Human Rights, 41
New York Metropolitan Council on Fair Employment Practice, 174
NHGIS, 270
Nixon, Richard, 150, 233
NOMINATE measure, 175, 309n84
Norris-La Guardia Act, 76
Norton, Mary, 218
NYCTA (New York City Transit Authority), 112
NYQMPA (New York Quartermaster Procurement Agency), 108–12

Obama, Barack, 222, 245, 312n1, 316n8, 316n10
O'Brien, Larry, 112, 122
O'Brien, Leo, 112
O'Dwyer, William, 105–6
O'Grady, Joseph, 112
O'Hara, Barratt, 55, 190–93, 195–96
Oliver, J. Eric, 291n92, 317n24
O'Neill, Tip, 53
one person, one vote, 1, 12
organizations (political). *See* Democratic Party; IHIs (institutions of horizontal integration); machines (political); Republican Party; traditional parties (as organizational IHIs); U.S. Conference of Mayors

Palin, Sarah, 222
Pearson, Kathryn, 185–86, 196–97, 307n41, 318n7
Pelosi, Nancy, 222
People's Lobby, 96
Pepper, Claude, 315n29
Perlstein, Rick, 243–44
Peterson, Paul, 11, 32, 37, 293n132
Philadelphia, 2, 44, 67, 78, 90, 108–11, 128, 130–35, 162, 180, 271, 274, 275, 303n112, 317n26
Philadelphia Quartermasters Depot, 299n38
Pike, Otis, 112
Pittsburgh, 78, 83, 85–86, 275
pivotal cohesion, 58–59
place character, 5, 9, 21–24, 29–31, 164, 204–6, 212, 214–16, 277–79, 315n37
Plotke, David, 12–13, 168, 282n36, 283n47
Policy Agendas Project, 309n85
political science, 9–10, 32–33.
    See also APD (American Political Development); specific measures and scholars
poll taxes, 162
pollution, 3, 204
Poole, K. T., 23, 175
Portland (OR), 243
poverty, 3, 93–98
Powell, Adam Clayton, 112, 298n12, 309n87
Pritcher, Lincoln, 270

Progressive Era, 4, 12–13, 36–37, 68–69, 72, 100–101, 105
Prohibition, 76, 170, 306n13
Pucinski, Roman, 120, 170
PWA (Public Works Administration), 94, 96

race: anti-integration riots and, 19; city representation and, 148–49, 195–202, 235–38; diversity calculations and, 126–28; double liberalism and, 38–43; Great Migrations and, 19, 67–68, 100–101, 156–65, 184–85, 266, 293n119, 310n99; group threat hypothesis and, 40–43, 156, 290n62; homeownership and, 191–92; IHIs and, 26, 145–47; immigration politics and, 100–101, 163–64; labor movement and, 72–73; measures of, 302n99; political responsiveness to, 6, 50–51, 164–75; Republican Party politics and, 100–101; rural areas' responses to difference and, 41, 174–83; scientific racism and, 312n140; spatial distribution and, 19, 35–36, 157–62, 192–93, 231, 267–75, 307n41; suburbanization and, 157, 159–64; unions and, 182; urban governance issues and, 24–25, 32–33, 163–75, 230–32, 238–40; violence and, 19–20; white supremacy and, 13, 15–18, 24, 64, 174–75, 199–200, 306n19. *See also* antilynching legislation; Democratic Party; fair employment practices; group pluralism; housing
racial liberalism, 19, 26, 41–43, 149–56, 160–75, 178–88, 190, 195–201
Randolph, A. Philip, 72
Reagan, Ronald, 150, 218, 246–50, 318n43
realignment (of parties), 149–53, 306n7. *See also* Democratic Party; race; Republican Party
Reciprocal Trade Agreements Act (RTAA), 113–17
Reconstruction (period), 149, 151
Reconstruction Finance Corporation, 71, 85, 87, 107
Red Scare, 98
redistribution, 11, 33, 35–37, 42–43, 60–61, 66, 92–95, 99–101, 289n43
Reece, Brazilla, 204
Reeder, Sherwood, 295n28
reformers (political), 6, 68–69, 74–75, 101
Reid, Ogden, 112
religious groups, 72
representation (political), 49; cities as unified constituencies and, 7–8, 21–24, 40–41, 43–52, 48, 52–63, 71–92, 95–101, 105–20, 133–44, 164–88, 203–4, 208–29, 240–50, 265–75; cohesion and, 25–26, 45–54, 61–62, 102–3, 133–44, 292n104; corruption and, 3–6, 18–19, 105–6; ideology's relation to, 5–6, 12–21, 24–33, 51, 59–63, 72, 105, 136–40, 146–56, 175–77, 197; IHIs and, 52–57, 102–5, 133–44; local organizations' power and, 4–5, 9–11; malapportionment issues and, 1–3,

24–26, 281n3, 317n36; metropolitan areas and, 240–45; one person, one vote and, 1, 12; race and, 6, 40–41, 148–49, 164–75, 181–88, 195–202; red-blue maps and, 5, 8, 20, 150, 202, 232–39; rural-city tensions and, 1–3, 8–9, 15–25, 27–31, 59, 62–63, 151–53, 202, 204–6, 208–27, 238–40, 284n7; spatial methodological techniques and, 15–21, 208–16. *See also* cities; city delegation theory; Democratic Party; federalism; IHIs (institutions of horizontal integration); Republican Party; roll call voting; rural constituencies

Republican Party: House of Representatives control by, 219, 221; party discipline and, 206; race politics and, 15–18, 150–53, 163–64, 166–67, 179, 188–95, 308n58, 308n61; rural constituencies and, 8–9, 27–29, 214–22, 225, 227–29, 283n51; schism of 1912 and, 100–101; suburbs and, 5, 17, 21, 209, 220, 243

Reynolds decision, 281n3
Rice cohesion scores, 129, 303n100
Richard, Scott F., 35, 37, 289n43
riots, 2, 160, 166, 200
Rochester, 2
Rockefeller, Nelson, 228
Rodino, Peter, 171
roll call voting, 22–23, 91–92, 134–35, 140–44, 175–95, 222–27. *See also* specific measures
Rooney, John, 55–56, 116, 201–2
Roosevelt, Franklin D., 15–16, 20, 74–75, 78, 86, 94, 105, 154, 157, 225, 229, 233, 235, 296n48, 296n69, 316n8
Roosevelt, James, 78
Roosevelt, Theodore, 75
Rosenthal, H., 23, 175
Rostenkowski, Dan, 56, 121–23
Rothman, Stuart, 112
Rousseau, Jean-Jacques, 32
Royko, Mike, 155, 189–90
Ruggieri, Bernard, 112
Rumsfeld, Donald, 243
rural constituencies: city politics' tensions with, 1–3, 8–9, 15–31, 59, 62–63, 151–53, 202–27, 238–40, 284n7; federal aid to, 80–83, 88–89, 102, 147, 246–50, 284n7; Great migrations and, 19, 67–68, 100–101, 156–65, 184–85, 266, 293n119, 310n99; Republican Party's relation to, 8–9, 27–29, 214–22, 225–29, 283n51
Ryan, Paul, 222
Ryan, Thomas, 167

Sabath, Adolph, 56, 169, 171, 217–18
San Diego, 44
San Francisco, 44, 78, 90–91, 275
Sassen, Saskia, 312n140
Scanlon, Thomas, 168
Schakowski, Jan, 243

Schickler, Eric, 161, 166, 185–86, 189, 193–94, 196–97, 283n43, 306n11, 307n41, 318n7
Schlozman, Daniel, 197
scientific racism, 312n140
Scott, Hugh, 111
seats disproportionality, 214–16
segregation, 35–36, 98–99, 103, 126–28, 157–59, 192–93, 231, 266–67, 310n92
Senate Banking and Currency Committee, 87
Shapiro, Ian, 200
Sheldon, James, 174
Simon, Raymond, 122
Sirovich, William, 108
slum clearance, 89–90, 95–96, 98–99
Smith, Al, 75–77, 86, 101, 152, 154, 225, 306n13, 315n40
Smith, Carl, 311n131
Smith, Joseph, 98
Snowiss, Leo, 121
Socialist Party, 136
Social Security Act, 95, 120–21
Sombart, Werner, 246–47
South, the: Democratic Party's relationship with, 5, 7, 12, 14–17, 26, 63–64, 74–76, 86, 97–98, 113, 148–53, 160–61, 164–75, 178–88, 206, 217–24, 231–32, 293n119, 315n37; labor movement and, 73; mutual exchange politics and, 60–61; white supremacy and, 15–17, 26, 67, 149–50, 230–32, 306n7. *See also* Great Migrations; realignment (of parties); rural constituencies
spatial analytic methods, 15–24, 33, 47, 48, 126–28, 157–59, 175–88, 210–11, 267–75
statism: double liberalism and, 4–5, 13, 25, 32–38, 54–55, 60–61, 80–81, 148, 222–27, 289n48, 290n60, 296n69; economic management and, 33–38, 42–43, 54–55, 60–61, 92–95, 289n43, 296n69; federalism and, 3–4, 11, 29, 33, 42, 63, 80, 85, 241, 244, 313n4; redistribution and, 11, 33–38, 42–43, 60–61, 66, 92–95, 99–101, 289n43. *See also* cities; double liberalism; Great Depression; South, the; United States
Steagall, Henry, 107
Stimson, James A., 151, 153, 165–66, 189
St. Louis, 44, 166, 275
Stratton, Sam, 112
Straus, Nathan, 97
Strauss, Nathan, 89–90
suburban district, 125
suburbs, 291n92; cities' declining power and, 10–11, 47, 62–63, 67, 70; delegations from, 5, 16–17, 125–33, 209, 220, 232–38, 317n30; Republican Party and, 5, 17, 21, 28–29; white flight and, 20, 157, 189, 229, 285n7, 310n99
Sumners, Hatton, 201
supralocalism, 4, 10–11, 25, 38, 45, 52–58, 146, 164, 240, 249, 290n58. *See also* cities; IHIs (institutions of horizontal integration)

Supreme Court (U.S.), 1, 96–97
Swanstrom, Todd, 62, 317n24

Taber, John, 114
Taft, Howard, 75
Tague, Peter, 166, 168
Tammany Hall, 75–77, 105–7, 295n39, 298n10, 299n23
TELs (tax and expenditure limits), 11, 36–37, 282n28
Textile Workers Union of America, 115
Third Amendment (to the Constitution), 191
Thompson, Bennie, 316n6
Thompson, William, 308n61
Thurmond, Strom, 152
Till, Emmett, 231
Tonnies, Frederick, 284n7, 287n14
Touhy, John, 122
TPO scores, 137–43, 181, 183–88, 194, 212–13, 304n122, 310n90, 310n101
traditional parties (as organizational IHIs), 56–57, 63, 71–80, 163–64, 172, 182, 185–86, 195–202, 213, 283n54, 292n101. *See also* Democratic Party; ideology; Republican Party; TPO scores
Trounstine, Jessica, 51
Truman, Harry S., 225
Trump, Donald, 232

UAW (United Auto Workers), 78, 146
unemployment, 3, 7, 66, 68–69, 86–87, 92–95, 296n64
unions, 6–7, 37, 56, 71–72, 78, 114–16, 118, 136–37, 146, 154–55, 238, 292n107. *See also* specific unions
United Hatters, Cap, and Millinery Workers International, 115
United Mine Workers, 115
United States: cities' political power and, 4–11, 16, 20, 28–29, 33–38, 57–67, 80–92, 102–3, 124–25, 137–44, 203–4, 223–32, 241–50, 285n7, 303n111; economic intervention and, 94–99; federalism and, 3–4, 11, 28–31, 33–38, 42, 63, 80, 85, 241, 244, 313n4; Great Depression and, 3–4, 7–9, 15–16, 20, 25, 54, 65–71, 84, 92–99, 106–7, 156; IHIs and, 102–20; local politics and, 32–33; mobility within, 3–4, 28–29; as polis, 11–15; rural aid emphasis and, 80–81, 83, 88–89, 102, 147, 246–50, 284n7
urban interlude (term), 7, 12–13, 21, 26, 218
Urban League, 72
urban renewal programs, 66–67

urban political order: definition of, 3, 283n47; liberalism and, 16, 201–202, 249; machines and reformers in, 6; partisan alignment and, 17, 100, 215–216, 228; shaping national politics, 11–15, 71–80; strategic considerations of, 58–63, 217–226, 241–245; unity of, 45
urbanicity measures, 136–37, 141–42, 147, 163–64, 175–88, 206–8, 210–11, 232–40, 250–64, 277–79. *See also* CSR datasets; density (population); heterogeneity
urbanization, 3, 11–13, 23, 30, 38, 65, 216, 284n7. *See also* cities; Great Migrations; group pluralism; immigration; mobility
U.S. Chamber of Commerce, 72
U.S. Conference of Mayors, 2, 4, 20, 25, 66, 71–80, 84, 89, 92, 97–101, 106–9, 118–19
U.S. Housing Authority, 89

Vorys, John, 1–3, 5, 19, 43, 102, 129, 281n5, 303n100
Voting Rights Act (1965), 157, 312n2, 316n6

Wagner, Robert F., 21, 56, 84–85, 101, 106, 171, 296n69, 297n98
Wagner, Robert F., Jr., 106, 108–13, 116, 118–19, 299n23
Wagner Act, 72–73
Wagner-Steagall Act, 97
Wallace, George, 150
Walsh, David, 78
Warren, Earl, 1
The Warriors (film), 285n7
Weir, Margaret, 62
welfare, 13, 37. *See also* redistribution
white flight, 20, 157, 189, 229, 285n7, 310n99
white supremacy, 13–18, 24, 64, 149–50, 157–64, 174–75, 199–200, 231, 306n19. *See also* Democratic Party; race; Republican Party; South, the
Wilson, James Q., 104, 131
Wilson, Woodrow, 75
Winthrop, John, 247–49, 318n43
Wirth, Louis, 34, 199, 284n7
WNYC (station), 240–41
Wolman, H., 62, 206–7, 220, 226–27, 251–52, 254, 259–64, 315n31, 315n41
Wolverton, Charles, 111
Wood, Fernando, 298n10
work relief, 93–95
World War II, 152, 250
WPA (Works Progress Administration), 54, 76–77, 94
Wright, Jim, 123